1

A Public
Betrayed

A Public Betrayed

An Inside Look at Japanese Media Atrocities
and Their Warnings to the West

Adam Gamble & Takesato Watanabe

Since 1947
**REGNERY
PUBLISHING, INC.**
An Eagle Publishing Company • Washington, DC

Copyright © 2004 by Adam Gamble

Library of Congress Cataloging-in-Publication Data

Gamble, Adam.
 A public betrayed : an inside look at Japanese media atrocities and their warnings to the West / Adam Gamble and Takesato Watanabe.
      p. cm.
 Includes bibliographical references and index.
 ISBN 0-89526-046-8
 1. Mass media—Objectivity—Japan. I. Watanabe, Takesato, 1944- II. Title.

 PN5417.O24G36 2004
 302.23'0952—dc22
                           2004012723

Published in the United States by
Regnery Publishing, Inc.
An Eagle Publishing Company
One Massachusetts Avenue, NW
Washington, DC 20001

Visit us at www.regnery.com

Distributed to the trade by
National Book Network
4720-A Boston Way
Lanham, MD 20706

Printed on acid-free paper.

Manufactured in the United States of America.

10 9 8 7 6 5 4 3 2 1

Books are available in quantity for promotional or premium use. Write to Director of Special Sales, Regnery Publishing, Inc., One Massachusetts Avenue, NW, Washington, DC 20001, for information on discounts and terms, or call (202) 216-0600.

Unless otherwise indicated, all photographs are by Adam Gamble.

For more information on *A Public Betrayed*, including supplementary and teaching material, see http://www.apublicbetrayed.com.

AG

To my wife, Rachel, who didn't work on this book,
but who allowed me to, by doing virtually everything else.

TW

To my wife, Hisako, my children, Takemasa, Hironori, and Natsuko,
and to my fellow Japanese citizens.

Contents

FOREWORD

This is a valuable book about a neglected topic. Japan is one of the most media-saturated democracies in the industrialized world. It has the highest newspaper circulation of all such major democracies. Any of its several biggest newspapers dwarf any Western country's newspapers. Its citizens watch more hours of television than any people except Americans. Surely, the relationship between media and politics in one of the world's most influential polities is a significant subject.

For years few on this side of the Pacific paid much attention, either in the scholarly or journalistic worlds, to Japan's mass media. Then, with Japan's rise to world prominence through economic power beginning in the 1990s we began to see books and articles in English about the mass media's and politics' influence on each other. Yet surprisingly I know of no previous major study of the *shukanshi*, Japan's ubiquitous and seemingly omniscient popular weekly magazines. In Japan, one sees them everywhere—on sale prominently displayed in bookstores and at train-station kiosks, and their advertisements, as authors Adam Gamble and Takesato Watanabe point out, hang in almost every subway car, with Japan's train-commuting public coming into contact with their sensational headlines every day.

And what headlines these are! Stories about crime and scandal, the foibles and personal and political lives of politicians, major issues of the day, important cases of history and national identity. You name it, if it's something that is happening that would attract people's attention and that they might care about, it's going to be in these weeklies and in the most sensational way possible to attract interest, advertised all over Japan. More serious than our checkout-stand tabloids, more scurrilous and sensational than any establishment press in Japan or elsewhere, we have no exact equivalent in the United States. As the authors note, millions of Japanese each day read them, and millions more come into contact with their headlines and form impressions and images through their ads. These characteristics alone, one would have thought, would make Japan's weekly magazines worthy of serious attention in the United States.

Why hasn't anyone thought to investigate this important media and political phenomenon and write a book in English about them before? A good question without a definitive answer, but I can hazard a few guesses. The reasons probably have more to do with our own "information elites" than with this significant subject itself. As I discovered in my own previous scholarly research about Japan's mass media and politics, academics may talk about the pernicious and extensive influence of the media on political life at cocktail and dinner parties, and rant against it in the privacy of their homes, but many disciplines rarely accord the mass media much respect as a serious scholarly endeavor. There is a subtle "high culture" bias in a profession that values books and reading, even though few academics would acknowledge this. And to journalists for reputable newspapers in the Western world, the same self-interested disdain for what they would consider a "tabloid" form of journalism would operate.

Even among those who study politics and should be interested in media's impact, one finds a very narrow definition of what qualifies as a legitimate media study. Political scientists in particular devote much attention to television's influence on voting behavior in the United States but only if its impact can be precisely measured with sophisticated survey-research techniques. I've always wondered if this isn't putting the cart before the horse—whether one can measure precisely the media's impact on individuals' beliefs or not, isn't it first necessary to know how the media is portraying reality to ascertain exactly what collective symbols, impressions, meanings, and information those individuals have available to them?

The nature of Japan's weeklies, and the stories they disseminate and how they do so, *are* very important and neglected subjects that need to be brought to the attention of people in the United States, Europe, and the world. Their role, and the information, true and false, that they disseminate are an integral and major part of Japan's postwar democratic life, and as the authors rightly point out, most likely *do* have some impact on its citizens' view of the world. Part of the weeklies' role in Japan's democracy is positive and valuable—doing "investigative" reporting and uncovering information that the establishment media, for reasons explained well in this volume, won't publish or air. Journalists in the establishment media are known to sell or give stories their own media outlets won't cover to the weeklies in order to get the information out.

But a major part of the worldview those citizens are getting is also an irresponsible and frightening one. The well-documented and perversely fascinating case studies in this book demonstrate clearly that whatever other valuable and less horrifying information and impressions Japanese are receiving from these weeklies, they are also getting much more: vicious persecutions of select individuals; legitimating anti-Semitic and holocaust-denial viewpoints; the distortion and denigration of Japan's own massive atrocities in China—few Americans realize that the Japanese killed more Asians, especially in China, than the Nazis killed human beings in Europe; and refutation of even the minimum recognition of the suffering of the victims of brutal sex slavery.

Bringing these cases of media irresponsibility to a Western audience alone would justify the book's publication and its receiving attention. These cases are also, however, embedded in a serious attempt to explain why such media thrive in Japan and produce such gross violations of journalistic and human ethics and morality. They accurately show how such publications fill a void and have incentives to do so in the otherwise overly "responsible," factual, and dry world of establishment journalism that eschews almost any kind of interpretation or human interest, and can be subject to subtle political pressures and extraordinary attempts to avoid alienating just about anyone. And there are political and commercial incentives for doing so.

In reading this book, you will learn a great deal about one of the most important media phenomenons in the democratic world, and much of what you will discover will, and should, frighten you. Given current trends in some media outlets in the United States toward more sensational "reporting," often with clear, politically biased as well as commercial agendas, one should not read this book as merely a case of some exotic and unique Japanese phenomenon. It describes many issues Americans need to confront now: Where does a free press's mission to propagate the "truth" end and propaganda begin? How does one define the line between legitimate interpretation and outright political bias? Does the media have a responsibility to be fair and "balanced," and what do these terms mean? Where does catering to the patriotic values of most citizens turn into nationalist propaganda and distortion of the facts of history? And where do the collective rights of the public to know become outweighed by the right of the individual to be treated fairly? I hope many Americans read it and think about its implications for their own society and media. I also hope it causes Japanese journalists, editors, and publishers to seriously reflect about their profession, standards, and the image of Japan they give to the Japanese public and to the world.

I will end this brief foreword where I began: this is a valuable book about a neglected subject.

—Ellis S. Krauss

Professor of Japanese Politics and Policymaking

Graduate School of International Relations and
    Pacific Studies

University of California, San Diego

Note on Language

As might be expected with an English-language study of the Japanese news media, a number of issues have arisen surrounding the interpretation of and translation between languages.

First, it ought to be stated that a fair number of the interviews conducted as research for this book required the use of interpreters. Moreover, a number of different interpreters were used. In all cases, every effort was made to clarify areas of doubt, and both the interpreters and the interviewees were often questioned repeatedly until an agreement was reached about the accuracy of each questionable statement.

Regarding the actual translation of material, a number of translators were used throughout the composition of the book. All translated material was triple-checked for optimal accuracy.

Because this book is written from a Western perspective, and directed toward a Western audience, all Japanese names have been Americanized, with given names first and family names last. Also, all Japanese words that are not proper nouns have been italicized. Regarding the use of macrons and other diacritical marks in transliterated Japanese, we have followed the advice provided in the *Japanese Style Sheet* (1983), published in Tokyo by the Society of Writers, Editors, and Translators. In books such as this one, which is directed toward a general audience, the *Style Sheet* finds "omission to be the better part of valor." For currency conversion between United States dollars and

Japanese yen, the ratio of 100 yen per dollar has been used throughout. At the time of publication in the spring of 2004, the current rate is between 105 and 108 yen per dollar. However, many are currently predicting the 100-to-1 ratio in the future, and this figure has been used for simplification purposes.

Finally, one of the major issues confronted in writing this book was how best to handle the reproduction of headlines from Japanese newsmagazines and other publications. To successfully make the point that these headlines are often completely unreliable, it seemed necessary to translate many of them into English. Others have been left untranslated but are reproduced as illustrations or images. In reproducing such headlines, no matter what the method, there is always the risk of passing along dubious or false information to the reader. To guard against this danger, a disclaimer has been added to the captions accompanying all questionable headlines and other similar information.

The Violence of Lies

In the uniformity of its interpretations of events, the Japanese press has the power to manufacture expedient realities that would suggest a comparison with the controlled press of the communist world if it were not that the latter is far less successful in convincing foreign observers. The Japanese press is the major source of information and misinformation about Japan.

—Karel van Wolferen, *The Enigma of Japanese Power*[1]

A Quintessential Example

Japan is the quintessential example of a rich, industrialized, democratic nation, with a news media that has betrayed its people. At seemingly every turn, the Japanese public is deluged with lies, misrepresentations, and distortions of the grossest sort—a situation that has become so commonplace that it primarily passes without comment. In trains and subways, on buses, at the corner newsstand, on the Internet, even in advertisements in the nation's most trusted daily papers, banner headlines attack foreigners and minorities, rewrite history, and misrepresent current events with little regard for consequences. It is all just business as usual for a most extraordinary species of journalistic enterprise, the Japanese weekly newsmagazine, or *shukanshi*.

That these periodicals can get away with passing off such irresponsible, libelous reporting as news is astonishing. The how and why are well worth exploring, though, for they reveal much about Japan: its culture, business practices, and the relationship between that nation's news media and its peculiar brand of democracy. This relationship is so fundamental to the way Japan works that only by examining it can we hope for more than a superficial comprehension of the country, its social norms, reading and buying patterns, system of government, and foreign policy.

Unfortunately, for anyone living in a Western democracy, the unethical aspects of the Japanese news media are likely to seem less foreign, strange, and exotic than one might expect. Indeed, they are imminently relevant. A closer look at the actual mechanisms involved in Japan's "media atrocities" yields sobering insights into the relationships between the news media and democracy in general. For it is often by studying the most extreme situations that the most universal truths are revealed. And though a significant body of insightful books and studies has been written on the news media's relationship to civil sovereignty in the West, such studies on Japan are in short supply, especially in English. A thorough look at the Japanese news reveals many of the ways that institutional, cultural, and structural factors together can undermine the relationship between media and democracy anywhere.

For instance, as more of the world's media companies merge and form partnerships and other intimate relationships, the cozy connection between Japan's government and its national news media (going back at least as far as the 1930s) appears less and less foreign in country after country. As a result, many people across the globe have grown deeply disillusioned with news media of virtually all stripes and national origins. Having "seen it all," a jaded public no longer finds anything particularly remarkable about the kind of intense emphasis on sensationalism and commercialism over journalistic ethics that one is assaulted by in Japan. Today, even the lurid headlines and anything-goes reporting of the Japanese weekly newsmagazines strike a familiar chord for news consumers in virtually every free-market economy. Many familiar with both Japanese and Western news industries believe that what has occurred in Japan is but a harbinger of what is occurring in other Western countries.

Of course, the mechanisms of corruption in the Japanese news media aren't just important because of what they reveal about other countries. Japan, after all, is indisputably one of the most powerful nations on earth—a fact too often underestimated and overlooked. In puzzling contrast with its vast wealth and power, Japan receives relatively scant international attention and plays a comparably tiny role in international politics and diplomacy. The country has been described as an economic giant but a diplomatic dwarf. It has even been compared to a dinosaur: in contrast to its humongous economic strength, it often appears to lumber along under the minimal guidance of a tiny brain, especially where diplomacy and international relations are concerned. The perception seems to arise from three main causes: (1) Japan's introspective and sometimes isolationist cultural tendencies and behavior; (2) the diplomatic protection it has received from the United States since the close of the Second World War, in exchange for cooperation with the U.S. cold-war security strategy; and (3) Japan's "no-war constitution," designed and imposed on it by the United States,[2] which has greatly curbed its participation in military conflicts.

Despite perceptions, however, Japan's international influence is extensive and should not be underestimated. In direct contradiction of its Constitution, it ranks number four in the world in annual military expenditures, behind the United States, Russia, and France, and ahead of Great Britain. Japan is also the leading holder of U.S. foreign debt, giving it significant power and influence over the world's lone superpower. It also constitutes the second-largest economy on earth, behind the United States. Japan even has the ninth-largest population on the planet, with some 128 million residents.[3] Indeed, the greater Tokyo-Yokohama metropolitan area is by one measure the largest single urban area on earth by far, with a population of 26.4 million as of the year 2000.[4] In short, serious troubles in Japan inevitably lead to serious troubles throughout the world. The damaging relationship between Japan's news media and its democracy deserves serious attention, not only because of its example but because of its profound repercussions.

This book considers that relationship through five main case studies. While each study is in itself an extreme example, none should be discounted as unrepresentative of the Japanese situation. Each was chosen because of its extreme nature. Rather than selecting examples that are less extreme, and thus potentially more easily dismissed, each illustrates just how dire the situation is.

The first case study is a comparison between two high-profile news-media victims: Yoshiyuki Kono, a Japanese who was also a victim of a sarin-gas terrorist attack, and Richard Jewell, an American security guard who put his life on the line to save others during the terrorist bombing of the 1996 Atlanta Olympics. Exploring how these two admirable individuals were each persecuted by the news media of their own countries provides a rich context for comparing the often-collusive relationships between the news media and law enforcement in both nations. As time has borne out, both men are heroes of the highest order. Unfortunately, having courageously faced horrific terrorist attacks, both were subsequently terrorized a second time, not by the initial perpetrators but by the police and "journalists" whose duties it was to protect them. While the two cases differ in some key ways, comparing them nevertheless shows in unmistakable terms how unchecked and arrogantly exercised law-enforcement and journalistic powers can conspire against human rights, democracy, and basic justice in both countries. Ultimately, not only did two innocent men and their families suffer tremendously, the public in both nations was completely misled about major terrorist strikes against them. As terrorist attacks appear to grow in frequency and destructive power across the democratic world, the examples of the senseless persecution of these two men grow in relevance.

The second case study explores the shocking prevalence of anti-Semitism in the Japanese media—a seemingly baffling phenomenon given that the country has virtually no Jewish population! In a high-profile case, a major Japanese newsmagazine featured a denial of the Holocaust on the fiftieth anniversary of the liberation of the infamous Nazi death camp at Auschwitz. The incident led to an international boycott of the magazine and to the publishing company's swift cancellation of the publication. However, it did not bring an end to anti-Semitism in the mainstream Japanese publishing world, nor did it resolve any of the myriad complex reasons for its ugly presence there. Several other examples illustrate the very real problem of anti-Semitic writing in Japan and confront the tremendous failure of Japanese journalists to rebut this blatant racism within their own ranks. A pattern emerges of xenophobic hate language traditionally used to support the Japanese system of governance.

The third case study considers one magazine's malicious campaign to smear the reputation of Daisaku Ikeda, leader of Japan's largest Buddhist sect and a powerful national figure. The magazine ran a lengthy, highly sensational series of dozens of articles supporting fabricated rape claims lodged against Ikeda by a disgruntled husband and wife who were former members of the Buddhist organization. Evidence clearly shows that the magazine not only had every reason to know that the claims were false but that the magazine's editorial staff had worked closely with the husband and wife to assist them in developing and trumpeting their claims. Indeed, when the Japanese courts eventually weighed in on the case, they were unusually decisive in their strong rulings against the couple. The case is one of the most extraordinary examples of how unfettered commercialism in Japan can combine with politics and feeble libel laws to leave little recourse for even seemingly powerful victims of defamation.

The fourth case study considers one of the most important stories of the twentieth century, the Nanjing Massacre, one of the most horrific war crimes in history, along with the ongoing war of words that has surrounded it in Japan and internationally. The baseless "controversy" surrounding the event has been at the center of concerted efforts by Japanese nationalists to whitewash their country's Second World War legacy. Thanks in part to the staunch support of certain Japanese magazines and other publications, the historical truth of the massacre remains obscured in Japan to this day—although a number of brave and persistent Japanese have dedicated themselves to exposing the terrible reality of what occurred. One of Japan's most accomplished journalists, Katsuichi Honda, has been at the forefront of this movement for truth and justice, and the attacks against him have been most telling. For decades, Honda, whose name and work are widely known in Japan, has been forced to hide his identity in public (to the point of donning a false wig and glasses) in order to avoid threats from violent Japanese ultranationalists.

The final case study considers the weekly newsmagazines' blatant denials of the sexual enslavement of the so-called comfort women by the Japanese military during the Second World War. In what represents one of the most underreported and shocking war crimes ever, as many as 200,000 teenage girls and young women were systematically "recruited" from occupied countries and held captive in "comfort stations," where they were repeatedly raped by soldiers, often for years on end, if they endured that long. Surviving victim Ok Seon Lee offers her shocking testimony, published here for the first time. The motivations for contemporary media attacks against survivors such as Lee include racism and sexism, which also conspire to support the broader Japanese system of governance.

Again, these egregious instances of journalistic malpractice are not merely aberrations of an otherwise healthy news industry and social system. They are at once causes and effects of a dangerous continuum of chronic cultural, legal, and institutional maladies.

It should also be noted that the phrase "media atrocity" is not used lightly. Certainly, the nature of these examples is terrible and shocking. But more to the point, the phrase underscores their genuinely violent natures. The childhood taunt—"sticks and stones may break my bones, but words will never hurt me"—may be a valid sentiment under certain circumstances. But in the giant mass-news-media melee of the modern world, language has the power to yield profound suffering in direct and immediate ways.

Lies in the mass media are also too often at the root of mass violence. For example, the militaristic Japanese Empire of the Second World War did not simply spring out of nowhere. The Japanese population of the time was intrinsically no more good or bad than that of other nations. However, the Japanese public was betrayed by both its leaders and its news media, and misled in drastic ways, just as the people of so many other nations have been and are misled by similar lies. Behind such national tragedies are none other than false philosophies and brutal fabrications—philosophies and fabrications that ultimately impact whole societies. As the saying goes, truth is often the first casualty of war. It is also often the first casualty of other forms of exploitation, domination, and destruction.

CHAPTER ONE

THE JAPANESE SYSTEM OF GOVERNANCE

The new constitution generated problems that were to beset Japan for the remainder of the twentieth century. One such problem was the great divide between the concept of the state held by Japan's political rulers in 1946–47, and the modern secular, demilitarized, civil state concept enshrined in the new constitution, in conformity with the wishes and aspirations of most Japanese.

—Herbert P. Bix, *Hirohito and the Making of Modern Japan* [1]

Blotting Out the Sun

Without some view of Japan's wider sociopolitical landscape, the examples detailed in subsequent chapters are likely to strike many Westerners as inexplicably strange or perhaps even incomprehensible. Some knowledge of Japanese governance is therefore required to understand how the case studies in this book are not disconnected anomalies but direct consequences and byproducts of a dysfunctional democracy.

Despite Japan's democratic constitution and many democratic institutions and traditions, it is just not the fully functional democracy that it is often presented as being and perceived to be. Indeed, Japanese governance combines democratic with nondemocratic institutions and methods in ways that offer important lessons about democracy—not only in Japan but throughout the world. A whole host of extralegal relationships and "institutional corruption" blunt citizen sovereignty and support the rule of elite power holders, especially business leaders, bureaucrats, and politicians.

Not that there has ever been an "ideal" democratic nation; nor are all of the world's other major industrialized democracies necessarily more democratic than Japan. There is no attempt here to rate Japanese governance with other democracies around the world. Although such an exercise could be enlightening, it falls outside the purview of this book.

What matters here is that the current method of governance in Japan, practiced fairly consistently throughout the postwar period, has failed in a multitude of ways to live up to its potential for the empowerment of everyday citizens. Similarly, the Japanese news media as an industry and Japanese journalism as a profession have failed to support the potential of the country to be a great democracy—to be a truly admirable "Land of the Rising Sun," where democratic principles shine forth. Instead, the less scrupulous aspects of the publishing industry combine with other elements in the system in ways that distort reality and obscure hope for true Japanese democracy—that blot out the sun, as it were.

Japanese Governance

This overview of Japanese governance is indebted to the work of a number of scholars and writers, including the groundbreaking analysis of Karel van Wolferen, author of *The Enigma of Japanese Power* (1989). While van Wolferen's work has its detractors, it has nevertheless been seminally influential on the way that Japan is perceived and written about by Japanese and foreigners alike.

Similar to many of those writers and scholars cited here, van Wolferen has been criticized for being too harsh in his assessments. However, a reading of his books and essays, as well as lengthy discussions with him, confirms that his work is not so much about criticizing Japan as it is about analyzing it as accurately as possible. What van Wolferen and most of the others quoted in this chapter advocate is a better understanding of an often seriously misunderstood country—even when it means exposing the ugliest abuses of power in that country.

One of the most respected scholars of contemporary Japan, Chalmers Johnson, who has made comparisons between Japan and its wartime ally Germany, writes about having been unduly censured for his analysis of Japan's international problems:

Germany has real political parties compared with Japan's facade of political accountability; Germany is embedded in the European Community whereas Japan has hardly begun to respond to its neighbors' concerns; Germany is actively engaged in helping a distressed area of the world, East Europe, whereas much of Japan's foreign aid is as valuable to its general trading companies as it is to the designated recipients; and Germany clearly expressed its differences with the [American] strategy toward Iraq while the Japanese debate centered only on what would satisfy the Americans. In light of these considerations Americans are tired of being called racists or Japan-bashers for trying to understand accurately what is going on in Japanese policy-making circles.[2]

Alex Kerr, an accomplished writer who has lived in Japan for much of his life, explains in an interview for this book why he has written such severe indictments about a country he so obviously loves. Addressing the now-cliché response that such criticisms constitute "Japan bashing," Kerr insisted:

First of all, it's not bashing Japan. It's speaking for the Japanese who are unhappy with their country. [My] book, *Dogs and Demons*, actually gives voice to that feeling about Japan. It's why I'm being flooded with requests to speak in Japan. It's the opposite of bashing. It's Japan helping. It's Japan supporting.[3]

In a similar vein, media scholar, journalist, and author Kenichi Asano stated in an interview for this book, "I have been seriously attacked for my criticism of Japan and the Japanese media. It is why I am no longer employed by a Japanese media company. But I do it because I want the country to be better. It's a journalist's duty to stand up for justice."[4] Echoing these sentiments, acclaimed journalist Katsuichi Honda says that, in spite of the decades of caustic and violent attacks against him—especially those that charge that he is "anti-Japanese"—in confronting injustice in his country, he ultimately considers himself a "Japanese patriot."[5]

Key Characteristics of Japanese Governance

During the Meiji Era (1868–1912), Japan established a number of important democratic institutions and traditions, and even experienced moments of robust democratic dynamism. By the Second World War, however, the country had descended into a complete militocracy. Thus, Japan can be thought of as a formerly nondemocratic country onto which outsiders grafted democratic ideals and institutions after the war. Although these institutions remain, and in ways have grown and developed impressively, it would be a misrepresentation to say that they have entirely flourished. Numerous nondemocratic and antidemocratic institutions and practices—many of which have been around for centuries—remain firmly rooted. For example, despite the stellar growth of the Japanese economy in the postwar period, most Japanese people simply have not gained their fair share of the rewards for their country's successes. While Japan does boast an impressive degree of economic parity between classes, the average Japanese does not enjoy a standard of living that reflects the country's status as the world's second-largest economy.

It should be no surprise that the relative lack of economic rewards for the average Japanese citizen is matched in democratic terms. The Japanese body politic exercises relatively very little influence over the way its government operates. As a result, the population has grown increasingly unhappy and filled with feelings of resignation and apathy. Van Wolferen has written three Japanese-language books on this very point. The titles of the first two translate roughly into "Why Can't the Japanese Love Japan?" and "Can Japanese Control Their Own Fate?"[6] In the third book, the title of which translates as "Bourgeoisie—The Missing Element in Japanese Political Culture," under the auspicious heading "A Plague of Gloom," he cites a survey that concluded that "no less than 90 percent of Japanese between the ages of 20 and 70 expect that they will face insecurity as they grow older." He further notes the striking statistic that "only 17 percent of Japanese parents in Tokyo thought that their children's generation would be happier than they had been, contrasting greatly with the more than 70 percent of respondents in Seoul who thought so."[7]

Bruce S. Feiler, who described his experience teaching Japanese students in a Japanese public school in his acclaimed book *Learning to Bow,* took a survey of his students that revealed that fewer than half of them expected to earn more than their parents. "Clearly these children were not being taught to reach for great challenges; instead, they are taught to get ahead by going along."[8]

Kerr corroborates this when he asserts that his longtime country of residence has failed to produce the kind of humane governmental system he believes its people deserve: "Few have questioned why Japan's supposed 'cities of the future' are unable to do something as basic as burying telephone wires; why gigantic construction boondoggles scar the countryside (roads leading nowhere in the mountains, rivers encased in U-shaped chutes); why wetlands are cemented over for no reason; why the movie industry has collapsed; or why Kyoto and Nara were turned into concrete jungles. These things point to something much deeper than a mere period of economic downturn; they represent a profound cultural crisis, trouble eating away at the nation's very soul."[9]

Of course, there will always be those fans of Japan, both foreign and domestic, who will argue that the Japanese are indeed doing quite well. However, an informal survey of pedestrians in Tokyo, taken in 2003 for this book, indicates serious discontent. Asked how they felt about the way their country is governed, and given the choice of four answers, they responded[10] as follows:

- Unhappy: 56%
- Somewhat Happy: 24%
- Happy: 8%
- Very Happy: 2%
- No Answer: 10%

When asked in the follow-up question, "Could you rate your personal level of happiness with Japanese governance on a scale of one to one hundred?" the average score was just thirty-seven. These statistics, while coming from an informal survey and being more anecdotal than scientific, corroborate other observations and conclusions. For example, a *Mainichi Shimbun* survey on January 4, 2001, showed that 80 percent of those questioned are "dissatisfied with politics."[11] Another survey of three thousand Japanese, conducted by *Yomiuri Shimbun* in 2003, revealed that some 82 percent of respondents distrust Japanese politicians and politics.[12]

It's impossible to avoid the conclusion that there is a serious disconnec-
tion between the Japanese citizenry and those who govern it, as well as widespread pessimism. To get at some of the root causes of these issues, first
consider some aspects of Japanese governance that make it less than ideal. A
short list might include the following:

- Continued dominance of the political process by a single party
- Lack of a clearly discernible core of national power
- Relative weakness of the rule of law
- Especially strong governmental controls exercised over the free
  market
- High emphasis on industrial output over other priorities
- Use of myths and false ideology to legitimize rule

Of course, none of these characteristics is unique to Japan. They each exist
in varying forms and degrees elsewhere. However, taken together, they do
define the Japanese system in significant ways.

Single-Party Dominance

Perhaps the most conspicuous manifestation of the Japanese system is, as
Richard Katz puts it, that "one corruption-ridden party, the Liberal-Democratic
party [LDP], has ruled the country almost continuously for the past four
decades."[13]

With the exception of a nine-month period in 1993–1994, the LDP has
been the dominant ruling party in Japan since the party's founding in 1955.
Although the LDP has had to forge coalition governments with minority parties, especially since 1994 and most recently with the New Komei Party in
1999, the LDP has maintained what amounts to an iron grip on politics. The
contradiction in describing any country with nearly half a century of one-
party rule as a healthy, working democracy is painfully obvious.

It has become commonplace in Japan to point out that the LDP, the Liberal Democratic Party, is neither "liberal" nor "democratic," nor even a real
political "party." The LDP has always put forth a conservative platform and
is anything but progressive. As for being "democratic," the LDP is more com-

monly considered—certainly by the majority of those who have studied it objectively—far more of a vote-getting machine than an organization dedicated to civil sovereignty. And as for being a "party," the LDP is regularly described as less a political organization composed of like-minded colleagues who share similar ideological opinions than as a loose coalition of competing and evolving power groups (*habatsu*) bent on retaining and increasing their political clout through the extraction of money from special-interest groups and the doling out of government pork.

The LDP can indeed be downright neonationalistic, such as when, just after the party's conception, it made the Second World War militarist and A-list war criminal Nobusuke Kishi prime minister in 1957. Patrick Smith writes scathingly of Kishi: "To put the matter simply, Kishi was a war criminal and a thug. During the 1930s, when Japan occupied Manchuria, Kishi was the second-ranked civilian in the colonial administration. In Hideki Tojo's wartime cabinet he held the industry portfolio and served, in addition, as

Former Japanese Prime Minister Yasuhiro Nakasone was the first in his position to worship, in his capacity as prime minister, at Yasukuni Shrine. The shrine was a prominent center of the state Shinto creed that had been used by Japanese militarists during the Second World War to justify their military aggression. It is also considered to be the place where the souls of Japanese war dead, including Class A war criminals, are enshrined. *(Photo courtesy of Mainichi Photo Bank.)*

vice-minister for munitions."[14] And Kishi's legacy has lived on. Yasuhiro Nakasone, for example, who served as prime minister from 1982 until 1987, was an unabashed apologist for his country's wartime aggressions, having reintroduced the practice of prime ministerial visits to the Yasukuni Shrine to offer his prayers as the country's leader for the Japanese war dead. Many have compared this practice with the hypothetical idea of a contemporary German chancellor worshipping at a shrine dedicated to the Nazis. Katsuichi Honda, with very little jest, has called the former prime minister "Nazisone."

Other examples of the LDP's extreme policies include a variety of incidents in which their top politicians have categorically denied the facts of Japanese military aggression during the Second World War, resurrected symbols of the war such as the rising-sun flag and national anthem, worked to dismantle the country's no-war "peace constitution," and rammed all sorts of legislation through the Diet against popular opinion. Not long before the publication of this book, the current LDP prime minister, Junichiro Koizumi, made his fourth visit as head of state to worship at Yasukuni Shrine, thus symbolically, and unabashedly, proclaiming his support for the country's militaristic past.[15]

Prime Minister Junichiro Koizumi worshipping at Yasukuni Shrine on August 13, 2001. As of the publication of this book in 2004, Koizumi had worshipped there four times as prime minister. *(Photo courtesy of Mainichi Photo Bank.)*

The eminently experienced "Japan hand" Ivan P. Hall, writing in his 2002 book *Bamboozled,* has labeled a major faction of the LDP as belonging to what he calls Japan's "New Old Right." According to Hall, these politicians may be "new" (contemporary), but they hold a core ideological kinship with the country's Second World War militarists. While Hall certainly does not imply that Japan is likely to return to its wartime aggression anytime soon, he does fear that the increasing popularity of the New Old Right within the LDP does not bode well for Japanese democracy. "The most critical divide in Japanese political values today runs not between the moderate and far left (as it long did) but between Japan's moderate conservatives and the unreconstructed old right. The key divergence lies in their attitudes toward World War II, especially Japan's defeat, and toward the democratic reforms that followed."[16]

As for the glue that holds the LDP together, at least since the financial scandals of the early 1970s surrounding former Prime Minister Kakuei Tanaka, it has been universally understood that the LDP runs, first and foremost, on "money politics." Commenting about Tanaka's infamous bribe-taking and corruption scandals, which will be discussed further in the next chapter, the *New York Times*'s William Safire described the situation in tough terms:

> [Japanese] prime ministers and high officials have been on the take for years; Mr. Tanaka stands accused of doing it more aggressively than most, and if convicted might blow the whistle on just about everyone of importance in Japanese business and politics... the politico-economic system of Japan is inherently corrupt. The combination of capitalists, power brokers and government leaders known as "Japan, Inc.," which produced an eye-popping rate of growth and catapulted a defeated island nation into the front rank of superpowers, cannot by its nature be anything but corrupt.... The price of this government sponsorship of business is the "free" in "free enterprise."[17]

J. Mark Ramseyer and Frances McCall Rosenbluth write in their 1993 book *Japan's Political Marketplace* that many scholars of Japan characterize the Construction Ministry as a "politically driven pork wagon."[18] In this vein, Alex Kerr has documented, in almost excruciating detail, the disastrous results of the collusion between bureaucrats, politicians, and the Japanese construction industry. According to Kerr, Japan spends between three and four times more than the United States on public construction each year, although Japan has only one-twentieth the land area and less than half the population.[19] Citing seemingly innumerable examples of Japanese public spending on unnecessary construction projects, he notes the amazing fact that, "by the end of the century, the 55 percent of the shoreline that had been encased in concrete had risen to 60 percent or more. Nobody in their right mind can honestly believe that Japan's seacoasts began eroding so fast and so suddenly that the government *needed* to cement over 60 percent of them."[20]

Ramseyer and Rosenbluth say that "the resulting system may strike observers as 'corrupt,' but it is an institutionally driven corruption."[21] One of the main reasons, they say, for the LDP's lengthy reign is that structural corruption provides incumbents with unmatched opportunities to exchange favors for support. And because the LDP was fortunate enough to grasp power early on after the Second World War, the party has been able to parlay that advantage, seemingly without end.

Note, however, that many also point a finger of responsibility across the Pacific. John Dower, for example, has written extensively in his Pulitzer Prize–winning history *Embracing Defeat: Japan in the Wake of World War II* on the many damaging policies of the so-called "reverse course" policies of U.S.-led occupation forces. Although occupation began with its remarkably altruistic policies of "demilitarization and democratization," plans were radically shifted around 1947 to meet the U.S. foreign-policy requirements of the early cold war.[22] At the expense of democratic reforms, the United States influenced the Japanese system in a manner that ensured that the U.S.-aligned LDP was able to gain dominance.

Patrick Smith, who sees the Japanese system as "the madness of a mutant democracy in which elections function to deprive voters of their democratic rights,"[23] points up recent research revealing that the Central Intelligence Agency (CIA) provided a considerable amount of support to the LDP for at least two decades following occupation in exchange for the LDP's obedience to U.S. cold-war foreign-policy requirements. For instance, an October 9, 1994, page-one *New York Times* article entitled "C.I.A. Spent Millions to Support Japanese Right in the 50's and 60's" says that one reason the CIA's support of the LDP remained secret for so long was that it was so successful.

The article includes corroboration from a number of top U.S. intelligence and other officials:

> "We financed them," said Alfred C. Ulmer Jr., who ran the C.I.A.'s Far East operations from 1955 to 1958. "We depended on the L.D.P. for information." He said the C.I.A. had used the payments both to support the party and to recruit informers within it from its earliest days.
>
> By the early 1960's, the payments to the party and its politicians were "so established and so routine" that they were a fundamental, if highly secret, part of American foreign policy toward Japan, said Roger Hilsman, head of the State Department's intelligence bureau in the Kennedy Administration.
>
> "The principle was certainly acceptable to me," said U. Alexis Johnson, United States Ambassador to Japan from 1966 to 1969. "We were financing a party on our side." He said the payments continued after he left Japan in 1969 to become a senior State Department official.
>
> The C.I.A. supported the party and established relations with many promising young men in the Japanese Government in the 1950's and 1960's. Some are today among the elder statesmen of Japanese politics.[24]

Given these revelations, Smith poses the loaded question: "And how did a small group of conservative politicians, closet xenophobes obsequious toward America but commanding no great enthusiasm among voters, hold power without serious challenge until 1993?"[25]

Indeed, when, on May 1, 2003, U.S. President George W. Bush, in a colorful quasi-victory speech (staged on the aircraft carrier USS *Abraham Lincoln*) after the takeover of Iraq, made comparisons between the stated U.S. goal of transforming Iraq from a dictatorship into a democracy and the way the United States did this in Germany and Japan after the Second World War, at least some Japanese took exception. Kenichi Asano, for instance, was quick to point out that some six decades after its defeat in the war, Japan can in many ways still be described as a U.S. protectorate, with nearly fifty thousand U.S. troops still stationed there. Asano, like many others, says that Japan remains far less than truly democratic, pointing out that Japan's government is often far more slavish to U.S. foreign-policy desires and demands than to the consensus of its own citizenry.[26]

Of course, the full extent to which the United States has directly supported the LDP and actively undermined opposing parties is yet another issue that falls outside the scope of this book. The key point is the LDP's predominance. Ichiro Ozawa, a former LDP politician, has been a key power player since the early 1990s in the movement to dislodge the party from power. He goes so far as to compare the task of beating the LDP with that of "overthrowing the [Tokugawa] Shogunate" that had controlled Japan for two-and-a-half centuries (1601–1868). According to Ozawa, defeating the LDP and putting it out of power is the only hope for his country. "Other than that, there will be no dawn in Japan. A new age won't arrive," he is quoted as saying in a 2004 *New York Times* article. "Therefore, the Meiji Restoration once more."[27]

Politicians and Bureaucrats

Even if one were to accept as true a statement made by LDP Lower House Diet member Ichiro Kamoshita, in an interview for this book, that the LDP's continued reign is the result of "the popular will of the Japanese people, who have freely and strongly supported this party over the years,"[28] it would still be false to assert that the Japanese public exercises much influence over the government through the LDP.

Former U.S. Vice President Walter Mondale, who served as ambassador to Japan from mid-1993 through 1996, is certainly not one to speak overcritically of Japan. In a telephone interview for this book, he described the country as having its own "brand or style" of democracy, but he also acknowledged that this was not just a matter of style or superficialities. "I would emphasize that [the Japanese] opened up to the world and became democratic and on their own terms. There are very deep trends that honor hierarchy and harmony there, where consensus is valued almost as much as the legal process. However, they've ended up with a system in which they do have elections and within which someone who is corrupt in Japan cannot bet that he won't be exposed. I think it has to be included as a free country." Mondale adds, however, "Of course, it is different from Great Britain or America. There is no question that the power of the bureaucracy versus the elected official is different, with the bureaucracy having more authority."[29]

According to Chalmers Johnson, the unelected Japanese bureaucracy dominates the mechanisms of government at the expense of civil sovereignty. Writing in 1995, he described the situation: "Who governs is Japan's elite state bureaucracy. It is recruited from the top ranks of the best law schools in the country; appointment is made on the basis of legally binding national examinations—the prime minister can appoint only about twenty ministers and agency chiefs—and is unaffected by election results. The bureaucracy drafts virtually all laws, ordinances, orders, regulations, and licenses that govern society. It also has extensive extra-legal powers of 'administrative guidance' and is comparatively unrestrained in any way, both in theory and in practice, by the judicial system."[30]

This view that unelected Japanese bureaucrats wield disproportionate power is widely held by many Japanologists. However, J. Mark Ramseyer and Frances McCall Rosenbluth present noteworthy arguments—steeped in so-called rational-choice theory—that the Japanese bureaucracy really is under the control of the LDP, especially when it comes to setting broad policy goals and to providing governmental favors to LDP backers. While the authors admit that an astonishing 75 to 95 percent of all legislation passed in the Diet originates in the bureaucracy and does not come from politicians[31] (a sky-high percentage when compared with most major democracies), they argue that this is only because the LDP has intentionally delegated this work to bureaucrats who initiate such legislation on the LDP's behalf, or at least with the LDP's best interests in mind. According to the authors, the LDP implements a host of control mechanisms (legal and otherwise) to regulate bureaucrats and to ensure that they take actions that help the party stay in power. They argue that if the LDP did not have strong influence over bureaucrats, the bureaucrats would not provide the massive pork projects and other favors to the special interests that support the party, and the LDP would subsequently not be supported by those special interests or be reelected decade after decade.

No Clear Core of National Political Power

In light of the analysis presented in the previous section, it would seem that a strange but legitimate question is: Who, ultimately, is at the reins of national policy in Japan? A number of highly influential English-language books have been written on the matter, including van Wolferen's *The Enigma of Japanese Power*, Johnson's *Who Governs Japan?*, and Ramseyer and Rosenbluth's *Japan's Political Marketplace.*

Whereas Johnson argues that the massive bureaucracy is the preeminent repository of national power, Ramseyer and Rosenbluth assert that the LDP wields the power. On the other hand, van Wolferen (who tends to agree with many of Johnson's overall assessments) goes on to point out that no specific political party, ministry, institution, or individual ultimately "rules," at least not in the way that presidents, prime ministers, and central parties are commonly considered to rule other nations.

According to van Wolferen, Japan is not so much "ruled" as it is "run" by a large and continuously evolving coalition of elite institutions, organizations, and individuals. Chief among them are "certain ministry officials, some political cliques and clusters of bureaucratic businessmen," with many lesser players, including "agricultural cooperatives, the police, the press and gangsters."[32]

Although governmental powers are spread among multiple institutions within any democratic country, van Wolferen says that in Japan ultimate sovereignty is especially diffuse. "It is important to distinguish this situation from others where governments are besieged by special interest groups, or are unable to make up their minds because of inter-departmental disputes," he explains. "We are dealing not with lobbies but with a structural phenomenon unaccounted for in the categories of accepted political theory. There is, to be sure, a hierarchy or, rather, a complex of overlapping hierarchies. But it has no peak; it is a truncated pyramid. There is no supreme institution with ultimate policy-making jurisdiction. Hence there is no place where, as Harry Truman would have said, the buck stops. In Japan, the buck keeps circulating."[33]

Some argue that the diffusion of political power in Japan is very much the result of that country's "culture of consensus," or predilection to make group decisions, and that this should be seen as an admirable, even democratic, trait. However, van Wolferen asserts that this arrangement has little to do with democracy, as the general citizenry has so little influence over these major players. Moreover, because Japan has no single institution, much less a single individual, with the capacity to implement major political decisions, Japanese rulers are often powerless to make meaningful changes when they are most needed. He argues that this absence of a final decision maker in the prewar and wartime periods is what allowed Japan to make the seemingly incomprehensible blunder of attacking the United States, a country that at the time had ten times Japan's industrial might. His analysis certainly goes some way toward explaining Japan's indecisiveness when confronted with issues surrounding its participation in the First Gulf War. That same absence of a decision-making center, says van Wolferen, is the key factor keeping Japan from implementing serious economic and political reforms in the postwar period.

Whether one agrees with Johnson that unelected bureaucrats dominate, with Ramseyer and Rosenbluth that special-interest politicians are ultimately on top, or with van Wolferen's assessment that "no one is essentially in charge," it is clear that Japan's elected officials are often either unwilling or incapable of implementing the popular will of the people.

Weakness of Rule of Law

Many Japanese and foreigners have observed that the rule of law is particularly weak in Japan—especially when compared with other major industrialized democracies—and that cultural, family, class, business, and other noncodified social relationships regularly take precedence over formal laws. Even international comparative-law expert John Owen Haley, who defends the Japanese legal system as a very good one, relatively, admits that in no other industrial society is legal regulation "as confined and as weak as in Japan."[34] Many have concluded that the weakness of the rule of law in Japan has yielded a society where social controls crush dissension and diversity, blunt individual rights, and curtail civil sovereignty—all in a manner that leaves many victims (usually those with the least power in society) without recourse.

This relative lack of rule of law can be seen at all levels of society. Perhaps the most blatant defiance of the Japanese Constitution is the longtime disregard of its famous Article 9, which says "land, sea, and air forces, as well as other war potential, will never be maintained." Despite this unambiguous prohibition, Japan boasts the world's fourth-largest annual expenditure on its military, or "defense forces." Moreover, recent legislation has further legitimized the use of Japan's "land, sea, and air forces" under "emergency" circumstances and in "peacekeeping" exercises, including the 2004 deployment of troops to Iraq. Whether or not one believes Article 9 to be reasonable or just (it remains a contentious issue both within the country and internationally), the flouting of the Constitution for more than half a century has plainly devalued the rule of law.

Also, while the Japanese Constitution guarantees judicial independence, Japanese judges have seldom shown much real freedom from politicians, bureaucrats, or business leaders. A half a century of LDP rule has resulted in a judicial system that could hardly be more sympathetic to the party's desires, if only because the LDP has appointed the Japanese judges it has wanted for decades now, including Supreme Court justices.[35]

Even after judges are appointed by the LDP, their careers remain at the mercy of the LDP-stacked Supreme Court, which is solely responsible for the oversight management of their careers through the office of the Supreme Court Secretariat, which monitors the actions of all judges, makes all job assignments, and doles out promotions. Subsequently, Japanese judges who regularly rule in a manner that displeases the LDP are apt to find themselves relegated to undesirable backcountry and family courts, with little prospect for promotion. According to Ramseyer and Rosenbluth, the current Japanese judiciary is even less independent today than it was during the repressive wartime period: "Before the war, the Ministry of Justice picked the judges; now the cabinet picks them. Before the war, the Ministry of Justice rewarded and punished judges; since the war ended, the senior judges at the Secretariat, who are beholden to the Supreme Court justices, who in turn are beholden to the cabinet, reward and punish them. Prewar judges at least had life tenure, whereas, since the war, the cabinet has had the option every 10 years of firing a judge."[36]

Another good example of the weakness of the rule of law in Japan, discussed at length in chapter 3, is Japanese libel law, which provides victims of media malpractice little recourse to justice and has long failed to properly punish the crimes of the media. Nor can common citizens expect to fare much better when wronged by the state. As a result, Japanese citizens seldom sue the government,[37] and the vast majority of instances where they do so end in findings for the state.[38]

The legal system also fails to protect those deemed by the police to have broken the law. Upon issue of a warrant, Japanese suspects can be held without access to a lawyer for up to twenty-three days.[39] This situation may appear somewhat less shocking in a post–September 11, 2001, world, where the United States has held its own citizens and hundreds of foreign nationals deemed terrorist threats for years without access to lawyers. However, the longtime, routine practice in Japan of holding suspects of all sorts of crimes for more than three weeks without legal counsel still gives one pause. Indeed, the Japanese criminal-justice system is infamous for its sky-high confession rate.[40] Murray Sayle, writing in the *New Yorker*, explains that in 1997 an incredible 92.3 percent of all Japanese defendants tried for serious crimes confessed! Sayle rightly calls this "a record that has only been matched, if ever, in totalitarian states" and continues: "As a consequence, Japan has very few trial lawyers—proportionately a twentieth as many as the United States—and Japanese judges have the most technical task of checking that confessions have been correctly obtained. (Of those who pleaded innocent, only sixty-seven—one in a thousand of those accused—have been acquitted.)"[41]

Even when members of the public are treated fairly by the courts, that treatment is almost always glacially slow. A case in point is the snail-paced trial of Aum Shinrikyo founder Shoko Asahara in regard to the horrific 1995 Tokyo sarin-gas attack. The *Japan Times* ran an insightful op-ed piece in November of 2003,[42] comparing Asahara's torpid trial with the relatively rapid one of Washington, D.C., sniper John Allen Muhammad in the United States. While both men were tried and sentenced to death for high-profile acts of domestic terrorism with similar death tolls and a preponderance of evidence against them, the Japanese case took many times longer than the American, at least when measured from the date of the initial arrest to the date of sentencing. In fact, the Japanese courts took more than six times as long. While it took the U.S. courts just sixteen-and-a-half months to convict Muhammad, it took the Japanese courts eight years and nine-and-a-half months to convict Asahara.[43] The repercussions of such routinely dilatory proceedings are difficult to diminish. The surviving victims, their families, as well as the Japanese public and the world community were forced to wait nearly a decade for justice to be done in the highly emotional and seemingly open-and-shut case, which was also one of the country's most closely followed criminal proceedings ever.

A dearth of lawyers, structural barriers against foreign-trained legal professionals, and social stigmas against pursuing justice through the courts all contribute to the legal system's endemic problems. Sadly, these very shortcomings are fundamental to the maintenance of the present Japanese system of governance. And it is important to keep them in mind when considering the case studies presented in this book.

Strong Controls Exercised over the "Free Market"

Chalmers Johnson has pioneered much original thinking about the Japanese political economy in the last quarter century, including coining the phrase "capitalist developmental state" (CDS) to describe it. According to Johnson, Japan is neither a traditional capitalist economy, such as those of the United States and the European Community countries, nor a centrally planned economy, such as that of the former Soviet bloc. Rather, it is a cross between the two. Although his theory has been controversial in some circles, by and large it has been borne out.

Central to the CDS model is the exceptionally close relationship between the bureaucracy and industry. The Japanese bureaucracy works in concert with the private sector to protect and nurture key industries and even to dictate market strategies, not only for individual companies but for whole industrial sectors. Japanese bureaucratic control can take a variety of forms, such as the implementation of strict tariffs and other protectionist methods designed to thwart foreign competition, or it can take the form of specific "administrative guidance" issued directly to industry leaders. The bureaucracy also secures massive low- and no-interest loans to leading companies in certain sectors that it deems worthy. Johnson puts it simply: the "Japanese economy is guided by a state strategy." He further explains:

> Japanese economic strategy requires that the public interest be elevated over
> private interests, and it delegitimizes the pursuit of private motives openly
> acknowledged.

The Japanese economic strategy is comparable to the American pursuit of a military strategy; and many norms of Japanese economic life—long hours, service to the group, wearing uniforms, equitable pay, and long-term goals—are perfectly familiar to the American military.[44]

Van Wolferen has extended Johnson's analysis, arguing that in the higher echelons of business and government in Japan, there is no fundamental difference between the private and public sectors. In most cases, the government may not directly own or operate private companies or even run the cooperative organizations that coordinate them, but the influence of the government can be so strong that it might as well own them. Augmenting this relationship is the common practice of bureaucrats retiring from government only to take lucrative positions in the very industries that they once regulated or to enter politics as a member of the LDP. The practice of taking early retirement from government to move straight into cushy jobs with companies in their industry is so commonplace that there is even a word for it, *amakudari*, which translates as "descent from heaven," implying with a golden parachute.

Richard Katz, in his book *Japan: The System That Soured,* presents a strong case that the Japanese economy has been extremely overregulated. Unlike Johnson, however, he does not believe that Japan represents a genuine alternative to the capitalist model. Instead, Katz argues that it has simply been in a different stage of development than that of the other major capitalist countries. He says that Japan's devastated early postwar economy required and benefited appropriately from the regulatory coddling provided by government officials in order to get the country back on its feet and make it internationally competitive again. Early postwar Japanese industry needed the infusion of cheap capital and protections from outside competitors to accomplish this. The problem, as Katz sees it, is that long after Japan's economy had grown and become robust, its bureaucrats made the error of continuing to apply the same strategies of overprotection. He writes, "The caterpillar, not believing it had turned into a butterfly, refused to leave the cocoon. No wonder it couldn't fly."[45]

Katz says that contemporary Japan has a "cartelized dual economy," wherein many of its international companies, having faced years of strong competition abroad, are both efficient and competitive. However, far too many of the country's domestic companies, having been spoiled by an overly friendly environment at home, are weak and inefficient. For Katz, Japan's economy is not really of a different category. It has just been overprotected to its own detriment.

Whatever jargon used to describe Japan—as a capitalist developmental state, a country with a free-market fiction, or a system that soured—it is indisputable that the government has overreached in its long campaign to direct the Japanese economy.

Overemphasis on Industrial Output

At the end of the Second World War, Japan was in utter ruins. Most of its major cities were reduced to rubble, and its industrial infrastructure was decimated. A primary concern during the early years of occupation centered on the looming dangers of famine. Given such circumstances, Japanese officials deliberately directed the nation's energies toward industry.

This was not a difficult task. For at least the previous two decades, increasing portions of Japanese society had been set on a path of total military mobilization. In the postwar period, everything was simply redirected from the creation and maintenance of a great national military industrial complex to a purely industrial complex. This may be an oversimplification, but in essence it is accurate.

Van Wolferen describes Japan's economy since the war as "a wartime economy operating in peacetime."[46] Katz argues that this emphasis on industrialization is the cause *both* of the "Japanese economic miracle" that occurred from the 1950s through the 1980s *and also* of the spectacular splat of the Japanese bubble economy in the early 1990s.[47]

The problem is that by having focused so intensely and exclusively on industrial growth at the expense of so many other potential national priorities—democratic rights, the environment, the arts, the establishment of a strong domestic consumer market—Japan's leaders failed to support their people. Rather than identifying industry as a means for the betterment of society and as a foundation upon which to build a rich, flourishing culture, they made industrial expansion the end itself.

A genuinely empowered, well-informed Japanese electorate simply would not tolerate this never-ending overemphasis on industry at their expense. While Japan remains one of the world's wealthiest countries, consumption as a share of gross domestic product (GDP) is notably lower than in other industrialized countries. Japanese citizens are regularly required to put in some of the lowest-paid workweeks in the advanced industrialized world, and death by overwork, or *karoshi,* remains a real problem. Placing industry above all other national priorities has meant that the quality of life for the average citizen has failed to keep pace with the Japanese "economic miracle."

For example, Japanese homes are physically 20 to 30 percent smaller than European homes, but about three times more expensive.[48] Moreover, they are infamous for their shoddy construction. The reduced size of Japanese homes is commonly credited to the misconception that Japan is a country with far too many people and far too little habitable land. But Kerr dismisses this argument as nonsensical. Who could legitimately argue, he asks, that Japan, with its immense wealth and technical expertise, could not reallocate land use in a way that provides people with homes that are more comparable to those of similar industrialized countries? In Kerr's assessment, Japan could easily create more, better, and larger accommodations for its people through such simple means as putting up taller buildings and by developing more hillsides and mountainsides. He insists that the Japanese incorrectly conceive of their country as exceptionally lacking in resources and space:

> When the Japanese describe their country, they will often use the word *semai,* "narrow," "cramped," "crowded." The idea is that Japan's landmass is too small to support its population properly. Of course, there are many nations with less habitable land and higher population densities, including some of the most prosperous countries of Europe and East Asia. Taiwan, South Korea, the Netherlands, and Belgium have higher population densities than does Japan; Britain and Germany have slightly lower but roughly comparable densities. *Semai* is not a physical property; *semai* is in the mind. It's the emotional consequence of Japan's rigid systems, which bind individuals and keep out the fresh air of new ideas from abroad.[49]

The Japanese have been duped into accepting less than they should in the name of national industrial growth.

The Use of Myth and False Ideology

To one degree or another, all societies nurture various myths and ideologies, both accurate and inaccurate, as part of their collective worldviews. Too often, unfortunately, these concepts are popularized and maintained because they serve those in power, while subjugating those not in power. Japan is no exception. Noteworthy, however, is just how divergent from Western notions of "common sense" these myths and ideologies can be.

Leading up to and during the Second World War, Japanese militarist leaders—in their creation of one of the most violent regimes in history—propped themselves up with a host of false myths. These Japanese wartime ideas are frequently referred to as the *kokutai* ("national essence") or *Yamatoist* ideology. The foremost concept within this ideology is that the Japanese emperor descended from an ancient sun goddess and was thus entitled, according to the Meiji Constitution, to his "sacred and inviolable" place at the head of the Japanese nation, or "family," as it was regularly described. Although postwar occupation reforms reduced the emperor to the official status of figurehead or "symbol of national unity," the god myth and a variety of related ideas have not completely lost their power.

This is not to say that significant portions of contemporary Japanese still view their emperor as a god—the vast majority certainly does not. Still, the continued deference shown to the imperial household adds an unmistakable aura of legitimacy to the Japanese bureaucratic structure. After all, in prewar times the bureaucracy was the primary national mechanism for implementing the imperial will.

Although the death of the Showa emperor in 1991 resulted in a noticeable erosion of the cultural taboo against publicly criticizing the imperial household, the taboo remains in place. In fact, the emperor's final illness and death brought many reminders of its power, as the Japanese word *jishuku*, which translates as "self-restraint," became a byword for news reporters and the populous as a whole. While reporters sat on death watch (sometimes for days on end without time off) awaiting the emperor's passing, the citizenry was strongly encouraged by the media to avoid any kind of celebrations or festivities, personal or otherwise, and to assume a posture of grief and mourning.

Although criticisms of the emperor and the Imperial Household Agency do occasionally see print (more often than not in weekly newsmagazines), such incidents are strictly avoided by mainstream journalists. (It is significant, however, that criticism of the current empress is not considered out of line, as she is a "commoner" and not of imperial blood.)

Myths at the Heart of the System

Perhaps more important than the emperor institution itself in Japan, however, are a number of other myths related to or derived from the emperor system. Again, this is not to say that all or even most Japanese believe these myths. Contrary to the first myth listed below, Japan has a rich diversity of thinkers. There may well be as many opinions about these myths as there are Japanese. Unfortunately, many of these false ideas and beliefs retain currency. Here are six:

1. The Japanese are naturally harmonious.
2. The Japanese are an essentially homogeneous racial group.
3. There is a spiritual dimension to being Japanese.
4. The highest virtues are social virtues.
5. There is value in accepting formal, superficial, and fake "realities."
6. Japan was as much an innocent victim of the Second World War as other nations.

It is easy to see how the now generally defunct belief in the Japanese emperor as a deity relates to a number of these myths. For instance, if the leader of the Japanese "race" were a god, there would be a deep spiritual connection among its members. It also follows that reverence toward a deified leader would be a great virtue, as would the expression of deference to social leaders in general.

Myth 1: The Japanese Are Naturally Harmonious

The idea that Japanese are naturally harmonious has been a most powerful tool in the hands of the country's elite, who have used it to discourage criticism. Related to this myth is the idea that Japanese are an essentially non-litigious people—that they not only naturally dislike turning to the judicial system to solve conflicts but tend to have far fewer run-ins with one another than do the citizens of other countries. But even the most cursory reading of Japanese history reveals that Japanese people—unfortunately, like the residents of most nations—have been fighting one another for centuries. There is also little doubt that if Japanese were given a more functional judicial system, one that fully supported individual rights and popular sovereignty, they would take more advantage of that system to right social wrongs.

This false emphasis on the "harmonious nature" of Japanese has also helped to discourage attitudes akin to the British concept of "the loyal opposition." Because harmony is stressed so intensely, it can be very difficult for individuals to disagree on the lesser details of issues while maintaining solidarity on larger issues. The dampening effect of such a myth on freedom of speech is profound and is especially troublesome for Japanese journalism.

Yoshibumi Wakamiya, a deputy managing editor at *Asahi Shimbun,* has been quoted on the effects of this false belief on his profession: "In Japanese society, it is difficult to hold healthy debates. The person you are debating will feel their personality is under attack, and will hold a grudge. That is Japanese society, and we have to get information from our politicians. If you ask sharp questions, you may end up being isolated, even from other journalists."[50]

Myth 2: The Japanese Nation Is an Essentially Homogeneous Racial Group

The related myth of the homogeneity of the Japanese population may well be one of the most dangerous of all those listed here. Before and during the war, the idea of Japanese racial purity was regularly invoked as part of an effort to unify the population against non-Japanese. The emperor's bloodline was considered to be the "purest" of all, with that purity becoming increasingly diffuse as one moved further away in relationship to the royal family. Although it is true that Japan is more homogeneous than many countries and that many Japanese share physical similarities, the idea that it is somehow a uniquely homogeneous country encourages denial of the facts. There are, for example, an estimated two million Japanese citizens with one or more parents or grandparents from Korea, although it is difficult to find solid data on this. Moreover, hundreds of thousands of Koreans in Japan find it so difficult to obtain citizenship that the great majority of them simply opt not to naturalize. Indeed, even after multiple generations of living in Japan—speaking only the Japanese language and knowing very little about their ancestral land of Korea—many Japanese residents of Korean descent do not have Japanese citizenship and are marginalized in society. A number of sources, including the book *Japan's Hidden History: Korean Impact on Japanese Culture,* document the reality that the Korean peninsula has played a pivotal role in shaping Japanese culture. As the authors put it, there has been a "deliberate cover-up of Korea's role in Japan's development" at least since the late nineteenth century.[51]

Of course, even among "pure" Japanese there are significant degrees of physical difference, especially among those from different parts of the country. While it is true that Japan is in many ways less racially diverse than many other countries, it is certainly not the only such country. Sweden jumps immediately to mind, for instance.

The denial of diversity in Japan often results in the denial of individuality. It also encourages a feeling of separateness, disconnectedness, and "differentness" of Japanese from the rest of the world and reinforces ideas of racial hierarchies, both inside Japan and even internationally. It contributes to a paradigm wherein non-Japanese are more likely to be viewed as "others," and that makes it harder for some Japanese to empathize with these "others." To put it bluntly, it encourages racism.

Myth 3: There Is a Spiritual Dimension to Being Japanese

The previous two false concepts of Japanese harmony and homogeneity are inextricably tied up with the false ideology that there is a spiritual dimension to being Japanese. For example, in May of 2000, then–Prime Minister Yoshiro Mori was quoted as stating, "Japan is a divine nation centering on the Emperor."[52]

Van Wolferen writes, "it is almost an article of faith among Japanese that their culture is unique, not in the way that all cultures are unique, but somehow uniquely unique, ultimately different from all others, the source of unique Japanese sensibilities and therefore safe from (if not off-limits to) intellectual probes by outsiders."[53] This myth manifests in a number of ways, one being the commonly asserted idea that non-Japanese cannot comprehend various aspects of Japanese culture.

Feiler writes, "But over time, I came to feel that the problem lay in a simple misconception: most Japanese believe that only they can understand Japan." He goes on to quote a retired Japanese teacher: "'But we are one race,' he insisted. 'We are unique. Only a Japanese person can understand the heart of another. You can't figure us out because you are a foreigner.'"[54]

Among duped foreigners, this false myth is manifest in the cliché that Japan is an exotically "mysterious" and "incomprehensible" land. It is even occasionally said (by both Japanese and non-Japanese) that when two Japanese are together, they hardly need to speak with one another but can "understand" each other with the barest of verbal and nonverbal cues.

Again, in blunt terms, this myth of Japanese spirituality is a subtle form of racism. It unfortunately plays out in unhealthy interactions between Japanese and non-Japanese, who may be discriminated against; and it can also create serious friction between those Japanese who ascribe to it and those Japanese who reject it or who follow other spiritual paths. Obviously, there is nothing in the Japanese gene pool or social group that makes Japanese more "spiritually connected" to one another or fundamentally different from any other subgroup of humanity.

Myth 4: The Highest Virtues Are Social Virtues

This is one of the oldest and most important myths to retain currency in Japan. Ruth Benedict, one of the most influential foreign writers about Japan, touches upon key aspects of this myth in her classic work *The Chrysanthemum and the Sword*.[55] Benedict famously categorizes Japan as a "shame culture," in contrast to the Western "guilt culture." The distinction is that many Japanese individuals are supposedly guided in moral matters by consideration of what actions are most likely to cause them to be shamed by society, whereas many Westerners tend to be guided by concerns of feeling guilty, an emotion based more on inner conceptions of right and wrong.

The Japanese "shame culture," as identified by Benedict, is at least partially rooted in the closed-door policies of Tokugawa Japan. The Tokugawa

Bakufu, or feudal, military government, which ruled Japan from 1601 to 1867, implemented a national policy of extreme isolationism, cutting the nation off from the rest of the world in a manner that few nations or peoples have ever experienced. The policy allowed the government full control over trade, including guns. However, in addition to addressing the fear of invasion by Western powers, this policy was also motivated by the desire to eliminate Christianity's influence in Japan and to assist authorities in controlling other philosophies already well established, such as Buddhism, for instance, which also advocates a reverence for transcendental beings, forces, and principles. The Bakufu did not want their subjects to conceive of anything greater than their earthly, human leaders. Ideas of absolute moral and spiritual truths, or of a "lord in heaven" to whom even earthly leaders were subservient, threatened the Tokugawa desire to rule absolutely.

Decades after the Tokugawa regime was ousted, state Shinto, the racist national religion propounded by twentieth-century militarists, offered its own version of this philosophy. According to state Shinto, nothing was more virtuous or worthy of reverence than the Japanese emperor. Although the emperor's status was drastically lessened after the war, the basic cultural tendency to emphasize social relationships over "universal truths" remains a significant aspect of Japanese culture to this day.

Obviously, the idea that loyalty to one's social superiors represents the highest virtue possible poses serious problems for democracy. Democracy places principles and laws above the dictates of individual leaders. If a significant number of people believe that social relationships reign supreme, then where exactly do ideas of ultimate truths or universal laws fit in?

This deference to social values over transcendental concepts has had profound repercussions for Japanese journalism. If one starts from the supposition that a journalist's role is to seek out and report the truth of the topics he or she covers, then a journalist's conception of "truth" is fundamental to the job. In fact, some might say that journalists are in the "truth business." This is no small point.

Of course, not all Japanese journalists hold social values in such high regard. Moreover, Western journalists are clearly influenced by social circumstances and relationships as well. Still, as the case studies in this book show, the Japanese myth that stipulates that the highest virtues that one can aspire to are social virtues has serious consequences.

Myth 5: There Is Value in Accepting Formal, Superficial, and Fake "Realities"

This myth is deeply rooted with the myth of holding social virtues above transcendental or absolute values. Chapter 3 contains a discussion of the well-known Japanese dichotomy known as *tatemae* (the formal and superficial) and *honne* (the intimate and real). For instance, let us say that someone makes a mistake, such as mispronouncing a word. As in the West, many Japanese social settings would dictate that others, in deference to the person's feelings, pretend that the error did not happen. This is an innocuous example of accepting a false reality (pretending that something did not occur) over the truth of the situation (that something did occur).

In Japan, however, this idea is regularly applied to all manner of social interactions, some of which are anything but innocuous. The most profound example may well be that of the Showa emperor, Hirohito. With the end of the war, Hirohito was suddenly presented (and presented himself) as just another human being, a mere mortal who only happened to be a symbol of national unity at an unfortunate time in history. This stark contradiction to the emperor's prewar and wartime status as a god with ultimate moral authority and power was blatantly apparent to the entire nation. Nevertheless, social circumstance dictated that this new reality be accepted with little or no discussion or dissension, and so it was.

Another example has already been mentioned: the contradiction between Japan's no-war "peace constitution" and the huge national expenditures used to maintain land, sea, and air forces. Although those on the extreme left and extreme right regularly point out this contradiction, for the most part it is simply accepted by the mainstream in Japan.

Herbert P. Bix touches on these issues in his Pulitzer Prize–winning book *Hirohito and the Making of Modern Japan*:

> The new constitution generated problems that were to beset Japan for the remainder of the twentieth century. One such problem was the great divide

between the concept of the state held by Japan's political rulers in 1946–47, and the modern secular, demilitarized, civil state concept enshrined in the new constitution, in conformity with the wishes and aspirations of most Japanese.

The political elites had not been the original drafters of the constitution they were duty bound to implement. Like Hirohito, they too did not believe in many of its ideals, including especially the notion of the demilitarized state and the principle of the separation of politics and religion.

The constitution of Japan also left unresolved the problem of the symbol monarchy's place in Japanese national identity.... How were the Japanese citizens supposed to regard their formerly divine emperor who remained on his throne, though now only a "symbol," and had never accepted responsibility for his earlier behavior?[56]

In Japan, the truth of a situation does not have to be based solely on empirical proof but is often considered to be situational, or based on social circumstances. The perpetuation of this thinking supports the system by creating intellectual space for elites (and journalists) not merely to give their "spin" on issues, but to present entirely fictitious versions of reality.

Myth 6: Japan Was as Much an Innocent Victim of the Second World War as Other Nations

Westerners are sometimes astounded to hear from seemingly well-educated Japanese that their nation was as much a victim of the Second World War as other nations. Of course, there is no disputing that many innocent Japanese suffered terribly under the militarist leadership and from the conflict. In particular, the tremendous suffering created by the firebombing of Japanese cities and the atomic bombing of Hiroshima and Nagasaki has played a critical role in Japanese thinking about the war. As a result, unfortunately, many Japanese have come to think of the war almost solely in terms of their nation's victimization, and they forget or ignore the ruthless aggression perpetrated by Japan that resulted in the deaths of a staggering twenty-two million non-Japanese Asians.

This way of thinking about the war has become increasingly common and has created many problems for Japan on the international stage. Many younger Japanese have little or no idea of the brutality unleashed by the militarists on military and civilian populations alike throughout East Asia. Indeed, many young Japanese today are more likely to refer to the war's "end" than to their country's "defeat." The war itself is often thought of as an unpredictable force of nature that manifested at that time rather than as the result of the actions of power-hungry, racist leaders who imposed their perverted philosophy and sick schemes upon the country.

One recent example of this mind-set is the frenzy of outrage that erupted against North Korea when it was revealed that the North Korean government abducted dozens of Japanese civilians in the 1970s and that many of them have since died. This was a horrible crime. Yet few Japanese seem to remember that as recently as the 1940s, during the living memory of many people today, the Japanese government abducted hundreds of thousands of Korean civilians into forced labor and even sexual slavery, torturing, maiming, and killing countless individuals. Meanwhile, the Japanese government persists in failing to pass legislation supportive of either the surviving abducted Korean laborers or the sex slaves.

Many express fear that Japan's "culture of amnesia" about the war will lead to a resurgence of Japanese militarism. This certainly is not impossible. However, the immediate problem is that it consistently undermines Japan's foreign policy with its neighbors, who continue to view Japanese power with deep suspicion.

Summary

For all the nondemocratic and antidemocratic aspects of the system described in this chapter, Japan is a far cry from the wartime military dictatorship it once was. Unfortunately, it is also anything but the democratic utopia it is sometimes wrongly portrayed as being. As the succeeding chapters demonstrate, the Japanese news media is especially culpable in creating and maintaining this dysfunctional status quo. It is also seriously influenced by the politics of power around it.

The Japanese people deserve far more from the country that they toil so diligently to support. And so do their neighbors in East Asia, as well as the members of the global community within which Japan is such a powerful influence. The various problems and issues enumerated in this chapter may manifest themselves in an assortment of ways, but they all result in one thing: the subjugation and suffering of people. And as this book shows, they are all closely related to exaggerations, misrepresentations, and lies masquerading as news in the Japanese media.

CHAPTER TWO

JAPAN'S CORRUPT NEWS MEDIA

Japanese press clubs are nothing more than transfer devices. They function and will continue to function as mouthpieces for those interests that hold power in this country, because all they [press club journalists] do is a rote transfer of the information they are provided by news sources. This is assured, because that is the way they are able to stay close to the powers they work with and from whom they are fed exclusive information. The newspapers, of course, find this to be a very low-cost option for filling their pages, and so from a market perspective, it's hard for editors and managers to resist.

—Tatsuya Iwase[1]

A Godzilla of the News

The Japanese news media is one of the largest and most technically sophisticated in the world. The nation's newspaper industry truly seems larger than life. The circulation of Japan's largest newspaper, *Yomiuri Shimbun,* for example, is the highest in the world with more than 10,000,000 daily readers of its morning edition alone, about the same as the combined circulations of the top ten daily newspapers in the United States. While the combined circulation for the top ten newspapers in the United States is 10,102,833,[2] the most recent figure available for *Yomiuri* was 10,180,981![3] As with most major dailies in Japan, *Yomiuri* still puts out a morning and an evening edition—a now-bygone practice in much of the world. Although those who receive the evening edition are mainly the same as those who receive the morning edition, the evening run accounts for yet another 4,065,203 *Yomiuri* papers distributed every day.

In fact, *Yomiuri's* main rival, *Asahi Shimbun*—the second-largest paper in the world—also has a circulation that is not far behind that of the combined top ten U.S. papers. *Asahi* puts out a morning edition with a circulation of 8,321,934 and an evening edition with a circulation of 4,003,570. Japan's five national daily newspapers are all among the twenty largest in the world.[4] According to the Nihon Shimbun Kyokai (NSK or Japan Newspaper Publishers and Editors Association), the average Japanese household subscribes to nearly 1.1 newspapers per day.[5] Indeed, 86 percent of Japanese citizens read one or more of the more than 70,000,000 newspapers sold there each day.[6]

The Japanese, who have a nearly 100 percent literacy rate, also appear to be significantly more influenced by the tremendous amount of news material they consume. In one study, just 20 percent of U.S. residents polled expressed high confidence in television and print news,[7] yet a *Yomiuri Shimbun* survey in 2000 found that 88 percent of Japanese respondents trusted the information printed in their newspapers.[8] The high degree of faith that many Japanese have in their newspapers may well stem from the most commonly voiced criticism of the Japanese education system: that while it can be superb at transmitting fundamentals such as literacy, memorization, and other skills, it has traditionally taught students to avoid criticizing those in positions of authority and to accept what they are told. Whatever its causes, this is a pivotal statistic and should not be overlooked by Westerners who might expect the Japanese public to have a similar attitude toward the media as readers in their own countries. Japan's news industry is not only one of the most massive, it is also one of the most powerful: a genuine Godzilla of the news.

Japanese Weekly Newsmagazines

Japan's unique weekly newsmagazines, or *shukanshi,* which include some of the most scandalous publications on earth, comprise a media genre without any real parallel in the Western world. For a more detailed look at some of these publications, see appendix B, Anatomy of *Shukanshi.*

These *shukanshi* are characterized by the bizarre (to Western readers) diversity of material found within their pages. It is as if text and photos from

Newsweek, the *New Yorker, People, Playboy,* and the *National Enquirer* had all been stapled together inside the same cover. For instance, *shukanshi* often present hard-hitting political exposés next to inconsequential gossip, relatively sophisticated cultural analysis right alongside the most sophomoric erotica. They feature short stories and literary reviews but also throw in a fair share of puerile jokes, vulgar innuendo, and obscene cartoons. They can even present the best investigative journalism Japan has to offer, making the weeklies virtual must-reads for Japanese who want to be in the know on the latest political scandals.

Diet member Mizuho Fukushima is a case in point. A leading Japanese feminist who is not inclined to appreciate the often lewd language and pornography in *shukanshi,* she nevertheless considers reading them indispensable, according to the *New York Times:* "Women should take the initiative in eliminating the nudity from these magazines," Fukushima said. "But I must buy them because they always carry stories on subjects that I need to know about, subjects that the newspapers don't cover."[9]

Similarly, Alex Kerr, a Western-born author who has won a major Japanese literary prize for his Japanese-language writing about Japanese culture, confirmed this viewpoint in an interview for this book. "Of course I read them. I get some of the best information from them. Of course, you have to be very careful with them, they are so unreliable," he warns.[10]

The weeklies are in some ways stepchildren of the daily papers, comprising a news category distinct from Japan's "establishment news media." This is not to say that they are not well-established publications enmeshed in the broader media and power structures or that they are not highly influential— they certainly are. They are not, however, permitted to join the Japanese press club, or *kisha kurabu,* system. This basic Japanese news-gathering institution can be described in broad terms as an exclusive social mechanism designed to facilitate intimate ties between government and corporate officials on one hand and the country's major news providers on the other. While Japanese weekly newsmagazines are excluded from it, the fact is that they could never exist in their current form were it not for the press club system.

The weekly newsmagazines take a very different approach to news coverage, both in content and style, than do the establishment media. The weeklies tend to be brash, sensationalistic, and irreverent, in glaring contrast to the establishment press, which is characteristically fact-oriented, staid, authoritative, and downright dull, giving very little interpretation or analysis of the news it reports. They are widely acknowledged to be less accurate than the establishment press. The informal, unscientific survey of one hundred Japanese taken for this book suggests that, on average, people estimate that less than half the material in the weekly newsmagazines is true—46 percent, to be specific, although responses to this question varied widely. (See appendix A.)

Two major issues in Japan further compound the worst excesses of *shukanshi*. First is the especially unrestrained nature of powerful news and publishing corporations in a country where libel suits are exceptionally rare and ineffective, and where individual rights are not always highly valued. Second is the intensely commercial and sensational nature of the magazine industry itself.

The worst material in the magazines is also troubling because the top headlines in each issue show up everywhere—on trains and subways and in the mainstream newspapers—in the seemingly ubiquitous advertisements that run for each issue. In this way, the influence of the magazines is multiplied many times over, reaching far beyond their actual readership to touch almost everyone.

The Japanese Establishment News Media

As noted, the weekly newsmagazines do not exist in a vacuum, and to understand them it is essential to consider the basic structure of the news media to which they belong. It is true that in many ways the weeklies serve as counterpoint to the Japanese establishment papers and broadcasters, although not necessarily in the ways that they claim.

The most defining features of the Japanese establishment news media are the uniformity of information and the bland manner in which it is reported. Sociologist and Japanese press historian Taketoshi Yamamoto has noted that "rare indeed is the capitalist nation that has print and broadcast media that carry such uniform news as Japan. If you were to hide the masthead, it would be virtually impossible to tell from the contents which newspaper you were reading."[11] In an interview for this book, Japanese journalist Katsuichi Honda described the situation in similar terms: "Japan's news is as uniform as that of the former Soviet Union. This is especially amazing, given that it is legally a completely free press."[12]

Regarding the dullness of the material presented, former *Washington Post* Tokyo Bureau Chief Tom Reid put it this way: "The first thing I would say about the Japanese media, particularly newspapers, is that they're boring.... [In journalism,] the first rule is to be accurate. But the second rule is to be interesting. Because if it's not interesting nobody will read it; and what's the point? It's just a waste of ink. I think it really both-ers me that Japanese newspapers are so boring."[13]

Japanese newspapers are so well known for their dullness in simply laying out facts that author Tatsuya Iwase has written an entire Japan-ese-language book about the phenomenon, with a title that translates into English as "The Reason Why Newspapers Are Boring."[14] He says, "News-papers here don't write lies, but they avoid deal-ing with uncomfortable truths. Japan has the hardware of the Western press, but there is no software. The inside is empty."[15]

Tatsuya Iwase is an experi-enced Japanese magazine writer and an eloquent critic of the Japanese press club sys-tem. He is also the author of the book *Shimbum ga omoshi-roku nai ri yuu* (The Reason Why Newspapers Are Boring).

Four major factors conspire to make the estab-lishment news media's reporting so uniformly drab: (1) the high concentration of power in Japanese media, (2) the marketing strategies of the major papers, (3) editorial tradition, and (4) the government's enormous influ-ence over the papers through a variety of institutions but particularly through the press club system.

The High Concentration of Media Power

The fundamental structure of today's Japanese news media can be traced directly to the militaristic government of 1931–1945, which saw the begin-ning of the China war and lasted until the end of the Second World War. The leadership of the time used the news media as a highly effective thought-control tool over the populace to focus all of the nation's resources toward

military goals—what came to be known as the National Spiritual Mobilization Movement, or Kokumin Seishin Sodoin Undo. The militarists enacted
drastic censorship, resource rationing, and other policies that drove thousands
of publishers out of business and successfully consolidated the industry in
short order. The structure that emerged included five major national daily
newspaper companies as well as "local" papers for the fifty-one prefectures.

Unlike other authoritarian regimes such as those of Germany and the
Soviet Union, the Japanese government permitted the continued private
(albeit intensely consolidated and intensively regulated) ownership of newspapers. This strategy proved wise: whereas the Nazi Party in Germany exerted
airtight control over the news, the Japanese press actually produced far more
effective propaganda. Japanese journalism historian Gregory Kasza explains
this situation in his superb book *The State and Mass Media in Japan*:

> [In Nazi Germany,] the ideological imperative of direct party control under-
> mined the effectiveness of propaganda in convincing the reader. Japan's pro-
> paganda machine did not labor under this ideological handicap. Since those
> actually writing the articles and moving the presses were the same old
> employees of the venerable *Asahi Shimbun*, journalistic quality was as good
> as ever, and outside the intellectual class, until very late in the war there is lit-
> tle evidence of widespread skepticism about what was being written.[16]

After the war, the U.S.-led occupying force, the Supreme Command for
the Allied Powers (SCAP), implemented some reforms but intentionally
elected not to dismantle most aspects of the wartime Japanese media, including its highly concentrated ownership. This is similar to the way SCAP chose
not to dismantle or seriously reform the Japanese bureaucracy. Indeed, both
Japan's contemporary bureaucracy and its establishment news media have
retained tight working relationships that have their foundations in the prewar period.

As with its decision not to dismantle the bureaucracy, SCAP chose to give
the Japanese news media a wide berth, not because it was considered best for
the fledgling democracy in the long run, but because SCAP wanted to use the
established and easily manipulated media structure to influence Japanese
public opinion to SCAP's own ends. John Dower writes extensively on this

topic,[17] strongly emphasizing the importance of SCAP censorship during the nearly seven long years that Japan was occupied after the war. He also shows that a major difference between the censorship by the Japanese militarists and SCAP is that SCAP censorship was not publicly acknowledged. Dower asks:

Can anyone really believe that no harm was done to postwar [Japanese] political consciousness by a system of secret censorship and thought control that operated under the name of "free expression"—indeed, waved this banner from the rooftops—and yet drastically curbed any criticism of General MacArthur, SCAP authorities, the entire huge army of occupation, occupation policy in general, the United States and other victorious Allied powers, the prosecution's case as well as the verdicts in the war-crimes trials, and the emperor's personal war responsibility once the victors pragmatically decided that he had one?[18]

Dower goes on to describe the profound repercussions of SCAP's engineered consensus through censorship, many of which reverberate to the present time in Japan and deserves serious consideration in regard to other U.S.-occupied lands:

This was not a screen for weeding out threats to democracy (as official justifications claimed), but rather a new chapter in an old book of lessons [the Japanese had learned] about acquiescing to overweening power and conforming to dictated consensus concerning permissible behavior. From this perspective, one legacy of the revolution from above was continued socialization in the acceptance of authority—reinforcement of a collective fatalism vis-à-vis political and social power and of a sense that ordinary people were really unable to influence the course of events. For all their talk of democracy, the conquerors worked hard to engineer consensus; and on many critical issues, they made clear that the better part of political wisdom was silence and conformism.[19]

Subsequently, to this day the Japanese news media continues to be dominated by just six major entities: the five daily newspaper companies (each of which has close ties with a major television station) plus the national broadcast organization, Nihon Hoso Kyokai (NHK), or the Japan Broadcasting

Corporation. This is an especially salient point, given: (1) the extreme and rapid news-media consolidation globally at the end of the twentieth century and beginning of the twenty-first, and (2) the tendency for many of the conglomerates that own the remaining (and increasingly powerful) global news-media companies to come from nonmedia backgrounds and to emphasize profitability over journalistic concerns.

All five of Japan's major daily newspapers put out a morning and evening edition, a practice that is almost unheard of today in the West. The five papers are: *Yomiuri*, with a circulation of about 10.2 million; *Asahi*, with about 8.3 million; *Mainichi*, with about 4 million; *Nihon Keizai*, with about 3.1 million; and *Sankei*, with about 2 million.[20] Again, these figures are just for the morning editions of the papers, as evening readerships tend to be smaller and mainly comprise the same individuals that read the morning papers.

Each of Japan's five dailies also has a direct link with one of the five national commercial television stations: *Yomiuri* is affiliated with Nippon TV, *Asahi* with TV Asahi, *Mainichi* with TBS (Tokyo Broadcasting Systems), *Nihon Keizai* with TV Tokyo, and *Sankei* with Fuji TV. These associations are subject to some legal constraints under the principle of avoiding excessive concentrations of media power, but the papers and their associated broadcasters do wield significant influence over one another all the same. Also, some of the rules were recently loosened to allow newspapers to own a higher percentage of television stations, a reality that mirrors the Western news-media paradigm of multimedia ownership.

When considering how the Japanese news media, under the control of the brutal militarists, were so effectively consolidated down to just six major companies, it is frightening to note that as of 2003, just six companies dominate the U.S. news media as well. Ben H. Bagdikian, writing in the most recent edition of his classic book *The Media Monopoly*, explains, "The top six firms, ordered solely on their annual media revenues, are Time Warner, Disney, Viacom (an amalgam of CBS and Westinghouse), News Corp, Bertelsmann, and General Electric. These six have more annual media revenues than the next twenty firms combined."[21] Interestingly, when Bagdikian's book was first published in 1983, he sounded an alarm because a mere *fifty* corporations dominated almost every mass medium in the United States at that time.

Today, the thought of a national U.S. news media with fifty major players strikes one as a cornucopia of diversity.

Of course, highly concentrated news industries do not automatically lead to dictatorships. Still, as Bagdikian points out, the situation does pose real dangers to basic democratic tenets:

> Major industries, including those controlling the media, have always been more comfortable with conservative politics. Now that these industries own their countries' daily printed and broadcast news, it is not surprising that their newly acquired staffs have come to understand that they remain in their employers' good graces by downplaying or keeping unwanted ideas out of the printed and broadcast news. With time, this shrunken social-political range becomes the accepted definition of what is news. The emerging picture has overtones, subtle or otherwise, of an Orwellian Big Brother, Incorporated. Such concentrated private power is not what the creators of the American democracy had in mind when they created the First Amendment guaranteeing free speech and free press.[22]

If even a portion of Bagdikian's assertions are true—that the depth and breadth of discourse is constrained by high concentrations of media power and that such media industries are easily manipulated by power holders— this is even more the case in Japan, where the press media has suffered from such high ownership concentration for some seventy years.

Marketing Strategies

In keeping with established Japanese business practice, newspapers there do not pursue short-term profits anywhere nearly as avidly as do firms in other capitalist countries. Instead, Japanese newspapers choose the longer-term approach of fighting for market share. In the newspaper business, this means that rather than striving to fill specific niches—and thus developing unique identities to do so—the emphasis is on having the largest number of subscribers. As a result, some 99 percent of Japanese newspapers (excluding the entertainment tabloid newspapers) are delivered directly to homes. Japanese newspaper-sales campaigns are broadly targeted at all demographic groups simultaneously and are promoted through intense door-to-door subscription drives. These drives often include visits from newspaper-circulation sales-people, who can be aggressively persistent and who often offer subscribers substantial gifts and other deals.

As part of this strategy, each national paper makes a conspicuous effort to offer articles on as many different topics as possible, all the while following an editorial policy that avoids offending any significant demographic group. This reinforces the tendency of journalists to emphasize facts over opinion, especially on controversial subjects. It also tends to yield an exceptionally boring take on the news.

Hajime Kitamura, former head of the Japan Federation of Press Workers' Unions, who has experience both as a seasoned newspaper reporter and a weekly newsmagazine editor, firmly believes that the marketing strategies of the papers make them boring. "At the newsstand, daily papers would not sell well at all," Kitamura explained in an interview for this book. "However, newspapers can afford to be boring for a certain number of days every week, as they are assessed by their readers, not on a per-issue basis but on a longer-term basis, perhaps on a monthly basis. . . . The papers don't have to try to grab people's attention."[23]

Editorial Tradition

The traditional market-share approach fits hand in glove with the Japanese editorial policy known as *fuhen futo*, which can be translated as "unbiased and nonpartisan" reporting. This policy was developed early in Japanese press history, during the Meiji period (1868–1912). Many newspapers were established at this time with the sole purpose of championing a particular political issue, party, or agenda. But the later shift away from their initial partisan causes to *fuhen futo* allowed papers to outlast their founding causes and take on lives of their own. In the best cases, *fuhen futo* led to an editorial policy that was, as the term indicates, "objective and fair." In too many cases, however, it was used as a justification for not criticizing anything except the safest targets, such as issues and individuals that met with government disapproval or perhaps those that other papers had already criticized without serious repercussion.

During the Meiji period, and in varying degrees up to the end of World War II, various Japanese laws and policies empowered government officials to censor and fine newspapers they disapproved of, and to imprison editors, owners, and even copy editors and printers. So it's not hard to see how the idea of a *fuhen futo* policy was a boon to Japanese publishers desperate for an editorial approach that would help them avoid costly run-ins with the authorities. Today, despite the fact that the Japanese Constitution provides for freedom of the press, this same editorial tradition continues, and for the same reason: to keep news-media members in the good graces of the authorities with whom they are so closely aligned.

Of course, the policy of *fuhen futo* also supports the papers' traditional marketing strategies by justifying bland, uncontroversial coverage that does not offend any broad readership base or advertising contingency.

Government Influence over News Media

The other major reason for the lockstep uniformity within the Japanese establishment news media is the government itself. Although its most infamous tool for influencing coverage is the *kisha* club system, the Japanese government has a wide arsenal of other methods at its disposal for keeping the press in line.

Ties between national papers and national broadcasters do more than simply hinder diversity in the news. For decades now, Japanese news companies have earned more income from the broadcast end of the business than from the printed word. Because the central government issues broadcast licenses on a renewable basis, the ruling party holds a lethal (albeit rarely used) weapon over the broadcasters and, therefore, against the newspapers too. For example, in 1993, after the Liberal Democratic Party (LDP) lost power for the first time since the party's founding in 1955, the news-division director of TV Asahi made a statement that almost cost the company its license. The director at that time, Sadayoshi Tsubaki, bragged at a meeting of the National Association of Private Broadcasters of Japan that TV Asahi's negative coverage of the LDP was responsible for the LDP's landmark loss. As a result, when the LDP regained power only nine months later, the president of TV Asahi was summoned before the Diet, where LDP politicians reprimanded him before the nation—a standard Japanese parliamentarian move to humiliate individuals. The LDP further underscored Asahi's tenuous position by seeing that the company's license was renewed for only one year rather than the standard five years. The message from the LDP to the news media was clear: Japanese newspapers and broadcasters who do not report the news in a manner acceptable to the ruling government jeopardize their very existence.

Another area of government influence over the news is the massive non-profit organization NHK, Japan's single largest broadcaster. Similar both in size and structure to Great Britain's BBC (British Broadcasting Corporation), NHK employs some ten thousand people and owns four TV stations: two that broadcast via satellite and two that use terrestrial signals. It is legally neither a directly state-operated enterprise nor a purely public corporation. Like the BBC, it is financially supported by a per-household viewing fee, which in 2002 amounted to about ¥3,000 (yen) per month (approximately US$30). NHK's total income in 1999 was ¥645 billion, or about US$6.45 billion. (In comparison, the BBC's income was about US$4 billion for the year 2000–2001.)[24] NHK's annual budget must be approved by the Diet, which also appoints its head officers, thus exerting a substantial influence over it.

Ellis Krauss's book *Broadcasting Politics in Japan: NHK and Television News* offers one of the most detailed studies available of NHK and its relationship with the Japanese state. The book documents the close relationship between the fortunes of the Japanese bureaucracy and the popularity of NHK. Through careful comparative analysis of NHK's 7 PM news broadcasts (the single most popular news source in Japan for many years), the book reveals how NHK's coverage consistently legitimizes the Japanese bureaucracy: "NHK's political coverage is unique among the major industrialized democracies' public and commercial broadcasters in that it provides disproportional attention to the national bureaucracy, portraying it as the prime actor engaged in governing, managing conflict, and making societal rules and as an impersonal and active guardian of the interests of the average citizen. It is also idiosyncratic in the extreme to which it carries its factual, opinionless and dramatically anemic style."[25] Krauss shows in no uncertain terms how this quasi-governmental broadcaster has played a profound role in supporting the Japanese system of governance throughout the postwar period. His conclusion that NHK's news coverage has been a boon to the Japanese power establishment (especially as it relates to the unelected bureaucracy) is all but unassailable.

Japanese Press Clubs

Karel van Wolferen, who has many years of experience writing as a foreign correspondent, comments that "the variation of opinion among newspapers is smaller [in Japan] than anywhere in the world that I have seen. Only in countries where regimes have dictatorial power over the press can you find such unanimity. It could hardly be otherwise in Japan, given the *kisha kurabu* [press club] system."[26]

Van Wolferen is not alone in this opinion. In recent years, a number of English-language books have been published that similarly denounce Japanese press clubs. The most focused of these are *Closing the Shop: Information Cartels and Japan's Mass Media* (2000), *A History of Japanese Journalism: Japan's Press Club as the Last Obstacle to a Mature Press* (1997),[27] and *Cartels of the Mind: Japan's Intellectual Closed Shop* (1998).[28] The main criticism of Japanese press clubs is their exclusivity. With few exceptions, only members of Japanese establishment newspapers, broadcasters, and news agencies are allowed to belong. Writers for all magazines, political and religious publications, and tabloid newspapers are banned, as are freelance journalists of all stripes. Until 1993, writers for all foreign news outlets were also excluded. Indeed, only after significant international pressure was brought to bear were they finally allowed membership in a limited number of the more important press clubs. Unfortunately, membership has included conditions that limit foreign journalists to the status of mere observers or that do not allow foreign journalists access to more-intimate interactions with sources. Moreover, even when granted unrestricted membership to the clubs, most foreign writers are unable to devote the time necessary to participate full-time in any given club (with the exception of some financial reporters who are active in finance-related clubs). Thus, the privileges of foreign writers remain limited at best. For example, foreign reporters in Japan who belong full-time to a given club routinely miss out on many important club activities such as "informal briefings" with news sources. And those foreigners who have rights to multiple clubs regularly find themselves scrambling from one to another in hopes of catching up with the news.

In October 2002, this exclusion of foreign journalists led to protests against the system by the European Union (EU), which called for the complete abolition of the Japanese press clubs. The EU rightly described them as "a de facto competitive hindrance" to both Japanese and foreign media organizations by denying fair access to what ought to be public information.[29] The EU continued applying pressure on this issue in December of 2003, stressing that its call for the abolition of the clubs had nothing to do with a misinterpretation of the functions of the clubs on behalf of the EU. "We reject the statement that our proposals are based on misunderstanding, cultural biases and misconception of facts," Etienne Reuter, a spokesman for the Delegation of the European Commission in Japan, told a news conference.[30]

At the time of publication of this book, it would seem that the EU's stand may be yielding some results, as Japan made a vague concession offer in February of 2004. Still, such a concession, if genuine, is not likely to substantially alter the nature of the clubs. Except for a tentative offer to provide foreign journalists (who register with the Foreign Ministry) access to press conferences sponsored by press clubs, there would be little change to the system domestically. Indeed, there is no offer to increase access to press conferences for Japanese citizens whatsoever.

Given that accountability, access, and transparency in government are cornerstones of democracy, the restriction of access to what should be public information to but a handful of private news organizations flouts the very ideals of popular sovereignty. Perhaps the most shocking aspect of the press club system is that Japanese journalists participate so willingly, even enthusiastically, in it. At its core, the Japanese press club system is about Japanese journalists excluding other Japanese journalists from what by all rights should be public information. It is about journalists suppressing journalism.

Tatsuya Iwase described press clubs in an interview for this book:

> On an individual level, I know Japanese reporters who are passionate about doing good investigative reporting, about pursuing the truth. But Japanese press clubs are nothing more than transfer devices. They function and will continue to function as mouthpieces for those interests that hold power in this country, because all they [press club journalists] do is a rote transfer of the information they are provided by news sources. This is assured, because that is the way they are able to stay close to the powers they work with and

from whom they are fed exclusive information. The newspapers, of course, find this to be a very low-cost option for filling their pages, and so from a market perspective, it's hard for editors and managers to resist.[31]

Each member of a press club tends to be inundated with the same large quantities of information provided by the club's news source that all the other members of the club receive. This information comes through press releases, lectures, press conferences, and the like, and is, of course, presented by the source in a calculated manner designed to put the source in as flattering a light as possible.

A few brave, altruistic Japanese like Iwase have spoken out and fought hard against their country's corrupt press club system. One of the pioneers of this movement is Ken Takeuchi, the former mayor of Kamakura, in Kanagawa Prefecture, an important coastal city about an hour's journey from Tokyo.

For some twenty-six years, Takeuchi served as a journalist for *Asahi*, widely considered Japan's most esteemed newspaper. Among his various positions, he was assigned to press clubs at the prime minister's office, one of the most prestigious assignments for any Japanese journalist. By the time Takeuchi made the change from writing about politicians to becoming one himself, he had acquired formidable knowledge of both occupations—knowledge that motivated him to be the first Japanese politician to loosen his own iron grip on "public" information through his mayoral press club.

Takeuchi opened his city's press club to free-lance writers and foreign correspondents—a move that was considered radical at the time, in 1996. Although he did not open it to the entire public, or even to every legitimate member of the press (for example, writers for party and religious-organ papers still were not allowed), his action was, at the very least, a bold symbolic step for an elected Japanese official.

The man to the right is Ken Takeuchi, the former mayor of the city of Kamakura. He was one of the first Japanese officials to successfully challenge the Japanese press club system. To his left is Masao Kunihiro, distinguished visiting professor at the University of Edinburgh. Kunihiro is a notable Japanese television personality and teacher of English. They were interviewed together for this book.

Takeuchi explained in an interview for this book that his decision was based on his own experience as a member of the prime minister's press club:

> The one thing I can tell you is that at the *Asahi* newspaper company, as a whole, something was not right. We were very much swayed and influenced by the government and the country's financial interests. I felt this way, and many of my colleagues had that feeling as well. I had a notion that reform was absolutely necessary. I wondered what I actually did for *Asahi* newspaper. Reflecting on my behavior, I see that my attitude was simply to chase after then–Prime Minister [Kakuei] Tanaka. Because I was so close to him every day, I was just seeking out information from him. Where was he going? What was he doing? What was he saying? In other words, I was utterly influenced by him. I felt that I was part of the authority of the government. My mind-set was to seek out the information that he offered, not to write critically about him or the existing structure surrounding him.[32]

Since Takeuchi's initiatives, another politician, Yasuo Tanaka, governor of Nagano Prefecture, has taken things even further, issuing a "Declaration of Departure from the Press Club System" on May 15, 2001, and subsequently dismantling the press club system in his prefecture. Like Takeuchi, Governor Tanaka is also a man of letters, not a news reporter but a novelist of some fame as well as a former freelance writer. He replaced Nagano's press clubs with a media center that is completely open to the public. Yasuo Tanaka explains his move:

> Is it possible to say that it is good for citizens to spend tax revenues on such a Japanese press club? Since I was inaugurated as a governor, I have repeatedly suggested that we should invite newspapers such as *Akahata,* the Japan Communist Party newspaper; and *Seikyo Shimbun,* the Soka Gakkai [see chapter 6] newspaper; and others to our press conferences. However, three kisha clubs in Nagano jointly controlled access to the governor's press conferences and refused to allow such a thing. . . . However, I am the person who gives the speeches. As a governor elected by a free and fair election, I could not stand this situation. There is no reason for a special group of people to own exclusionary rights over space in a public building. Why should anyone be excluded

from the press conferences of a public official? I presented this matter over and over to the members of the local press club, but they never took action. They just said that they would consider it. That's why I made the change.[33]

In an interview on the matter with Kenichi Asano, the governor went so far as to liken the press club to the Japanese bureaucracy for its vague, non-committal responses to his initial proposals, feeling that this justified his action. "The press club's reply that they would 'consider the issue' was just like the standard reply of a typical Japanese bureaucrat. Very few Japanese citizens know the actual conditions of Japanese press clubs, because the mass media do not report on their actions at all. In fact, not one major Japanese newspaper dealt with my decision to eliminate the Nagano press club in an editorial."[34]

Ivan P. Hall has commented on the matter by stating, "the Nagano governor's move was an enormously bold break with the past. But the response of playing down coverage and discussion of it was a classic defensive ploy of the Japanese press against criticisms of its ways. This is how they have gotten away with it again and again!"[35]

Yasuo Tanaka, governor of Nagano Prefecture, enters his "glass-walled" governor's office. Tanaka was the first major Japanese politician to do away with his local press clubs. Unfortunately, virtually no other politicians have followed his lead, and the mainstream news media has written very little about this radical step toward a healthier Japanese news corps. *(Photo courtesy of Mainichi Photo Bank.)*

Restricting Access and Dictating "The Story": The Prime Minister's Press Club

An example of a major failure of the Japanese establishment press, one that is deeply related to press clubs, involves former Prime Minister Kakuei Tanaka, arguably the most powerful Japanese prime minister of the postwar period. His story is also a key instance of admirable journalism on the part

Former Japanese Prime Minister Kakuei Tanaka at Tokyo District Court on the day of the ruling in the Lockheed trial. He was found guilty and sentenced to jail. *(Photo courtesy of Mainichi Photo Bank.)*

of a magazine journalist. Kakuei Tanaka was a self-made man who reached the pinnacle of Japanese power from humble beginnings by sheer tenacity—a particularly unusual route to the top in Japan, where a degree from the prestigious Tokyo University is all but a prerequisite for high political positions. And in a political environment where financial corruption is so rife that most postwar Japanese prime ministers have been tainted by money-related scandals, Kakuei Tanaka's "money politics" stand out as legendary. Serving as premier starting in 1972, he was forced to resign from the office two years later (although he retained his Diet seat as well as immense political influence) because of allegations, first published in the magazine *Bungei Shunju,* that he bilked the government out of a small fortune through illegal land schemes.

Later, in 1976, Tanaka became the center of one of the worst political scandals in Japanese history, the so-called Lockheed scandal. He was found guilty of accepting more than US$2 million in bribes from the U.S. aircraft manufacturer to help smooth the way for Japanese sales of Lockheed's TriStar planes.

Although Ken Takeuchi had been working as a highly privileged press club reporter during Tanaka's tenure as prime minister and was thus afforded intimate access to Tanaka, neither Takeuchi nor any of his press club colleagues broke either scandal about Tanaka. The land-scheme allegation was revealed by a team of *Bungei Shunju* reporters led by freelance writer Takashi

Tachibana. *Bungei Shunju* is the flagship magazine of Bungeishunju Ltd., the publisher of *Shukan Bunshun* weekly newsmagazine, and a company whose journalistic approach will be considered in fair detail in this book.

Freelance writers in Japan were (and still are) often looked down upon and derided. Yet, there it was: a freelance writer working for a mere magazine toppling Japan's larger-than-life Prime Minister Tanaka!

Kengo Tanaka, former president and CEO of Bungeishunju Ltd., was involved on the editorial side of the magazine when the scoop broke. He spoke about the overriding censorship by the prime minister's press club in an interview for this book. "The spirit of the press clubs has always been to ensure that all the member reporters receive and release the same information at the same time, so as to avoid anyone scooping anyone else," Tanaka explained. "At the time of the Tanaka scandal, the prime minister's office was the most closed off of all. I tried to approach the prime minister's office myself a number of times, in order to get information. Sometimes various government officials working for the prime minister would actually ask the press club for permission to speak with me, because I was a magazine journalist. But every time the press club disallowed it. The press club told the prime minister's office that they couldn't speak with me."[36] The profundity of this statement should not be missed. According to Kengo Tanaka, the press club journalists dictated to the prime minister to whom he could and could not speak. One might think that this is an exaggeration, but it is a well-known fact that Japanese press clubs regularly influence their sources in such powerful ways.

Former Mayor Takeuchi explains the mentality that ruled the prime minister's press club when he covered Prime Minister Tanaka: "The one hundred or so journalists [in the club] were just like a single entity. We were one thing, and we shared a common notion that our job was simply to get new information from the prime minister of Japan. That group consciousness dominated our thinking, so acting individually in such an environment was almost impossible. We were individuals, yet we were one. Doing something individually just wasn't our culture. We all knew that Prime Minister Tanaka was corrupt. We all knew it. All the information that Takashi Tachibana used in his *Bungei Shunju* scoop was public information. He just analyzed it and put it together in a way that we did not have the mind to do as members of the press club."[37]

Amazingly enough, even after *Bungei Shunju* first broke the scoop against the prime minister, the mainstream press continued to ignore it. It wasn't until the prime minister was seriously questioned on the matter by a group of foreign press members led by *Los Angeles Times* reporter Sam Jameson, at a press conference at the Foreign Correspondents' Club of Japan, that Japanese establishment news writers finally picked up the story.

Similarly, despite all the attention heaped on Prime Minister Tanaka during the 1974 scandal, Japan's elite writers failed to catch him in any other significant scandal to follow, including the outrageous Lockheed scandal of 1976. It took a U.S. congressional subcommittee investigation and the U.S. Securities and Exchange Commission to break that story overseas before the Japanese establishment news media picked it up.

Maggie Farley, writing in *Media and Politics in Japan,* makes some interesting comparisons between the Tanaka scandals and Watergate.[38] For instance, both Nixon and Tanaka were powerful national leaders who stepped down within just a few months of each other in 1974. Of course, Tanaka retained significant power as a Diet member, in contrast to Nixon, who was forced out of public office altogether. Moreover, in defense of the American press, it might also be added that while Tanaka had been incriminated in an ongoing pattern of shady and illegal dealings for years, the Nixon scandal initially focused on a single criminal incident.

Terry MacDougall, writing in *The Politics of Scandal: Power and Process in Liberal Democracies*, a fascinating book that compares nine major scandals in nine different democratic nations, observes, "the sluggishness of Japanese newspapers in developing issues of political ethics stands in sharp contrast to the zeal of the *Washington Post* and other American newspapers in their exposure of the Watergate incident."[39] Still, it is interesting to note that relative "outsider" journalists were responsible for toppling both leaders. Watergate reporters Bob Woodward and Carl Bernstein were not members of the elite Washington political press at the time but were relatively low on the journalistic ladder as mere metropolitan beat reporters for the *Washington Post*. Farley also notes that neither the Japanese nor the U.S. press was especially adept at analyzing the "big-picture issues" involved in either scandal, focusing instead on the personalities of the individual men rather than the wider systemic and cultural issues that permitted both shocking cases.

Anatomy of a *Kisha* Club

Japanese press clubs are entirely different from Western press clubs, which are essentially social clubs. "The term press club is an absolute misnomer," writes William De Lange in *A History of Japanese Journalism*. He adds, "In sharp contrast with the leisurely activities of press clubs in the West and, indeed, even the foreign press club in Japan, Japanese press clubs have from their very inception been the focal point between the authorities and the media."[40]

As exemplified by Takeuchi's experience, the press club system not only engenders but also enforces collusive relationships between journalists and their establishment sources. These relationships are even policed by the journalists themselves. Laurie Freeman, author of *Closing the Shop: Information Cartels and Japan's Mass Media*, the most thorough English-language book on contemporary Japanese press clubs, claims that "the close relations political journalists have with their sources make it very difficult for them to write unfavorable pieces about them." Freeman goes on to point out correctly that "in fact, political journalists in Japan have been known to feel quite protective of the political 'bosses' they cover."[41]

Of course, as almost everyone familiar with Japanese journalism will agree, Japanese journalists are, on the whole, as diligent and intelligent as any reporters in the world. It is simply that their press club system focuses their thoughts and energies in directions that are unavoidably supportive of those in power while constantly working to undermine whatever conceptions of journalistic ethics they may have.

According to Brian Covert, a U.S. journalist who has written for four different English-language papers in Japan, "It is said in Japan that if you belong to a *kisha* club, you are certain not to get the scoop—and if you don't belong to the *kisha* club, you don't get the story."[42]

At least 800[43] press clubs dominate the establishment press in Japan. Although they are governed by Nihon Shimbun Kyokai (NSK, the Japanese Newspaper Publishers and Editors Association), which claims that one of its prime functions is to "conduct research on Japanese journalism," NSK claims it does not know exactly how many clubs exist. Each club is a semiautonomous organization, governing itself for the most part.

Membership in major press clubs is often restricted to reporters from the country's 17 dominant news organizations: the 5 daily national newspapers, the 6 national broadcast stations, NHK, the 2 major news agencies (Kyodo and Jiji), and the 4 "block" or major regional papers. Local clubs usually also include reporters from local papers. Most organizations permitted club membership assign 1 to 10 reporters to a club. Once assigned, most reporters then spend the bulk of their time at their assigned club cubicle or desk. Total membership in a club usually varies between 15 and 150 individual reporters. However, the largest club, the Diet club, has thousands of member journalists from a multitude of news organizations, while the prime minister's club currently has about 500 member journalists from approximately 100 member organizations.

Japanese press clubs are attached to most significant government agencies, political parties, prefecture and city governments, police, and other offices. Many major corporations, such as Toyota and Mitsubishi, also sponsor press clubs, as do the Tokyo Chamber of Commerce, Narita Airport, and Tokyo University. Even NHK has its own press club.

Most press clubs are physically attached to, or located within, the buildings that house their sources. Additionally, a club's facilities are usually paid for or subsidized by the source to which it is attached. This point is particularly contentious in the case of government-attached press clubs, as noted earlier by Governor Yasuo Tanaka, because the voting public foots the bill for these private club facilities.

Freeman explains that in most situations the sponsoring agency provides "the physical space for the club, the *kisha shitsu*, desks, tables, chairs, bookshelves, telephones, and payment for outside calls. Frequently, television sets, subscriptions to popular magazines, and parking spaces or exemptions from parking restrictions are also provided. Free photocopies, fax machines, and copies of each of the papers' morning editions are other common items, as are mah-jongg, shogi, and igo, popular games journalists rely on to while away the time between scheduled events. In 1993, 60.8 percent of clubs surveyed stated that government sources also provided and paid for a permanently staffed assistant."[44]

Many clubs also provide journalists with their own sections, equipped with desks and chairs, and one can sometimes also find a "refrigerator filled with beer and drinks which are gifts from news sources."[45] Journalists are also sometimes given complimentary train passes and even passes to entertainment events, such as movies or sporting events.[46] Small gifts from sources to journalists are also not uncommon, and many sources host regular social events designed specifically to provide a casual atmosphere for sources and journalists to develop cordial relationships.

While precise figures are not available on how much money Japanese news sources spend supporting press clubs, Iwase has gathered a great deal of fascinating information in his book *Shimbum ga omoshiroku nai ri yuu* (The Reason Why Newspapers Are Boring), published in 2001. Iwase sent out 800 questionnaires mainly to public institutions,[47] asking them how much money they spent on office space, furniture, telephone and fax bills, rent, labor, and so on for the press clubs connected to them. Having received 529 responses,[48] the author detailed a staggering total of ¥11 billion, or approximately US$110 million at current exchange rates. This is an astonishing subsidy of the Japanese mainstream news media by governmental and other public-oriented organizations, especially as the news media is generally already considered a very profitable industry.

While apologists for the system might describe this annual expense as an "investment" in the country's news media that merely facilitates the flow of information to the populace, others decry it as institutional bribery, a payoff to ensure that mainstream Japanese news companies disseminate the kind of information that establishment institutions desire.

Of those surveyed, only 164 answered Iwase's inquiry as to how much money is spent simply to entertain club journalists by sponsoring social events, meals, parties, buying gifts, and the like. Of the 164 responses to this question, a total of ¥50 million (or about half a million dollars) was shown to be spent on such things annually. The fundamental conflict of interest in Japanese journalists taking half a million dollars' worth of entertainment from their sources could not be any clearer. And with only 164 of 800 institutions answering this question, one can only imagine how much more is actually spent by sponsors on Japanese journalists for these kinds of perks.

Of course, in addition to the amount spent on press clubs and journalists, most major Japanese government agencies and major corporations also have substantial public-relations budgets dedicated to churning out press releases, fielding inquiries, coordinating press conferences, and so on. Moreover, these PR departments are almost always located directly adjacent to the press club associated with such organizations, making it especially easy for PR officials to feed journalists the information they want them to have. It also means that PR staff and journalists are likely to spend long hours together, month after month, year after year, developing intimate relationships. According to Asano, "One European correspondent once told me that 'Japanese news reporters are between public relations officials and journalists.' However, I regard many Japanese mainstream journalists as press-spokespersons themselves.... There is no need for sources to 'buy' Japanese journalists in order to get them to cooperate. Cooperation with sources and competitors is a fundamental part of club membership."[49]

Structural Incapacitation:
The Ministry of Foreign Affairs Press Club

An apt example of the public relations–press club arrangement is the press club at the Ministry of Foreign Affairs (Gaimusho), one of the most important Japanese organizations. The ministry is housed in one multistory building, where the public-relations department and press club share the same floor, separated by a press-conference room.

Discussions with reporters from major Japanese newspapers who belong to the press club reveal that many of them commonly spend as many as fourteen hours per day at the press club, six and sometimes even seven days a week. This means that for the standard two to four years that these reporters are assigned to the club, the vast majority of their waking lives takes place within the walls of the ministry they are assigned to cover.

When asked in an interview how members of the club go about double-checking the information given to them by the minister of Foreign Affairs, one veteran club reporter explained that the standard method is to check one ministry official's information by surreptitiously asking a second ministry official to corroborate! According to the reporter, he and his colleagues rarely sought out any sources of information whatsoever outside the Ministry of Foreign Affairs—indeed seldom left the building at all, except perhaps for meals. Although not all press club reporters work as closely with their sources, the situation is by no means exceptional.

According to Hajime Kitamura, former head of the Japan Federation of Press Workers' Unions, "Japanese news reporters who are skilled and talented don't use just the press clubs. They may only use their press club sources for as little as 30 percent of their information, and they double-check their facts."[50] However, even Kitamura admitted that those journalists who are members of press clubs attached to national-government ministries tend to be the least likely to check facts or find alternative sources. He also said that those reporters who are not "skilled and talented" might regularly rely on their sources for 100 percent of their information.

Journalists Policing Journalists

In addition to the enforced intimacy between news sources and press club journalists, there are many club rules and practices designed to ensure journalist cooperation. Those who break them can be punished or even expelled from the club by their fellow journalists. Obviously, reporters who are expelled from clubs find themselves in a difficult situation, since they are denied access to information pertaining to their beat and must explain to their employers that they can no longer do their jobs.

One rule is the so-called blackboard agreement (*kokuban kyotei*), designed to ensure that no one press club journalist is likely to scoop the other members of the club. If, for instance, a source informs the captain (or journalist in charge) of a club that there will be a press conference or other event pertaining to a particular news subject, the captain will often write that subject on a blackboard or otherwise post it in the club. Assuming no member of the club objects to the subject being posted, all the journalists in the club are thus prohibited from writing on the topic until the event is held, at which point all members will have received the same information at the same time. This not only kills many scoops, it puts a damper on the desire of reporters to strive to get scoops. It also provides news sources with time to spin information on topics in ways that are favorable to them.

Of course, the Second Gulf War offers a number of examples of Western reporters keeping information to themselves. A more controversial, high-profile example, however, came soon after the war, when the broadcast-news channel CNN revealed that its reporters had withheld significant information it had gathered about the former ruling Iraqi Baath Party in order to ensure that the organization's reporters would not be expelled from the country by the Iraqi government. Indeed, NPR reporter Anne Garrels, who was in Baghdad throughout and immediately after the war, has stated that many Western journalists in Iraq engaged in substantial self-censorship to avoid trouble with Iraqi officials.[51]

It is also not so unusual for individual Western reporters to agree with individual sources not to write about certain things in exchange for some other information from those sources. In such cases, journalists need to make a value judgment about what is right and wrong, and which information is more important to their audience. While many of these agreements may be ethical, some undoubtedly are not.

Another important instance of journalistic ethics played out during the 2003 invasion of Iraq was embedding reporters, a practice that fundamentally alters the relationship between reporters and their information sources/subjects. For instance, embedded reporters are rightfully required to withhold certain information, such as the locations and plans of the troops they cover. This example at least makes intuitive sense, as the obligation of journalists to inform the public would not seem to extend to endangering the journalists' country or allied nations' troops.

On March 19, 2004, one year after the declaration of the war, the National Public Radio (NPR) show *On Point* aired an "audio diary" of the formerly embedded NBC correspondent Chip Reid. Reid's eloquent remembrance of his experience as an "embed" underscores many of the difficulties faced under such circumstances. It is worth examining briefly here for what it illustrates about the nature of intimate journalist/source relationships.

Reid traveled with the Third Battalion, Fifth Marine Regiment, living side-by-side with the soldiers he was assigned to cover. According to him, one pitch-dark night, the Marines exchanged automatic-weapons fire with Iraqis. After the fighting was over, a girl's cry could be heard in the distance. In the morning, the bodies of two dead Iraqi girls were discovered nearby. According to Reid, the Marines investigated and concluded that the Iraqi fighters had used the girls as "human shields" the night before and that it was the Iraqis' fault that the Marines had apparently shot and killed the girls. The incident was a very emotional one for at least some of the Marines. Reid explains:

> That incident presented one of my biggest journalistic challenges of the war. There was no doubt in my mind that the story of the two girls' deaths was newsworthy. Civilian casualties are a tragic but important part of war. But after I reported it, a couple of other marines asked me why I put it on air? They said it would make the Marines look bad. They were surprised, they said, because they thought I was their friend.
>
> I was taken aback and don't remember exactly how I responded. I hope I told them that just as they have duties as Marines, I have duties as a reporter, including the duty to report the story as fully and accurately as I can—even if it means putting people I like and respect in a bad light. Truth be told, telling the bad news wasn't easy, especially when I was reporting it, as a group of young marines stood nearby listening to every word. But I tried like hell just to tell it like it was, and I think I succeeded. I believe that by the time I left even the skeptical ones understood and accepted my role.[52]

Reid goes on to explain that after the war many of the family members of the Marines offered him heartfelt thanks for keeping them informed of what was going on. They even presented him with a scrapbook filled with thank-you notes, an item that Reid says has become one of his most prized possessions. He concludes that embedded reporters are likely to be a part of future U.S. military actions, not only because of the information provided to the public but because of the intense desire of military family members to hear about their relations.

Reid's story addresses many of the issues involved with embedded journalists. He explains how difficult it was for him to report on the death of the girls, apparently killed by the Marines, with the Marines looking on at him while he issued his report. He was even called to task by some Marines and put in the awkward position of justifying his work. Reid emphasizes that he had a "duty to report the story as fully and accurately" as possible, "even if it means putting people I like and respect in a bad light." His story makes one wonder, however, how the situation may have been different if, for instance, the Marines were not people he liked and respected or if he had to do more than just put them in a "bad light." What would the dynamics have been if he exposed serious corruption or other abuses perpetrated by those with whom he was embedded? Reid also does not discuss his intense dependence on the Marines he was covering. Not only was Reid dependent on the soldiers as sources; he was dependent on them for his basic safety.

Reid's story, of course, concludes on an upbeat note for the most part. The soldiers he covered were generally successful in their mission and most of them had a homecoming back in the United States that autumn, which Reid attended. One has to wonder how things might have been different for a reporter embedded with troops that failed in their mission—lost their battle or their war. Indeed, one has to wonder how a reporter that was less experienced, less independent of mind and character, or perhaps less cognizant of his journalistic duty than Reid would have handled his assignment. This example is important because in Japan, it is hardly a ridiculous stretch to say that many press club reporters are in fact "embedded" with their sources, whether that source is the prime minister, a police department, or a corporation. As noted, Japanese press club reporters often spend the vast majority of their waking hours working next to and with their sources. Indeed, while combat-embedded reporters usually are not assigned to the same troops for long and extended time periods, Japanese reporters are typically assigned to their press clubs, and thus to their sources, for years. Japanese press club reporters may not depend on their sources for the safety of their lives, but they do depend on them for their livelihoods. The clubs provide those in power with a host of mechanisms, both subtle and brutal, for manipulating the reporters who depend on them. On top of that, they provide a myriad of motivations for press club journalists to avoid intensely critical coverage of their sources.

One common defense of both embedded reporters and Japanese press clubs is that they can both be very effective mechanisms for news gathering, when used in concert with a wide variety of other sources. For instance, in the case of embedded reporters, many news organizations point out that their "embeds" are just one of many sources they are likely to use to cover a military conflict. Similarly, Japanese news organizations sometimes claim that their press club–derived information is often combined with that from other sources. However strong such arguments seem in theory, in practice it is obvious that news organizations often become exceedingly reliant on such reporters, especially in the case of Japanese press club reporters. Nonofficial-source information is not only much more difficult and expensive to gather, it is also often less reliable and far more likely to come under attack from authorities. The simplest and safest way to gather news in Japan is through press club reporters, and, by and large, this is how it is accomplished.

Other Problematic Aspects of Mainstream Japanese Journalism

Further hampering the Japanese journalist's ability to write objectively is, as noted, the systematic encouragement by his or her employer to develop close personal relationships with sources. Kenichi Asano has made public a handbook, originally produced by the *Mainichi* newspapers for its reporters, that officially outlines the type of journalist the company desires. Freeman has published a translation of part of this handbook:

> You should try to be the kind of journalist the family [of your source] will come to think of not as a "journalist who makes visits in terms of his own interests and benefits" but rather, as a "journalist who comes visiting as an intimate friend." Human relations formed in this way become the journalist's

own personal asset. . . . If your opposite number likes alcohol, take along some whiskey or other alcoholic beverage; if they don't drink, take candy or fruit.[53]

Again, it would be absurd to imply that Japan is the only major democracy in which journalists rely intensely on their establishment sources. For instance, Leon V. Sigal, in his dated but still relevant 1973 book, *Reporters and Officials*, concludes from a detailed analysis of stories that, at that time, a startling 78.3 percent of all news stories published by the *New York Times* and the *Washington Post* were derived from official sources.[54] In Japan, that figure is estimated to be well over 90 percent.[55] Bob Garfield, host of the NPR show *On the Media,* made the following observation in a telephone interview for this book: "I do think that there are some objective truths about journalism, notwithstanding cultural differences. One of them is that there needs to be at least an arm's length of distance between a reporter and his source. If journalism is being practiced with a series of sub-rosa interlocking relationships, it is simply not journalism. It is something else."[56]

Whereas press clubs constitute one of the most widely decried aspects of Japanese journalism, an equally important yet more frequently overlooked difference from the West is the almost complete absence of schools of journalism in Japan. Only a handful of today's working Japanese reporters have received any university training in their profession. Asano estimates that of the approximately 20,000 working journalists in Japan, perhaps only 200 to 300 (1 to 1.5 percent) actually have degrees in journalism. He further states that even among the tiny number who do have such degrees, perhaps only a fraction of them have an understanding of journalistic ethics as is regularly taught in the United States. "There are probably only 10 or 20 working Japanese journalists with the equivalent of a U.S. degree in journalism in the entire country," he says.[57]

In fact, Japan has just 4 schools of journalism, and even they do not offer much training in the actual craft. (In contrast, the United States, according to one count, has some 337 undergraduate and graduate journalism schools, departments, and programs.[58]) The Japanese schools are at Doshisha University, Sophia University, Nihon University, and Tokyo University. Actually, the school at Tokyo University is called an "institute of social information," and its journalism class is only available as a postgraduate course and does not teach hands-on reporting skills. The schools at the other 3 universities offer only limited training and focus mainly on media criticism and similar topics. Only about 1 in 4 journalism students in Japan actually pursues a career as a reporter, and these graduates often find that their degree is a demerit! Masanori Yamaguchi, a veteran reporter for *Yomiuri*, put it this way: "The major media firms prefer not to hire journalism graduates, because they come with all kinds of annoying baggage—things like a background in journalistic ethics. Thus, most Japanese news media companies prefer to train new recruits 'on the job.'"[59]

One Japanese journalist who has both Japanese and American degrees in journalism (and who, ironically enough, asked not to be named) explained in an interview for this book how her training hurt her chances of landing a reporting position. After multiple interviews at *Asahi* newspaper, she was finally taken aside by one of her interviewers, who explained that the decision makers were debating hiring her. He explained that even though some of his colleagues felt she would make an excellent reporter, a number of them were quite concerned that her degrees in journalism would make her "a difficult employee to manage."

Of course, the existence of schools of journalism in a given country is no guarantee that journalists will perform their jobs well. Many European countries do not have schools of journalism. In fact, such schools are sometimes criticized for narrowing the imagination of young reporters and for weeding out those with heterodox opinions and views from those of their privileged professors and fellow students. Also, by hiring a predominant number of graduates from such schools, news organizations limit their pools of reporters to people of similar backgrounds, thus narrowing journalistic approaches and viewpoints.

Still, the virtual absence of schools of journalism in Japan must be recognized as a problem. The fact is that many Japanese journalists simply are not adequately trained. The internationally acclaimed journalist Katsuichi Honda, for instance, has made this cutting observation: "Foreign reporters who can't speak a word of Japanese can nonetheless do excellent reporting by using a translator, while the converse—journalists who can speak Japanese but can't write decent articles—is not at all rare."[60]

Once in the workplace, Japanese journalists often also hold a vastly different conception of their work and careers than do Western journalists. In many countries, the occupation of journalist is viewed as a lifelong career or profession. However, in Japan it is more often thought of as training or early career work, to be performed on one's way to becoming an editor and then, if successful, a manager in the company hierarchy. This is no small distinction. Whereas in the West most journalists think of themselves in terms of their profession, in Japan they tend to think of themselves as employees of their companies.

Kiyoshi Takada, a seasoned Japanese magazine editor and freelancer, put it this way: "In Japan you apply for and choose a job because of the company, and you go to work for the company. You are a company employee first and a reporter second. Japanese have a very difficult time establishing their own individual identities separate from their companies, so it's very important to belong to a company. That's where a Japanese reporter gets his identity."[61]

In fact, when top journalists do move from one employer to another, it is often the result of a move from journalism to politics. The former mayor of Kamakura, Ken Takeuchi, is a case in point, having been an accomplished reporter for *Asahi Shimbun* before his move into politics. Terry MacDougall, a specialist in Japanese politics and foreign affairs, has observed that "many Japanese reporters serve, or hope to serve, as political secretaries to influential politicians, a political ambition that can work to restrict the reporting of some news. In effect, the newspapers, however critical they may be at times of the government, are part of the political establishment; they will not take actions lightly that might shake the equilibrium of Japanese politics."[62]

Indeed, Japanese journalists are often extremely well-paid individuals. Given the close relationships they develop with their powerful press club sources, the many perks and fringe benefits of their jobs, and the potential for positive career advancement, it is no wonder that many develop an elitist view. Given the often long hours involved in Japanese reporting, during which time most reporters are confined to the small world of their individual beats, it is no wonder that many of them lose touch with the plight of average, everyday Japanese.

Other issues also conspire to make journalism in Japan different from that in the West. For one thing, in Japan it is still not standard practice to use bylines in most articles, although they are becoming more common, particularly for foreign correspondents. This is in part because the journalistic process, like so many other activities in Japan, is more of a team effort than in the West. In Japan, it is common for reporters to go out in the field and gather material, but for an editor (often called an "anchor") to write up the article based on the material gathered, conforming it to the in-house style and viewpoint. While this process can be effective (and was formerly used in the West), one result is that both reporters and editors are, for obvious reasons, likely to feel less responsible for what eventually sees print. Indeed, it is a common belief among Japanese journalists that the Western tradition of using bylines in newspaper and other news pieces is not so much about keeping Western journalists accountable for what they write as it is about their selfishness and vanity in wanting to see their names in print and in putting themselves before their companies.

Similarly, citation of sources is also inconsistent in Japanese journalism. Although this is also a problem in the West, where references to "unnamed sources" have become increasingly commonplace, it is especially so in Japan. Brian Covert explains, "There is also a tendency in Japanese news organizations to delete from news stories the names and identities of the corporations, business officials, or government spokespersons who may be adversely affected by the news stories.... Why not [include the names]? 'Because then they would cut their ties to our paper, and we don't want them to do that' is the most common refrain heard in Japanese newsrooms."[63] Ivan P. Hall, among others, believes that this Japanese tendency is a "hugely important point." He explains, "Anonymity is the sturdiest defense for Japan's power holders, identification by name the most feared weapon against them. The press's deletion here is a major blow to democratic transparency and accountability."[64]

A final shortcoming well worth mention, and one emphasized by many of those interviewed, is the consistent failure of Japanese journalists to delve into detailed analyses of events. To be sure, Japan is not the only nation whose news media is criticized for superficiality. According to many, however, it is a particularly big problem in Japan. Van Wolferen, for example, writes about how the Japanese press covers scandals in great detail yet fails to analyze the broader context that allowed such scandals to occur: "Press behavior during a big scandal makes me think of a big frustrated dog. He is ultimately loyal to his boss (in this case the official establishment), but his owner must throw him a bone once in a while so that he can relieve his frustration by exercising his teeth with a lot of growling."[65]

Sam Jameson, who has been called "the dean of American journalists in Japan" because of his more than thirty years as a foreign correspondent there, has a similar take on the matter: "They have honed their skills in fixing blame and pillorying scapegoats. They can topple prime ministers, destroy careers, and make life miserable with invasions of privacy. They can set an outer boundary for permissible action. But somehow they have not yet developed the ability to uncover the facts needed to expose, uproot and correct social ills, corruption and inefficiency."[66]

Despite the obstacles, exceptionally fine journalists do exist in Japan. Indeed, those quoted in this chapter—Iwase, Honda, Takeuchi, Takada, Asano, and others—have had admirable careers. The industry, however, is structured and run in such a way that it both undervalues and undermines such exemplars. The *kisha* club system combines with market forces, cultural influences, journalistic tradition, financial influences, and legal factors to yield what is undoubtedly one of the weakest and least independent national press corps among the world's leading industrialized democracies. Unfortunately, with the exception of the press club system, many of these same factors are in play, to one degree or another, in every democracy around the globe.

CHAPTER THREE

JAPANESE WEEKLY NEWSMAGAZINES

Japanese weekly newsmagazines dislike and attack people who try to be different in this country. They don't want to have a Japanese with a different opinion from the mainstream Japanese. This is true not only for people who are against war or who want the economy to be different. Anyone who is different from the mainstream, they attack. This is a big problem, especially when the mainstream is wrong.

—Japanese novelist and activist Makoto Oda[1]

What Are Journalists For?

Journalists exist because people require far more information than they are likely to acquire through their own efforts. Even though communication and travel are cheaper and faster than ever before, nearly everyone still must rely on news broadcasters and publishers for information about the broader world outside their immediate environment. Thus, journalists are tasked with the vital service of collecting and disseminating relevant information, usually of a timely nature—"news"—that would not otherwise be readily available to the average person. In an ideal world, this information would always be selected based on its usefulness in helping people make informed decisions and live better lives.

Recognizing the public's need for such knowledge, the United States Constitution, the Japanese Constitution, various United Nations declarations, and most other modern democratic constitutions provide certain guarantees of freedom of expression. These bodies of law mandate such freedoms because access to knowledge is considered fundamental to the democratic process through which, ideally, a citizenry exercises sovereignty over its government. The authors of these constitutions and declarations, as well as the representatives who ratified them, have recognized that voting is a productive act only if those who vote are properly informed. Thomas Jefferson, widely considered the father of modern democracy, famously declared, "Were it left to me to decide whether we should have a government without newspapers or newspapers without a government, I should not hesitate a moment to prefer the latter."[2] Of course, freedom of speech and of the press are not enshrined solely so that we are informed enough to vote. Indeed, they are generally recognized as basic human rights in and of themselves.

Journalism's role can be broken down into nine principal functions, many of which have little to do with voting issues:

1. To provide accurate information
2. To offer opinions (editorialize)
3. To serve as a forum for the exchange of views among citizens
4. To educate
5. To spearhead a broad array of campaigns on a society-wide basis
6. To entertain
7. To provide a medium for advertising and public relations
8. To serve as a tool for social interactions, such as discussions among friends or colleagues
9. To inform the public about emergency situations, such as natural and man-made disasters

Walter Williams's famous Journalist's Creed, extolled by the National Press Club in Washington, D.C., also asserts that there is much more to journalism than merely providing democratic information. He declares, "I believe in the profession of Journalism. I believe that the public journal is a public trust;

that all connected with it are, to the full measure of responsibility, trustees for the public; that acceptance of lesser service than the public service is a betrayal of this trust."[3]

In 1946, shortly after the end of the Second World War, the Japan Newspaper Publishers and Editors Association (Nihon Shimbun Kyokai), commonly referred to as the NSK, adopted the Canon of Journalism, later revised after occupation in 1955 and then revised again in 2000. The Japanese canon, based on U.S. concepts of journalism, was created with the aim of reforming the Japanese news media from a propaganda tool of the dictatorial militarists into a genuinely free press. According to part VI of the canon, which addresses guidance, responsibility, and pride, "the principal difference between newspapers and other commercial enterprises is that newspapers in their reportorial and editorial activities exercise great influence over the public. The public depends on newspapers as their chief source of information and consequently newspapers affect their [sic] judgment of public events and problems. From this distinction arise the public character of journalistic enterprises and the special social status of journalists."[4]

The canon also states, "In order to realize this mission in the fastest and most effective manner possible, it is necessary for every newspaper in the nation to adhere to a high ethical standard, elevate the prestige of its profession, and carry out its functions to the fullest."

Both Williams's creed and the Canon of Journalism describe journalism as a profession and insist that journalists contribute to society. Media scholar Jay Rosen, an advocate for "public journalism," also sees journalism as a profession. In his book *What Are Journalists For?*, Rosen writes that "unlike law, medicine, or accounting, there is no licensing procedure or standardized training; nor do journalists own the newsroom. And because the First Amendment protects the charlatan and the scrupulous alike, the press has no power to expel wayward members." Rosen continues, "But journalism is like the most honored professions in other ways. It expects the individual practitioner and the practice as a whole to serve the general welfare—not through the invisible hand of competition, but directly, through acts of journalism that amount to pubic service. If a professional is one who hears a calling in the opportunity for a career, then most journalists I know consider themselves professional, serious people serving the public good."[5]

Many see one of journalism's functions as perhaps the most important of all: to guard against abuses by government and by other high concentrations of power. According to this view, journalism in many modern democracies is a "fourth estate" or "fourth power," serving as an added check against the three branches of government: executive, legislative, and judicial. Though discussion on this subject could fill libraries, it suffices to say here that journalists should, as their prime purpose, serve the public good; they should therefore strive to serve as a check or "watchdog" against all destructive social powers, not just governmental powers.

In practice, of course, not every bit of news that is published or broadcast serves the public good—far from it. Rosen's book, like the Journalist's Creed and the Japanese Canon of Journalism, was written because so much that passes for journalism not only fails to contribute to, but actually erodes, the public good. Jefferson, for example, despite his praise of the press, knew all too well how destructive "news" can be. "Nothing can now be believed which is seen in a newspaper," he wrote. "Truth itself becomes suspicious by being put into that polluted vehicle. The real extent of this state of misinformation is known only to those who are in situations to confront facts within their knowledge with the lies of the day."[6]

So how to categorize news coverage that, as Jefferson described it, not only fails to serve the public good but actually damages it? There are stories created simply to increase ratings and circulation, or filed for no better reason than to keep a reporter in his employer's good graces, and articles that support selfish special interests—even entire "news" publications devoted to violent and hateful philosophies. Put simply, such material is not journalism. It is merely bad writing posing as journalism.

No doubt such writing will always be with us. The real problem occurs when, successfully passed off as journalism, it becomes systemized and institutionalized as part of the wider news-media industry and society. A study of how this has happened in Japan provides a wealth of lessons to anyone interested in truth and accuracy in public reporting, not just in that country but in any modern democracy.

Although the Japanese weekly newsmagazines, with their unique brand of journalism (too often composed of bad writing posing as journalism), serve to support the least democratic aspects of the Japanese system, it is not by design. There is no grand scheme, no devious plot hatched by Japanese power brokers colluding with magazine writers, editors, or publishers. Indeed, the best place for that sort of conspiracy theory would be in the weeklies themselves. What has happened in Japan is that a number of weekly newsmagazine publishers have found market niches wherein bad writing posing as journalism yields great rewards. This, combined with other factors such as weak legal constraints against libel, lax professional ethical standards within Japanese journalism, intense concentrations of media power, commercial pressures, and the like, has resulted in a terrible assault on civil sovereignty and human rights by *shukanshi*. Worst of all has been the slow but steady spread of a Japanese neonationalistic fundamentalism throughout society since the end of occupation that insists upon its own warped worldview. Needless to say, Japan is hardly the only democratic nation where similar factors circulate. Indeed, the Japanese example can serve as a key to unlocking the complicated mechanisms of troubled news-media sectors in liberal democratic nations everywhere.

Japanese Weekly Newsmagazines

In many ways, the Japanese weekly newsmagazines constitute their own genre. As noted in chapter 2, they are often described as bizarre blends of various types of U.S. magazines, such as *Newsweek*, the *New Yorker*, *People*, *Penthouse*, and the *National Enquirer*. They are similar to *Newsweek* or *Time* in that they often present more-detailed coverage of selected topics from each week's news than is offered on television or in most newspapers. They can be a bit like the *New Yorker*, however, in that they carry a fair amount of literary and cultural commentary, albeit usually less sophisticated than the *New Yorker*'s best material. In their fluffy celebrity gossip, they also resemble *People*, and yet, like *Penthouse* (and similar men's magazines), many feature pornography and target (with but a few exceptions) men. And like the U.S. "supermarket tabloids," such as the *National Enquirer*, they are widely acknowledged to be less reliable than more establishment-oriented news publications.

Tabs or Not Tabs?

This last point has led many Japanese intellectuals and Western visitors to dismiss *shukanshi* as mere tabloids, unworthy of serious consideration. This is a grave error. Although the weeklies' standards of journalistic ethics may be low and their sensationalism quotient high—and although they often contain lowbrow, even downright sleazy material—they are a far cry from U.S. or even most British tabloids. Not only are Japanese weeklies different from the Western tabloids, they are also far more influential. For example, *shukanshi* are absolutely nothing like the U.S. supermarket "tab" *Weekly World News,* which commonly features tales about alien matings and Elvis Presley sightings, and regularly runs headlines such as:

"Grossed-Out Surgeon Vomits Inside Patient!"

and

"I Watched a Wild Hog Eat My Baby!"[7]

to quote the titles of two recent books on the U.S. tabloid industry.

In fact, *shukanshi* feature a far wider array of material than the celebrity-oriented gossip that makes up the bread and butter of the *National Enquirer,* the *Star,* and other popular U.S. weekly tabloids; or of the *Sun,* the *Daily Mirror, Sport,* and the other British tabs. *Shukanshi* run serious political news, book reviews, and fiction, as well as social commentary. Moreover, depending on the magazine, much of the material can adhere to good or even very high literary standards—something not often found in the U.S. or British tabloids.

Writers such as Bill Sloan, S. Elizabeth Bird, and Jim Hogshire[8] have argued persuasively that the influence of U.S. supermarket tabloids is greatly underestimated. They argue that many readers take the tabloids very seriously, often relying on them as their sole source of written news, and that many readers' worldviews and sometimes even politics are heavily influenced by them. Hogshire in particular cites a number of examples of flag-waving by the U.S. supermarket tabs that have helped to rally readers behind various national causes. No doubt the U.S. and other Western tabloids regularly capitalize on nationalism. Perhaps most important, however, all three authors point out that the total circulation for the top six U.S. tabs was more than ten million in 1997. This is greater than the combined circulation of all fifteen Japanese weekly newsmagazines and comparable to the total circulation of the top ten national U.S. daily newspapers (as well as *Yomiuri Shimbun*). Still, for all their readers, the U.S. supermarket tabloids are simply not as influential on the national political scene as the *shukanshi* are on Japanese politics. The U.S. tabs rarely if ever cover social, cultural, or political issues as thoroughly or regularly as Japanese weeklies do. This has become particularly true in recent years, as U.S. tabloids have further narrowed their focus on celebrity gossip and bizarre human-interest stories.

Even though Japanese weekly newsmagazines do have a distinctively tabloid flavor to them—some more pungent than others—this is but one aspect of the industry. And while it is true that British tabs can be political, and even politically influential, they rarely carry the kinds of fiction, erotica, literary reviews, or thoughtful social commentary that some Japanese weeklies do. In short, the Japanese weeklies are a breed apart.

One reason for this difference is that Japanese news consumers comprise a significantly different demographic from Western consumers. Western countries often have a much more "polarized" readership, with a small proportion of readers that confine themselves to the highest level of sophisticated reading material and a larger proportion of readers consuming less-sophisticated material. In contrast, Japan tends to have a very large middle set of readers, with significantly smaller proportions than in the West of readers who confine their reading to "intellectually elite" publications or to the tabloids. Ivan P. Hall explains the situation with the same "dinosaur analogy" that was used in a different context in the introduction to this book: "It's a mass-middlebrow audience—with the bulge higher on the scale of intellectual sophistication and reader education, as contrasted to the "dinosaur" configuration of Europe and America (with national variations, to be sure)—a small head of limited highbrow papers and magazines attached to a huge lowbrow, mass-circulation body. . . . I see the Japanese weeklies as the underbelly of this huge national mass-middlebrow market, rather than as genuine lowbrow or trash-level stuff on the Anglo-American tabloid level. Tokyo University professors read the weeklies, and I knew at least one famous political scientist who reads them faithfully, he told me, so as not to miss anything of real importance that the respectable press had chosen to ignore."[9]

Types of Japanese Weeklies

Japan's weekly newsmagazines fall into two principal types, one produced by major newspaper publishers and the other produced by other publishers, such as those that primarily publish books. Technically, the Japanese-language edition of *Newsweek* forms a third type. *Newsweek* doesn't qualify as a

shukanshi. This is true partly because it is published by a non-Japanese company and also because it tends to offer a far wider spectrum of international stories than the domestically focused weeklies. It is also generally aimed at internationally minded readers, such as travelers and businesspeople. The Japanese *Newsweek* is also printed in full color and on a higher-quality paper than the pulp used in *shukanshi*, whose interiors are almost exclusively black and white. *Newsweek* also has a rela-

This newsstand adjacent to a gate at Narita international airport sells *shukanshi* side-by-side with English-language Western newsmagazines like *Time* and *Newsweek*.

tively small circulation in Japan, around 100,000, compared to 300,000 to nearly 700,000 for typical *shukanshi*.

Table 3.a briefly describes eleven of the fifteen weeklies published in Japan, as listed in the Japan Magazine Advertising Association (JMAA). Those not owned by newspaper publishers tend to present the boldest and raciest coverage and, as one might suspect, have the reputation of being far less reliable. They also boast larger circulations than the newspaper-owned magazines. The weeklies owned by newspaper publishers tend to base much of their coverage on that offered by their associated newspapers and therefore are considered less independent than those owned by nonnewspaper companies. Indeed, although they should not be ignored entirely, the newspaper-owned magazines generally follow the editorial policies of their newspapers and thus are much tamer than the non-newspaper-owned magazines.

The four weeklies not listed in table 3.a are categorized by JMAA as being "general" magazines and have not been included in the table because they do not tend to publish a significantly large proportion of their weekly content that can reasonably be described as news. These four magazines—*Asahi Geinou*, *Shukan Jitsuwa*, *Shukan Taishu*, and *Weekly Takarajima*—are more accurately categorized as men's, or perhaps even soft-pornography magazines than newsmagazines per se.

Table 3.a further denotes whether each newsmagazine features pornography. Those that do tend to de-emphasize serious literary and journalistic coverage. Although many Japanese frown on pornography, it is generally less derided in Japan than in most Western countries, especially the United States, where it is often judged through the lens of Judeo-Christian values.

Table 3.a Major Japanese Weekly Newsmagazines

Non-Newspaper-Publisher-Owned Weekly Newsmagazines

The headlines in this image may or may not be reliable.

Shukan Post
Circulation: 682,072   *Features Pornography:* Yes

"Boasts the largest circulation among general interest weeklies. The magazine features political and economic articles aimed at elite urban businessmen between the ages of 25 and 40. Articles report on what will happen in Japan and the world and also in the business and corporate worlds."

The headlines in this image may or may not be reliable.

Shukan Gendai
Circulation: 618,161   *Features Pornography:* Yes

"*Shukan Gendai* is aimed at businessmen in their 30's in middle management positions (93% of the readers are male). The varied content of the magazine covers politics, economic and social issues, international affairs, and sports news. A series of articles by astute critics provides intelligent and perceptive comment on current issues. The magazine has considerable influence on decision-making of readers."

Table 3.a, continued

Shukan Bunshun

Circulation: 602,569 *Features Pornography:* No

"*Shukan Bunshun* focuses on the social, political, economic, sports and health issues of the nation. Feature articles include opinions of world renowned novelists, critics and essayists. The majority of readers are upper class, wealthy and intellectually inclined."

The headlines in this image may or may not be reliable.

Friday

Circulation: 520,000 *Features Pornography:* Yes

"*Friday* is a weekly pictorial newsmagazine focusing on social events, crime, accidents, entertainment and sports of national and international interest. Over 60% of the readers are in their 20's and 30's and 70% are male."

Shukan Shincho

Circulation: 489,206 *Features Pornography:* No

"*Shukan Shincho* is a general interest weekly which for more than three decades has featured various subjects written from an independent, authoritative and creative point of view. The average reader is 41.4 years old, 34.2% are white collar, and 60.9% own their own homes."

The headlines in this image may or may not be reliable.

Flash

Circulation: 461,000 *Features Pornography:* Yes

"*Flash* is a pictorial news weekly targeted at males whose average age is 29 years. Articles are selected mostly for entertainment value. Regular columns are also very popular among the readers."

The headlines in this image may or may not be reliable.

Spa!

Circulation: 300,000 *Features Pornography:* Yes

"*Spa!* is the only magazine dealing with relevant issues of phenomenon which the existing paradigm has collapsed. It also sends the current topics with its original viewpoints to readers aged 20's."

Newspaper-Publisher-Owned Weekly Newsmagazines

Shukan Asahi

Circulation: 305,984   *Features Pornography:* No

"Shukan Asahi is a general interest weekly first published in 1922, popular among a wide range of readers. Using its own *Asahi Shimbun* national and international news bureau network, this magazine features the latest news coverage. With its editorial slogan being 'information source which links the office to the home', the magazine enjoys a wide readership from businessmen to housewives, in higher income and educational brackets."

Aera

Circulation: 300,000   *Features Pornography:* No

"Since its launch, *Aera* has been a leader among weeklies in the quality of its news coverage, for which it has earned high marks from its readers. People see it as a weekly with international recognition, and many of its readers are well-informed leaders, not only in opinions but also in consumption habits. One of its distinctive features is the fact that 40% of its advertisements are placed by foreign companies."

Yomiuri Weekly

Circulation: 270,000   *Features Pornography:* No

"This weekly magazine, based on *Yomiuri Shimbun*, pursues different news from those in the newspaper with readers' points of view. Making hard news more understandable, and feeling signs of trends from light news it encourages people in rapidly changing society."

Sunday Mainichi, The

Circulation: 104,296   *Features Pornography:* No

"Japan's most venerable news weekly, it naturally covers the broader issues of Japanese society from politics and economics to crime. However, it also includes areas of public interest, such as sports, fashion and entertainment. It even challenges accepted values by touching on taboo topics, including the geisha scandal involving former Prime Minister Uno and the election campaign of the Aum Shinrikyo cult."

Source: Descriptions and circulation figures from *An Advertiser's Guide to Magazines in Japan 2002–2003, No. 14* (Tokyo: Japan Magazine Advertising Association, 2002), pp. 12–15.

The headlines in this image may or may not be reliable.

The Genesis of *Shukanshi*

The first weekly newsmagazine in Japan, *Sunday,* was published in 1908 and carried mainly gossip and human-interest stories. In 1922, *Asahi* and *Mainichi* newspapers began publishing weekly newsmagazines as well, with the aim of covering some of their stories in greater depth and from other angles and points of view than in their more fact-oriented newspapers. Both newspaper-owned weeklies are still published today.

In 1956, just three years after television had been introduced in Japan and just four years after the end of the occupation, the prominent book publisher Shinchosha Ltd. initiated its weekly magazine, *Shukan Shincho*, considered by many the first true Japanese weekly newsmagazine, or *shukanshi*. From the start, *Shukan Shincho* differed from anything else in the Japanese news media. It simply did not have the same newsgathering infrastructure or experience as its newspaper-owned competition. Having been relegated to a distinctly "outsider" position, but inspired by the exciting new visual aspects of television, *Shukan Shincho* introduced a controversial, sensationalist stance that gained immediate popularity. *Shukan Shincho* broke new ground in adopting both a language and a political stance that appealed directly to everyday Japanese. Although today the magazine is generally considered the most "literary" of the weeklies, often using comparatively sophisticated language that does not shy from obscure literary and other references, its use of informal language early on made it fresh and appealing.

Shukan Shincho may also be responsible for introducing in Japan what today is referred to as "narrative journalism," or journalism that tells a story. The dubious nature of *Shukan Shincho*'s brand of narrative—sometimes referred to as the *Shukan Shincho* "literary art style," or "literary-narrative journalism"—will be considered in detail later in this chapter. In broad terms, this style represented a bold departure from the unequivocally formal, staid approach used by most other Japanese news gatherers. Daringly, it featured informal Japanese language, which was not associated with the presentation of news, but which was easier and more enjoyable for everyday readers. The narrative style adopted also called for a significant amount of interpretation, often even serious exaggeration and invention of facts by reporters, in order to ensure that each story was as intriguing to readers as possible, although the story itself might only have been pieced together from a handful of established facts. Of course, the style is naturally suited to scandals or other stories that deal with moral failures.

This preoccupation with scandals was not unprecedented at Shinchosha Ltd., *Shukan Shincho*'s publisher. One of the company's founders, Giryo Sato, had previously established a publishing company called Shinseisha in July 1896. Shinseisha put out a magazine called *Shinsei,* as well as a number of books. In July 1899, Sato himself wrote and published a particularly interesting book entitled *Bundan Fubun-ki,* which translates as "A Record of Rumors in the Literary World." In subsequent years, the magazine *Shinsei* also published scandalous information about a famous poet of the time, Tekkan Yosano, for which the poet sued the company. In 1903, Sato eventually gave up on a struggling Shinseisha, with its ownership transferred to new owners, but he restarted his publishing ventures the following year under the new name Shinchosha.

In addition to *Shukan Shincho*'s literary-narrative journalism, the magazine was also successful in identifying and capturing the resurgent feelings of Japanese national pride that began to emerge in the 1950s. As the Japanese economy regained its feet after the war, and with the end of more than six years of occupation, a growing sense of resentment against the United States began to simmer among the population. The feeling was compounded by issues surrounding the fact that the United States had not yet relinquished control of Okinawa and other Japanese islands. This anti-American sentiment was perhaps best symbolized by the clean-cut "all-Japanese" wrestling star Rikidozan, who, like so many other Japanese cultural icons, was of Korean descent. Rikidozan routinely beat up on American wrestlers, especially his archenemies the Sharpe Brothers, to the great delight of Japanese fans.

Thus, while *Shukan Shincho* is known today for its staunch support of the ruling LDP and its unapologetically pro-U.S. stance on international policy, the magazine's early years were marked by a distinctively anti-American slant. Not that *Shukan Shincho* was filled with heady op-ed pieces against the United States—it simply capitalized on an undercurrent of resentment by featuring inflammatory articles that portrayed the United States in a negative light whenever possible. Articles on the various transgressions by U.S.

military personnel stationed in Japan were a favorite and a big seller. Jun Kamei, a former career *Shukan Shincho* writer and assistant editor, recalls that in his early years at the magazine it was well known that anti-Americanism was an overt part of *Shukan Shincho*'s early editorial policy.[10]

This fundamentally pro-Japanese policy played a pivotal role in popularizing *Shukan Shincho* and in laying the foundation for its antiestablishment stance, still struck by the magazine today. Documents at the U.S. National Archives show that in the late 1950s the U.S. State Department, focused as it was with fighting the cold war, had made specific moves to co-opt the Japanese government into a covert policy to engender positive feelings there about the United States. This scheme was clearly laid out in the so-called Draft Psychology Strategy Plan for the Pro-U.S. Orientation of Japan and the National Psychology Program for Japan.[11] The success or failure of these programs, as well as the extent of participation by the Japanese government with them, will bear further research and is beyond the scope of this book. However, and especially in light of revelations that the CIA secretly provided the LDP with millions of dollars to help keep it in power (see chapter 1), there is no doubt that many portions of the Japanese establishment worked (especially through the mainstream press) to encourage amity toward the United States at that time. As a result, the Japanese news-media marketplace was wide open for the fledgling, populist *Shukan Shincho* to garner a readership through anti-American news coverage. This was true until at least 1972, when the normalization of Japanese relations with China appears to have resulted in a shift in politics at the magazine, which has been decidedly pro-U.S. ever since.

Soon other nonnewspaper *shukanshi* publishers took their cues from *Shukan Shincho*'s profitable model, especially its populist approach to the news, its antiestablishment slant, and its use of a literary-narrative journalistic style. Today, however, the antiestablishment posturing by *Shukan Shincho* and its imitators is only that: posturing. For they are anything but antiestablishment. Indeed, they are firm fixtures of the Japanese power-elite status quo. Hajime Kitamura, former head of the Japan Federation of Press Workers' Unions, former editor in chief of Sunday *Mainichi* weekly newsmagazine, and current head of public relations for *Mainichi Shimbun,* made an important point along these lines in an interview for this book. According to Kitamura, when Japanese weekly newsmagazines started out, they were so small, especially in comparison with the dailies, that they had little choice but to use unconventional methods to gather news and attract readers. However, they have since become quite powerful and well established. Unfortunately, he says, they still act like—and are largely perceived as—relatively small, outsider forces and thus have not changed their original tactics and approach:

> The weeklies in Japan began with their ability to use what I would describe as "guerrilla-tactic journalism." But they are no longer guerrillas. Their influence has grown tremendously. The dailies learned about the potentially destructive nature of their power during World War II, when they helped galvanize public opinion behind the militarists. They know how easily they can influence things or ruin people socially. So far, however, the weeklies do not seem to have come to fully appreciate their powers. I think that if they had more self-awareness, they would hold back quite a bit. I think we are at a point where we really need to step up and evaluate. The weeklies have been criticizing the dailies for some time now, but the dailies on the whole just ignore the weeklies. They haven't acknowledged the power of the weeklies either. But it's time the whole industry, and society at large, acknowledges their power.[12]

Other Important Characteristics of *Shukanshi*

Some 93.8 percent of mainstream Japanese newspapers are purchased through subscriptions,[13] while more than 90 percent of Japanese weekly newsmagazines are purchased at newsstands. (The few actual subscriptions to weeklies are generally bought by businesses that place them in waiting rooms and lounges.) Of the vast majority that sell at the newsstand, a substantial portion go to commuters who read them on the subway or train. According to one source, 30 to 40 percent of all *shukanshi* sales occur at the approximately four thousand kiosks located within train stations across the country.[14] The bulk of the rest of the magazines are sold at bookstores and convenience stores (many of which are located near train stations).

This reliance on commuters means that the average weekly magazine reader is urban and of working age. Indeed, the *shukanshi* industry would suffer gravely were it not for the country's army of train and subway riders. This commuting readership often defines the editorial stance of newsmagazines, just as massive subscription bases drive newspaper content. Whereas Japanese newspapers strive to present broad-based, inoffensive material to massive numbers of committed readers, each week the *shukanshi* must entice what amounts to a brand-new readership to stop in their tracks and make a special purchase from a newsstand or similar outlet. Therefore, unlike Japanese newspaper editors, who have almost no motivation to produce enticing headlines, the newsmagazine editors and writers are required to formulate new, attention-grabbing headlines every week, to be reproduced in advertisements in the national daily papers and on posters in trains and on subways. Given the huge popularity of cellular phones that include game and imaging capacity, which many young Japanese are using on trains, one can only speculate about how

This April 3, 2003, ad for *Shukan Bunshun* was prominently displayed in a window at the headquarters for Bungeishunju Ltd. not long after the start of the Second Gulf War. The head on the left is that of Japanese baseball hero Hideki "Godzilla" Matsui of the New York Yankees. The small heads to the right of him are U.S. Secretary of State Colin Powell and Secretary of Defense Donald Rumsfeld. Two heads over from Rumsfeld is Japanese Prime Minister Junichiro Koizumi. Next, of course, is U.S. President George Bush, with Saddam Hussein on the end.

In typical *shukanshi* fashion, the ad promises information not to be found in Japan's mainstream press. The headline along the right edge, for instance, reads "Iraq War That Newspapers and TV Don't Report: The Ten Major Scoops." To the left of that is the headline "CIA Secret File." Also of note, the headline above Powell and Rumsfeld announces "Scoop Report: Iraq Attack, Self Defense Force's Alliance Plan with U.S. Military."

shukanshi sales may suffer once the phones start featuring television (as is now possible in South Korea) and other more sophisticated entertainment features.

Many *shukanshi* also brandish their publishers' names on their front covers as part of their names. This serves to bolster the credibility of the magazines, which also sometimes serve as de facto emissaries for their parent companies. For example, Shinchosha Ltd. and Bungeishunju Ltd., publishers of *Shukan Shincho* and *Shukan Bunshun,* respectively, are prodigious book publishers, each releasing several hundred new titles

Many Japanese, faced with long, tedious commutes on public transportation, regularly read weekly newsmagazines to pass the time.

each year. Shinchosha Ltd. has published such Western classics as *Jane Eyre* and *War and Peace,* and Bungeishunju Ltd. has published *The Bridges of Madison County* and the Japanese-language edition of *The Diary of Anne Frank.* Obviously, the names of these publishers add a veneer of credibility to their magazines.

Dave Spector, a well-known "Western" television personality and pundit in Japan, known for his eloquence in Japanese, has contributed to such weekly newsmagazines as *Shukan Bunshun.* He participated in a panel discussion on Japanese newsmagazines and tabloid newspapers held at the Foreign Correspondents' Club of Japan in 2002, where he observed that "there is a tremendous vitality to the weeklies here. And the reason for that is because newspapers are so boring...incredibly boring. There are no columnists to speak of. You don't curl up in bed with the Sunday edition like you would with the *New York Times* or the *Financial Times*...so I think the magazines make up for the tremendous dullness of the normal newspapers."[15]

Spector's point is fundamental. The *shukanshi* present the kind of material they do, in the way that they do, because of the bland nature of the establishment Japanese news media. Japanese newspaper coverage tends to be so noninterpretive, boring, and supportive of the establishment that readers are

Pictured here is a typical kiosk in a Tokyo train station. There are approximately four thousand such kiosks in Japan, with weekly newsmagazines being one of the top-selling items. The magazines for sale at kiosks are usually placed prominently, face up or face out, so that many times the number of customers read the headlines on the newsstand than actually buy the magazines.

often left feeling as though they just aren't getting the full story on what is happening. As a result, many turn to the weeklies, which loudly proclaim to have all the details.

The *Tatemae* and *Honne* of the News

The dichotomy of *tatemae* and *honne* is such an important concept in the Japanese culture that most books on Japanese culture for non-Japanese include at least some discussion of it. *Tatemae* refers to the official, outwardly acknowledged aspect of things; *honne*, to what is really going on. In other words, *tatemae* characterizes formal communication that often deals with issues on superficial and cosmetic levels, while *honne* is more intimate, substantial, and truthful. In the chapter 1 example of someone mispronouncing a word, the *tatemae* response might be to ignore the error, but the *honne* response would be to acknowledge it openly. In another simple example, someone gives a gift that the recipient dislikes. In a *tatemae* response, the recipient might express thanks and praise the gift as wonderful—a superficial but socially appropriate response. In a *honne* response, however, the recipient might avoid all pretenses and come right out and say that he or she dislikes the gift. Such a response might or might not also include expressing thanks for the thought that was behind the gift. Either way, *honne* would express the recipient's genuine feelings.

These examples are benign enough, but as Alex Kerr, author of *Dogs and Demons: Tales from the Dark Side of Japan,* has pointed out, the practice of *tatemae* and *honne* becomes a truly profound problem when applied to broader social issues: "*Tatemae* is a charming attitude when it means that everyone should look the other way at a guest's faux pas in the tearoom; it has dangerous and unpredictable results when applied to corporate balance sheets, drug testing, and nuclear power safety reports."[16] Frighteningly enough, and to the great detriment of the Japanese citizenry, the *tatemae/honne* dichotomy is indeed regularly applied by journalists and publishers whose job is supposed to be to disseminate genuine information but who too often choose instead to offer only superficial, formal, *tatemae* news.

In comparing the Japanese weekly newsmagazines and the mainstream press club newspapers, two primary *tatemae* explanations are likely. The first is simply that the press club newspapers are authoritative and respectable, whereas the weeklies are unreliable, sensationalistic, and trashy. For example, Nobuaki Hanaoka, a former senior editorial writer for *Sankei* newspaper, recently defended the Japanese press club system in a panel discussion at the Foreign Correspondents' Club of Japan: "The clubs are our hard-won achievement in the battle against the government over a century. Of course we need them."[17] And Hajime Kitamura stated in an interview for this book that "press clubs were established so that papers could maintain a presence and monitor activity from within those actual agencies. They work within those agencies to ensure that the officials are not up to any chicanery."[18] Japanese media scholar Ellis Krauss has noted that "the Japanese media defends the clubs, citing the collective nature of the club and its institutionalized rules as a way to protect the individual reporter from intimidation or manipulation by the source."[19] According to those who agree with these assertions, Japanese press clubs are a "means for the media to jointly press reluctant public officials to disclose information."[20] Given the collusive relationships between the Japanese establishment news media and government and corporate sources, as enforced by the press club system, it is obvious that these are all *tatemae* explanations. The Japanese establishment press and press clubs may at times function according to some of these rosy descriptions, but their primary functions are thornier, to say the least. In this case, not only are they superficial and formal, they contradict reality.

A second *tatemae* explanation of the relationship between the Japanese news media and the weeklies is that, contrary to the explanations above, press club journalists are mere mouthpieces for the establishment, spouting little else but the official views *(tatemae)* of the news, whereas the writers for weekly newsmagazines are bold outsiders courageously investigating and printing the truth *(honne)* of the news.

Kengo Tanaka, the former president and CEO of Bungeishunju Ltd. and a former editor in chief of *Shukan Bunshun*, gave an example of this view in a personal interview for this book. "I fail to think that *Shukan Shincho* and *Shukan Bunshun* are delving into seriously scandalous issues today," he commented. "There was a period of scandalous writing, but this only lasted as long as it would sell. To my mind, this is no longer the case. Such sensationalism appears mainly on the so-called wide-shows [a popular type of Japanese TV talk show]. I have the impression that *Shukan Shincho* and *Shukan Bunshun* have toned down their coverage of scandals quite a bit and that they perform good journalism and are taken very seriously today."[21]

Of course, this second view of the newsmagazines, as related by Tanaka, is just as *tatemae*, or formal and superficial (and, in fact, false), as the previous stories mouthed by those who support the establishment newspapers. Japanese weekly newsmagazines beget an extraordinarily sensationalistic version of the news that seldom takes hold of the *honne*, or substance, of the way things really are in Japan. They may cover stories in more entertaining and titillating ways than the press club media, and they sometimes present subjects in greater depth. They have even been known to break important political scandals. However, they rarely offer much in the way of genuinely important journalism. The *New York Times*'s Howard W. French, writing in the year 2000, sums this situation up nicely: "Indeed, a growing body of press criticism says Japan's mainstream dailies suffer from their cosseted relationships with the government and other powerful institutions, while the fat, glossy-covered weeklies pull some of their punches out of fear of Japan's huge and omnipresent advertising agency, Dentsu, an integral part of a deeply conservative establishment."[22]

Another veteran American writer (who requested not to be named) with longtime, close ties with Japanese weeklies described the coverage by *shukanshi* in an interview for this book. "When it comes to the establishment, they never go beyond certain boundaries. They don't challenge the way things are done beyond a certain point. It's like the difference between boxing and sumo wrestling. Real journalists are like boxers. They are out for blood. But the weeklies are like sumo wrestlers. There's a lot of huffing and puffing, and a lot of weight thrown around; people sometimes even get hurt a bit, but they are certainly not out to do any real damage."

Jun Kamei, a former *Shukan Shincho* reporter and assistant editor with some twenty years at the magazine, resigned because of what he describes as the unethical news coverage of his former employer. Since then, he has written extensive exposés on Japanese newsmagazines, including his book *Shukanshi no Yomikata* (How to Read *Shukanshi*).[23] As an assistant editor, Kamei's livelihood depended for many years on his ability to understand exactly what kind of readers his magazine targeted—and how. In an interview for this book, he explained the appeal of *Shukan Shincho* and similar weeklies:

> Unlike the newspapers that have their press clubs, through which they are completely piped into the big companies and the government agencies, and who are essentially public-relations apparatuses for these businesses and agencies, the weeklies take a position that says, "We're not those bureaucrats, and we're not their proxies either. We're not those big fat capitalists, and we're not their proxies either." The regular man on the street in a busy city sees so many of their ads everywhere. It's like the magazines are whispering to people, "Do you want the real scoop? This is the real scoop. Do you want to know the truth? We've got the truth." They work so hard to convince their readers that they've got the genuine information, but it's just a sleight-of-hand trick. They don't publish the truth.[24]

This outsider posturing of the magazines actually makes them the perfect vehicles for supporting the Japanese establishment's *tatemae*. Although marketed as alternatives to the establishment press, they are nothing like real alternatives. As the examples in this book show, their politics are decidedly conservative in almost every way. They are strongly supported by Dentsu and other Japanese advertisers. They regularly run pieces that support nationalist thinking and that attack feminists, foreigners, opposition parties, advocates for human rights, and others.

Again, this does not imply in any way that there is a conspiracy within the weekly newsmagazine industry to manipulate public opinion. On the contrary, many weekly magazine reporters take great pride in the fact that their papers regularly run humiliating information about specific politicians, business leaders, and other elites of various affiliations. However, almost all take a decidedly conservative position on social and foreign-policy issues. Moreover, they almost never challenge major Japanese institutions in a serious way, let alone question the fundamental ways in which those institutions interact.

The Japanese weekly newsmagazines' relatively bold approach to the news means that they could, theoretically, be strong forces for journalistic and democratic reform in Japan. For instance, if they were truly dedicated to real journalism, they would rail against the corrupt press club system that denies them direct access to official sources. But they do not.

Gathering Material

Because journalists from the weeklies are banned from the press clubs, they are unable to offer their readers the same timely official information provided by press club journalists. Instead, they have to gather material through a variety of alternative methods. Although this may sound like a difficult situation for *shukanshi* writers and editors, it actually suits them just fine—so much so that their industry-wide organization, the Japanese Magazine Publishers Association, does not even complain about its members' exclusion from the clubs. In fact, if weekly magazines did belong to Japanese press clubs, not only would they have to pay much more money to support the staff required, but one of their presumed raisons d'être would be eliminated—they would no longer be able to pose as an "outsider" or alternative press.

Of course, the best way for magazine reporters to get material outside the press clubs is to follow the traditional journalist work ethic of chasing leads and tracking down information. Excellent journalism often requires that reporters go around official sources anyway. Also, it is not impossible for non–press club reporters to arrange interviews with government and corporate sources in Japan; it is just more difficult and time consuming.

Author and press club critic Tatsuya Iwase, who has many years of experience writing for Japanese newsmagazines, prides himself on performing just such investigative reporting. Iwase believes that good, investigative reporting is gaining favor with the Japanese public because readers have grown increasingly frustrated with the establishment press and overloaded with the barrage of sensationalism coming from television, radio, and elsewhere. Although Iwase is no starry-eyed optimist, he says that the newsmagazine industry is slowly starting to improve. In an interview for this book, he predicted that investigative journalism will eventually make up as much as 20 to 30 percent of the contents of many Japanese weekly newsmagazines. However, Iwase also estimates that currently only about 3 or 4 percent of all the material in a given weekly newsmagazine could be categorized as solid investigative reporting. He qualified this statement by estimating that, unlike in the establishment press where 90 percent or more of all stories are derived from government and corporate sources, as many as half of the stories (at least in non-newspaper-published weeklies) are on original topics that were not initiated by a press release or similar official source.[25]

However, if Iwase and the many who agree with him are correct, and only a tiny percent of all the reporting in Japanese weekly newsmagazines is made up of worthwhile reporting, how do these publications fill their pages each week?

One common information-gathering method employed by weekly newsmagazines is simply to bribe press club reporters to "leak" information from the clubs. Indeed, newsmagazines commonly pay press club reporters to write entire stories anonymously, a fact confirmed repeatedly in interviews with numerous newspaper and magazine reporters. Although frowned upon by establishment-media companies, this practice can be a boon for the press club reporters themselves. Not only are they able to earn extra income while plying their trade, they also are provided a much-desired outlet for the hottest insider information, which they can obtain as club members, but which club rules and other restrictions often prevent them from disclosing in the establishment press. Yasunori Okadome, the publisher and editor in chief of the monthly scandal magazine *Uwasa no Shinso* (Truth of Rumors) for twenty-five years, until its discontinuation in 2004, has estimated that 30 to 40 percent of all the articles in his magazine "come from information leaked by newspaper reporters who feel they cannot write about much of the information they have in their own publications."[26]

Another method is simply to repackage public information already reported in the establishment news media by putting a different spin on it. This usually means making the information somehow more sensational. A good example is a *Shukan Shincho* article that repeated accusations already widely reported against an innocent man, Yoshiyuki Kono (see chapter 4). It is obvious that writers working for the magazine simply added to this public information by interviewing some of Kono's neighbors and acquaintances and researching his parents' and grandparents' histories. Although the information collected was fundamentally innocuous and had no bearing on the validity of the accusations against Kono (all of which later proved false), *Shukan Shincho* ran its story about "The Originator of the Poisonous Gas and His Macabre Family Line"[27] as though it had achieved an inside scoop that demonstrated Kono's guilt in an original way.

A variant on this technique is to rehash news already reported elsewhere in the media and then simply hire experts to comment on it. This can be a popular format among Japanese readers, who do not often encounter detailed news analysis in the opinion-shy establishment press. Although nothing is fundamentally unethical about this approach, a particularly ugly example appears in chapter 8. The *Shukan Shincho* article quoted opens with a criticism of *Asahi* newspaper's coverage of the "comfort women" story and then simply recounts the opinions of so-called experts (some of whom are nothing but neonationalist cranks), who variously accuse the surviving women of being prostitutes and opportunists.

Yet another popular *shukanshi* method for gathering material is simply to report hearsay, rumors, or other unreliable sources as news. Such unsubstantiated claims, collected from various neo-Nazi and other Western sources, became the basis for a freelance writer's "proof," published in a Japanese newsmagazine, that no Jews were gassed at Auschwitz (see chapter 5).

Of course, the easiest and least expensive way to produce "news stories" is simply to invent them, a common practice in the *shukanshi* industry. Dave Spector explains: "They will use fuzzy expressions like *'A kankeisha ni yoru to...'* ('According to source A...'), and they will make up many things. It's so obvious they are making up things. And they are not even interviewing anyone. They are just thinking it up in the editorial room there. Rather than saying they go overboard, I think it's a lot of sloppy journalism that would not cut the mustard in other countries."[28]

The practice of false reporting is so commonplace among the nonestablishment Japanese press that journalists have coined a term for it: *netsuzo*, or "the manufacturing of the news." In one documented case, a group of sportswriters, wishing to quote the unavailable baseball player Hideo Nomo, agreed on a common statement on the basis of what they "thought the pitcher would say if he were there" and then falsely attributed it to him in print. The National Press Club of Japan even published an account of the incident, written by one of the very sportswriters involved, without any comment that it had been a breach of journalistic ethics.[29]

These are just a few of the more popular methods Japanese newsmagazine reporters commonly employ to get around the lack of access to official sources through the press clubs. Some of these methods are, of course, perfectly legitimate, and certainly none of them are unique to the *shukanshi*, for they have all been employed by reporters around the world. What is interesting in the case of the *shukanshi*, however, is that any given issue can include articles that run the gamut of journalistic scruples: from top-notch investigative work to formulaic techniques, to bald-faced lies. This range of quality is perhaps matched only by the magazines' range of subject matters. It is in itself dangerous, since it puts the readers of the weeklies in the difficult position of never being sure how much credence to give what they are reading.

The Massive Influence of the *Shukanshi*

The influence wielded by Japanese weekly newsmagazines is far more pervasive than is usually recognized. A primary reason for this is their advertising campaigns, which are structured so that twenty, forty, or even eighty times the number of people who actually buy the magazines are influenced by their content. These advertisements do not merely promote the magazine as a brand or just give the latest issue's top story. Rather, they feature the table of contents with the headlines of most of the major stories carried in each week's issue. These advertisements are blazoned across posters, displayed prominently on trains and subways around the country, mounted on the inner walls of the cars, or hung from the ceilings. Moreover, the weeklies' tables of contents are regularly advertised in the major national daily newspapers.

One informal group of Japanese media scholars who meet at Doshisha University in Kyoto have conservatively estimated that the table of contents of each issue of the Japanese weekly newsmagazines *Shukan Shincho* and *Shukan Bunshun* are seen by between 10 million and 20 million people each week. This range reflects the dynamic nature of the magazine's advertising campaigns, which vary according to their advertising budgets and the effectiveness of their campaigns. Nevertheless, even the lower figure of 10 million is quite substantial. Given that Japan had a population of about 128 million in 2003, this means that between 7.8 and 15.6 percent of the Japanese public is exposed to the table of contents of each newsmagazine every week.

The estimate is not hard to get at, as both magazines—like most of their fellow *shukanshi*—advertise their tables of contents in the morning edition of two or three of the five major national daily newspapers. Depending on just which two or three newspapers the magazines advertise in, this portion of the campaign alone means that they are seen by between 5.1 and 20.5 million people. Adding to those that see the advertisements in newspapers are the millions more who see their ubiquitous advertisement on Japanese public transportation—on trains and on buses. For example, ninety-nine of the one hundred individuals in Tokyo who took part in an informal survey for this book (see appendix A) said that they regularly read advertisements for weekly newsmagazines that are hung on trains and subways. Indeed, the lone individual who said he did not read the advertisements explained that he probably would read them if only he did not suffer from vision problems!

Thus, while only fifty-two people of the one hundred surveyed said that they read *shukanshi* regularly, nearly all of them said that they regularly read the headlines in the advertisements for them, and seventy-six admitted to being influenced by them to some degree. Of course there is also the roughly half a million people who buy *shukanshi* each week, as well as those who are likely to browse through them in waiting rooms and the like. Given the previous factors, the estimate of 10 million to 20 million is clearly a conservative

This photograph of a *Shukan Asahi* ad (front left) offers a good perspective on the number of advertisements posted on Japanese trains. *The headlines in this image may or may not be reliable.*

one, and it may well be that some weeks many more millions of Japanese are exposed to these headlines.

One might suppose that many Japanese might ignore these advertisements. In reality, though, it is quite likely that most Japanese do read them when they see them, if only because they are so provocative and sensational. Jun Kamei explains the popularity of the ads:

> Weekly magazines are very influential, and the reason is the advertisements. The headlines reproduced in ads on trains and in other publications are nationwide. Millions see them every week. And they are very, very clever at getting those one-liner headlines down so that they deliver their messages, be it serious sensationalism or a political agenda on those headlines. They can be very searing, and they can be very seamy. A huge chunk of people in Japan who never buy the periodical walk away thinking that they know about what they are writing every week.[30]

The headlines in the advertisements are often far more sensational than the actual content of the articles. David Kaplan, a freelance journalist with experience in Japan, confirms this reality: "Even those solid reports would get headlines (translated into ad placards) that absolutely lied about the contents. It's pure hype and typical of Japanese magazine publishing."[31]

When it comes to the headlines of the weeklies, the cart is regularly before the horse. Kensuke Nishioka, an accomplished reporter for *Shukan Bunshun*, explains that coming up with a good headline may well be the single most important aspect in researching and writing a story for a weekly: "Headlines are the bread and butter for the weeklies. The editor in chief's biggest prerogative is making the advertisements each week. We are always told to write stories with the headlines in mind. If you can't come up with an enticing headline for a story, don't write it."[32]

The tremendous dependence of the newsmagazines on ads to drum up their readerships each week also means that at least some headlines are composed in advance of the news articles themselves. This isn't always the case, and interviews with weekly newsmagazine editors and writers indicate that some magazines have systems in place that help to mitigate the problem. However, the fact remains that a number of each week's articles are completed at the last minute. In these cases, headlines must be written for the advertisements *before* their corresponding stories have been put to bed, sometimes even before they have been properly researched. Thus, it is not uncommon for there to be a serious disconnect or incongruence between advertised headlines and the content of stories. The real

The headlines in this image may or may not be reliable.

Shown here is the October 4, 1999, advertisement for *Shukan Post*, as it appeared in *Asahi Shimbun*. It also appeared in *Mainichi Shimbun* and *Sankei Shimbun*. The angled headline in the top right corner (in largest type) reads, "FINALLY UNVEILED! THE HUMAN NETWORK OF JEWISH CAPITAL THAT DEVOURS FIVE TRILLION YEN OF OUR HARD-EARNED TAXES THROUGH THE LONG-TERM CREDIT BANK OF JAPAN." See chapter 5 for more information about this horrendous anti-Semitic article. The total circulation numbers for the three newspapers is more than fourteen million.

problem arises when the advertised headline asserts something that is not in the story at all or that even contradicts the actual article. In such cases, the millions of people who read the ads but not the stories are completely misled.

Exacerbating the situation is that Japanese newsmagazine headlines are often exceptionally sensational. Keigo Takeda, editor in chief of the Japanese-language edition of *Newsweek,* who has experience in both U.S. and Japanese journalism, says that even a relatively reserved magazine such as his regularly sexes up its headlines. Takeda is especially aware of this, since the Japanese edition of *Newsweek* often runs stories that were originally written in English. He says that the original English-language headlines often just aren't sensational enough for the Japanese market. He claims that, unlike the English-language version of *Newsweek,* which has a broad base of subscribers, the Japanese industry's reliance on newsstand sales demands provocative headlines.

A case in point is a cover story about the insider-trading scandal involving American do-it-yourself icon Martha Stewart. Soon after the story broke in the summer of 2002, both the U.S. and Japanese editions of *Newsweek* carried the same cover story on the subject. The article was originally written in English and then translated into Japanese. Both editions of the magazine featured the same photograph of Stewart on their covers. The cover of the U.S. edition offered the words "MARTHA'S MESS" below Stewart's photo, with the words, "AN INSIDE TRADING SCANDAL TARNISHES THE QUEEN OF PERFECTION" next to her image. However, Takeda and his editorial team in Japan felt that this was just too weak for the Japanese magazine market. As a result, the Japanese edition used the more inflammatory language:

"MARTHA STEWART: CORRUPT QUEEN"

and

"THE BEHIND-THE-SCENES SUSPICIONS OF THE CHARISMATIC HOUSEWIFE. THE ENDLESS GREED OF WALL STREET"

Unlike the U.S. edition, the Japanese edition was also widely advertised with posters on subways and trains. The poster ad for this particular issue not only featured the Japanese cover with its two significantly stronger, more damning headlines, it also sported an additional two headlines:

"Martha Stewart Falls off Her Pedestal
as America's Charismatic Housewife"

and

"The Shocking Scandal: Her Insider Trading
with Her Dubious Circle of Friends"

It is true that the four Japanese headlines do more than simply sensationalize the story. They also contextualize the story for Japanese readers, who are typically less familiar with Stewart than their U.S. counterparts. Still, the example is revealing. Where one relatively plain headline sufficed for the U.S. magazine, four were required in Japan, two on the actual cover and two more on the ad poster.

Martha Stewart was found guilty of four crimes related to the scandal. However, it is worth noting that until May 2003, some ten months after the article appeared, no formal charges were lodged against her. If Stewart were later found innocent, the difference in the U.S. and Japanese headlines would be even starker. For example, as the U.S. cover was not widely advertised, the lone headline published there primarily only reached those people who were actually in physical proximity to the magazine. Those who saw the magazine headline but who did not read the article only learned from the cover that Stewart was involved in a "mess," a relatively mild accusation. Only those U.S. readers who actually took the time to read the article in question learned anything else from *Newsweek*.

In Japan, however, the more inflammatory headlines presumably reached many more people than did the actual magazine. Many of those who read the headlines on the advertisements simply did not have the benefit of being in the physical proximity of a magazine and, by extension, had a much smaller chance of reading the actual article associated with those headlines. Given that this case involved *Newsweek*, a "reputable" magazine that is so comparatively tame that it cannot accurately be categorized as a Japanese "weekly," it is easy to imagine how overblown the headlines on domestic Japanese newsmagazines can be.

The English-language edition of *Newsweek* shown here appears rather tame in its treatment of Martha Stuart during the summer of 2002, when her insider-trading scandal initially broke.

The Japanese-language banner advertisement for the same article, which is dated July 3, 2002, was widely displayed in Japan on public transportation and was likely seen by dozens of times the number of people that read the actual Japanese magazine. As can be seen, the cover of the magazine is actually part of the ad. The cover features the headlines: "THE TRUE BEHIND-THE-SCENES SUSPICIONS OF THE CHARISMATIC HOUSEWIFE. THE ENDLESS GREED OF WALL STREET" and "MARTHA STUART: CORRUPT QUEEN," which are unquestionably more sensational than the language on the American magazine cover. Along the right edge of the Japanese banner ad is the headline, "SHOCKING SCANDAL: INSIDER TRADING SCANDAL WITH DUBIOUS CIRCLE OF FRIENDS." The headline adjacent to it in large type reads "MARTHA STUART FALLS OFF HER PEDESTAL AS AMERICA'S FAVORITE HOUSEWIFE." To the left of the large type is the question, "CAN YOU BELIEVE THIS LOVEABLE HOME-FURNISHING MAVEN AND STAR OF TV AND MAGAZINES IS CAUGHT IN THE MIDDLE OF THIS WALL STREET DISASTER?"

The contrast between the two illustrates just how different Japanese magazine reporters tend to approach stories, in comparison to Western reporters. Without a doubt, the Japanese industry produces more sensationalism, especially on its popular and highly influential banner advertisements.

With *shukanshi*, it is not at all uncommon for a single fact to be misrepresented and exaggerated, first in the body of an article, a second time in the headline for that article, and then a third time in the advertisements for the magazine—and this doesn't even take into account the possibility of an especially hot or provocative article being posted on the Internet or repeated by word of mouth. Moreover, each level of exaggeration tends to reach a geometrically larger, and less well-informed, group of people.

Of course, it would be foolhardy to think that all Japanese readers patently believe what they are exposed to by weekly newsmagazine headlines, or articles, for that matter. However, it would be equally naïve to suppose that the millions who read the headlines just dismiss them. As noted in chapter 2, studies indicate that Japanese tend to put far more faith in what they read than do Westerners. Media professor and author Kenichi Asano states it simply: "People say that they don't believe Japanese weekly newsmagazines, but they do. It's impossible to read them or their headlines all over the trains and in ads and to simply assume that everything is false. It's only natural to believe that there is truth to things that are published so widely by national publishing companies."[33]

Shukan Shincho and *Shukan Bunshun*

Many of the case studies in this book focus on *Shukan Shincho* and *Shukan Bunshun* for two reasons: these two publications are especially egregious offenders of journalistic ethics, and they are widely considered to be the most influential *shukanshi* in Japan. Neither weekly has the largest readership in the industry. In fact, of the eleven Japanese newsmagazines listed in table 3.a., *Shukan Bunshun* has only the third-largest circulation, and *Shukan Shincho* the fifth. Nevertheless, *Shukan Shincho* and *Shukan Bunshun* appeal to more influential readerships than do the other magazines. They also appeal to those readerships in a manner that gives their news coverage more credence than the others.

Of all the *shukanshi,* these are the only two that specifically target men in their forties—given the patriarchal leanings of Japanese society, a quite powerful readership. In contrast, all the other major non-newspaper-owned weeklies appeal to audiences that are either less specific or younger. For example, *Shukan Post* targets men between twenty-five and forty; *Shukan Gendai,* men in their thirties; and *Shukan Asahi,* "a wide range of readers."[34]

In addition to being older men and thus more likely to be in influential social positions, readers of *Shukan Shincho* and *Shukan Bunshun* are relatively well-off. *Shukan Bunshun*'s entry in the *Advertiser's Guide to Magazines in Japan,* for example, claims that "the majority [of its readers] are upper class, wealthy and intellectually inclined." *Shukan Shincho,* on the other hand, claims that its "average reader is 41.4 years old, 34.2% are white collar, and 60.9% own their own homes."[35] Although neither magazine has a truly powerful audience—for example, neither targets company CEOs, intellectuals, or other social leaders—their audiences are relatively important, especially when compared to the readers of other *shukanshi.*

Credibility

Shukan Shincho and *Shukan Bunshun* are the only major nonestablishment weekly newsmagazines that do not feature pornography. This makes them the magazines of choice for men who want to read so-called alternative news (from sources other than the major newspapers and broadcasters), but who do not want to look at (or be seen looking at) pornography. As in most cultures, many settings in Japan, such as professional-office and family environments, are inappropriate for pornography. As a result, *Shukan Shincho* and *Shukan Bunshun* are in many ways more respected and socially acceptable than their competitors.

Both weeklies further reinforce this relative respectability with their layouts. The text pages of both magazines are mainly printed in black and white on paper that is common to many other weeklies—a rough, pulpy stock (although glossy pages are becoming more common)—but both also spurn the standard weekly newsmagazine practice of running a picture of a young woman, surrounded by sensational headlines, on their covers. In fact, their front covers are nothing short of handsome and dignified. They tend to carry a single clean, contemporary fine art painting or photograph, usually of a nondescript, vaguely evocative subject such as a landscape, flower, window, or the like. They present the artwork, name of the magazine, date, and issue number—and that is all. One might think that the omission of headlines from their covers would be a detriment to sales, but both more than make up for this by widely disseminating each week's headlines through their aggressive advertising campaigns.

The left and center covers are from *Shukan Shincho*. The right cover is from *Shukan Bunshun*.

These two factors—the absence of pornography and a dignified layout—also make *Shukan Shincho* and *Shukan Bunshun* especially popular in the waiting rooms of doctors, lawyers, and other professionals, which, of course, adds further to their credibility and influence. However, the old adage could easily be paraphrased "don't judge a *shukanshi* by its cover" in the case of *Shukan Shincho* and *Shukan Bunshun*. While they appear dignified, and may even be considered so by some readers, their writing is too often debased and debasing.

Not everything published in *Shukan Shincho* and *Shukan Bunshun* is as disreputable as the examples given in this book. In fact, many of their severest critics emphasize that they regularly proffer a lot of solid, even sophisticated

material. Unfortunately, this makes them still more dangerous. Asano explained the paradox in an interview for this book: "The problem with magazines like *Shukan Shincho* and *Shukan Bunshun* is that they have lots of decent articles, interesting ones, but then they slip in the poison, total lies. It's very strange. It's like a healthy plate of food, but laced with arsenic. The average Japanese person doesn't know. That's how they get you. And the strange thing is that they don't have to do it. Their publishers make lots of money selling very good books."[36]

Kenichi Asano is the author of many books about the Japanese news media, including the best-selling *Hanzai Hodo no Hanzai* (The Crime of Crime Reporting). He is a former Kyodo news service reporter and is now a professor of journalism at Doshisha University.

When asked what he meant by "poison," Asano cited a number of examples used by many Japanese critics of the two publications. These fall into two basic categories: (1) coverage that unnecessarily disparages or defames individuals and groups, and (2) material designed to support nationalism, either by casting the contemporary nationalists in a beneficial light or by justifying the excesses of the Japanese military during and before the Second World War.

Support of Nationalism

Shukan Shincho and *Shukan Bunshun*, for all their outsider posturing, are especially well known for their nationalistic ideologies—something their staff members freely admit, although by various terms. Bungeishunju Ltd.'s former president Kengo Tanaka, for instance, put it this way:

> First of all, magazine journalism is inherently conservative and therefore inherently nationalistic. Now, it goes without saying that that can be in conflict with ideas of human rights. Language is the means of communication. I mean, there is a continued conversation among the postwar Japanese. We have had left-wing thoughts forced on us, and there has been an intentional effort to continue to do so. So in that respect, in countering these left-wing ideas, Bungeishunju is nationalistic. It's part of an effort to ensure that the left wing does not get out of hand.[37]

Hiroshi Matsuda, former editor in chief of *Shukan Shincho* throughout much of the 1990s, likewise described his magazine as "benevolent conservative." In a similar though more severe vein, a former assistant editor of *Shukan Shincho,* Jun Kamei, described both magazines as "blatantly supportive of the far right."[38]

Both magazines are well known for their tenacious campaigns to "reinterpret" the well-documented history of Japanese atrocities during the Second World War. In doing so, they support the same extreme Japanese nationalism that was espoused by the militarists leading up to and throughout the war.

Bungeishunju Ltd.'s tendency to whitewash Japanese war crimes is nothing new. It is true that most Japanese publishers who were in business before and during the war supported the militarists. If they were not supportive, they were driven out of business. However, Bungeishunju Ltd. stands out as one of the most zealous advocates of Japanese militarism at that time, certainly among publishers. The famous Hiroshi Kikuchi, founder and president of Bungeishunju Ltd. in the 1930s and 1940s, also helped to organize the so-called Pen Corps, a team of propagandists and co-opted journalists who banded together under the auspices of a Japanese military-intelligence unit. The Pen Corps followed Japanese troops in their brutal campaign into Mainland China during the late 1930s and were even present in Nanjing at the time of the horrific massacre there. An October 1938 issue of *Bungei Shunju* declared: "You might dream of such organizations as the Nazis and Fascists. Keep in mind, however, that it is the people, united and centered on Hitler

and Mussolini, who are moving the world." In December 1941, the month
the United States declared war on Japan following the Pearl Harbor attack,
Bungei Shunju further urged:

> Unless and until we sweep away every and all influences of democracy and
> internationalism, we Japanese will not be able to see the truth.... We should
> eliminate any suspicious thoughts that lurk within academia and the
> press.... It is *Bungei Shunju*'s position that freedom of speech and publica-
> tion must be strictly controlled.

Unfortunately, after the war Mr. Kikuchi was not purged from the industry but stayed on at Bungeishunju Ltd., where he continued to exercise considerable influence on the content and the reporting of their magazines.
Many observers point to this legacy, unbroken as it was by the end of the war,
as a major contributing factor to the continued "revisionist" stance of *Shukan
Bunshun* to this day.

Although *Shukan Shincho* shifted away from its initial anti-American bias
in the 1960s, thereby aligning it with the LDP's decision to follow the U.S. lead
in virtually all things international, it has nonetheless remained nationalistic
throughout its life. This brand of nationalism, however, has been distinctly different from what one might categorize as patriotism. For while patriotism (at
its best) tends to emphasize a given country's assets, nationalism often focuses
on other countries' problems. Indeed, nationalism in Japan today has a
markedly xenophobic streak. For instance, during its early years, *Shukan Shincho* ran many articles disparaging the United States. Today, hardly an issue is
published without articles that are harshly critical of North Korea or China.
Another small but obvious example is *Shukan Shincho*'s continued support of
prime-ministerial visits to worship at Yasukuni Shrine. As noted in chapter 1,
Yasukuni Shrine was a spiritual center and a pillar of the state Shinto creed and
emperor worship that served as the theological foundation of Japanese militarism up through the Second World War. It is also said to be where the spirits of Japanese soldiers are enshrined, including fourteen Class A war criminals
of the Second World War, such as Prime Minister Tojo. When contemporary
Japanese prime ministers worship there in what clearly appears to be the official capacity of their nation's head of state (although there are some technical

questions as to what comprises an "official" visit), critics of the act see it as comparable to a contemporary German leader brazenly worshipping at a hypothetical shrine to the Nazis. Not only do many Japanese protest these visits, but the visits usually elicit censure from the country's Asian neighbors, who take serious offense at what they perceive as the prime minister's support not just for Japan's dead soldiers but for the brutal war crimes many of them perpetrated under the influence of state Shinto and emperor worship. Like other prime ministers before him, Koizumi claims to visit Yasukuni in order to pray for world peace (Yasukuni means "to bring peace to the nation"), but, as Ian Buruma, one of the most eloquent Westerners to write about Japan, has commented in his book *The Wages of Guilt*, "It is a peculiar concept of peace."[39] It's also no coincidence that *shukanshi* such as *Shukan Shincho* have been so adamantly supportive of these visits.

The fact is that the prime minister of Japan could pay respect to his country's war dead in any number of ways, symbolically or otherwise. He could sing their praises; he could give compensation to their surviving family members; he could build new memorials. In worshipping at Yasukuni, however, the prime minister is able to salute the neonationalist and emperor-worshipping philosophies that his far-right neonationalist supporters continue to believe and expound. Indeed, this is really what his visits are about, and it is also what *Shukan Shincho* supports when it runs its positive coverage of those visits.

The headlines in this image may or may not be reliable.

This January 15, 2004, *Shukan Shincho* article celebrates the prime minister's recent visit to Yasukuni Shrine with the headline "PRIME MINISTER KOIZUMI WHO DARED TO PAY A VISIT TO THE YASUKUNI SHRINE ON NEW YEAR'S DAY." The piece blames the Japanese mass media for covering the international outcry and includes quotes from various Japanese who are pleased that he is worshipping there.

Actually, on April 7, 2004, the Fukuoka District Court ruled that the first visit to the shrine made by Prime Minister Koizumi in his premiership on August 13, 2001, violated the constitutional separation of church and state in the country. However, the 211 plaintiffs in the case were not awarded the monetary damage for "psychological suffering" that they claimed resulted from the visits. Moreover, the prime minister has insisted that he will continue his annual visits there. At the time of the publication of this book, a number of similar cases are pending on the matter.

In addition to supporting Japanese neonationalism, *Shukan Shincho* and its parent company, Shinchosha Ltd., are well known for trampling on human rights. The Japanese judicial system recently acknowledged the extreme nature of the company in a landmark ruling in February 2002 by the Osaka District Court. At issue was a case wherein Shinchosha Ltd.'s weekly magazine *Focus* was sued by Masumi Hayashi, the woman famously convicted of killing three people by lacing curry with poison at a community event. Despite knowing full well that it was illegal to do so, Shinchosha Ltd. sent a photographer with a hidden camera into a courtroom during the trial to take Hayashi's photo and then ran it in *Focus*. When Hayashi sued, the magazine (reveling in the fact that it was being sued by a woman on trial for murder and widely presumed to be a murderer) responded by running an illustration of her in a subsequent magazine that boasted the caption "How will she respond to this?"

The Osaka District Court ordered Shinchosha to pay the incarcerated woman the substantial sum of ¥6.6 million (yen), or about US$66,000. Although the specific case illustrates little more than Shinchosha Ltd.'s juvenile sense of humor and adolescent defiance of authority, the court ruling was most revealing, as it also took the extraordinary action of finding Shinchosha Ltd.'s president, Takanobu Sato, personally guilty of negligence in his oversight of his company's magazines. The court justified its decisions, not just by citing the Hayashi incident, but with the following laundry list of his magazine's offenses: (1) the repeated publication of photographs taken illegally with hidden cameras inside various courtrooms, (2) the company's loss of some sixteen defamation cases under Sato's supervision, (3) five warnings issued to Shinchosha Ltd. by the Legal Affairs Bureau for publishing the names of minors charged with crimes, and (4) three other warnings issued to it for infringement on human rights. While it is certainly not unusual for a Japanese publisher to lose a court case, it was heretofore unprecedented for a court to find the president of a major publishing company guilty of negligence in his duties as a corporate officer.

Media *Ijime*

Vicious attacks against individuals and organizations are a hallmark of *shukanshi* journalism. While this practice frequently focuses on supposedly corrupt power holders, reformists, minority groups, foreigners, and women, it is in no way limited to them. These attacks are as much about punishing those who threaten to destabilize the Japanese system as they are about anything else.

Jun Kamei, whose understanding of Japanese weeklies is based on his two decades of writing and editing articles for *Shukan Shincho*, says that a major part of the magazine's appeal to its readership is its brutal attacks on individuals and groups, both foreign and domestic.[40]

The Japanese term *ijime* may be translated as "bullying," but it is also used to refer to "group bullying," an even uglier social phenomenon. The word is regularly used to describe the behavior of a group of children or young people persecuting one of their peers, although it can apply to the behavior of individuals of any age. The victim of *ijime* is not simply "picked on" but is often physically brutalized by the group. In Japan, where group identity and social approval have especially high value and where independence and individuality are often frowned upon, children who are different or unusual are prime targets of *ijime*.

Bruce S. Feiler, in *Learning to Bow*, his book about his year as a teacher in a Japanese junior high school, records the suicide of a ninth-grade boy while Feiler was teaching there. The student jumped to his death off a balcony at the school. According to Feiler, the suicide was the result of *ijime*. Feiler considers the phenomenon:

> While it would be an exaggeration to say that Japanese students go to school in an atmosphere of violence, it is fair to say that schools generate a high level of stress in the form of pressure to conform and comply with the rules. This

invisible violence in schools, like "white noise" in cities, lingers in the air, constantly reminding students of the threat of force that surrounds them at all times. A growing number of children, called "school refusers," have responded by staying home. Other students take out their anxiety on one another in the form of teasing, taunting, or bullying.[41]

Feiler eloquently describes the results of the *ijime* pattern of violence, which he sees as "fairly well established":

It begins with minor taunts—"You stink," "You're a germ," "You don't belong in this school." Then it moves on to petty crime—forcing a student to steal candy from the 7-Eleven or a pack of cigarettes from the railroad station. And it often escalates to the level of physical abuse—cigarette burns on the arms or punches to the head. Much of this goes unseen by the teachers, who know it exists but do not actively try to stop it. Most of the victims never speak out. Instead, they learn to live with their torture as just another price for being different from their peers. Occasionally, however, a victim will lash out, and the consequences are dramatic: a seventh-grade student beats himself to death with a hammer; an eight-grade girl hangs herself in her home; a ninth-grade boy jumps off the balcony of his third-floor homeroom class.[42]

John Nathan dedicates the entire first chapter of his superb 2004 book, *Japan Unbound,* to the "epidemic" levels of juvenile delinquency and suffering among contemporary Japanese youth.[43] He includes a number of his interviews with Japanese young people that leave little doubt that the bullying of children who don't fit in remains a terrible problem to this day.

Of course, group bullying is hardly unique to the Japanese but seems to be a universal human dynamic. For example, many commentators have noted that the teenagers who perpetrated the Columbine High School attack in the United States had histories of being victimized by their classmates and that one of their motivations was a perverted concept of revenge against their peers. Still, the problem is widespread enough in Japan that a specific term for it has long been a household word.

One explanation for *ijime* is that groups often identify themselves by what they are not. By singling out an individual who is different, the group is able to define itself more clearly and unify in its campaign against that victim. Thus it is not surprising that *ijime* occurs so frequently in Japan, where social coherence is known to be stronger than that of most other large countries. Jun Kamei explains:

> It's called *ijime*. It's a Japanese word that I believe is also used in English. And it exists particularly in elementary and middle school. But it's also in the wider community. It's a kind of group psychology where *that* person is considered odd. The question is, Has this particular school kid or person done something bad to deserve being persecuted? The answer is almost always no. He might just be socially inept for some reason. Or perhaps he is a crybaby, or perhaps he doesn't cry, so that's why that individual gets bullied.[44]

Kamei went on to focus on the "different from us" aspect of *ijime*:

> It can be anything that sets that individual apart. Actually, the difference is very often foisted upon the target. There's some sort of action going on, where you always have a group and that group is always trying to identify small dissimilar elements within that group.[45]

Kamei says that *Shukan Shincho* and *Shukan Bunshun* regularly instigate or participate in what amounts to "media *ijime*." In these instances, the magazines heap abuse on an individual to a degree that far exceeds any reasonable amount of criticism, or even condemnation, that the individual can be said to deserve. Examples include the media frenzies around corrupt former Prime Minister Kakuei Tanaka, accused murderer Kazuyoshi Miura, Masumi Hayashi (mentioned above), sarin-gas victim Yoshiyuki Kono, outspoken journalist Katsuichi Honda, Kenichi Ino (the father of a murder victim), Buddhist leader Daisaku Ikeda, former Democratic Party leader Naoto Kan—and the list goes on and on. Kamei explained in an interview how media *ijime* affects the readers of the *shukanshi*:

> Why do the masses love it when the magazines persecute someone? The readers of *Shukan Shincho* and *Shukan Bunshun* are not really powerful people. They are men in their forties, but many of them aren't secure about their positions in society. Some are. A few are. But the great majorities are insecure "wannabees."

They read these magazines to think, "Hey, this guy is being bullied so badly it's unbelievable, and I feel sorry for him. But at least I am not him."

So then these readers feel superior. They feel better than the victim. As readers they become part of a superior group looking down. So, *Shukan Shincho* and *Shukan Bunshun*—what are they doing? They are selling this euphoric aura of superiority for three hundred yen per copy. You can buy an awful lot of this feeling for three hundred yen. It's cheap. That's what I peddled as an assistant editor at *Shukan Shincho*.[46]

Kamei's concept of media *ijime* is widely acknowledged by many in the industry, although not necessarily by the same term. Kazuyoshi Hanada, for example, was the longest-reigning editor in chief of *Shukan Bunshun,* having served in that position from 1988 to 1994 before being transferred to *Marco Polo,* a highly controversial monthly magazine published by the same company. Hanada, who lost his job for publishing the Holocaust denial discussed in chapter 5 and who no longer works for a *shukanshi,* candidly confirmed the existence of media *ijime*:

I think the idea that there is a great deal of media *ijime* often initiated by the weekly newsmagazines is a correct assessment. You have to have a criterion that begs for the public good. There should be a notion of serving the public interest. On the other hand, there is a reality that the weekly magazine market is plagued by commercial demands.[47]

Indeed, while Hanada made it clear that he is not proud of it, he admitted that he had been an active participant in the execution of the practice during his career. He further noted, "It is possible that I had been somewhat desensitized from the week-to-week battle of coming up with headlines and fighting to come up with sensational stories."[48]

A current senior editor for one of the major *shukanshi* (who consented to be interviewed only on condition of anonymity) also agrees that the practice of media *ijime* is a major aspect of his industry. He admits that his magazine participates in it and that, as an editor, he has some personal responsibility for it. However, he explained that, in some ways, the highly competitive nature of an industry reliant on sensational headlines forces it:

You see, first one publication writes about someone. Then another publication follows up, and then the rest of the media jump into the fray. Before you know it, it's too late, because we are all basically fighting for position with the other media. So even though it should be just a tiny point, it just blows up.

As Jun Kamei points out, articles that aggressively rail against, mock, and attempt to humiliate their subjects appeal to readers of the weeklies.[49] Put simply, they sell magazines. Of course, at the same time, the practice plays an important function in supporting the least democratic aspects of the Japanese system. Just as *ijime* is often tacitly supported in Japanese schools by teachers, parents, and children who pretend not to see it, or who even overtly support it, media *ijime* is supported both by the establishment news media and by the broader society, which either actively participate in it or silently tolerate it.

Keeping the System Sound and the Wheels Well Oiled

The enlightening 1988 book *The Politics of Scandal* presents nine case studies on the role of scandals in nine different liberal democratic countries around the globe. Editors Andrei S. Markovits and Mark Silverstein make the argument that scandals play critically important functions within liberal democratic nations, where there is inherent tension between the power of the citizenry, with their individual rights, and the power of rulers. According to them, scandals function (not unlike the case of media *ijime* mentioned previously) to define the norms of the system. They write:

> In addition to reaffirming and ultimately strengthening the bonds of a common morality, scandals help to create the scapegoats, enemies, and pariahs needed by all communities.... While a scandalous act invariably challenges the norms and values of the community, the public ritual of investigation, discussion, and punishment ultimately serves to reinforce the primacy of those shared norms and values.... The ritual of scandal and punishment provides social systems with a means for self-legitimation and purification. Scandals, in short, constitute an important opportunity for reaffirming the social order.[50]

Karel van Wolferen, who has written at length about the role of scandal in Japanese society, argues that because the rule of law in the country is so especially weak, scandals are required to serve as a moderating force against excesses of individuals—especially members of the ruling elite—that threaten the balance of power and thereby threaten the stability of the system. Where the law fails to curb these excesses, such as an individual or an institution making a move for new power, scandals step in. The behavior of the individual in question may or may not be legal; that is beside the point. What matters is that the ultimate target of the scandal is seen to overstep accepted norms of behavior.[51]

Van Wolferen goes on to argue convincingly that, unlike those in many other liberal democracies where scandals tend to lead at least to reforms that mitigate similar scandals in the future, in Japan this is rarely the case. Because "extralegal" and "non-codified" relationships are so dominant, there is little motivation for power holders to reform the system or to make other fundamental changes in the way things operate. Scandals function to punish those whose behavior challenges the status quo and to reaffirm the dominance of the system, not to change or reform the system. Van Wolferen explains, "By preventing destructive excess, Japanese scandals make it possible for the System to survive."[52]

Howard W. French puts it this way in the New York Times: "The weeklies seem to serve more as pressure valves for burdensome matters in a society that shuns open disputes and confrontational debate, than they do as journalistic crusaders for the truth."[53]

Alex Kerr described the situation in an interview for this book: "If a bureaucrat or a politician gets too greedy, then they get slapped down and dragged through the mud. And then they have to quit.... But what doesn't actually happen is change to the system. So it's a way actually of keeping the system sound and the wheels well oiled, because anyone who gets too far out of line gets punished. But the low-level constant institutional bribery and corruption go right on.... It's an automatic way of controlling or moderating the system."[54]

Kensuke Nishioka has earned a reputation as a top Japanese weekly magazine reporter and has even written a notable autobiographical book on the subject.[55] He currently investigates scandals for Shukan Bunshun, a role that he acknowledges is important in moderating the excesses of power among the Japanese elite. Nishioka, like the more successful of his colleagues, relishes the fact that his work provides him with the opportunity to challenge power holders. When asked how *shukanshi* reporters determine what to investigate, his reply was refreshingly straightforward. "If you are a big fish, someone with power, like a government or corporate leader or in charge of some outfit that is in the news constantly, you are a target," he explains. "Or maybe you are a celebrity or someone who publicly acts like he lives his life better than others. We get good results by crucifying people. I guess what it boils down to is simply how famous you are. As a reporter, I don't try to make a determination of how good or bad you are. It doesn't really matter to me."[56]

While Nishioka agrees that the *shukanshi* tend to appeal to a conservative readership and even to have some nationalist bias, he says that he is not driven by any political leanings. Celebrity and salability are the dominating factors in his choice of subjects, or "targets," as he calls them. "The fact is that there are a lot of small fish out there, a lot of unknown people who are really bad, far worse than the big fish, but we don't target them. Our targets are the big fish. Of course, sometimes it's smart to remember what a small fish is doing, because eventually small fish become big fish!"[57]

Obviously, it is not just the elite who are attacked by Japanese weekly newsmagazines or who fall victim to media *ijime*. While the old maxim "the bigger they are, the harder they fall" remains true, anyone who challenges Japanese society is a fair target of media *ijime*.

Kiyoshi Takada, who has worked as a magazine editor and writer in Japan for more than thirty years, says that editorial decisions on whom to target are often driven by editorial bias. He offered the following analogy:

Let's say there is a bottle of sake, and the editorial staff at a publication gets the idea that it is a bad bottle of sake. They send a reporter out to investigate why it is such a bad bottle of sake. The reporter is told to go find the information that supports the supposition that it's a bad bottle of sake. But let's say that this reporter goes out and does his research and he determines that it is actually a good bottle of sake. It is made in a good way with good ingredients and has a good role to play in society. But, in terms of a sales strategy for the publication and the editors, it has been decided that it's best if there is an article that shows how bad the sake is. So, the editors will tell the reporter that if the reporter wants to write his story based on his research, he should do so somewhere else.[58]

It is almost needless to say that since the editors and publishers of *shukanshi* are well-paid, privileged members of Japanese society, it is only natural for them to select targets that do not fit in with the status quo of which they are a part. Takada explained that once a target has been selected, decision-making policies of the typical *shukanshi* editorial room make it almost impossible for reporters to change that policy, regardless of what the research yields. Takada continues the analogy:

> Now, when editors tell a reporter that he should take his story somewhere else, they don't really mean it, because in Japan it's impossible to take a story somewhere else. If you work for a company, it's almost impossible to quit and find employment somewhere else. So, the reporter ends up having no choice, because if he leaves his organization his livelihood is going to be risked. Somehow the reporter must resign himself to finding information that shows that the sake is poor-tasting. It's that simple.[59]

Makoto Oda is a Japanese novelist and activist of international renown whose prize-winning books *Hiroshima* and *The Breaking Jewel* are available in English. A champion of many social causes over the years, in the 1970s he was a national leader of the anti–Vietnam War movement in Japan. Having been a target of *shukanshi* since that time, he too concurs wholeheartedly with Kamei's idea of media *ijime*, which he spoke about in an interview for this book: "Japanese weekly newsmagazines dislike and attack people who try to be different in this country. They don't want to have a Japanese with a different opinion from the mainstream Japanese. This is true not only for people who are against war or who want the economy to be different. Anyone who is different from the mainstream, they attack. This is a big problem, especially when the mainstream is wrong. Anyone like this is a very good target for these magazines that function to support the mainstream. In this country, everyone is supposed to have the same opinion."[60]

While commercialism is obviously a driving force for the Japanese week-lies, Oda believes wholeheartedly that he has been attacked by *shukanshi* because his politics contradicted those of the pro–Vietnam War Japanese leadership. He says, "*Shukan Shincho* and *Shukan Bunshun* have always attacked me. Even now they... are waiting for opportunities to attack, but mostly they attacked me when I was active in the anti–Vietnam War move-ment here. They wrote scandalous stories about me, about women and money. They regularly publish half-truths as truths, and then build their cases from there. Why did they attack me? It was their goal to disgrace our move-ment against the establishment."[61]

While the overriding driving force behind the editorial policies of the weeklies is unquestionably one of commercialism, it is not difficult to under-stand their predilection to target individuals who threaten to destabilize the Japanese system of governance in some way, be they politicians who are per-ceived to have overstepped the reasonable bounds of their positions, pro-gressives who advocate reform, writers who expose systemic problems, foreign powers, immigrants, or others. Indeed, the mere fact of being differ-ent can be a threat to a system that prides itself on false myths about harmony and homogeneity. Given their nationalistic history, conservative readership, and aggressive nature, it is not surprising that *shukanshi* focus their exagger-ated coverage on individuals and elements that do not fit in with the estab-lished order.

Feeble Libel Laws

One of the major legal loopholes that permit Japanese weekly newsmagazines to function so far outside the boundaries of reasonable journalistic ethics, both in their use of media *ijime* and in the sheer outrageousness of the distortions they print, is the historical impotence of Japan's libel laws. Although awards in defamation cases in Japan have increased significantly in 2002 and 2003, they are still comparably very weak and are only just becoming a deterrent to any sort of scurrilous reporting. And even now, the increased fines are being applied mainly to defamed celebrities and other famous individuals. In 2001, for instance, a study panel of five judges from the Tokyo District Court released a report concluding that compensation for defaming a publicly known figure should be set between ¥4 million and ¥5 million (approximately US$40,000 and US$50,000). According to the *Japan Times,* "the panel said the amount should be set in accordance with the public status of the targeted person, truthfulness of the reporting and other factors."[62] And, in fact, Japanese libel law has long placed high value on the social position of the individual who has been wronged, so that an average citizen who has been defamed is seen in the eyes of the law as deserving less compensation than a famous or powerful individual who is similarly defamed. Time will prove how this history plays out under the new climate of higher awards, but for the purposes of this discussion, readers should assume that award amounts apply primarily to celebrities, politicians, and other powerful individuals. Of course, these are the individuals who are most likely to be unfairly attacked in print.

Until sometime just after the start of the twenty-first century, the average judgment against a defendant losing a libel suit was a mere ¥1 million (approximately US$10,000). Even though awards to successful plaintiffs have increased significantly in recent years, they currently average only about ¥1 million to ¥5 million (US$10,000 to US$50,000), with a few as high as the ¥5 million to ¥8 million (US$50,000 to US$80,000) range, and only one in excess of ¥8 million (US$80,000). This largest single award in a Japanese libel suit was just ¥19.8 million (US$198,000) and was given in October of 2003. Not surprisingly, the case involved Shinchosha Ltd., which was required to pay a chairman of the board of a medical corporation for an extensive series of twelve articles in Shinchosha's now-defunct magazine *Focus.* The articles alleged, implied, and insinuated that the man had murdered his wife and three other women to collect life insurance proceeds. In point of fact, the Tokyo District Court gave a smaller award, but when it was appealed, the high court found the breach of ethics to be so egregious that it increased the amount.

The next-highest award ever in Japan, significantly lower than the record breaker above, was in September of 2001, when Kondan-sha Ltd., the publisher of the magazine *Shukan Gendai,* was required to pay ¥7,700,000, or about US$77,000. A survey by the NSK (Japan Newspaper Publishers and Editors Association) found that between August 2003 and February 2004, the media (mainly newsmagazines) were defeated in nineteen damages suits, including ten in which the amount of compensation was more than ¥3 million.[63]

There have been only a limited number of high-award cases yielding pay-outs of more than ¥5 million (US$50,000). Needless to say, even the record-breaking award of ¥19.8 million (US$198,000)—which is more than double the next highest and a highly unlikely outcome for most plaintiffs—is still not a truly serious blow for a major multimillion-dollar publishing company such as Shinchosha. Indeed, though many in the media have complained that the new increased awards are unfair, the current standard award range of between ¥1 million and ¥5 million (US$10,000 to US$50,000) is not likely to seriously chill Japanese newsmagazine writing. While there will obviously be a transition period while *shukanshi* and other publishers adjust their editorial stances to the new libel-exposure risks, it is still safe to say that defamation awards in Japan remain too low. Indeed, as the weeklies have long chosen to run dubious and even fallacious "scoops" in the face of ¥1 million awards, it seems unlikely at best that they will profoundly alter their ways now that the award range is closer to ¥1 million to ¥5 million.

Defenders of Japan's historically low libel awards often point out that the judgment is sometimes accompanied by a court order that the guilty defendant issue a public apology to the plaintiffs. This argument supposes that in Japan such apologies carry great weight and that they not only go a long way toward righting the situation in the eyes of victorious plaintiffs but actually serve as a real punishment to the defendant. While it is true that many successful plaintiffs are usually deeply gratified to receive apologies for having been wronged, such acts of contrition do not often make up for the damages suffered by victims. Nor do court-ordered public apologies serve as a serious deterrent or punishment to contemporary Japanese publishers. While such apologies may once have brought profound social shame upon those forced to issue them, the modern corporate structure creates a situation whereby the employees of large publishing companies tend to be unaffected. In a news industry where articles are routinely written by teams of writers and editors, where most pieces are published without bylines, and where editorial decisions are made through group consensus, court-ordered apologies have little consequence.

Indeed, the prospect of being sued can sometimes even be a boon to publishers. Legal proceedings initiated against them not only draw attention to the "controversial" nature of the publication—a truly virtuous quality for *shukanshi*—the court proceedings themselves also often provide writers with new and valuable material.

According to Hiroshi Sato, a libel lawyer based in the Akasaka area of Tokyo, the legal costs of suing a defendant for libel currently average around ¥1,666,700, or about US$16,667—no small investment for the average Japanese. Moreover, legal costs increase as plaintiffs sue for higher awards, so that seriously damaged plaintiffs are required to spend more. And, it may take up to two years to receive an initial resolution to a case. Thus, if a Japanese libel victim were to pay the average fee of US$16,000 to sue a publication, and were to win an amount that falls within the new, increased award range of ¥1 million to ¥5 million (approximately US$10,000 to US$50,000), he or she would actually walk away with significantly less, perhaps even losing money.

Even if a plaintiff can afford to risk losing US$16,000 or more in bringing the case, except in the cases of affluent individuals, he or she is unlikely to be able to afford the same quality of legal representation that the publisher has at its disposal. Many Japanese publishers have tremendous financial resources as well as seasoned legal teams who are adept at fending off such charges.

Of course, even relatively wealthy libel victims may well choose not to risk suing a publisher, since such a course of action brings with it such serious risks. For instance, if the victim were to lose on a technicality, it could open the way for a countersuit. And even if the publisher does not countersue, the initial lawsuit is often an open invitation for the publisher, in its coverage of the lawsuit, which might last for years, to rehash again and again the same libelous accusations that brought on the suit in the first place, thus compounding the initial damage many times.

Criminal Libel Law

In countries such as the United States, libel law is exclusively a matter of civil law and concerns itself with disputes between two or more parties: usually a plaintiff, who claims to have been libeled, and a defendant, who is accused of having perpetrated the libel. The primary purpose of U.S. libel laws is to determine whether libel has occurred and, if so, what monetary awards might be in order. Awards in the United States tend to fulfill three main functions:

(1) to serve as compensation to the injured parties, (2) to punish the guilty, and (3) to deter further similar actions by the guilty defendant and by others in society.

In contrast, Japan has two types of libel law: criminal and civil. Theoretically, criminal responsibility falls upon anyone who behaves in an illegal manner. Responsibility for criminal behavior is owed to the public, not to the injured party; therefore, the state is responsible for trying criminal cases. Defendants who lose such cases risk incarceration. Japanese criminal libel law therefore focuses on punishing those who commit libel and on deterring libel.

Japanese civil law, however, is designed to address grievances between parties. Therefore, civil libel law focuses not on punishment or deterrence but (once libel has been established) on restoring the injured party's social status. Traditionally, this has been quite important in Japanese society, which is far more cohesive than most Western societies and hence far more influenced by concepts of public and social shame. Historically, the legally prescribed method for correcting such injuries in Japan has focused not on the payment of monetary damages but on public apology.

However, rather than render justice for the injured party, this separation of criminal and civil law actually means that those who commit libel in Japan almost never receive punishment under criminal law. This is true for a number of reasons. First, even though the victim may file criminal charges, only a public prosecutor can bring the case to court, and prosecutors rarely bother with criminal libel cases. This is not only because they are so difficult to prove, but, critics say, because of an establishment culture that does not value the individual rights of victims. Instead of championing victims' causes, most prosecutors prefer to steer complaints to the civil courts.

Second, the standards required for a guilty verdict in a criminal libel case are exceedingly difficult to meet. (For example, if the defendant can show that there was some "trustworthy data" to justify the assertions in question, that defendant cannot be convicted.) Third, even in the rare instance that prosecutors act, the difficult standards are met, and a verdict of guilty follows, the defendant is unlikely to serve jail time, since courts have made it a regular policy to suspend such sentences.

A fourth obstacle to real justice in cases of criminal libel is the fact that many Japanese are simply unaware of the option or the procedures for lodging a criminal libel complaint and thus don't take it up. In Japanese society, litigation is generally a less accepted course of action than in the West.

Indeed, Japanese criminal libel laws are generally so ineffectual—especially in regard to the news industry—that in spite of Japanese magazine writers' well-earned reputations for malicious deceptions, only three writers in just two separate cases have been successfully convicted under that law in more than three decades. The most recent example occurred in October of 2001, when Yasunori Okadome, the founder, editor in chief, and publisher of the famous monthly magazine *Uwasa no Shinso* (Truth of Rumors), and one of his writers were both found guilty of criminal defamation for false material they had run about a Japanese science-fiction writer.

When Okadome recently terminated his magazine after the April 2004 issue (which marked the twenty-fifth anniversary of its founding), he had the gall to blame Japan's unfair libel laws as a key reason for his action. According to Okadome, he has been sued some forty different times.[64] Media professor Kenichi Asano, a strong supporter of freedom of speech in Japan, was quoted by the *Japan Times* as saying that magazines like Okadome's have no one to fault but themselves. According to Asano, magazines like *Uwasa no Shinso* have failed to establish any system for hearing and responding to complaints other than through the courts.[65]

At any rate, the fact that only three Japanese magazine writers in two separate cases have been successfully committed under criminal libel law in the last three decades underscores the reality that it is neither a significant punishment nor an effective deterrent.

Civil Libel Law

Japanese civil libel law tends to focus mainly on restoring the social status of victims, not through financial rewards but through requiring offenders to apologize publicly. A 2002 article entitled "Damage Control" in the *New York Law School Journal of International and Comparative Law* summarizes the situation:

Japanese damage awards are exceedingly low. The courts in Japan, unlike those in the U.S., do not utilize juries to set damages. Rather the Japanese courts promote remedies such as apologies that seek to correct falsehoods and restore good reputations.

This traditional Japanese approach, however, is not as relevant today as it used to be. Private Japanese television networks, vying with one another for larger audiences and advertising revenues, are feeding viewers a once-shocking diet of scandals, gossip and fads. According to numerous Japanese commentators, Japan has become an increasingly "selfish and materially obsessed society." It is a nation altering the dynamic most people consider to be quintessentially Japanese—the relationship between the individual and society, and between the desires of self and the duty to the social whole. As Japanese publishers and broadcasters are increasingly obliged to convey salacious material in order to attract consumers, it must be questioned whether quaint apologies are enough to keep their libelous excesses in check.

Although the values of the Japanese people and the role of their press have altered dramatically since World War II, the approach of Japanese courts to cases of libel have changed little.[66]

The growing but still relatively small risk of meaningful legal consequences for libel is a key factor in the abuses by *shukanshi* and other media members. Although many in the Japanese news media are currently decrying the increases in judgment awards, one must keep in mind that the Japanese news media has been held almost completely unaccountable for much of the post-war period. In Japan, scandal and media *ijime* play too important a role in keeping in place the status quo of ruling elites, institutions, and traditions. The ever-present threats of the *shukanshi* and the broader media to beat up on, shout down, discredit, and delegitimize virtually anyone who steps out of line are so beneficial to the current Japanese establishment that reform is unlikely.

Chapter Four

Terrorizing Victims
of Terrorism

*The Japanese media treated me worst. At least when the terrorists were caught,
they expressed remorse for what they had done. And it made sense that the
police would act aggressively in trying to catch the criminals. But it was the
media's job to protect me, a common person. Yet they purposely attacked me.
The media was definitely the worst.*

—Yoshiyuki Kono, victim of sarin-nerve-gas terrorist attack,
the Japanese police, and the Japanese news media[1]

The Jewell and Kono Case Studies

The Japanese media watchdog organization JIMPOREN (Liaison Committee on Human Rights and Mass Media Conduct) opens its mission statement
with a severe indictment of the country's journalism, citing one of the most
flagrant cases of media malpractice in that country's recent history:

It is one of those distinct ironies perhaps found only in Japan that the news
media of a democratic society, rather than crusading for the rights of citizens, often campaigns to infringe upon them. Nothing better illustrates this
than the case of Yoshiyuki Kono. On June 27, 1994, the people of Matsumoto,
a sleepy city some 200 kilometers west of Tokyo, awoke to the stunning news

that seven residents had died and 144 others were hospitalized from what was later determined to be sarin, a lethal nerve gas developed by the Nazis in World War II.[2]

The mission statement goes on to explain that not only was Kono an innocent victim of a terrorist attack who was also falsely blamed for the attack, but that many members of the media exploited his tragic predicament by defaming him with other sensational accusations as well.

Of course, Japan is not the only modern democracy in which innocent citizens are exposed to unfounded persecution, in the media or otherwise. JIMPOREN also notes that a disturbingly similar "trial by media" occurred in the United States, just two years after the Kono case. Richard Jewell, a security guard at the 1996 Olympics in Atlanta, Georgia, was thrust into a comparable "media-inspired hell" by being accused of a crime that he did not commit.

These two case studies, which occurred on opposite sides of the globe, in countries with the two largest economies on earth, reveal some of the most troubling aspects of the news media in both nations. Although the differences between them underscore important distinctions in the nature of the media in the two countries, together they expose critical aspects of what some have decried as an "unholy alliance" between the news media and government officials—particularly law-enforcement officials—in both countries. The litany of similarities between them, moreover, shines a bright light on some of the most imminent threats to democracy the world over. Rather than representing strange aberrations of journalism gone awry, the cases reveal serious systematic failures that deserve far more attention than they have received to date. Indeed, each example highlights a number of the most insidious ways that the news media in each country often function to support nondemocratic and antidemocratic components of their respective systems of governance.

Despite their appalling similarities, few detailed comparisons between the cases have been made—thanks to a general lack of self-reflection by the media. Kenichi Asano, a former Japanese crime reporter and best-selling author who is currently a media professor at Doshisha University in Kyoto, is credited with the most insightful comparison to date. In addition to interviewing both victims individually, he also arranged for Jewell and Kono to meet and participate in interviews together. Asano's work on the two cases shows how more than mere coincidence was at play:

> I've been to the U.S. twice in recent years, once when two of my students and I interviewed Richard Jewell. After studying the situation there, my new phrase has become "the Japanization of the U.S. media." Ten years ago, the U.S. media provided a good text for me [to make comparisons to the way the Japanese media could be], but nowadays, *USA Today*, CNN, and the Internet's twenty-four-hour reporting has made the U.S. more like Japan. In the U.S., there was a good tradition of skepticism toward authorities and officials and a healthy respect for the role of journalism in democratic societies. There were fundamental principles recognized by most good journalists. Now it seems that it has become an information industry, not journalism. This situation has become even worse since September 11, 2001.[3]

Richard Jewell and Yoshiyuki Kono underwent almost eerily parallel persecutions; but they were different ordeals, and they occurred in very different countries. As the saying goes, the devil is in the details.

The Terrorist Bombing of the 1996 Olympics

An Olympic celebratory party was held at Centennial Olympic Park in Atlanta, Georgia, on Friday night, July 26, 1996. Thousands of people joined in the festivities, which included live music and dancing. Richard Jewell was working at the event as a private security guard. It was his job to patrol a particular part of the park that included a five-story light-and-sound tower and special VIP facilities. His duties included monitoring access into the tower, keeping watch on the crowd, being prepared to respond to disturbances, and looking out for safety hazards.

It would have been easy for Jewell to become complacent that night. He had suffered from stomach problems earlier in the evening, and the party continued well after midnight. Then, too, the general level of concern nationwide about terror attacks was considerably lower than in today's post–

September 11, 2001, world. But Jewell stayed vigilant and focused, and he spotted a backpack that had been left unattended near the tower in his patrol area. He asked around to see if anyone knew whose it was. Satisfied that the backpack's owner was not around, he followed the prescribed procedure and promptly alerted police to the discovery of a "suspicious package."

Unbeknownst to Jewell, only two minutes earlier, authorities had received an anonymous telephoned bomb threat. Thus, officials took Jewell's call seriously, and law-enforcement officials were quickly dispatched to the scene. Once there, they decided to call in a bomb specialist from the U.S. Alcohol, Tobacco and Firearms (ATF) Agency. They also started casually moving people away from the package. Acting on his own initiative, Jewell proceeded to the nearby VIP area, where he informed people that although nothing was certain, they could conceivably be in a dangerous situation. Jewell told everyone to remain calm but to be prepared in case they were asked to evacuate the area. He then returned to the vicinity of the backpack, where he watched an ATF agent inspect it. Based on the agent's behavior, Jewell felt fairly certain there was a bomb. In a CBS News interview, he explained: "He [the ATF agent] was laying flat on his stomach and was undoing the top of the bag with his hand and he was doing his flashlight like this and all of a sudden, he just froze. What really made me think, 'Uh-oh, this is bad'—there was, like, a little line in training that they taught you, that [they] would instill in you: 'If you see an ATF agent running, you better be in front of him.'"[4]

But instead of running, instead of quickly moving to safety away from the ATF agent and what Jewell had every reason to conclude was a bomb that might explode at any moment, he single-handedly went through the five-story tower and evacuated everyone from it. He then remained nearby to assist in crowd management, calmly trying to move park patrons away from the vicinity of the bomb.

Jewell saved many lives that night, not only by alertly noticing the suspicious package in the first place, but by adeptly following procedure and then by evacuating everyone from the tower and helping to clear the area, even though it meant keeping himself in harm's way. Had Jewell been any less competent, or less courageous, the bomb could have killed and injured hundreds of people. Jewell was an authentic hero.

Atlanta Journal EXTRA

TUESDAY, JULY 30, 1996

FBI suspects 'hero' guard may have planted bomb

Back to 'the people's park'

Service at reopening honors bombing victims

This is a reproduction of the July 30 *Atlanta Journal-Constitution* special edition that first reported that Richard Jewell was a suspect in the 1996 Olympic bombing. Unfortunately, the piece does more than simply report that Jewell is a suspect. It leads readers to believe that Jewell is very likely guilty. In actuality, of course, he was not only innocent of the bombing; he was a genuine hero who put his own life on the line to save many others.

Media Treatment of Jewell

Thousands of media members were in Atlanta covering the Olympics, and a media circus ensued after the bombing. Over the next three days, Jewell's employer was approached by many different media organizations requesting interviews with the security guard who first spotted the bomb. Despite this demand for interviews, Jewell only agreed to ten interviews and a photo opportunity. He granted these requests because he felt that his employer wanted him to do so. He was not paid for any of them.

Then, on Tuesday afternoon, July 30, the *Atlanta Journal-Constitution* began distributing its special afternoon Olympic edition of their paper, featuring the lead story:

> FBI SUSPECTS "HERO" GUARD MAY HAVE PLANTED BOMB
> By Kathy Scruggs and Ron Martz, Staff Writers
>
> The security guard who first alerted police to the pipe bomb that exploded in Centennial Olympic Park is the focus of the federal investigation into the incident that resulted in two deaths and injured more than 100. [*Note:* While one woman died from the bomb, a camera man rushing to cover the story also died due to a heart attack.]
>
> Richard Jewell, 33, a former law enforcement officer, fits the profile of the lone bomber. This profile generally includes a frustrated white man who is a former police officer, member of the military or police "wannabe" who seeks to become a hero.

Jewell has become a celebrity in the wake of the bombing, making an appearance this morning at the reopened park with Katie Couric on the Today Show. He also has approached newspapers, including *The Atlanta Journal-Constitution*, seeking publicity for his actions.

He has told members of the media that he spotted a suspicious knapsack near the tower that was damaged in the blast. He said he reported the find to the FBI agent and helped move people from the area.

FBI agents are reviewing hours of professional and amateur videotape to see if Jewell is spotted setting down the military-issue backpack that contained the bomb. Acquaintances have told agents that he owned a similar knapsack. Agents have not seen Jewell in the tape of the 20 minutes following the blast.

Three undercover law enforcement cars were parked outside his mother's apartment on Buford Highway this afternoon. He refused to open the door when a reporter from *The Atlanta Journal-Constitution* knocked.

Jewell resigned two former law enforcement jobs in north Georgia, the latest at Piedmont College on May 21. He also was a deputy sheriff at the Habersham County Sheriff's Department, where he received bomb training.

Just before the Olympics Jewell got a job with Anthony Davis Associates, a Los Angeles security firm hired by AT&T after the company dismissed Borg-Warner Security Corp. after allegations of theft by employees.

Investigators are checking to see if his voice matches that of a 911 caller who phoned in a warning of the park bomb. The call was placed from a phone a few minutes' walk from the park.

Agents also are checking an earlier report from a plumber that pipes were stolen from his construction area near the park.[5]

Soon after, or perhaps even while the special edition of the paper rolled off the presses, an advance copy was delivered to the nearby world headquarters of CNN News. There, the anchorman interrupted the scheduled broadcast to read the story as requested, verbatim, on live television. The *Atlanta Journal-Constitution* also released the story on its international wire service, where news outlets worldwide picked it up.

Although the article is accurate in stating that Jewell was a suspect in the bombing, it features a number of flagrant errors. Perhaps most importantly, there was no "profile of the lone bomber" developed by investigators. Indeed, the article does not explain just who came up with such a "profile" or how they might have concocted it, although law-enforcement officials are implied. Further, Jewell did not even fit the "profile of the lone bomber."

Just two minutes before Richard Jewell reported the suspicious backpack, someone called in an anonymous bomb threat from a pay phone a few blocks away, or, in the words of the *Atlanta Journal-Constitution*, "a few minutes' walk from the park." Law-enforcement officials eventually determined that this pay phone was simply too far away from the site for Jewell to have made the call and then returned to his post in the crowded park in time to make his report to police there. Thus, even if Jewell had participated in the bombing in some way (which he did not), he certainly could not have fit any profile of a *lone* bomber who may have committed that crime. The simple fact is that Jewell would have required an accomplice, so a profile about a lone or single attacker shouldn't have been applied to him.

Although the *Atlanta Journal-Constitution* article highlights circumstantial evidence implying that Jewell made that call, it clearly failed to thoroughly check the accuracy of this evidence before printing it. Instead of assuming Jewell was "innocent until proven guilty," or following the commonly espoused journalistic principle of protecting ordinary people against centralized power holders, the paper rushed to print untrue information, the source of which was not identified but which was apparently "leaked" by police—and which vilified Jewell. Indeed, CNN and the rest of the news media that picked up the story were equally at fault for not double-checking the basic question of whether Jewell could have made the initial bomb threat.

Two other inconsistencies in the article also relate to the alleged profile. First, Jewell was not the "frustrated" person that the profile presupposed. He was a dedicated individual who performed his job diligently, and although it is true that he had recently changed jobs a couple of times, the newspaper did not cite any concrete evidence that one of his primary personality characteristics was his being frustrated.[6] But, even if Jewell was "frustrated" to some degree, as many people no doubt are, there was absolutely nothing about his history to imply that he was frustrated enough to plant a lethal bomb in the midst of a dense crowd during an international celebration.

Additionally, the paper offered no explanation why the so-called profile "generally includes" a white man. Given the ugly history of racism in the United States, one might expect a newspaper based in the capital of Georgia to be more skeptical about such race-based profiling. But it doesn't appear that any media member of any state or nation seriously questioned this inexplicable aspect of the supposed profile.

Another blatant inaccuracy in the *Atlanta Journal-Constitution* piece is the statement that Jewell "approached newspapers, including the *Atlanta Journal-Constitution*, seeking publicity for his actions"—a point that the newspaper should have known was dead wrong because the *Atlanta Journal-Constitution* contacted Jewell's employer and requested an interview with him, and one of their own photographers had himself approached Jewell and asked him to pose for a photo. Indeed, not only did Jewell not seek out attention from the *Atlanta Journal-Constitution*, he did not seek out any publicity whatsoever from anyone. The media initiated all eleven encounters with Jewell—a fact that could have been corroborated by any journalist covering the story. Although the equivalent of a small army of journalists was in Atlanta at the time, Jewell only met with eleven media members in three days. If, as the *Atlanta Journal-Constitution* article asserts, he had been actively pursuing publicity, surely he would have managed to tell his story to dozens of outlets during that time period.

In fact, and as a later article in the *Atlanta Journal-Constitution* duly noted, Jewell was confronted by "more than 17 television cameras and a horde of reporters" on the Tuesday evening following the *Journal-Constitution*'s original article implicating him.[7] It is a telling commentary on the media in America that a mere eleven organizations successfully contacted him during the three days that he was presumed a national hero, yet hordes surrounded him within hours of his being identified by the *Atlanta Journal-Constitution* as under investigation.

Another aspect of the case that passed without media scrutiny was the inconsistency between Jewell's supposed motivation and his actions. As noted, the theory circulated by the press was that Jewell had secretly planted the bomb in order to discover it himself and thus be proclaimed a hero. If that were the case, however, it seems strange that he would plant such a terribly dangerous bomb only to remain in the vicinity until it exploded. Surely his discovery of a bomb less dangerous to himself would have sufficed just as well to make him a hero. If the theory were accurate, then Jewell would have been a deranged criminal indeed—not only for seeking attention in such a violent fashion but for hanging around and needlessly risking his own life and limb in the process. Nothing in Jewell's past indicated that he was such a person. Still, the media failed to challenge the inconsistencies of the theory. They were simply too caught up in their race to break the latest, leaked, official-source information.

The article also fails to point out that the "bomb training" Jewell received at the sheriff's department was nothing more than the basic training police officers around the country routinely receive. Jewell, in fact, had no special training in making bombs and no more knowledge of them than the average American police officer.

The final point about the *Atlanta Journal-Constitution* article is its "voice-of-God" tone and "hot scoop" style. Even if all the other errors made by the paper were to be overlooked as understandable mistakes (which they should not be), the tone is difficult to ignore. As noted, the paper could have simply and objectively declared that it had reasons to believe that Jewell was under investigation. Instead, the language of the piece was crafted in a way that clearly implied that the *Atlanta Journal-Constitution* was breaking the scoop that Jewell was not only under investigation but that he was very likely guilty—an idea reinforced and emphasized by its having been run as the lead front-page story of a "special edition" of the paper with a banner headline containing sarcastic quotation marks around the word "hero." Rather than focus on discovering and reporting the truth

Richard Jewell, shown here before the United States House Subcommittee on Crime of the Committee of the Judiciary on July 30, 1997. Lawyer L. Lin Wood, who represented Jewell, can be seen behind him. *(Photo courtesy of AP/Wide World Photos.)*

and on serving the public good, journalists Kathy Scruggs and Ron Martz put together a story that gave unofficial police leaks undue deference and thus led readers to conclude that Jewell was the bomber. Moreover, the piece's voice-of-God tone presented the story as unequivocally fact-based, when indeed it wasn't. At best, it was a cobbled-together, subjective story based on unreliable details and poorly scrutinized logic. Even one of Jewell's attorneys, L. Lin Wood, a seasoned libel attorney, says that when he first read the story—before he became involved in the case—he assumed that Jewell was guilty.

Richard Jewell commented on the article himself, saying, "You read this [newspaper] and think 'He wanted publicity,' 'He wanted to be on T.V.,' 'Maybe he wanted it bad enough to put the bomb under the bench.'... You take away the bomb training, you take away the profile, and you're left with the story that [the] FBI suspects that he might have done it. And that is it. There is nothing else. Which means that [if you took away all these false suppositions] you might not believe that I did it. But as you read it, you think 'Now I know why they're looking at him. This is the guy!' "[8]

Arguably the worst article published on the matter was an op-ed piece that appeared in the *Atlanta Journal-Constitution* on August 1, nearly a week after the bombing. The article compares Jewell with the infamous convicted Atlanta child murderer, Wayne Williams. Written by Dave Kindred, it reads in part:

> Once upon a terrible time, federal agents came to this town to deal with another suspect who lived with his mother. Like this one, that suspect was drawn to the blue lights and sirens of police work. Like this one, he became famous in the aftermath of murder.
>
> His name was Wayne Williams.
>
> This one is Richard Jewell.[9]

The piece, which cites no concrete evidence against Jewell, concludes: "Richard Jewell sits in the shadows today. Wayne Williams sits in prison forever."

Other Media Errors

Whereas most news-media outlets were guilty of vilifying Jewell only insofar as they either reprinted stories or quoted from other publications such as the *Atlanta Journal-Constitution,* a number of other very notable media gaffes compounded the situation. Even though the facts proved contradictory, Tom Brokaw stated on *NBC Nightly News* on July 30th, "They probably have enough to arrest him right now, probably enough to prosecute him, but you always want to have enough to convict him as well. There are still holes in this case."[10]

And, although it was stated in the context of comedy, the *Tonight Show*'s Jay Leno made a crack that no doubt added to the national consensus against Jewell. Comparing him to the infamous postal bomber, Theodore Kaczynski, better known as the Unabomber, Leno called Jewell "the Una-doofus," and his mother, who was also forced into the media spotlight, "the Una-Momma."[11]

For the next eighty-eight days, the media assembled en masse outside the Jewell home—until Jewell was finally cleared by the U.S. Justice Department. For a time, a consortium of television networks even paid $1,000 a day to a tenant in a neighboring apartment complex for the right to use the unit for their stakeouts. Jewell described the situation: "I would look out the window and see about 150 to 200 press people. Then it would drop to five or six on the hill. They had one person sitting up there at all times with their binoculars.... They were over there with high-intensity zoom lenses. They had people over there who could read lips. They had a sound dish. They could hear everything that we said. They had a person writing down everything we said. I saw them."[12]

The Jewells simply could not carry on with their daily lives. Even minor errands became major trials, with journalists hounding them at all hours of the day and night for nearly three months. This intrusive media presence was tacitly condoned by the FBI, which also kept both Jewells under around-the-clock surveillance.

Here were an utterly innocent U.S. citizen—a hero, in fact—and his mother, neither of whom had been charged with any crime whatsoever, pursued by a small army of journalists and a team of federal agents, yet with absolutely no recourse. The FBI condoned the media's behavior, just as the media condoned the FBI's.

Police Treatment of Richard Jewell

Earlier on the day that the initial *Atlanta Journal-Constitution* story ran, FBI agents approached Jewell and told him that because he was so skilled in spotting bombs, they wanted to elicit his help in making a "police-training video" on the subject. Upon their request, Jewell gladly accompanied them to a police station, where he was told that he would be filmed answering some simple questions about the identification of dangerous packages.

But then, upon starting the video recorder, the FBI agents surprised Jewell by reading him his Miranda rights and then initiating an aggressive line of questioning about the terrorist bomb. According to Jewell, the agents' questioning turned unmistakably hostile when he suggested that he should have his attorney present.

Fortunately, Jewell had contacted an attorney friend, Watson Bryant, soon after the bombing to discuss a book proposal another media person had approached him with the day after the bombing. Thus, the two of them had been in contact regarding the event. At about the same time that Jewell was being interrogated by the FBI, Bryant had come across the infamous issue of the *Atlanta Journal-Constitution* insinuating that Jewell was the bomber. Bryant, who immediately tried to contact Jewell, soon learned Jewell was at the police station and was thus able to come to his defense. In retrospect, Jewell credits his relationship with Bryant as being absolutely critical to the eventual establishment of his innocence.

During the three months following the bombing, Jewell and his mother were subjected to many injustices. The FBI plucked twenty-five hairs from Jewell's head, as samples to aid them in their investigation.[13] The FBI impounded his truck. They also aggressively interrogated his family, friends, and associates, even coercing a number of them to undergo polygraph tests. In Jewell's own words:

For eighty-eight days, from July 30 to October 26, the FBI wasted millions of dollars and thousands of man-hours following me, my mother, my attorneys, my friends—always with three or four cars, sometimes with as many as five or six cars—sometimes with airplanes. The FBI followed me twenty-four hours a day. The FBI followed me into restaurants, into hardware stores, into grocery stores, to my lawyer's offices, to my friends' homes, to the funeral home where I went to say good-bye to a close friend who had been a father figure to me for many years. They even followed me to the Little League field where I coached football for ten-year-old kids.[14]

This alliance between powerful law-enforcement agencies and media companies was probably at its ugliest when FBI, ATF, and other law agents performed a painstaking search of the Jewells' town house, with hundreds of media people looking on and live television cameras rolling. The police then held a press conference in the parking lot in front of the Jewells' town house. Sadly, few law-enforcement officials or media members—all of whose job it is to protect the rights of innocent citizens—considered anything amiss with this treatment of Jewell and his mother. The police did not ask the media to back off on its aggressive surveillance and harassment of a common man who had not been charged with any crime. Likewise, the media failed to make any truly significant criticisms of the police's misguided investigation. In fact, the media essentially egged the police on in their investigations, just as the police encouraged the media in their speculations against Jewell.

The police and government benefited from the media coverage, because rather than appearing confused and helpless about a terrorist attack that they were indeed confused and helpless about, they looked as if they were making steady progress. In return, the media were spoon-fed all the drama they needed to keep their ratings and subscriptions high.

This was in many ways a self-reinforcing relationship. The police certainly knew that if they didn't offer up a suspect, they themselves were likely to feel the heat of the media's inquiries. Journalists, no doubt, knew that if they failed to use information leaked to them, the police would likely leak it to other journalists instead and perhaps leave them out of the loop. Serious analysis of the core questions raised by the bombing was sadly lacking, with few asking anything about the vulnerability of the United States to terrorist attacks or what steps might be taken to mitigate that vulnerability in the future.

Fortunately, in most cases reporters did back off their intensely critical coverage of Jewell soon after the FBI search of his residence yielded no corroborating evidence. And on August 22, some three weeks after Jewell's ordeal began, ABC News did initiate a media movement that led to serious questions about the suspicions against Jewell. To its credit, ABC aired a "Viewpoint" special, hosted by Ted Koppel, entitled "The Bizarre Case of Richard Jewell," and featuring a discussion with Jewell's attorneys. In September, CBS's *60 Minutes* aired an interview with Jewell conducted by Mike Wallace in a segment that was openly critical of the media and the FBI for its treatment of Jewell.

Jewell Seeks Justice

On October 26, 1996, soon after Jewell's mother made an emotional public appeal to President Clinton on behalf of her son, the U.S. Justice Department issued a statement asserting Jewell's innocence in the bombing. Since then, Jewell and his legal team have pursued civil damages in about eight legal actions against defendants that include CNN News, Tom Brokaw and NBC, *Time Magazine,* the *New York Post,* WABC AM radio of New York, 96 Rock FM (owned by City Casters of Atlanta), Piedmont College and its president Ray Cleere (who reported questionable information to the FBI about Jewell), and the *Atlanta Journal-Constitution* and members of its editorial team. All these defendants, with the exception of the *Atlanta Journal-Constitution,* settled their cases out of court. Although the extensive and byzantine details of the ongoing court battle between the *Atlanta Journal-Constitution,* which is owned by Cox Broadcasting, and Richard Jewell are more than can easily be presented here, Jewell's attorney L. Lin Wood admits that some aspects of the case have not gone well for Jewell, particularly a ruling that deemed Jewell to be a "public figure" because of his participation in the ten interviews and one photo shoot. Wood says that the matter could take many years to resolve completely and makes a powerful argument that it is becoming exceedingly difficult in the United States for victims of media defamation to successfully sue the powerful corporate conglomerates that own the media. He argues that while this is true for all such victims, it is especially true for ordinary people like Jewell as opposed to wealthy individuals such as certain celebrities, politicians, and other elites.

Regarding those who have settled out of court with Jewell, however, it would appear that he has fared reasonably well. The press has reported that Jewell's settlements with the media organizations have exceeded $2 million—a figure that has not been challenged by any individual or entity.[15] Of course, whatever Jewell has received from out-of-court settlements has been shared with his legal counsel—a split that in the United States is usually one-third of the settlement after expenses.

The Distortion of an American Hero

As a result of the events outlined here, Jewell has become what some have described as "a poster boy for those wrongly accused" in the U.S. media. Unfortunately, the one fact that has been almost universally missed about Jewell is that he is truly an American hero of the highest caliber. Like so many public servants who responded to the attacks of September 11, 2001, Jewell also put his life on the line to save innocent people in the face of a terrorist strike against his country.

"People still come up to me and give me a nudge and ask, 'Did he really do it? Did he get away with it?' " says Jewell's lawyer Wood in an interview held six years after the attack.[16] Wood has also served as a lawyer for such other high-profile clients as John and Patsy Ramsey, parents of the murdered six-year-old JonBenét Ramsey, and former Congressman Gary Condit, who came under scrutiny in connection with the disappearance of murdered Washington intern Chandra Levy. According to Wood, the fact that the U.S. government publicly vindicated Jewell has not prevented many people from continuing to associate him negatively with that terrorist attack:

> That's why neither Bill Clinton nor George W. Bush is going to put his arm around Richard Jewell and say "thank you." That's why the Olympic Committee is not going to give him an honorary gold medal or even give him the chance to carry the Olympic flame and let him run one mile here in America with it. He was so tainted by the media that he is viewed as damaged goods to this very day, and no one wants to be associated with him. That's what the media has done to him. He is damaged goods. And, don't forget this has all happened to a guy who is absolutely innocent and who did nothing but act heroically.[17]

That Richard Jewell is now seen as "damaged goods" is the result of what Wood describes as "the shout of guilty and the whisper of innocent," referring to the news media's practice of dedicating prominent coverage to initial stories that implicate suspects of high-profile crimes and then providing minor or even no coverage of later exonerations. The result is that many people who initially encounter accusations in the press fail to notice the retractions. According to Jewell and Wood, one survey revealed that 26 percent of

U.S. respondents still thought Jewell was guilty of the bombing *after* he had been publicly vindicated by the government and in the media.[18] Anecdotal evidence today—seven years after the event and just after a new suspect has been charged with the crime—indicates that while many Americans remember Jewell as having been wrongly accused of the bombing there, virtually no one remembers his heroic behavior.

"It's like yelling 'Fire!' in a crowded theater, then mumbling 'Just kidding' under your breath," Wood says. "The U.S. media have become so arrogant, so filled with a sense of privilege, that they find it very difficult to admit when they've made a mistake. The media in this country view themselves as part of the establishment."[19]

Things like special access to power holders, employment with some of the world's wealthiest and most influential companies, and lifestyles that increasingly separate them from poor people all put journalists in a position where they are likely to view events from the perspective of power holders—a position that increasingly alienates them from the plight of everyday citizens, both in the United States and in Japan.

Asked who treated him the worst throughout his ordeal—the news media or the police—Jewell replied, "They are all responsible for leaking my name. I think when they report suspects' names, they really should be careful. They are responsible for investigating what really happened. But they didn't, so I think both of them are equally bad."[20]

The Matsumoto Sarin-Gas Attack

It seemed to be just another summer evening in the attractive mountain town of Matsumoto, located in central Japan. Yoshiyuki Kono and his wife had sent their three children off to bed when their lives were changed forever.

Little did the Konos suspect that while they were enjoying a quiet family evening, members of the now infamous religious group Aum Shinrikyo (Supreme Truth Sect) were just yards away, in the small gravel parking lot adjacent to their home.[21] The group, formed in the mid-1980s by its leader Shoko Asahara, had an estimated one thousand full-time followers living in communes and as many as ten thousand less-active followers in Japan and other countries.

Shoko Asahara (center with beard) is shown in this November 30, 1989, photograph along with members of Aum Shinrikyo, the religious group he founded. Asahara and other members of Aum Shinrikyo have been found guilty in the 1994 sarin-gas attack in Matsumoto, Nagano—where Yoshiyuki Kono and his wife were injured—and of the 1995 Tokyo sarin-gas attack. *(Photo courtesy of Mainichi Photo Bank.)*

In 1994, finding itself involved in a legal controversy over a land purchase and in an attempt to preempt an unfavorable ruling, Aum Shinrikyo decided to murder the three judges overseeing the case. It seems that the members also concluded that the assassinations would be a perfect opportunity to test their new capacity to produce the chemical weapon known as sarin nerve gas. Unfortunately for the Konos, the targeted judges were residing just across the street from their home, in housing provided by the government.

The Aum Shinrikyo members drove a converted delivery truck from their main center in Matsumoto to the parking lot, where they used an improvised sarin-dissemination system, consisting of a heater, a fan, and a drip system, to vent the invisible vapor from the window of the truck for an estimated twenty minutes.[22] Although the three judges were unharmed, the Konos' resulting experience, as recounted by Kono himself, was horrifying:

> My wife began to complain to me, saying that she didn't feel well. About the same time, there was some noise in the backyard. I got up and looked out into the backyard and saw that one of my two dogs had collapsed. He was foaming at the mouth and his body was shivering. My other dog was dead. My immediate thought was that someone must have thrown poison into my backyard and poisoned them.
>
> I immediately went back and told my wife that I thought we should call the police. But she had lost consciousness.

I now realize that the sarin gas had blown into our backyard and got our dogs. But when I went to look into the backyard, the gas must have come into the room where my wife was.

That's when I called the ambulance. Then I tried to attend to my wife by loosening her clothes, but I began to suffer as well. The first symptom that I experienced was that everything started to go dark. It was just like I had put on sunglasses. After that, things started to look warped and distorted. Then whatever I saw danced and fluctuated, just like a TV screen that doesn't work correctly. The next moment I was ready to vomit. Soon I could not stay on my feet.

When the ambulance arrived, I could hardly move. But still I exerted myself to crawl out to the ambulance. I later learned that by the time the paramedics reached my wife, her heart had stopped beating. It was only about twenty minutes from the time that I looked at my dogs until the time that I was taken to the hospital.

I told the ambulance driver three things: First, please take care of my wife; she is in critical condition. Second, I told them that I was not right, so please take care of me. Third, I told them our dogs were ill, so something must be wrong in this area.

So I got into the ambulance. Physically I was in trouble. But spiritually I was still awake and fighting.

I was put in the ambulance first, and then my wife was carried in, but because her heart was not beating, the paramedics worked on her heart.

When I reached the hospital, I was vomiting profusely. Things kept coming up, so the doctor first suspected that this must be a horrible case of food poisoning. I felt horrible and I couldn't keep my eyes open. It seemed like the kind of experience that I imagine people on LSD have. There was this confusion of my vision. It was like everything was pouring down, just like water. It was so unnatural. I understand that because of these symptoms, the doctor judged that whatever happened was related to organic lead.

Soon after, terrible spasms went through my entire body. The doctor began to inject certain sulfide compounds as treatment. As I said, we were poisoned at about 11:00 PM. My seizures lasted until about 2:00 AM. Then my vision started moving from left to right in color. It was like I was recollecting many familiar scenes from my life. I developed a very high fever, and my mouth became terribly dry. Then, with the passage of time, the color vision faded into black and white.

Next, my vision started flashing like a lighthouse. This series of illusions occurred for two days. Not only visions but my hearing had illusions. In my case, someone was reciting a Buddhist sutra. In my eldest daughter's case, who was also poisoned, she heard the sound of oxygen being sucked in and out, and she heard a voice saying, "You better die. You better die." But another voice yelled, "You better try. You better live."

I felt that I was bordering on death. It was truly a life-and-death experience for me. One thing that went through my mind is that I recognized that all the memories in my mind are so vague, so nebulous, so dubious. It became clear to me that human memory is very vague.

I understand that a typical symptom of sarin-gas poisoning is memory loss. Another woman who was a victim of this incident even forgot her own name, that much of her memory was damaged.

During the experience, I saw many familiar things, but I could not remember their names.

Also with sarin-gas poisoning, one's nervous system can become so active that you cannot sleep. For that reason I was awake for two or three days in a row. I had to take medicine to sleep, but I was only able to sleep for two or three hours at a time.

When I was taken to the hospital, one of the attending nurses had gotten very close to me. As a result she was immediately affected by the sarin gas, too, and she was unable to sleep for two days.

Another symptom is a horrible headache. Also diarrhea. Also you cannot control your temperature. Even though eight years have passed, my body still cannot control my temperature properly and I still develop fevers every day.[23]

At the time of the publication of this book, Kono's eldest daughter had achieved a complete physical recovery. His son and youngest daughter were not poisoned, because their bedrooms were out of harm's way. Kono's wife, Sumiko, however, remains in a coma nine years after the fact. Her doctors say that, due to a lack of oxygen, her brain has been reduced to a fraction of its normal size.

Still, her facial expressions do change in response to sounds, and medical tests
have confirmed alterations in her brain-wave patterns at those times. Mr. Kono
therefore makes a point of playing music and speaking to her on his daily visits.
He also updates her on the status of their children and is often heard telling her

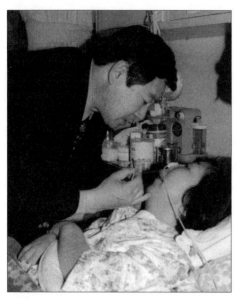

how beautiful she looks. Many
observers have commented that
one of Kono's most dominant
traits is his continued affection for
and devotion to his wife. One of
the books he has published about
his ordeal is appropriately entitled
*Tsuma yo! Waga Ai to Kibo to
Tatakai no Hibi,* which translates
into English as "My Wife! Days of
My Love, Hope, and Struggle."[24]

After the attack, Mr. Kono
remained hospitalized for thirty-
three days, during which time he
learned that he had been
misidentified by the media as
having created the sarin gas himself. Newspapers as well as televi-

Yoshiyuki Kono has visited his wife, Sumiko
Kono, on a daily basis since the Matsumoto sarin
attack of March 20, 1995. She has not regained
consciousness since then. *(Photo courtesy of Kyodo
News Agency.)*

sion and radio news programs throughout Japan reported that Kono had
probably concocted the poisonous gas accidentally by mixing chemicals. The
event was usually referred to as an "incident" or "accident," with no particular accusations that Kono had intentionally committed a terrorist act. But
eventually, the accusations emerged.

Although it is a relatively difficult process to create sarin gas—and all but
impossible to make it accidentally in a home environment such as the Konos'—
the theory that Kono did so was leaked to the news media by police authorities.
The truth, however, is that the police were merely making an early guess at what
might have happened and were stymied by the case. Just as with the U.S. media
in Jewell's case, most Japanese journalists simply reiterated what the authorities told them, with little or no scrutiny or analysis of the actual facts.

The police had the following evidence for their theory that Kono had created the gas: (1) Kono was the first person to report the case; (2) the area of chemical release appeared to be near his home; (3) with his engineering background and professional experience, he was licensed to handle a number of restricted chemicals; and (4) the police located a variety of gardening and photo-processing chemicals in his home.

This evidence is not as strong as it may at first appear, however. First, all of the containers that held the gardening and photo-processing chemicals at Kono's home were discovered by the police in a closed storage area and were covered with dust, showing that they had not been used for quite some time. Second, there was no evidence whatsoever that chemicals had been mixed at Kono's home in the recent past. Third, as noted, sarin gas is not easily manufactured in a home environment such as Kono's but usually requires laboratory equipment. Finally, and critically, as investigators ascertained, none of the chemicals at Kono's home could have been mixed to create sarin or any similar nerve gas. Thus, although it was reasonable for the police to investigate Kono, no evidence existed whatsoever that he was anything more than a victim of the incident, and their leaking of his name was therefore inexcusable.

While in the hospital, Kono tried to avoid the media and to focus on his recovery. Just a few days after the attack, however, his son brought him a videotape of an evening news broadcast that included footage of their home and identified it as the source of the gas. Kono was so outraged that he determined to sue the television station.

Not long afterward, Kono's daughter also showed him an article from the newspaper *Chunichi Shimbun,* which quotes Mrs. Kono as saying that she had helped her husband mix chemicals and in so doing caused a cloud of smoke to billow up above the house. This, of course, was a total invention, because Mrs. Kono never recovered from her coma and thus could never have said anything to anyone.

Kono's Legal Defense

While recovering in the hospital, Kono remained steadfast in his determination to sue the news media for falsely accusing him. Because he did not have any relationships with lawyers, he asked a good friend to help him find one.

His friend was able to refer him to one, but when this lawyer, Tsuneharu Nagata, arrived at the hospital, he shocked Kono by advising him that he was not there to help him sue the media but to assist him as a criminal-defense attorney. Until then, Kono had complete faith that the police must know he was innocent and that they would protect him. He simply could not fathom that they might actually pursue him as a suspect.

By seeking out the services of a lawyer, Kono had acted in an unusual manner for a Japanese citizen. In Japan, the ideals of social harmony and obedience to authority, combined with the common practice of finding extralegal solutions to problems, the high cost of legal counsel, and the relative scarcity of lawyers, meant that the very idea of a common person engaging a lawyer to sue the media struck many individuals as unusually confrontational. As a result, *Shukan Shincho* made special note of Kono's decision to retain legal counsel, as if his hiring a lawyer confirmed his guilt.

Nagata's decision to represent Kono was also unusual in Japan. There, lawyers can be permanently stigmatized for taking on high-profile criminal clients, especially those who are accused of heinous crimes. Such lawyers often suffer from "guilt by association" by representing such clients—even when their clients have not been determined guilty by a court or even officially charged with a crime, as in Kono's case.

Nagata was strongly advised by friends, family, and colleagues not to assist Kono. Interestingly, it was even more difficult for Shoko Asahara, the leader of the Aum Shinrikyo group that actually perpetrated the sarin-gas attack against Kono, to retain a lawyer when charges were eventually brought against him. The Bar Association of Japan failed so completely in its search for a lawyer to take Asahara's case that it eventually gave up altogether and requested the state to assign someone. Needless to say, in countries such as the United States, where "guilt by association" does not affect lawyers, a number of high-profile lawyers would fight for the chance to defend a client such as Asahara.

Hiroshi Saito, a Japanese lawyer who has studied Kono's case in detail, commented on Nagata's decision. "Since I too am a lawyer, I asked myself many times if I could have taken the same action as Nagata had I been placed in a similar situation. Even today," he went on, "I can't say clearly if I would have acted as Nagata did. Nagata persisted in his belief and fulfilled his duty beautifully. . . . It seems so miraculous to me that a lawyer like Nagata existed within Kono's reach."[25]

"Miraculous" may seem an awfully strong word to describe the willingness of a lawyer to handle a high-profile case, especially in the United States, where O. J. Simpson–defender Johnnie Cochran and others have made their careers with such cases. But in Japan, "miraculous" is no exaggeration. There, the stigma that goes with the mere accusation of wrongdoing is often enough to ruin not only the accused but anyone associated with him or her.

Media Coverage of the Matsumoto Sarin-Gas Attack

The "media-inspired hell" surrounding Kono began soon after the Matsumoto sarin attack, when the press learned from the police that they had identified Kono's home as the source of the gas. As in the Jewell case, journalists from around the country quickly descended and bivouacked outside Kono's home, where they set up continuous surveillance.

But, unlike the Jewell case, when the Japanese police had completed the search of their suspect's home and failed to find any corroborating evidence or to press any formal charges against their suspect, the Japanese press did not tone down their critical coverage of Kono and his family. And, whereas negative coverage of Jewell only lasted eighty-eight days—and more positive coverage actually began within three weeks—seriously negative coverage of Kono lasted more than six months. It was not until January 1, 1995, when traces of sarin were found in Yamanashi Prefecture, that people finally began to realize that someone else may have been behind the Matsumoto gassing. Moreover, although coverage of Kono cooled on January 1, he was not vindicated until the tragic Tokyo sarin-gas attack of March 20, 1995, some nine months after the Matsumoto attack.

Not surprisingly, the most negative and personally damaging coverage about Kono came from Japan's sensational weekly newsmagazines, the worst of which was that of *Shukan Shincho,* published by Shinchosha.

Juichi Saito, the founder of *Shukan Shincho* and its longtime chief editor and "editorial advisor," was considered the driving force behind the magazine's "literary-narrative" editorial direction from its inception in 1956 until his

The headlines in this image may or may not be reliable.

A selection of the many magazine articles written about Yoshiyuki Kono.

death in 2000. Saito had a reputation for dictating to his staff that stories in the magazine be told from "imaginative" angles that were often caustically critical of their subjects. In a July 31, 1997, interview with the weekly newsmagazine *Shukan Bunshun* (*Shukan Shincho*'s main competitor), Saito emphasized the commercial nature of his editorial approach. Saito was asked about his company's weekly photo magazine, *Focus*, which had recently run a photo of a fourteen-year-old boy who was then suspected (later convicted) of a series of violent attacks against younger children, including the murder and beheading of a sixth-grade schoolboy. The entire nation had been shocked at the end of May 1997 when the victim's head was discovered propped in front of the main gate of a Kobe middle school, a taunting note to the police stuck between its teeth. Saito was asked why the magazine, under his direction, elected to run the photograph of the suspected boy, in spite of the country's Minor's Act, which everyone in the business knows forbids publishers from publicizing the identities of suspects under the age of sixteen. The magazine was recalled from newsstands as a result, although the photo is apparently still available in various locations on the Internet.[26] The question posed to Saito by *Shukan Bunshun* was, "Isn't it a reflection of your commercialism that the *Focus* photo-essay magazine, which is also your baby, ran a picture of the boy, a suspect who killed a grade-school child in an elementary school in Kobe?"

Saito's reply was, "Of course, we are coming from commercialism. We do anything to sell our magazine better."

In the same article, Saito describes his stance this way: "Human rights? They may be important, but we can't publish anything if we are attached to them. There is something that is more important than human rights. It is human existence itself. I mean human nature itself. Therefore, I will publish anything that I feel reflects human nature, even if doing so is criticized as an infringement upon human rights."[27]

Kazuyoshi Hanada, a former editor in chief of *Shukan Bunshun* who competed directly against Saito within the industry for years, knew Saito's editorial style as well as anyone. In an interview for this book, he confirmed the well-known fact that Saito dictated *Shukan Shincho*'s editorial direction with an iron grip (including during the magazine's attacks against the innocent Kono):

> Juichi Saito was the guardian of the gate at *Shukan Shincho*. He decided what would be published. He would write the table of contents, and he would say what the articles had to be like, and all the writers would have to come up with the stories to match his headlines. He would cut out any contents that he felt detracted from the magazine. He was a stellar editor. He essentially put the whole magazine together in his head, and then the stories were written to his order. It was essentially his opinions that were put in place in the form of *Shukan Shincho*'s news stories.[28]

Shukan Shincho's former assistant editor, Jun Kamei, who worked for Saito for twenty years, stated that the Kono case was a prime example of Saito's policy, as well as of media *ijime*, or group bullying by the media. According to Kamei, "they are selling a product that is a consummate essence of superiority. And that article against Kono is 100 percent consistent with that. It is designed, like many others, to give readers the feeling that you get when you think, 'I'm not that poor slob.'"[29]

Kamei, who eventually resigned his position at the magazine and wrote two books exposing the immoral editorial policies of Japanese weeklies, elaborated on this point: "By deliberately infringing on the rights of ordinary people, their stories sell better. They've learned that every time they appeal to their reader's baser instincts—that sense of sadistic voyeurism latent in all of us which delights in the suffering of others—circulation soars."[30]

Shukan Shincho began its coverage of the Kono story rather late, with its first piece not appearing until the July 14, 1994, issue, some seventeen days after the Matsumoto attack. But what *Shukan Shincho* lacked in timeliness, it attempted to make up for in originality. The story was titled:

THE ORIGINATOR OF POISONOUS GAS AND HIS MACABRE FAMILY LINE[31]

The *Shukan Shincho* writers interviewed Kono's neighbors, investigated his family's ancestors, and then essentially tacked the most negative information they were able to collect onto the known published "facts" about the case. The article is based on the premise that Kono not only was guilty of creating the poison gas but had done so purposefully and with malicious intent. The slant of this article made *Shukan Shincho*'s coverage the most critical of Kono thus far and gave it a "scoop" quality it didn't deserve.

The article, which does not carry a byline, states that "Kono's past personal record is quite queer"—an assertion that the magazine failed to back up with

These photos in *Shukan Shincho* accompanied what Mr. Kono described as the most malicious story about his predicament by any news company. This is no small statement, as there were literally hundreds if not thousands of news pieces composed about Kono. The headline of the photo layout reads "EERIE SECRETS OF THE KONO FAMILY." (*Shukan Shincho*, July 14, 1994.)

any evidence, just as the *Atlanta Journal-Constitution* failed to back up its accusation that Richard Jewell was "frustrated." The Kono article also recounts various negative stories (some false and others previously unknown even to Kono) about Kono's grandfather and great-grandfather, and features photographs not only of Kono but of his deceased grandfather as well.

Shukan Shincho even went so far as to imply that there was something unseemly about the way Kono's wife had been found. "When the paramedics went inside the house, his wife was lying on her back in the living room. All she had on were her shorts and a girdle. She was almost naked, with an undergarment lying across her bare upper body." This description is worked into the article without any explanation that Kono had loosened his wife's clothing in an attempt to help her breathe more easily; it simply appears within the sordid context of a crime-scene description. The article even goes so far as to suppose that "if he [Kono] was a victim, it does not seem that he would need an attorney." Kamei critiqued the article:

> This article about Mr. Kono is one of the most unforgivable articles that *Shukan Shincho* has ever printed. . . . They were intentionally hurtful of him. It doesn't just say that Mr. Kono was suspicious, which wasn't true anyway. It says that the whole Kono family is macabre and bizarre. In other words, it's the imagery they use in that article. They talk about an old home with a large, dark tree, dank and dark. But if you think about it, any home that has been around for a long time is likely to have a tree that is probably pretty large in the yard. And if it's large, it's likely to be pretty dark and dank, too. And then *Shukan Shincho* published an aerial photo of Mr. Kono's home in black and white so that it looks scary, like the home of the devil or something. And then they drop gratuitously insulting captions on the photo. It's very childish, the whole journalistic approach. But it is also seriously hurtful to this poor injured person who is on the receiving end.[32]

When told that Kono felt that *Shukan Shincho*'s coverage of the story was the most vicious of all, Hiroshi Matsuda, the magazine's editor in chief at the time of the attack, said in an interview for this book that he simply did not think that was the case. He described *Shukan Shincho*'s accusations against

Kono as a simple, honest mistake, one made by many members of the news media, and certainly no worse.[33]

Literary-Narrative Journalism

Matsuda explained that his magazine is not just a newsmagazine, devoted to altruistic journalistic ideals: "There is sort of a heroic motif to journalism. Frequently, people try to draw equivalents between journalists and heroes or workers for justice. We have a slightly different policy. We are looking at the human interest. So, we get into some of the more seamy sides of things, like scandals with women."[34]

According to Matsuda, *Shukan Shincho* is unlike U.S. newsmagazines in that it is a cross between a newsmagazine and a "literary" magazine. He explained in great detail that the magazine writes what may be described as literary-narrative journalism. This does not include intentionally fabricating material, Matsuda maintained, but it does include "contextualizing facts" in a way that makes them as intriguing as possible:

> This is quite a substantial difference between the U.S. and Japan. For instance, in the U.S. you have the weekly magazines *Newsweek* and *Time*. The substance that you see in *Newsweek* and *Time*, if you brought that kind of editorial policy over to Japan and published it in a magazine, you would probably be bankrupt in three weeks. We really try for a multifaceted approach, and what we are trying to do is make sure that it's an interesting read for our patrons. There aren't any novels that are running in *Newsweek* and *Time*, but in weeklies in Japan we have them, as well as essays, and we have serial publications as well. So, the weeklies are pursuing more than just news. They are literary titles, and they are pursuing essentially what is most preferred by Japanese readers. So, in that area, you can't ignore the fact that there is a tendency for sensationalist pieces to be highlighted.

Matsuda elaborated on this point in great detail. According to him, Japanese weekly newsmagazines don't simply sensationalize facts in a common tabloid fashion. What they do is combine the literary principles of storytelling with journalistic techniques:

However, we have to be careful about what we mean by "sensational." It does not mean fabrication. It really refers to a certain kind of exaggeration. In other words, it is a style of expression and writing whereby Japanese find it very easy to identify with what's being written. That's using simile or metaphor. So, the metaphorical method can cause what you have described as being a slightly exaggerated expression. So, what I see here is that looking at the actual headlines and the content in these weeklies today, what's going on is that instead of covering the facts, just the plain old facts, there's an emotional element to the approach. I would say, it's this emotional expression, not what you term sensational, that is what is added or what flavors the facts. And this is something that the readers use to find a way to identify with what they are reading.

Matsuda illustrated his assertions by comparing *Shukan Shincho*'s coverage with that of the Japanese establishment news media:

For example, you have some sort of political corruption on some level, the news coverage is very cool and bland—just the facts. What we try to do is try to come up with the story. The politician involved—what was his background? Why did he do what he did? What we are trying to do is give attention to the whole spectrum. And the readership finds it acceptable, and there is definitely a response. In other words, if you are looking at the fundamentals of journalism, you are looking at who did what, where, when, why, and how. But if you look at the feature articles of a weekly magazine, each piece goes through the four phases of a story: the initial plot, then the second part of the story, then there's sort of a flip, and then there's a conclusion. So it becomes a very readable story. There are many weeklies in Japan. But in particular, the *Shukan Shincho* and the *Shukan Bunshun*—these publications are constantly struggling with their literary expression, so that they can retain high sensibilities. They don't want to degrade the expression.[35]

Here Matsuda summarizes a key point made earlier: Japanese newspapers and broadcasters tend to present the news in such a boring, fact-oriented fashion that many Japanese long for news coverage that is more analysis and opinion. The literary-narrative journalism described by Matsuda fulfills this desire among readers. Given this dynamic, one cannot help but wonder what would happen to the popularity of the weeklies if the Japanese establishment press were more interesting.

One editor for a major weekly newsmagazine, who asked not to be identified, described literary-narrative journalism in an interview for this book:

> What we [newsmagazine writers and editors] do is get all of the facts and then we try to actualize them in print, to make them more real. We sort of imagine the flow of what happened. And we do this simply because otherwise the reader is not going to be able to follow the story. And that's true for *Shukan Shincho* and other magazines as well. Of course, we have to keep it within the limits of being sued. This way, the story is going to be easy for the reader to digest.

Given this editorial policy, it is not hard to see how *Shukan Shincho*'s coverage of the Matsumoto sarin-gas incident could be so damaging to Kono. Like the many Japanese establishment papers that regurgitated the false information provided them by police, *Shukan Shincho* also presented incorrect data. But, in its attempt to add an "emotional element," to "flavor the facts" and "imagine the flow of what happened," *Shukan Shincho* decided to write about "the originator of poisonous gas and his macabre family line." This, of course, also fits well with Kamei's assessment of *Shukan Shincho*'s appeal to "that sense of sadistic voyeurism latent in all of us which delights in the suffering of others."

Hajime Kitamura, a former newspaper journalist who has also served as editor in chief of the weekly newsmagazine *Sunday Mainichi*, has an intimate understanding of the use of literary-narrative journalism. He confirmed that this style, initiated by *Shukan Shincho* in the 1950s, has come to dominate the weekly newsmagazine industry. "The writing style of *Shukan Shincho* had a significant impact on Japanese newsmagazine reporting," he said. "What *Shincho* proposed was to touch on subtleties. It doesn't offer 100 percent fiction, or 100 percent fact, but a blend of fact and fiction. They have a method of 'adorning' the facts."[36]

Asked about the pros and cons of this policy, Kitamura acknowledged that it has inflicted very real harm on a number of individuals covered by the weeklies. Asked to estimate how much of a given weekly newsmagazine article is based on fact and how much on fiction, he admitted that it varied from piece to piece and from magazine to magazine. Although he said some articles can be completely accurate and that he cannot personally point to one that is utterly fictitious, he admitted that "the kernel of truth in a published weekly newsmagazine story may well be as low as 20 percent verifiable fact."[37]

Other *Shukan Shincho* Coverage

Sadly, the July 14 article was just the first of many pieces run by *Shukan Shincho* portraying Kono as a criminal. The magazine's August 4 article boasted the following headline:

> SURREPTITIOUS INFORMATION OF CRIMINAL WHO PRODUCED
> HEINOUS SARIN GAS AND THE ONLY CONCEIVABLE SCENARIO
> THAT CAN ENABLE A BREAKTHROUGH IN INVESTIGATION[38]

This article argued that there is no other logical way for the gas to have been created than for Kono to have concocted it.

Another particularly damaging piece by the magazine ran in their joint issue for August 11 and 18, 1994, sporting this headline:

> FIRST PERSON WHO REPORTED INCIDENT REVEALS HIMSELF[39]

This article referred to statements by Kono, wrongly declaring that they exposed his guilt—an assertion repeated in the September 8 issue.

All these pieces were printed after the police had fruitlessly searched Kono's home and in spite of the fact that he was never charged with a crime. Just as in the Jewell case, not a single scrap of credible evidence was ever found to implicate Kono.

Unbeknownst to Kono, the negative media coverage began in the Japanese press club system, which all but ensures that the Japanese media present criminal stories in the way that the police and other authorities desire. Japanese crime reporters spend a majority of their working hours in intimate contact with police authorities through the press clubs. According to journalists who have worked in the clubs, rather than take a critical approach to the police or even strive for an objective view, many Japanese crime reporters think of police officials as colleagues or even members of the same team. For the most part, police authorities tend to be the exclusive information sources for crime reporters.[40] Although not every Japanese reporter fails to question official sources—indeed, Kitamura says that some are very good about double-checking their information—most reporters assigned to the police beat are new and inexperienced and thus particularly vulnerable to manipulation by the police. Once a suspect is charged with a crime, moreover, it is actually illegal for journalists to interview that person, thus reinforcing the press's reliance on information provided by the police. Indeed, it is rare for Japanese crime reporters to write anything seriously critical of the police or to do any independent investigations of crimes.

Of course, when Japanese police–press club members do write negatively about their assigned law-enforcement agency, they naturally jeopardize their relationships with their primary sources, a difficult situation for a new reporter to be in. Needless to say, mutually beneficial police-media relationships develop naturally in other countries as well, the Jewell case being a prime example. But, in Japan these relationships are anything but informal. Rather, they are institutionalized and reinforced through the press club system, within which editors often coach reporters to create close, friendly relationships with their sources.

As noted previously, the dynamic of this uniquely Japanese arrangement deserves special attention from those interested in media ethics in the United States and throughout the world, especially in light of the United States government's embedding of reporters with American troops during the Second Gulf War, thus instituting a similarly intimate relationship between reporters and those responsible for implementing government public policy through force.

This is not to say that "embedding" is unacceptable, only that most embedded U.S. media outlets acted uncannily like Japanese press club members, who do not temper the information gleaned from their establishment sources with much in the way of outside material. As noted by many critics of the U.S. news media during the war, most outlets relied overwhelmingly on former and current U.S. military sources and analysts, so that the U.S. military point of view was emphasized far and away over nonestablishment sources. The problem lies not with using official sources and analysts, but with relying on them to the exclusion of others.

As in the Jewell case, the Japanese police had strong motivations for leaking information to the news media to the effect that they had identified a suspect. With seven dead and more than a hundred ill, the Japanese police may well have appeared inept were it widely known that they had no credible evidence, no significant leads, no idea what motivated the attack, and (for the first days, at least) no idea even what type of gas was involved.

Thus, the truckling behavior of the press served the police by keeping attention off their ineffectualness, just as the underhanded behavior of the police provided the press with a ready-made story. And just as in the Jewell case, the perfidious police-press alliance is self-reinforcing. American police are especially aware that if they don't provide a suspect of some sort, they are likely to be barraged with tough questions from a press corps hungry for a scoop. Even in Japan, where press clubs dampen the desire of mainstream news reporters to scoop one another and where few sources find themselves barraged with tough questions, law-enforcement officials are nevertheless certain to feel real pressure to look as if they are solving crimes, especially in high-profile cases, such as terrorist attacks. Unfortunately, rather than pressuring police to fully justify their implications against suspects, news-media members are often too quick to accommodate police sources. Journalists in both countries know that if they fail to use information leaked to them by the police, their chief source of information might well prove to be less than accommodating in the future.

Kono's Treatment by the Police

When Kono was finally discharged from the hospital on July 30, 1994, after a thirty-three-day stay, he was still recuperating, struggling with severe fatigue and other symptoms. But recovering from sarin-gas poisoning, caring for a comatose wife, and supporting three children were not the worst challenges before him.

Soon after his release, Kono was called to the police station, where he was aggressively interrogated and given a polygraph test. Kono explains that this experience transformed his thinking about Japanese law enforcement. "I was

released from the hospital on July 30th," he said. "Soon after, I was interviewed by the police, and through this experience I concluded that the police
are the people who produce criminals, not simply people who protect citizens. What they tried to do was force a confession out of me."[41]

Eventually, fed up with the aggressive questioning police were putting him
through, Kono demanded to see the evidence that the police claimed to have
against him, upon which the police abruptly released him. Kono explains that
of all the injustices done to him, the way the police treated his son, a teenager
at the time, was worst of all. "The most horrible thing for which I cannot forgive the police is that they had three policemen interrogate my [teenage] son,"
he recalled. "These officers told him that I had confessed and that he should
admit to the truth as well. This I cannot forgive. If my son had felt weak or
was swayed by the police, I would have been arrested that day."[42]

The police also leaked false stories to the press, such as the rumor that a
taxi driver had identified Kono as having bragged about his ability to make a
weapon "worse than an atom bomb."

According to Kono, one of the strangest aspects of his interrogation is that
the police presented him with newspaper clippings of stories such as the
Shukan Shincho pieces that recounted the very fabrications that they themselves had leaked to the media, as if to say, "Here is our proof that our accusations about you are true—they are in the newspaper." The police not only
manipulated the media to draw attention away from their fruitless investigation; they also manipulated the media into publishing their false theories,
which they then attempted to use against their suspect. Needless to say,
Kono's mistreatment by the police received no attention in the Japanese news
media during their investigation of him and only scant mention even after
he was vindicated. Not a single member of the press seriously investigated the
leaking of false information about Kono, and no police were ever held
accountable for having done so.

Unfortunately, this type of interaction between Japanese police and journalists fits with the understanding of scholars of Japanese media. Laurie
Anne Freeman, in her book *Closing the Shop: Information Cartels and Japan's
Mass Media,* notes that "criminal suspects in Japan have little opportunity
to voice their views once arrested, and since journalists are prohibited from

interviewing them (and are expelled from the club if they do), news stories are frequently based almost entirely on information handed to them by police officials in the relevant press club."[43]

This situation might seem shocking to readers in Western democratic countries were it not for events such as those following the initiation of the "War on Terror," in which the U.S. government has treated so many prisoners as badly or worse (not allowing them to visit lawyers or family members for years on end), and with little effective objection by mainstream journalists.

Kono Seeks Justice

Nine months after Kono, his wife, daughter, and neighbors were poisoned, on March 20, 1995, Aum Shinrikyo struck again, this time releasing sarin in the Tokyo subways in the midst of the morning rush hour. Twelve people died and some five thousand sought medical help, hundreds of whom were seriously injured. Other attacks soon followed: the attempted assassination of the chief of the National Police Agency, and more gas attacks on trains in the Tokyo-Yokohama area, resulting in still more deaths and injuries. When members of Aum Shinrikyo were finally prosecuted for the Tokyo attacks, a number of them confessed to having perpetrated the Matsumoto attack, thus officially vindicating Kono.

By coincidence, the day of the Tokyo attack was also the day that Kono brought his first lawsuits against the media. He sued *Asahi,* the country's second-largest and most prestigious daily newspaper. Ironically, Kono received a telephone call that very day from an *Asahi* reporter, who said, "Congratulations, Mr. Kono, you have been proven innocent by today's attack."[44]

Asked why he had singled out *Asahi,* Kono explained that it is widely considered the most prestigious paper in the country, and that by making an example of it in court, he could send a signal to the entire news industry.

In the end, Kono did not have to follow through with his suit against *Asahi,* as the newspaper readily agreed to his demand that it print an apology. Indeed, all but two of the many publications and broadcasters he demanded apologies from complied. The two that refused were the *Shinano Mainchi* newspaper—the most important regional newspaper in the Matsumoto area—and *Shukan Shincho.* According to Kono, *Shinano Mainchi* was at first only willing to publish what amounted to a partial apology and refused to admit its full culpability, so he took the paper to court. Eventually, he prevailed over *Shinano Mainchi* and forced a proper apology, but he never received a single yen in compensation from any Japanese publication for all they had put him through.

Kono explains that things went a bit differently with *Shukan Shincho*. He says that because *Shukan Shincho* published photographs of his ancestors, he demanded that the magazine do more than simply publish a written apology. He demanded that *Shukan Shincho* publish an apology featuring a photograph of their company president, Ryoichi Sato, as well as a photograph of the magazine's editor, Hiroshi Matsuda. He also requested that the magazine list its apology to Kono in its table of contents for that issue, as well as on the advertisements for the issue that were hung on trains and subways and reprinted in newspaper advertisements. Although *Shukan Shincho* refused to publish photographs of Sato and Matsuda, the magazine did eventually agree to publish a full apology in the president's name and to list it in the table of contents and in that issue's advertising campaign—a compromise that Kono reluctantly accepted.

But, when *Shukan Shincho*'s apology ran, it was in Matsuda's name only and not in Sato's, and was not listed in the table of contents or in its advertisements—omissions that Kono continues to resent. Moreover, with respect to the actual wording, Kono feels that rather than issuing a proper apology, what *Shukan Shincho* published was little more than a list of excuses.

"*Shukan Shincho* was the only publication that did not keep the promise it made in our dialogue," explained Kono in his interview for this book. In the end, he simply gave up in disgust.[45]

Asked about this situation in an interview for this book, *Shukan Shincho* editor Matsuda said that he knew nothing about it. According to him, as far as he knew, the magazine had done its duty by publishing the apology in his name—another prime example of the "shout of guilty, whisper of innocent" practice described by Wood. *Shukan Shincho* readers had been fed page after page of damaging photographs, hurtful headlines, and out-and-out lies about Kono, but once the truth was known, they saw nothing more than a single sedate apology. Moreover—and of no small consequence—headlines for many of *Shukan Shincho*'s false articles about Kono were also widely advertised on trains and in daily newspapers, each advertisement reaching between ten million and twenty million people.[46] Needless to say, *Shukan Shincho* failed to feature its apology to Kono in any of these ads, so only those who read the actual issue containing the apology were likely to see it—a tiny fraction of the tens of millions who read the many caustic headlines.

The most striking part of Kono's quest for justice was that he never received any monetary compensation from the Japanese press for all that it cost him, despite all that the various publications gained in running their false stories about him. In contrast, Richard Jewell has received unconfirmed damages of at least $2 million, and possibly more.

Asked why he only brought two suits (against *Asahi* and *Shinano Mainchi*) and why he settled for mere apologies from most of the publications rather than demanding financial satisfaction for the suffering they caused him, Kono explained that it would not have likely benefited him: "In Japan, even though you win in court, the damages you can receive are small. They are so small that even if you win, you may not be able to pay the court and legal fees that it cost you to win. Therefore, by suing somebody, you can actually damage yourself financially, even if you are victorious."[47]

As noted in the previous chapter, rewards for libel victims in Japan have increased somewhat in 2002 and 2003, since the Kono case. However, it still costs an average of about US$16,000 for a victim to retain legal counsel and to sue. Victims can only reasonably hope today, if victorious, to receive between US$10,000 to US$50,000. So, while the costs are quite substantial (at least to ordinary people), the financial risks for big media are virtually inconsequential. But, again, the situation was even worse when Kono was victimized. He could not even reasonably hope to recoup his legal expenses. Although the situation in Japan seems to have improved somewhat, in reality it is still weighted tremendously against regular citizens and in favor of big media.

The Birth of a Japanese Reformist

Before his ordeal, Kono had faith both in the reliability of Japanese journalism and in the righteousness of Japanese law enforcement. Now, however, he is skeptical of his country's news media and has concluded that Japanese police don't just capture criminals but also sometimes create them by forcing confessions.

As a result of this fundamental shift in his beliefs, Kono has made a career change, from salesman to full-time social reformist. He has written three books and coauthored two more with Kenichi Asano. He currently works with various organizations advocating media and law-enforcement reform, having become a popular public speaker. He also received the honor of an appointment as public-safety commissioner on Nagano Prefecture Governor Tanaka's local police-oversight board. Seats on such boards are traditionally given as political favors only and members of these boards are not expected to be of reformist inclinations, so the appointment underscored Kono's growing influence.

Kono has been the victim of three powerful forces: terrorist outlaws, the police, and the news media. When interviewed for this book, he was asked how he views these forces, to which he replied that he was most disappointed by his country's news media. "The Japanese media treated me worst," he said. "At least when the terrorists were caught, they expressed remorse for what they had done. And it made sense that the police would act aggressively in trying to catch the criminals. But it was the media's job to protect me, a common person. Yet they purposely attacked me. The media were definitely the worst."[48]

Helen Hardacre, director of the Edwin O. Reischauer Institute of Japanese Studies and a professor of Japanese Religions and Society at Harvard University, feels that the Japanese media bear some responsibility for the violence caused by Aum Shinrikyo. Writing in a Japan Policy Research Institute Working Paper entitled, "Aum Shinrikyo and the Japanese Media,"[49] Hardacre points out that—both before and during the investigation of the Matsumoto attack—the Japanese news media failed to properly investigate the Aum Shinrikyo group or to press the police to do so. In fact, as many commentators have noted, the Matsumoto sarin-gas attack was not Aum Shinrikyo's first serious criminal act, not the first time that the police failed to properly investigate the group, and certainly not the first time that the group had come to the attention of the national news media. The Aum Shinrikyo attacks have revealed serious and systematic problems with both the police and the news media.

Some Conclusions

The Jewell and Kono cases are eerily similar:

- Both Jewell and Kono were the first to report deadly terrorist attacks that claimed similar numbers of victims. (Seven were killed and 144 hospitalized in the 1994 Matsumoto sarin-gas attack in Japan; 1 was killed and 110 injured in the 1996 Olympics bombing in Atlanta.)
- Both attacks revealed critical public-safety issues concerning the vulnerability of each country to terrorism.
- Although neither man was ever arrested or formally charged with any crime, law-enforcement officials in both countries set off media campaigns against the men through the dubious practice of leaking incriminating information to reporters.
- Law-enforcement authorities in each country attempted to coerce confessions out of each man through unethical, if not illegal, means.
- Due to incorrect reporting in the news media, both men were widely assumed to be guilty in their own countries and throughout the world long after each event. Indeed, both men's reputations remain scarred to this day.
- Although various members of the media worked tirelessly to dig up and disseminate negative details of each man's personality and history, there was a dearth of reporting about the positive aspects of either man's character. As a result, both men's families have suffered tremendously.
- In both cases, the substantial time, money, and effort that the police and media dedicated to investigating these innocent men required resources that could have been allocated to following up other leads and in this way hindered the pursuit of the actual criminals.
- Incorrect reporting on both cases also took media pressure off law-enforcement officials who were stymied and unable to come up with legitimate suspects for some time afterward.

- Although there have been some token apologies in both cases, neither man has ever received a genuinely adequate apology, either from his government's top officials or from those specific media members who slandered him the worst.
- No media members or government officials in either country suffered any serious repercussions for their wrongdoing.
- No significant legal or other reforms have been implemented in either country that are likely to prevent similar or worse injustices against innocent citizens in the future.

With such a litany of similarities, one unavoidable conclusion from the Jewell and Kono cases is that law-enforcement authorities in both countries found it far too easy to place false information in the press. Reporters in both countries, in competition with one another and highly reliant on the authorities for easily collected information, happily accepted public statements and "anonymous leaks" with little skepticism or analysis. In this, journalists in both countries effectively supported the establishment powers while neglecting their duty to protect those without power, namely Jewell and Kono.

Both cases also reveal a serious lack of accountability, both in law enforcement and in the media. Although there was a hearing on the Jewell case held by the United States House Subcommittee on Crime of the Committee of the Judiciary on July 30, 1997, no significant investigation, report, reforms, or other significant action resulted. According to Wood, the hearing was little more than a "photo-op" for the committee members.

The dire lack of accountability in law enforcement is underscored by the decisions of both Jewell and Kono not to take any legal action against law enforcement, despite both men's strong feelings that police authorities had profoundly wronged them. Both men, after consulting with legal professionals, concluded that action against the authorities would be fruitless and prove little. To compound the matter, the media (with a few notable exceptions) have remained conspicuously silent about the lack of investigation by government officials into either the information leaks or the specious interrogations and shabby treatment of Jewell and Kono. In both cases, the news media supported grave failures by one of the most powerful forces in society: law enforcement. They did this not only by tolerating those failures but by cranking out the sensational information that distracted the public's attention from the truth of the situation as well as from broader issues.

Both the *Atlanta Journal-Constitution* and *Shukan Shincho* benefited considerably, at least in the short term, from printing sensational, inaccurate information about innocent men. Both publications struck postures of having produced hot scoops. Yet neither publication has been required to pay any compensation whatsoever to its victim.[50] Neither publication, moreover, has run any meaningful accurate, positive coverage that could be said to balance out the false, negative information that it printed previously.

From the victims' perspectives, it seems important to emphasize that both Jewell and Kono testified that they could have suffered far worse fates, perhaps even being found guilty of criminal charges, were it not for their good luck in quickly retaining excellent legal help. This point is particularly unnerving in the Kono case because it is so difficult for defendants in Japan to retain good legal counsel. The problem of access to legal representation has more immediacy now in the United States as well, especially when we consider the circumstances that led to the persecution of Kono and Jewell: high-profile terrorist attacks. Since September 11, 2001, the possibility of such attacks has been cause enough for the United States to hold hundreds of people—U.S. citizens, green-card holders, and foreign nationals alike—for years at a time without any legal representation whatsoever. Seen in hindsight, the unnecessary persecutions of Kono and Jewell seem to be forerunners of a dangerous trend that seriously threatens the rule of law in both countries.

It would be a misrepresentation of the facts, however, to imply that the degrees of injustice in the Kono and Jewell cases are equal. Although Professor Asano may be correct in his assertion there has been a "Japanization" or dumbing down of journalism in the United States, these case studies show that Kono was treated worse than Jewell. Without drawing too broad conclusions from these specific examples, we can nonetheless see at least three key points that show the Japanese press as significantly more dangerous and irresponsible than that of the United States, at least during the mid- to late 1990s.

First, Japanese news coverage against Kono was harsher and more sustained than U.S. news coverage of Jewell. For one thing, the mainstream press in Japan was typically uniform in its critical coverage of Kono, which lasted more than six months after the fact. In contrast, there was some diversity in the U.S. coverage of Jewell. ABC News, for instance, came to Jewell's defense (albeit three weeks after the fact). CBS News did likewise (albeit two months after the fact), and the *New York Times* showed comparative discipline in not jumping to conclusions and in holding stories. Also, in the extreme cases of negative coverage exemplified by the stories in the *Atlanta Journal-Constitution* and *Shukan Shincho*, the latter appears to have been the more malicious. Even though the *Atlanta Journal-Constitution* did run a comparison between Jewell and a convicted child murderer, this appeared in a relatively short feature column and was represented as the thoughts of one writer only. In contrast, *Shukan Shincho* presented its piece about Kono's "macabre family line" and other stories in lengthy, investigative-style news pieces, whose headlines were advertised nationally before tens of millions. This point also comes out in the distinct responses of the two victims. Whereas Jewell perceives U.S. law enforcement and news media to be equally to blame for his mistreatment, Kono has asserted that Japanese journalists were worse than the police— worse even than the violent terrorist group that left his wife in a coma.

Second, whereas Jewell was able to use the U.S. news media itself to help force public vindication (most effectively with his mother's appeal to the U.S. president and his interview with Mike Wallace), Kono was essentially a victim of the entire Japanese news media (with very few exceptions) until evidence implicating others in the crime came to light. In addition, even though no other suspect in the Olympic bombing case was caught until the summer of 2003 (when Eric Robert Rudolph was arrested), Jewell actually did receive some positive media attention relatively early on. If the Aum Shinrikyo group had not been involved in similar attacks later on, who knows when, if ever, Kono would have received a public vindication by the Japanese news media.

Professor Asano comments, "It was not long before the U.S. media started to correct their former news stories [about Jewell]. The U.S. media also tried to respond very quickly when Jewell was no longer a suspect. In contrast, it took nearly a year for the Japanese media to admit that their half a year of reporting was wrong."[51]

The third and perhaps most critical difference between the cases is that once he was vindicated, Jewell was able to use the U.S. courts and libel laws to receive financial compensation for the damages inflicted on him by the news media. Kono, on the other hand, has received no compensation for his suffering. Not only do U.S. media victims have a more realistic opportunity to recoup some of what was taken from them, but those awards seem to serve as a deterrent to libelous writing. In Japan, the possibility of compensation for slander victims remains slim. This has led to the situation in Japan in which many members of the press, particularly *shukanshi*, often find it more profitable to run libelous stories than accurate ones—"profit by libel." Thus, Richard Jewell eventually received some justice, whereas Kono received precious little. However, if Asano's observation that the United States media is becoming more like Japan's is true, as many believe is the case, then media victims in the United States ought to beware.

In both the United States and Japan, the news media can easily destroy the lives of innocent individuals. They may even profit handsomely from defaming the innocent, especially when such attacks benefit powerful establishment forces, such as law enforcement. Here it is also worth noting that neither the police nor the news media in either country appear to have had any confrontational relationship with Kono or Jewell before the incidents in question. Circumstances just happened to put these two ordinary citizens in vulnerable positions that police and journalists could exploit to their mutual benefit. One can only imagine their treatment had either of them been on confrontational terms with power holders—if, for instance, either had somehow been deemed to be a serious enemy of some sort.

CHAPTER FIVE

ANTI-SEMITISM IN A COUNTRY WITHOUT JEWS

So, I asked him, why would you run an article like this that denies the Holo-caust? And do you know what he said? He said, basically, that it sells magazines. That's it!

—Rabbi Abraham Cooper[1]

Japanese Anti-Semitism

When Westerners learn about the problem of anti-Semitism in the Japanese media, the question that almost invariably arises is, quite simply, why? After all, there are almost no Jews in Japan. The answers to this question provide many penetrating insights into Japan and the Japanese media; but perhaps more importantly, they also speak volumes about the nature of the mass media in modern democracies.

Of course, many Japanese, like people everywhere, consider bigotry of any sort repugnant, and indeed, full-fledged anti-Semites make up only a tiny minority of the population. Still, the relatively widespread disparagement of Jews in portions of the mainstream Japanese media is in many ways remarkable, as is the failure of other media members to repudiate the practice. Both phenomena continue to baffle many observers within and outside the country. Japan truly stands out as a non-Arab country with a significant amount of anti-Semitic writing and speech, but with few Jews.

According to some sources, of the 128 million people in Japan, only about 1,500 are Jews.[2] This means that only about .0016 percent of the population is Jewish, an essentially negligible demographic. Tom Brislin puts the total somewhat higher in his thorough 2003 study of Japanese anti-Semitism entitled "Anti-Semitic Articles and Books Not Uncommon in Japan." He says most Jews in Japan are businesspeople, students, and diplomats,[3] and there appears to be only a minuscule number of Japanese-born converts to Judaism. Nor has there ever been a significant Jewish population in the country.[4]

Japan further stands out among the world's major industrialized democracies—certainly among what were formerly called the Global Seven, or G7, countries (Canada, France, Germany, Italy, Japan, the United Kingdom, and the United States)—for its acceptance of anti-Semitic writing in its mainstream publishing. In these other countries, Holocaust denials and similar anti-Semitic tracts do show up occasionally, though only in extremist circles and not in the commercial press, which roundly condemns it. In Japan, however, when a Holocaust denial appeared in a popular weekly newsmagazine in the mid-1990s, none of the mainstream newspapers or broadcasters raised any meaningful voice of protest. In fact, Japan's major national dailies have long histories of carrying advertisements for anti-Semitic articles and books, although the practice has waned in recent years.

Examining how mainstream Japanese journalists could be so complicit in tolerating such egregious violations of decency on the part of their media colleagues is even more fascinating—and perhaps even more important than understanding anti-Semitism in Japan as a phenomenon in and of itself. For, ultimately, the worst "media atrocities," in Japan and throughout world history, have been made possible through the silence of those in the mainstream. Journalists, of course, are especially culpable in such situations, given their mission to collect and publish information relevant to the public good.

Denying the Holocaust

January 27, 1995, marked the fiftieth anniversary of the liberation of Auschwitz, the infamous Nazi death camp where a million Jews were murdered and which has become a world symbol of terror, genocide, and the Holocaust. To coincide with that event, the popular Japanese monthly newsmagazine *Marco Polo* published an article in its February 1995 issue (distributed in mid-January) denying the Nazi mass murder of six million Jews in camps such as Auschwitz. The article featured a gruesome photo of corpses of death-camp victims with the following caption spread across it:

> January 27 will be the fiftieth anniversary of the "Liberation" of the Auschwitz concentration camp. But this event conceals the greatest taboo of the postwar period. The fact of the matter is that significant doubt is now being cast on the "Holocaust," the theory that there was a mass murder of Jews.

Marco Polo was founded by one of Japan's leading publishing houses, Bungeishunju Ltd. In 1995, the monthly newsmagazine was edited by Kazuyoshi Hanada, a former editor of Bungeishunju Ltd.'s leading weekly newsmagazine, *Shukan Bunshun*. Excerpts from the five-page story, which led to the demise of *Marco Polo*, appear below:

THE GREATEST TABOO IN POST-WAR HISTORY:
THERE WERE NO NAZI GAS CHAMBERS[5]

by Masanori Nishioka

On January 14, the Auschwitz Concentration Camp commemorated the fiftieth anniversary of its "liberation.". . . In fact, the "Holocaust" (a theory of the Nazi genocide of Jews) is now beginning to be greatly questioned. It is indisputable that Jews died tragic deaths. But what is questioned is that there was a systematic genocide plan using gas chambers. No gas chamber was found from the concentration camps in the territories that belonged to the West after the war. . . .

I am sure that everyone will be surprised if I tell you that the story of genocide by gas, which has been told again and again for nearly fifty years, is in fact fabricated. I myself was astonished when I first read this story in English six years ago.

I am just a medical doctor who happened to get to know this controversy, and read some of the literature in Western languages. And I have become convinced of the following.

First, forget everything that the Japanese newspapers and TV say. Also forget for a moment *Schindler's List*. The "Holocaust" was a fabricated story. No gas chambers for execution existed in any concentration camp including at Auschwitz. The "gas chamber" that is open for the public at the former Auschwitz concentration camp in Poland was made up by either the communist regime in post-war Poland or by the Soviet Union who dominated the country. The "genocide of the Jews" by "gas chambers" had never occurred either in Auschwitz or any territory that Germany occupied during WWII.[6]

The author, Masanori Nishioka, states that he is in no way a "neo-Nazi" but simply a rational man, a medical doctor, who has studied the matter and whose research is based solely on facts and logic. This "reasonable-man" approach is common among historical revisionists and especially Japanese revisionists, who often graciously concede minor points only to argue strenuously for a broader picture that denies reality. The formula for this line of argument calls for the insertion of small bits of truth into an otherwise fallacious supposition. In this case, Nishioka admits that the Nazis "unfairly discriminated and oppressed Jews," only to insist later on that the Nazis never actually intended the systematic murder of the Jews. He says that the Nazis merely gathered the Jews together at places such as Auschwitz to "relocate" them.

Later in the article, Nishioka posits that it was impossible to kill large numbers of people with poisonous gas because, among other reasons, such gases are very difficult to produce. Ironically and tragically, on March 20, 1995—less than two months after the *Marco Polo* article first appeared—the effectiveness of murder by toxic gas was proved in the horrific Tokyo subway poison-gas attack (see chapter 3), in which twelve people died, hundreds were seriously injured, and five thousand required medical help. This issue of *Marco Polo*, moreover, came out during the same time period that Yoshiyuki Kono was being persecuted by the media for supposedly having created sarin gas in

This noteworthy piece of news-magazine journalism appeared in the February 1995 issue of *Marco Polo*, right alongside the Holocaust-denial story discussed in this chapter. The headline for the story reads "THE MATSUMOTO SARIN INCIDENT IS A TERRORIST'S CRIME: ASSOCIATE DEAN OF THE U.S. CHEMICAL WEAPON RESEARCH INSTITUTE CONDUCTS A THOROUGH VERIFICATION IN MATSUMOTO."

That this article could appear in the same magazine as a Holocaust denial is tragically ironic on at least two levels. First, had the Holocaust-denial not appeared with it, *Marco Polo*'s publisher, Bungeishunju Ltd., could have theoretically bragged about the fine achievement of having featured the story. Not only does it successfully identify the Matsumoto gassing as a terrorist attack—and not merely an "incident"—it explicitly warns Japanese readers that a future terrorist attack is likely. Tragically, just two months after this article hit newsstands, the same terrorists that gassed Kono and his neighbors perpetrated the famous Tokyo sarin-gas subway attack on March 20, 1995, just as Olson presaged.

The appearance of this article is also ironic in that one of the main premises of the Holocaust denial is that the gassing of Jews in mass numbers was, according to the article, not technically possible because poison gas is supposedly so difficult to manufacture and to handle properly. Yet as the same magazine highlighted, Kono had still not been cleared of having supposedly single-handedly gassed his wife and neighbors in an event that killed 7 and injured 110. Clearly, if the editors at Marco Polo were even mildly interested in double-checking the claims about poison gas put forth in the Holocaust denial, they could have easily asked Olson about the issue.

---

his home and then killing and injuring many of his neighbors. Amazingly enough, the very same issue of *Marco Polo* containing this Holocaust denial also included an excellent story about Kono's experience written by Kyle B. Olson, a United States expert in weapons of mass destruction. The article's title is translated into English as "The Matsumoto Sarin Incident Is a Terrorist's Crime: Associate Dean of the U.S. Chemical Weapon Research Institute Conducts a Thorough Verification in Matsumoto."[7] Not only did the article defend Kono and assert his innocence at a time when he had still not been cleared, it included a strict warning from its author to the Japanese that the perpetrators of the Matsumoto attack were probably still at large and likely to strike again. Indeed, had the February 1995 issue of *Marco Polo* not included Nishioka's abominable Holocaust denial, Bungeishunju Ltd. could well have boasted of having defended Kono while forewarning the nation that the Matsumoto incident was only a precursor of the more devastating attack that followed.

That such an excellent piece would be crammed inside a magazine cover next to Nishioka's propaganda is sadly typical of the unfortunate state of the Japanese magazine industry. While Olson relies on actual scientific data for his conclusions, Nishioka invokes lunatic-fringe rumors and hearsay to challenge the authenticity of the actual physical evidence of the Holocaust, including (but not limited to) the great piles of shoes and human hair of the victims, which were recorded in films that were shot immediately after the liberation of the camp. Nishioka writes:

> If I were to collect great quantities of shoes and hair and then go on a TV station and claim, "My neighbor transformed his bathroom into a gas chamber and is killing people," would they broadcast what I said as news? . . . This is the "Holocaust."
>
> The difference between the above story and the "Holocaust" is that those who said that they "found" piles of shoes and hair were not me, but the Allied forces. I do not think people would believe me if I showed shoes and hair, but when the Soviet Union did the same thing in Poland, the entire world did believe it. Why? Because the media all over the world broadcast it. I will not discuss the reasons why the world mass media, including the U.S. media, believed the Soviet announcement without scrutiny. But I want readers to notice the way that people believe weak "evidence," simply because it is reported by the mass media. That is what sustains the "Holocaust."
>
> Regarding the "gas chambers," there is no material evidence.

One of the more interesting assertions in this excerpt is Nishioka's statement, "I will not discuss the reasons why the world mass media, including the U.S. media, believed the Soviet announcement without scrutiny." The reason most revisionists claim that the media swallowed the supposed lie of the Holocaust is that they believe the world's media are controlled by a conspiratorial network of Jews. Unfortunately, anecdotal evidence does show that this myth is alive and well in Japan today, even outside revisionist circles.

Toward the end of his article, Nishioka almost casually questions the number of those killed in the Holocaust. He writes, "Six million as the number of the victims is also groundless. Someone has pointed out that there were only four million Jews in all the territories Germany occupied." Challenging the number of victims of an atrocity is a standard rhetorical tool implemented by historical revisionists throughout the world. This practice is especially common in Japan, as will be seen in chapter 7, which deals with the Nanjing Massacre. The goal is to reduce the number of fatalities to the point that the entire event can simply be dismissed as unremarkable. In the case of mass atrocities, this can be an effective ploy because the exact number of victims is often difficult to prove, thus opening the door for argument.

Note also the unnamed source ("someone has pointed out") of information on the Jewish population of the Nazi-controlled countries. Although Western reporters commonly cite unnamed sources, particularly in cases of government and corporate leaks, this nebulous reference to the source of hard demographic information represents a blatant omission to Western readers and would stand out like a sore thumb on the page. Unfortunately, this kind of spurious reference is standard practice among journalists in many Japanese weekly and monthly magazines. Similarly fudged references can even be found in the national dailies, where citation of sources is far less a formal practice than in the West. Although he is less than thorough in his citations, Nishioka appears to have drawn primarily from such internationally known Western deniers of the Holocaust as the California-based Institute for Historical Review and the infamous Fred Leuchter, whose work has been duly debunked and dismissed by Western mainstream scholars, historians, public officials, and others.

Nishioka closes his piece with the following words, once again relying on the "reasonable-man" approach to solicit empathy for his claims: "Because we who live now do not have the right to forget these tragedies, the truth must be revealed and lies should not be told. I want to dedicate this article to the souls of those who vanished as Jews in Auschwitz and other places."

Marco Polo

This article did not appear in some newsletter or Web site of the extremist fringe, popular only among hate groups. It was featured in *Marco Polo,* a glossy, influential newsmagazine widely available at newsstands throughout Japan and boasting a readership of a quarter million. Its well-known, powerful publisher, Bungeishunju Ltd., also publishes a long list of classic books including *Anne Frank's Diary*.

Marco Polo featured advertisements for luxury cars, airlines, credit cards, watches, clothing, and computers. According to the *Advertiser's Guide to Magazines in Japan* for 1993–1994, the magazine was aimed at younger businesspeople and dealt with "lifestyle, love, fashion, cars, entertainment, domestic and international politics and economy."[8] It was marketed to "an affluent, well-educated male audience" and resembled such American periodicals as *Esquire* and *Gentlemen's Quarterly*.[9] In fact, an earlier edition of the magazine carried, on its cover beneath its name, the following words in English (a mark of its internationalism and appeal to educated readers): "To Business People in Their 30's. MARCO POLO changes. We will make new Marco Polo more exciting and more useful than ever."

The magazine also gained a reputation for taking chances and challenging authority. For example, the previous issue of the magazine included a list of Japanese institutions *Marco Polo* pledged to investigate, including major political parties, media companies, religious groups, and corporations.

The Nishioka article was not presented as gossip or rumor, or even as an opinion piece, but as a featured, legitimate historic piece. It even included editorial comments, such as the extensive photo caption quoted earlier. An unspoken agreement between the magazine and its audience assumed that, at the very least, the article was based on more than the musings of a crackpot fascinated with American neo-Nazi propaganda. By running it, *Marco Polo*—and by extension Bungeishunju Ltd.—had essentially put its stamp of approval on the piece. And in so doing, the publishers fundamentally betrayed their readers' trust in favor of their own self-serving purposes—namely, to capitalize on a cultural undercurrent of stereotypes, hatred, and fear in order to sell more magazines.

Tom Brislin explains, "Because of the differentiated structure and values of the Japanese press system, conspiracism also has found a place in magazines that are within, or on the periphery, of 'mainstream journalism,' giving the articles the cachet of objective truth."[10]

Of course, as in all the *shukanshi* articles presented in this book, the *Marco Polo* piece's influence extended well beyond the magazine's circulation alone. Brislin emphasizes that the advertisements for the article were perhaps even more dangerous than the article itself. As has been noted, these advertisements reach tens of millions of Japanese who see them in public transportation and in daily newspapers.

Brislin interviewed Arie Dan, first secretary for press and information of the Israeli Embassy in Tokyo, on the matter in 1995. Dan noted that "Japanese high school students do not study World War II. They have no sense of their, or anyone else's, history," adding that in regard to *Marco Polo*'s "No Gas Chambers" story, "millions saw it—statements that 'There were no gas chambers. Jews are lying.'"[11]

Bungeishunju Ltd.

Bungeishunju Ltd.'s senior managing editor, Mitsuyoshi Okazaki, in a speech delivered at a media conference in 1995, claimed that *Marco Polo* "was not discontinued because the feature it carried was untrue" or because of the expected loss in advertising income resulting from the threatened curtailment of advertising support from various international companies. Okazaki went so far as to make the absurd claim that Bungeishunju Ltd. stopped publishing *Marco Polo* because the company had learned from "a certain source" that Japanese expatriates would be targeted by Jewish terrorists outside Japan because of the article.[12] In other words, he claimed that Bungeishunju Ltd. stopped publishing the magazine out of selfless patriotism to protect Japanese citizens from Jewish terrorists!

As it turns out, Bungeishunju Ltd. did not support Okazaki's statements and took actions to distance itself quickly from the article. In an interview for this book, Kengo Tanaka, then CEO and president of Bungeishunju Ltd., said that while he remembered that Okazaki's bizarre statement was made by "someone" at his company, he could not remember the details surrounding it. According to him, publishing the Holocaust denial was an error, fundamentally the result of a cultural and factual misunderstanding on the part of his editor, Kazuyoshi Hanada. Tanaka explained, "The article was definitely not an intentional insult to Jews. It was a signed article written by an outside

Kengo Tanaka is currently president of Japan Book Tokens Inc. He was the president of Bungeishunju Ltd. at the time that one of its many magazines, *Marco Polo*, ran a well-publicized Holocaust denial.

contributor. I'm not saying that that makes a big difference for the editor, Hanada. He obviously had the means and the ability to review the article before he printed it. He simply lacked the ability to go through it correctly."[13]

As dubious at this may appear, it is not entirely absurd for Tanaka to claim that Hanada, a seasoned editor of major national magazines in a country that is a major world power, may not have had the "cultural background" to fully understand the seriousness of a Holocaust denial. As we shall see, the Japanese concept of the Jewish experience is entirely different from the Western. In an interview for this book, Hanada made this very claim in his explanation of why he chose to run Nishioka's story:

> I personally read most of the manuscripts that come to the magazines I write for. I think most editors don't. At that time, I had only a general knowledge of World War II history, the same knowledge most Japanese have. I honestly had no prejudices regarding Jews. And I read the manuscript, and it included a lot of different things that were interesting to me, based on my knowledge. At least superficially, it seemed fairly intriguing. So I had a couple of my editors read the copy. And we evaluated the document, and the three of us shared our impressions with one another. So, we decided to ask Dr. Nishioka to explain some of the points we were unsure about. Over the course of the next five months, there was an exchange between Dr. Nishioka and our editors, and during this time Dr. Nishioka also went back to Auschwitz to do some more research. There was no plan to publish it on the anniversary of the liberation of Auschwitz. But we had an article that month that didn't come through. By this time we had decided it was a credible piece of research. So we published it.[14]

Actually, Hanada has apologized a number of times for this article—including in his resignation from the company. He further explained:

As I said, at that time I had a limited understanding of the subject, pretty much just what the average Japanese might have. I take responsibility for this, of course. I should have been more tuned in, especially in terms of the headlines and titles used. They were obviously excessive. So, I personally feel responsible for that. As a result I was released as editor in chief and I left Bungeishunju as well.... The point I really regret is my lack of understanding of the feelings of the Jewish people. I really understand this. In other words, if we had had a different understanding of the matter, a different story would have been published.[15]

Hanada's words notwithstanding, the article's caption announcing the anniversary of the liberation of Auschwitz forces one to wonder just how ignorant he and his staff really were about what they were publishing. In his interview for this book, he talked about having personally interviewed Holocaust survivor and Nazi hunter Simon Wiesenthal. Indeed, according to Hanada, he had written an unpublished article based on that interview around 1993, "because the movie *Schindler's List* was popular at about that time." According to Hanada, it was purely the result of chance that Nishioka's Holocaust denial made it into print, while his own Simon Wiesenthal interview article did not.

Additionally, in December of 1992, during *Marco Polo*'s first year of publication, before Hanada took the reins there in April of 1994, the magazine ran a piece about Auschwitz "from the eyes of a young Jew who visited there" entitled "'Auschwitz Hangs by a Thread': The Shadow Created by Poland's Democratization."[16] The article gives many details about the sufferings at Auschwitz during the war and makes the case that this international landmark to one of humankind's worst atrocities has been neglected by a cash-strapped Polish government. Perhaps the most striking thing about this article is that it is graphically designed and laid out in a manner very similar to the magazine's 1995 Holocaust-denying article. Both pieces use a faded photograph of corpses as a background on the opening page, and both use an identical shade of red as a highlight on their initial opening pages.

It could hardly be more indicative of Japanese journalism as a "profession" that a major national Japanese newsmagazine could run, within the span of

Pictured here are the opening pages of two articles from Bungeishunju Ltd.'s *Marco Polo* magazine. The top article from the February 1995 issue of the magazine denies that the Holocaust occurred. In contrast, the spread below it, from December 1992, discusses the reality of what actually did happen at the notorious Nazi death camp at Auschwitz. Note that while the two articles present diametrically opposed stories, they were laid out and graphically designed in a notably similar fashion. Both feature sensational images of corpses; and although they are reproduced here in black and white, they both also utilize what appears to be the identical shade of red as a highlight.

just two years and two months, both a well-done article sensitive to the victims and legacy of the Holocaust and an amateurish article denying the Holocaust, both focused on the Auschwitz death camp and both using similar graphics to illustrate their contradictory worldviews.

And while Hanada was not the editor in chief at *Marco Polo* at the time of the first article, whatever else might be claimed of him, the fact remains that he was a knowledgeable editor, working for one of the country's top publishing companies, with significantly more than a bare-minimum understanding of what he was publishing.

Indeed, despite all the interactions he has had with and about Jews since the demise of *Marco Polo*, including the loss of his job, Hanada still does not seem to understand the fundamental problem with Nishioka's article. Certainly, the fact that it deeply offended many people is an issue, and the fact that he has apologized for not understanding "the feelings of Jewish people" is significant. But, the real breach in journalistic ethics in the 1995 article was that it was false. Hanada put his thoughts on the matter as follows: "I do take issue in terms of the following, though. As to the propriety of handling that kind of topic in a magazine, I think it should be able to be discussed. Now, the U.S. media are said to be largely controlled by the Jews. And in Germany there are laws that prohibit dealing with these issues, which is probably understandable. What I question is whether or not there should be some reason not to discuss the topic at all in the media here in Japan. Again, I have to attribute my mishandling of the topic to my lack of understanding."[17]

Not only does Hanada not know better than to repeat, in an interview conducted by an American about his Holocaust-denial article, the false and ugly
stereotype that the U.S. media is "largely controlled by Jews," he misses the point
that the Holocaust did actually happen and that to deny that fact is simply an
untruth. In an interview with the Associated Press in 1995, he commented similarly, "It's not good for everything about a certain subject to be taboo. Maybe
Israelis and Japanese have different ways of thinking about that."[18]

As noted previously, in Japan there is a tradition wherein some individuals
hold a different concept of what "truth" is than do most Westerners. Instead
of relying on scientific-method-based rationale, the Japanese tradition sometimes ascribes greater value to "social truths" that are independent of observable phenomena or logic. This means that some journalists can sometimes feel
justified in recounting what various parties claim to be true, regardless of the
reality of the situation. As will be shown in subsequent chapters, Japanese
magazine writers and others regularly quote statements and assertions, which
are easily proven false by available observable, quantifiable data, simply
because those statements were uttered. Indeed, this is exactly what Hanada did
in running his Holocaust-denial story. In spite of having previously interviewed and written an article about Simon Wiesenthal himself, in spite of his
magazine having run an article about the truth of Auschwitz just two years
previously, and in spite of mountains of evidence available in books and articles, on the Internet, and elsewhere, Hanada chose to run Nishioka's false story.
And he continues to state his view that there is nothing wrong with publicly
debating whether or not the Holocaust happened. The indisputable fact that
it did happen is not as important, in his view, as the reality that quacks like
Nishioka want to deny it. Nishioka, and those like him, deserve no more attention than would someone who would deny that atom bombs were dropped
on Japan. It is a journalist's job to confront such individuals with facts and to
share those facts with the public, not to support such bogus theories by publishing them as sensational scoops. But determining whether Nishioka's claims
were based in any way in reality was obviously less important to Hanada than
the fact that the story was likely to sell magazines. When it comes to Japanese
magazine reporting, the truth is too often a secondary concern at best, and this
is why Hanada's expressions of regret, like those of his former employers at

Bungeishunju Ltd., focus on his "lack of understanding of the feelings of the Jewish people" and not on his failure as an editor and journalist to weed out a ridiculously fallacious article.

Moreover, as the case studies in this book clearly show, Hanada is not an anomalous Japanese magazine editor. For example, Bungeishunju Ltd. also has a storied history of denying Japanese atrocities committed during World War II, even in the face of irrefutable evidence. Seen in this light, *Marco Polo*'s denial of German atrocities is in many ways just another manifestation of this tradition.

Kengo Tanaka, a former Bungeishunju Ltd. magazine editor, lost his position as president and CEO of Bungeishunju Ltd. soon after the *Marco Polo* article. He also freely admits that he considers thoroughly documented World War II atrocities to be "debatable issues." He is also proud of the fact that his former company's magazines are strongly nationalistic, and he further explained in an interview for this book that "magazine journalism is inherently conservative and therefore inherently nationalistic. Now, it goes without saying that that can be in conflict with ideas of human rights."[19]

Like the editors and executives at *Shukan Shincho*, Tanaka has come out strongly against the idea that journalists should strive after idealistic goals. For him, journalism is a practical job—much more a trade than a profession—and there is nothing wrong with writing news stories with the express intention of supporting nationalism. "It is in fact more dangerous when a journalist is imbued with a sense of justice. That's because justice can at times assume the work of the devil,"[20] he says.

The Simon Wiesenthal Center

The Simon Wiesenthal Center, an international Jewish advocacy center headquartered in Los Angeles, played the linchpin role in rebutting the *Marco Polo* article and thus in shining a light of international scrutiny on Japanese journalism. Simon Wiesenthal was a Holocaust victim who survived many Nazi persecutions, including internment in a concentration camp. Eighty-nine members of his family and his wife's family died in the Holocaust. An architect by training, he gave up his profession after the war and became engrossed in a quest for justice that focused on seeking out and assembling evidence against Nazi war criminals. Wiesenthal's efforts led to the 1960 capture of Adolf

Eichmann, chief of the Gestapo's Jewish Department, who was responsible for the implementation of the so-called Final Solution to annihilate the Jews.

The Simon Wiesenthal Center describes itself as "an international Jewish human rights organization dedicated to preserving the memory of the Holocaust by fostering tolerance and understanding." The center, founded in 1977, has a membership of 400,000 and offices in cities around the world. Located amid the urban sprawl of greater Los Angeles, its headquarters are next to the well-known Museum of Tolerance, which offers interactive exhibits designed to spur ethical thinking about the nature of prejudice. One of the centerpieces of the museum is a walking tour through exhibits that portray the evolution of anti-Semitism in Germany leading up to the war.

Rabbi Abraham Cooper, associate dean of the Wiesenthal Center, has actively opposed anti-Semitic writing in Japan for more than a decade. His office overlooks the entrance to the Museum of Tolerance. In an interview for this book, he shared many intriguing insights based on his years of close experience with both anti-Semitism and the Japanese news media. Because his insights into the industry are so relevant, extensive selections from that interview are quoted here. Extraneous information has been deleted for readability:

Q. Could you talk a little bit about the Simon Wiesenthal Center's dealings with Japanese anti-Semitism?

A. First of all, I want to say that I'm an admirer of Japan. I like the Japanese people a lot. I've been there about twenty-five times. There are vast cultural differences, which sometimes make our relationship a self-perpetuating cycle that needs to be broken. I don't pretend to know what makes that place tick. But if you are looking for commonality, baseball is a great place to start. I love Japanese baseball. . . .

At any rate, our approach to this whole thing has been to acknowledge that there are universal truths. There are universal values. If you really believe in universal truths and you have a deep respect and acknowledge that there are cultural gaps and differences between Japan and the U.S., then you have a place to start.

As for Japanese anti-Semitism, it's unusual. There are only about fifteen hundred Jews living in Japan. When you [as a Jew] get off the plane, there is no issue. When you walk around Tokyo, other than being an Anglo, no one looks twice at you. Nobody knows what a Jew is there.

But they still seem to have Jews on the brain. It's this sort of conspiratorial, overblown thing. No one can get a real handle on it.

You know, the whole idea of the museum is personal responsibility, personal empowerment. Unfortunately, these are not always universal values in Japan.

As for the Simon Wiesenthal Center, what you see is what you get. We are what we are. Whether we are giving a fun lecture to a receptive crowd or having a contentious discussion with a messenger for the chairman of the board of Bungeishunju, our message is more or less the same. We expect mutual respect. If you are a media corporation, you are expected to have integrity and honesty; and if you cross the line, you are going to hear from us.

Q. What was your first experience with anti-Semitism in Japan?

A. The first incident occurred, I believe, when [the financial newspaper] *Nikkei* ran a full-page ad on *Protocol*-type books [books based on the infamous anti-Semitic tract *Protocols of the Elders of Zion*, which alleges an international Jewish conspiracy bent on controlling the world]. We protested to them. The Japanese Foreign Ministry found out about it, and we were invited to go to Japan.

There we met with the board of *Nikkei*. They bowed. They apologized.

We asked for a meeting with the guys that run their advertising department. But when we met with them, it became very clear that they had no idea why we were upset. In other words, the people placing the advertising said, "Our job is to place advertising. Why would we have an obligation to check the content of the ad? It's not our job to check the content of an ad. This is how we pay for our paper. Someone pays us for the ad; the ad goes in. Why are you upset with *Nikkei* over our printing ads for anti-Semitic books?"

The whole idea of corporate responsibility simply isn't there.

Now, don't get me wrong, these are very capable people. Many media people work fourteen or eighteen hours a day—whatever it takes to get the job done. But the whole concept of connecting an individual's responsibility to the corporate just isn't there. Committees and group decisions are part and parcel of the way things are done. Personal responsibility and initiative are not valued.

I would say that part of the reason that the number of incidents of Japanese anti-Semitism have gone down in recent years, besides the obvious fact that they don't want the negative publicity or the headaches that go with publishing this stuff now, is that there is some growing understanding of what bugs human-rights groups and the Jewish community. It doesn't negate all incidents, but it helps. I guess the culminating incident was the *Marco Polo* magazine article. As it turns out, it was a watershed.

Rabbi Abraham Cooper of the Simon Wiesenthal Center led the international protests against *Marco Polo* magazine's Holocaust denial.

Q. How did your involvement with the matter unfold?

A. The *Marco Polo* article came almost simultaneously with the terrible January 1995 earthquake. What I usually did when a publication like the *Marco Polo* article came out was to make a courtesy call to the Japanese ambassador in Washington. But in this case, I knew his office would be very busy fielding phone calls from family members. . . .

What happened was that our source in Japan brought the article to my attention. So I asked the source to translate the ads for the major advertisers in that issue of the magazine: Volkswagen, Cartier, Mitsubishi Motors, some others. The Wiesenthal Center then forwarded a copy of the article with a translation of it to each of the CEOs of all those corporations with advertisements in the issue. We accompanied it with a note signed by me, basically saying, "This is what happened. It's the fiftieth anniversary of the liberation of Auschwitz, and this is the material your advertising dollars are supporting. Do you want to be supporting this?" [See appendix C for a copy of this letter.]

If I remember correctly, we sent these out on a Tuesday. By that Thursday night, I got a call from a Japanese guy. He said, "I'm the new North American representative for Bungeishunju, and I must see you as soon as possible. I must fly out to L.A. to see you tomorrow."

And I said to him: "What's Bungeishunju?"

I had literally never heard of the company before. . . . Anyway, we spoke, and he said he had a letter from the chairman of Bungeishunju that he wanted to deliver to me.

We met the next day, at which point he gave me a letter of apology from Kengo Tanaka, Bungeishunju's president and CEO. He also brought me official notice that *Marco Polo* magazine was being closed down and that all its 130 employees were being reassigned throughout the Bungeishunju. It was only at that point that I began to piece together what had happened.

As it turns out, one of the first people who responded to our letter about their article was the chairman of Volkswagen, in Germany, where it is illegal to publish something denying the Holocaust. Well, he didn't need any prodding from the Wiesenthal Center. What I am given to understand is that the CEO of Volkswagen contacted the CEO of Bungeishunju directly and told him what he thought. This was a big deal, because Volkswagen was buying advertising not just in *Marco Polo* but also in forty-one of Bungeishunju's publications. Apparently, a number of companies all weighed in, and the implication was clear: that Bungeishunju's entire empire could crumble because these advertisers were going to walk, and not just from one publication but from their entire relationship with Bungeishunju.

And then you start to do some research, and you find out that the Bungeishunju also publishes *Shukan Bunshun*, which denied the rape of Nanjing, that the company was a big supporter of the militarists during the war, and then, of course, there was a very quick learning curve. . . .

I told Bungeishunju that I was very concerned that many people at their company could be thrown out of work. I told them that we should have a press conference explaining to the world that we are no longer at war.

So they asked when it would be good for Mr. Tanaka to come here for a press conference. I explained that we definitely wanted Mr. Tanaka to visit the Museum of Tolerance, but that there was no reason for him to come here for a press conference. I said we should do a joint press conference in Tokyo.

Now, the reason I knew enough to make that suggestion is that we had experienced enough of the bait and switch of the Japanese media on all of these issues in the past. It works like this: They make great statements in the U.S., where all the American papers cover everything they say. But when you ask for printouts of what the five major daily papers in Japan have run on these same U.S. press conferences, the answer is zippo. The U.S. press conferences don't get mentioned back in Japan. I wasn't going to play that game again.

So we held a press conference in a major hotel in Japan with four hundred members of the press there. It was in simultaneous translation. Everybody was there. It was a two-and-a-half-hour thing. And, again, in some ways I was just an observer. The thing built up slowly, so that the toughest questions only came to Tanaka after two hours, becoming more and more personal toward him. My thing was just to announce that we had a truce.

Q. What kinds of questions were asked?

A. The first question to me was from a Japanese reporter. He asked, "Doesn't this press conference prove Jewish power?"

I said, "You know, there's a Japanese writer named Masami Uno who wrote all these best-selling Japanese books in the 1980s about the Jews and Jewish conspiracies. He blames the Jews for every Japanese problem. He is a total, visceral anti-Semite and very popular. As you know, the Japanese love to read. Love culture. Love literature. So it's really disappointing to see all these publications attacking Jews, attacking Koreans, attacking any ethnic group. It can be a crushing experience. . . ."

So anyway, at the press conference I pointed out that none of the chairmen of any of the major corporations that the Wiesenthal Center contacted [about the *Marco Polo* article] were Jews. I said that this press conference is about a publishing company that knowingly took a piece of hateful propaganda, promoted it, and published it. That violates the basic, universal responsibilities of the media. That was the point.

Now, I would say that 99 percent of the people at the press conference understood what I said, but I think that at least a few of them were still wondering. . . .

Q. So what happened after the press conference?

A. I'm still not entirely sure about their motivation in running the article in *Marco Polo*. I guess Jews still sell. I never really got a full answer. I understand the editor was a very respected guy in Japan. Kazuyoshi Hanada. He was no small guy.

But we asked for more than just an apology. These tend to be very talented people in their fields. So we came in and did some courses for 130 of Bungeishunju's top executives, including the editor, Hanada. Actually, Hanada was interesting. For the first full three days, he just sat in the back of the room with his feet up. Then, out of nowhere, at the end of the whole course, he volunteered the fact that he had been to Auschwitz and that he was very moved by what he saw there.

So, I asked him, why would you run an article like this that denies the Holocaust? And do you know what he said? He said, basically, that it sells magazines. That's it!

The very last question we were asked by one of their executives, after we got through with our entire presentation at Bungeishunju, and it was a really heart-felt question, was, "Why did you contact the advertisers in our publications?"

The man just didn't understand. Finally, I just had to say, "Because it works."

Q. Are you saying that the primary motivation for the *Marco Polo* article was commercialism?

A. You know, along the way we learned that there are virtually no subscriptions for these Japanese magazines. Each issue is basically do-or-die. It's just an unbelievable sword hanging over the heads of all the people in the magazine industry. It's unbelievable. If you don't have something to bring people to your magazine this week, forget about it.

When I was at Bungeishunju, I asked to see their operation and was given a complete tour. One of their entire floors is dedicated to the publication of kids' books. Just children's books. So I take a look in, and they're working on a book on Mother Teresa. Mother Teresa! It was a good-looking book. And suddenly it occurred to me that some people in that company truly understand what a quality publication is. It's very interesting....

Q. Kengo Tanaka [then president and CEO of Bungeishunju Ltd.] still stands by his statement at the time that the editor, Kazuyoshi Hanada, was "just unlucky" to have lost his job over the *Marco Polo* piece. According to Tanaka, Hanada just made an honest mistake based on his misunderstandings of history. Do you know about this comment?

A. All I can say is that if you are asking what the bottom line is, the bottom line is that it's a global village. If they cross the line and make an attack against our community, they are going to hear from us, and it's going to be very unpleasant.

Q. So do you think the Wiesenthal Center has made progress with Japanese anti-Semitism?

A. What we are interested in are things like the Friedleburger Brandeis Children of Terezin presentation, currently being held at the Tokyo Fuji Art Museum. Or our traveling exhibition of Anne Frank and the Holocaust that's been going since 1994. About 1.8 million Japanese people have seen it. That's the stuff away from the headlines. That's the kind of educational work we want to do in Japan. It's things like that that make a difference.

Part of the reason that I am upbeat about Japan these days is that we found good people there, people like Daisaku Ikeda and the Soka Gakkai, that support what we are doing. The Japanese have so many strong points. The fact is that good people will find each other.

You know, the whole ideal of the rainbow is diversity. God does not want everybody to be that one ray: red, black, green, white. The whole idea is the refraction of light. It is in diversity that we find each other. That is how I try to approach Japan. I know I will never really understand that place. But if I believe there are universal truths that shine through, I will find people that relate to them—and I have.

The Japanese, regardless of whatever they did to their neighbors, they harbored more than twenty thousand Jews during the Second World War. They turned down the Nazis who wanted these people sent back to them.

The explosion of interest in [Chiune] Sugihara has also helped a lot. He is known as a sort of Oskar Schindler of Japan for having helped Jews escape

Europe. Last year, we showed a documentary on Sugihara at the Diet. It was amazing. At the event, one of the more senior LDP [Liberal Democratic Party] guys came up to me with tears in his eyes. He was so moved. He said to me, "This is the first time in my life that anyone outside of Japan has ever come here and held up a Japanese citizen, not just for financial accomplishments but for humanitarian actions."

Q. What is your overall assessment today?

A. The good news is that for the most part we've been able to focus more on the proactive good stuff. The bad news is that among certain elements in Japan, the stereotype still is that Jews control Washington and that if you want something from the U.S. you have to go through the Jews.

The ratio of insane books about Jews and Judaism to legitimate books about Jews and Judaism has also gone way down.

Still, I don't want to dismiss the situation and pretend we don't have a problem anymore. We do. Recently I did an interview with one of the monthly newsmagazines, *Foresight* [published by Shinchosha Ltd., the publisher of *Shukan Shincho* weekly newsmagazine]. *Foresight* basically e-mailed me eight questions, very straightforward questions about anti-Semitism in Japan, to which I wrote up responses. They published exactly what I said, exactly. They didn't change a single word. But then, right after my piece they put in a commentary basically saying that they are sick and tired of having to worry about the Jews telling them what they can and cannot print.

It's a classic Japanese media thing. They place a perfectly legitimate story right next to one that's completely absurd. . . .

The Asia and Pacific Rim Institute

The Simon Wiesenthal Center has received a lot of attention for its work against anti-Semitism in the Japanese media, particularly with the *Marco Polo* magazine issue, but they are not alone in their work. The American Jewish Committee (AJC), the oldest Jewish human-rights group in the world, has been grappling with the same issues in Japan for even longer than the Wiesenthal Center. The AJC developed its Asia and Pacific Rim Institute in 1989, as an arm of the committee, to challenge anti-Semitism in Japan and throughout Asia. Since August 2002, the institute has been monitoring the Japanese media on a daily basis, not only to keep track of straightforward anti-Semitism but also to understand better how the Israeli-Palestinian conflict is being portrayed there.

Whereas the Simon Wiesenthal Center concluded that the *Marco Polo* magazine issue required an aggressive response, the Asia and Pacific Rim Institute has kept its focus on a less-confrontational approach. Neil Sandberg, founder of the Asia and Pacific Rim Institute, explained in an interview for this book that he has been to Japan some twenty-five times as part of AJC delegations entrusted with the goal of building long-term relationships with key Japanese leaders:

> The delegations consist of AJC leaders, so they include people active in their professions: lawyers and business leaders as well as some academics and intellectuals. We meet with counterpart groups in Japan. The foreign minister has been very helpful from the start. We pointed out to them that the widespread presence of anti-Semitic writing in Japan was creating a hostile atmosphere toward Japan in the U.S. Of course, they want to be friends, and we do too. And they also understood that we are a prominent group in the U.S., so they paid attention to us.[21]

According to Sandberg, work has been slow and steady for his institute but has nevertheless yielded powerful long-term results. In particular, he takes credit for helping to expedite the end of the Japanese embargo of Israeli goods, as well as for helping to build business relationships between the Japanese and Israelis.

Regarding anti-Semitic writing in the news media, Sandberg says that one of the first things his institute accomplished was to have a meeting with the Japan Newspaper Publishers and Editors Association (Nihon Shimbun Kyokai [NSK]) in the early 1990s. "I had what I thought was a historic meeting with them on issues of free speech. The AJC strongly supports free speech. But we pointed out that no major publisher in the U.S. would publish a book that denies historical fact. You don't make a living by publishing racist or bigoted literature."

According to Sandberg, a lot of Japanese anti-Semitism is borrowed racism. "As we looked at it more closely, we found that in Japanese culture, the acquisition of many things reflected what was happening in Europe and the U.S. The Japanese noted a certain degree of anti-Semitism generally in the U.S., so they felt free to print it there."

Another influence, Sandberg notes, is that the Japanese do not have a strong tradition of multiculturalism:

> Diversity is not an understood concept in Japan. Contrary to what some Japanese might say, they are not a monolithic culture. They have a large Korean population, for instance, and there are other regional differences. But in fairness, they are a relatively uniform population, one where conforming to a cultural standard or norm is the way. If you don't conform to it, you can be looked down upon. They also have a history of not getting along with other countries. So when it comes to foreigners, they don't really know how to deal with us. I think Japanese anti-Semitism can be a result of this.

Sandberg also notes two other motivations for Japanese anti-Semitism. One is the purely commercial basis for such writing. "There is a tradition in the Japanese media of paying attention to exotic and different and sensational things.... Anti-Semitism fits into that tradition." Also, he notes, many Japanese simply do not understand what a Jew actually is, and thus they mistakenly confuse the term with all things Western.

Sandberg offers the story of a prominent Japanese businessman, whom he prefers not to name. This man wrote a number of topical books, with such titles as *Get Rich Like Jews*. When Sandberg met the man, it quickly became clear that he had a great affinity for Westerners and Jews. He even went so far as to describe himself as a "Japanese-Jew," pointing out how much he loved Western architecture, food, culture, and the like. As amazing as it may seem, it had never occurred to this man that his writing could be perceived as anti-Semitic until Sandberg pointed out to him that his books were encouraging negative stereotypes of Jews as greedy people. According to Sandberg, from that time forward, the man never wrote a similar book.

A number of Japanese observers have noted that while the Wiesenthal Center had great success in challenging the *Marco Polo* magazine article, it was not without negative backlash. Sandberg, for one, says that many Japanese journalists now tend to avoid writing anything about Jews altogether, positively or negatively, because they do not want to risk offending Jewish groups. Some say that this has led to even more ignorance in Japan regarding Judaism. "The missing element remains: the disseminating of positive articles and images, a difficult prospect in the face of a publishing philosophy that it is better, and safer, to print nothing," says Tom Brislin.[22] Moreover, a number of Japanese journalists have characterized the Wiesenthal Center's actions as an immoral threat against free speech in their country—one that has created new resentments against perceived "Jewish power."

Still, most would agree that the Wiesenthal Center did far more good than harm. Both Sandberg and Rabbi Cooper say that there has been a general shift away from anti-Semitic writing in popular Japanese publications since the early 1990s, although the problem still exists and deserves attention.

Shutting Down *Marco Polo*

The official position of Bungeishunju Ltd. was that it cancelled *Marco Polo* in response to the threat of international advertisers to withdraw their advertising budgets from all Bungeishunju Ltd. publications. The move was put forth as a sign of the sincerity of the publisher's regrets that such an article was published in the first place. Some have described it as a "ritual magazine suicide"[23] performed to save the face of the publisher (as a shamed Samurai might "save" his family's name or lord's reputation by committing hara-kiri).

However, as pointed out by Rabbi Cooper, no one ever asked for the cessation of the magazine, a move that has led to a significant amount of resentment on behalf of Japanese who feel that Bungeishunju Ltd. was forced to do so by Jewish pressure and that Jewish groups went too far in their response to the article. Indeed, the ridiculous comment by Bungeishunju Ltd.'s senior managing editor, Mitsuyoshi Okazaki, that the magazine was closed to avoid the supposed danger of Jewish terrorists responding violently to it against Japanese citizens is an extreme example of this sentiment.

As noted, one result is the general avoidance by Japanese journalists and others of articles of any type (positive or negative) about Jews.

The slick, attractive cover of this February 1995 issue of *Marco Polo* belies the fact that it carries a serious ten-page Holocaust-denial article based mostly on Western neo-Nazi and white-supremacist propaganda. In addition to the anti-Semitism featured, a number of other articles in it are typical of Japanese magazine publishing and are worth a brief examination. The headlines on the cover are:

- "THE MATSUMOTO SARIN INCIDENT, ELUCIDATING THE TRUTH"
- "REPUTATION OF THE MAN THAT HONAMI SUZUKI CHOSE"
- "JAPAN'S 'DARK SOCIETY' WHITEPAPER ON CRIMES BY FOREIGNERS, AN ALL-OUT FEATURE: IS IT O.K. TO LET THIS MATTER TAKE ITS COURSE?"
- "SPEED A GREAT HIT, AN EXCLUSIVE INTERVIEW WITH KEANU REEVES"
- "THE COMPLETE LIST OF 150 FAMOUS FOLLOWERS OF NEW RELIGIONS: THEIR MOTIVATIONS FOR JOINING, A HISTORY OF THEIR ACTIVITIES, AND THEIR LEVELS OF CONTRIBUTIONS"

Notice that the top story listed here is a solid piece of journalism. Written by a U.S. weapons expert, it strongly vindicates sarin-gas victim Yoshiyuki Kono of the Matsumoto gassing that he had been falsely accused of perpetrating (see chapter 4). Published about two months prior to the Tokyo sarin-gas attack of March 20, 1995, the author goes so far as to warn the Japanese that another attack is imminent.

In contrast to this excellent article, of course, is the lighter material featured on the cover regarding actress Naomi Suzuki's romantic life and actor Keanu Reeve's latest movie, *Speed*.

Unfortunately, not all of the material is as innocuous. The cover also features—in the largest type size of all—the headline for a typically Japanese xenophobic article, about the supposedly problematic issue of crimes committed by foreigners in the country. Actually, this claim is anything but unique to *Marco Polo* and has been perpetuated by the government for years, "despite incontrovertible evidence that foreign crime rates are actually lower than those of Japanese," says the *Japan Times* in an October 7, 2003, article entitled "Time To Come Clean on Foreign Crime Wave." The *Japan Times* article says that foreigners are less likely to commit crimes in Japan than Japanese citizens, but that the Japanese government propagates fear of foreigners as part of its "tough on crime" posturing.

Similarly, the last story highlighted on the cover also singles out a "nonmainstream" segment of Japanese society. The piece focuses attention on "famous people" who belong to so-called new religions. Related to anti-Semitism in the Japanese news media, there is also a noteworthy trend toward negative coverage of domestic minority religious groups, which are regularly treated with distrust and disdain.

Another theory is that at least some executives at Bungeishunju Ltd. were happy to use the debacle as an excuse to cancel *Marco Polo*, which had been underperforming financially anyway. Editor Kazuyoshi Hanada, for example, did not deny the credibility of such a theory when interviewed about it for this book, noting that while circulation had improved under his leadership, it was not ideal.

Tom Brislin has put forth the idea that the cancellation of *Marco Polo* was at least in part the result of the inability of Bungeishunju Ltd. executives to effectively handle such a direct confrontation from outsiders, as well as from forces inside Japan. Brislin, among many others, questions the publisher's move. Would it not have been far more productive for a subsequent issue of the magazine to have included an apology as well as articles explaining where the magazine had erred, how it planned on improving, even some accurate pieces about the horrors of the Holocaust? Unfortunately, Bungeishunju Ltd. was quick to dash such possibilities. By shutting the doors of the magazine, it also effectively shut down the issue. And, it must be said, the international community, in allowing such a form of "apology," missed an opportunity.

Shukan Post's Jewish Financial-Conspiracy Theory

In 1999, the most widely read Japanese weekly newsmagazine, *Shukan Post*, ran a blatantly anti-Semitic article. Through advertisements in the country's major daily newspapers and on the subways and trains, *Shukan Post* proclaimed that its upcoming issue would reveal the way that Jews had recently taken control of billions of dollars of Japanese taxpayers' funds. When the issue finally hit the newsstands, the five-page article sported the headline:

FINALLY UNVEILED!
THE HUMAN NETWORK OF JEWISH CAPITAL THAT DEVOURS
FIVE TRILLION YEN OF OUR HARD-EARNED TAXES
THROUGH THE LONG-TERM CREDIT BANK OF JAPAN[24]

Amazingly enough, the actual text barely mentions Jews. The article claims that by "tracing the network involved in the buyout we have discovered the shadow of Jewish capital looming [over the deal]. What are they after, now that they've succeeded in establishing a beachhead in Japan?...By examining sources in both Japan and the U.S., we have uncovered the reality behind the takeover that you won't find in your daily newspaper."[25]

The vast bulk of the article was about fairly standard political-influence peddling, and, in fact, the word "Jew" was not even used until the last page. Even then, the supposed connection between influence peddling and Jews was not substantiated in any way. The reason for this is that the article's author, Takao Toshikawa, did not originally prepare the piece as an anti-Jewish article or even as an article about Jews. It was first published as a straight economic article in the New York–based economics newsletter *The Oriental Economist*.[26] As written by Toshikawa, the article was a legitimate exploration of the political ties between Ripplewood Holdings, the equity fund that spearheaded a takeover of the Long-Term Credit Bank of Japan (LTCBJ), and leaders of the Democratic Party in the United States. Unfortunately, after Toshikawa provided the article to *Shukan Post*, the editors there saw fit to

The headlines in this image may or may not be reliable.

Shown here is the October 15, 1999, cover of *Shukan Post*, Japan's number-one-selling weekly newsmagazine, with a readership that has fluctuated between six hundred thousand and more than a million. The large headline running vertically along the right edge reads "FINALLY UNVEILED! THE HUMAN NETWORK OF JEWISH CAPITAL THAT DEVOURS FIVE TRILLION YEN OF OUR HARD-EARNED TAXES THROUGH THE LONG-TERM CREDIT BANK OF JAPAN."

Once inside the magazine, readers are treated to the article that starts with the page spread pictured here. Although then–Vice President Al Gore is not Jewish, he is identified in the piece as a pivotal player in the supposed "Jewish conspiracy."

ostensibly transform it into a Jewish-conspiracy piece by adding the gratuitous headline and a short section at the end of the piece blaming the whole thing on Jews.

Among those implicated as being part of this so-called "Jewish connection" were U.S. Vice President Al Gore and Ambassador Tom Foley, neither of whom is Jewish. Not only did the *Shukan Post* use a drummed-up racist theory to hype the article, it also misled its readers, who expected to read a piece focused on such connections but instead found an article about run-of-the-mill Washington influence peddling, with only a passing mention of Jews. The article reads, in part:

> What all the parts of this network of brokerage houses and investment banks that surround Ripplewood Holdings and support [Vice President Al] Gore have in common is that they are Jewish. In other words, the strong will of Jewish finance capital, which prides itself on its enormous power and which has constructed a network that covers the world's financial markets like a fine net, was behind the buyout of the LTCBJ.[27]

As is always the case with the weeklies, the damage came not just from the article itself but from the magazine's advertisements. In fact, the advertisement for this article took the most prominent place in the week's ads for *Shukan Post* and featured Al Gore's face under the headline.

TV Asahi Commentator Claims Jews Control U.S. Media

One of the most recent incidents of Japanese anti-Semitism in the mainstream media occurred near the end of 2001, not two months after the terrorist attacks of September 11, and concerned the anthrax mailings in the United States at that time. A regular commentator on TV Asahi's *Super Morning* show, Koji Kawamura, asserted on the air that the "common thread linking the targets of anthrax attacks was that they were Jews" and declared that "Jews were targeted for anthrax attacks because they control the U.S. media."[28]

Interestingly, none of the early victims, nor any of the prominent personalities who were targeted (such as NBC's Tom Brokaw or U.S. Senate Majority

Leader Tom Daschle), was Jewish. Ultimately, it is difficult to judge which is most outlandish: the claim that Jews control the U.S. media, the factually incorrect statement that the anthrax terrorist targeted Jews, or the fact that a popular commentator could make such claims on Japanese national television without losing his job or otherwise being seriously publicly reprimanded. At the end of 2002, Kawamura refused repeated requests for an interview for this book on the grounds that his schedule of television appearances was too heavy.

To make the TV Asahi matter worse, the apology, signed by Masao Asano, director of public relations for the entire Asahi National Broadcasting Company, stated (in English that had not been thoroughly proofread): "There is no doubt that the program nor Kawamura himself did not have a slightest anti-Semitic intention." (See appendix D for a copy of this letter.) Asano also refused to answer questions or to participate in an interview for this book, stating that his and TV Asahi's position on the matter had already been established and that nothing needed to be explained. Given that it is Asano's job to handle public relations for a powerful company that earns much of its revenue from its perceived ability to inform the public about what is going on, his flat-out refusal to be interviewed is interesting. This is especially true because TV Asahi never offered a reasonable explanation about why Kawamura's statement should not be seen as anti-Semitic. Kawamura's statement that Jews "control the U.S. news media," like Kazuyoshi Hanada's remark noted previously in this chapter, clearly implies that Jews have been working in concert as part of a planned network or conspiracy to control the U.S. media. TV Asahi's assertion that such a statement is without "slightest anti-Semitic intention" ought to be explained. Indeed, Kawamura can't even cry ignorance in this case, as Hanada and Bungeishunju Ltd. did about their *Marco Polo* article. Kawamura is the former director of TV Asahi's office in Cairo, Egypt; he is a former New York special correspondent; and he is described as an "expert" on Middle East issues on TV Asahi's Web site in 2004.[29] Kawamura is obviously well acquainted with both Jewish issues and American media issues. He knew full well what he was saying, as did TV Asahi. The station's insistence on sweeping the issue under the rug with pat apologies is yet another sorry example of the Japanese mainstream news media's culture of tolerance when it comes to stereotyping foreigners and minorities. As Nagano Governor Yasuo Tanaka made clear when he compared Japanese journalists to Japanese bureaucrats, rather than working to find and disseminate the truth, they are too often more than happy to cover it up.

Jews in the Japanese Mind

David G. Goodman, who wrote the fascinating book *Jews in the Japanese Mind: The History and Uses of a Cultural Stereotype* (relying heavily on the research of his coauthor Masanori Miyazawa), follows the evolution of Japanese anti-Semitism in sometimes minute detail, yet offers sweeping views on the broader phenomenon. Perhaps most startling is just how much writing the Japanese have produced on the subject of Jews, given the scarcity of Jews in that country. Miyazawa has actually collected Japanese material on Jews produced from 1877 through 1988—some 5,500 items in all, enough to fill a small library.[30]

Goodman and Miyazawa define Japanese anti-Semitism as "the persistent, chimerical belief in a global Jewish conspiracy bent on destroying Japan."[31] A massive body of Japanese literature supports this preposterous idea, but the authors say that it would be wrong to claim that anti-Semitism is more than a minor influence on the society as a whole.

Roots of Modern Japanese Anti-Semitism

Goodman and Miyazawa identify a number of intriguing trends in Japanese thinking about Jews. According to the authors, the roots of modern anti-Semitism can be traced back to the early nineteenth century, well before there was any significant Japanese awareness of a people known as Jews. Japanese xenophobes of the time warned of the appearance of foreign adherents of a menacing "occult religion" determined to destroy Japan.[32]

This fear of outsiders actually contributed to the general undermining of the Tokugawa military government, to the development of the national Shinto emperor cult, and thus to the development of modern Japan. Goodman and Miyazawa refer to it as fears of "proto-Jews," citing similarities between those fears and later fears against actual Jews. Actually, the fears may have been based on fears of Christians who, as Jesuit missionaries, had visited Japan and proselytized as early as 1582.

In 1883, *The Merchant of Venice* was the first Shakespearean drama performed in Japan. The play obviously touched a chord in the Japanese psyche,
and it has virtually been an important fixture in the education system ever
since. Unfortunately, *The Merchant,* as it is often called, is usually interpreted
in Japan as portraying Jews as simplistically fixated on business and money.
This has resulted in the planting of negative stereotypes of Jews in the minds
of generations of Japanese students, who were exposed to very few other rep-
resentations of Jews. A familiarity with the play's text is expected of every lit-
erate Japanese. According to Goodman and Miyazawa, the work was so well
known in 1985 that Katsuhito Iwai, a prominent economist at Tokyo University, published a serious and commercially successful study of modern
capitalism based entirely on *The Merchant of Venice.*[33]

Goodman and Miyazawa have also identified many bizarre-sounding but
nonetheless influential theories about Jews dreamed up by Japanese Christians starting in the early twentieth century. These include sophisticated common-ancestry theories in which Japanese are claimed to be the descendants
of Jews, often one of the "lost tribes of Israel." Other theories inverted the
relationship, arguing instead that the Japanese are actually the ancestors of
Jews. Some also claim that Japan is an important unnamed biblical place,
alluded to in various scriptures as "a land in the east." As strange as these ideas
may sound to Western readers, Goodman and Miyazawa show that these
schools of thought have been important sources of the Japanese preoccupation with Jews. The theories derive much of their power, the authors say, from
the idea of a divinely "chosen people"—a fundamental tenet of both Judaism
and Japanese indigenous beliefs. Such common-ancestry theories for the Jews
and Japanese are not difficult to find on the Internet today.[34]

Another important text to influence Japanese anti-Semitism is the *Protocols
of the Elders of Zion,* first published in Japanese in 1924.[35] The *Protocols* is a propaganda text created by the Russian secret police at the end of the nineteenth
century that has helped fuel worldwide anti-Semitism ever since. Purporting
to document the words of "elder" Jews involved in a centuries-old conspiracy
to control the world, it ranks with *Mein Kampf* as one of the primary texts of
modern anti-Semitism. The idea of an international Jewish financial plot for
world domination, as espoused by the *Protocols,* remains common to this day.

(Indeed, Kawamura's and Hanada's comments that Jews control the U.S. media can rightly be seen as a variation of the *Protocols* theme.)

Fortunately, Japanese anti-Semitic language did not lead to the substantial persecution of Jews by the Japanese leading up to or during the Second World War. There is even an important case in which many Jewish refugees—some of them the Lithuanian refugees referred to further along in this chapter—were actually saved *because* of anti-Semitic stereotypes. A group of Japanese officers believed that Jews were so influential with Roosevelt and Washington that, prior to Pearl Harbor, Jewish refugees were given safe haven in Japan in the hope that the lenient treatment of them would convince Roosevelt to be less hostile to Japan. Plans were even formulated for the settlement of a Jewish colony in Japanese colonial Manchuria, where the Japanese hoped to exploit what they believed to be special Jewish financial resources and technical skills. After the bombing of Pearl Harbor brought an end to any plans of appeasing the United States, the Jews were settled in Shanghai, in the belief—based on stereotypes again—that the Jews were so economically and financially astute they could contribute to Japan's development plans in conquered China. The original plan to give Jews safe haven in Japan before December 1941 was called the "Fugu Plan" after the poisonous blowfish, which is considered a delicacy after its lethal poison sacs have been removed by trained, licensed chefs. The metaphor was that Jews were like the fugu: dangerous—in that they might turn their imagined powers against Japan—but if handled and used correctly, beneficial to Japan. In 1979, American Rabbi Marvin Tokayer and writer Mary Sagmaster Swartz wrote an interesting book, called *The Fugu Plan,* about this strange episode in Jewish and Japanese relations.[36]

And while Japanese militarists did not actively persecute Jews, they did exploit anti-Semitic propaganda to help solidify domestic public opinion against their enemies throughout the war. Historian John Dower has also noted an outburst of "anti-Jewish race hate" by the Japanese during the war in his powerful book on the mutual racism between Japan and the Allies (particularly Britain and the United States) entitled *War without Mercy: Race and Power in the Pacific War.*[37]

Goodman and Miyazawa wrote about the news media's involvement in the Japanese wartime campaign:

Takeda Seigo, author of a 1944 book titled *Newspapers and the Jews,* defined Japan's newspapers as "a weapon of war to destroy the Anglo-American-Jewish enemy"; and he expressed his "profound hope that our newspapers and news agencies will valiantly charge forward toward victory in the ideological war against Anglo-American-Jewish thought." Among other functions, Takeda saw it as the role of Japan's newspapers to "completely expunge Anglo-American-Jewish influence" and "join forces with the news organs of our ally Germany to launch a frontal assault on journalistic plots of the Anglo-American-Jewish foe."

All of Japan's major newspapers carried anti-Semitic articles. The *Yomiuri* ran stories blaming "war fever" (*senso kaze*) on the Jews and claiming that Commodore Matthew Perry [albeit not a Jew] had spearheaded a Jewish invasion of Japan. It even featured articles on the theme of "The Inhuman Machinations of the Jewish Vampires." The *Asahi* carried an article by Navy Lt. Fukui Shinzo urging people to beware of the Jewish influence that threatened to undermine scientific thought.

Of all the major dailies, however, the *Mainichi* was the most enthusiastic promoter of Nazi ideology.... In sum, by the 1940s, anti-Semitism had become an integral part of ultranationalist thought actively disseminated and promoted by Japan's major newspapers with the approval of the Japanese government. It reached every corner of the country.[38]

As this passage shows, anti-Semitic writing is not new to the Japanese news media. Moreover, wartime Japanese anti-Semitism was often lumped together with anti-American and anti-English sentiments—the so-called "Anglo-American-Jewish influence." As dramatized by Sandberg's anecdote about the Japanese businessman and author, as well as by both the TV Asahi and *Shukan Post* examples given earlier, many Japanese continue to confuse Jews with Westerners in general.

Postwar Japanese Sympathy for the Jews

After the war, in the 1950s, Japan seems to have had a period of some serious discussion and writing on Jews and Jewishness, culminating in the Eichmann trial of the early 1960s. However, Japanese thinking about Jews also took an especially strange twist at about this time.

Ian Buruma, in his comparison of Japan and Germany, *The Wages of Guilt*,[39] touches upon some of the same themes as Goodman and Miyazawa in *Jews in the Japanese Mind*. Both books document the fact that after the war many Japanese actually identified strongly with the Jewish plight, viewing themselves as similar victims of international violence during the Second World War.

Many Westerners may find it surprising to think that the Japanese—having been allied to the Jew-hating Nazis during the war and having perpetrated a race-based aggression against their Asian neighbors that led to more than twenty million deaths—could possibly identify themselves with the Jewish victims of the Holocaust. This identification is commonly manifest in the Japanese tendency to equate the Holocaust (sometimes even more specifically Auschwitz) with the dropping of the atom bombs on Hiroshima and Nagasaki.

This comparison is inappropriate for at least two reasons. First, whereas the two atom bombings occurred much more suddenly than the Nazi Holocaust, the Holocaust claimed many times more lives. Another crucial difference, pointed out in Richard Rubenstein's fascinating book *The Cunning of History*, is that the killing of Japanese with atom bombs stopped when Japan surrendered, whereas the killing of Jews by the Nazis *began after* the Jews surrendered and were helpless.[40] Other writers, such as Ivan P. Hall, argue that the atom bombings are most fairly compared with other horrific World War II bombings of cities by the Allies, such as that of the German city of Dresden.[41]

None of the writers mentioned here attempts to downplay the incomprehensible, tragic suffering resulting from the atom bombs or to justify their use. However, they all stress the importance of contextualizing the reality of the bombings within the flow of history. They see the equation by many Japanese of the two atomic bombings with the Jewish Holocaust as deeply tied to the failure of many of those same Japanese to come to terms with their country's wartime aggression. Goodman and Miyazawa write:

The Japanese identification of Hiroshima and Nagasaki with the Holocaust
has led only seldom to an understanding of the Jewish (or, for that matter,
the Japanese) experience. It strives instead to bestow on the entire Japanese
wartime experience a moral stature that is simply not appropriate. It seeks to
blur the elementary distinction between victim and aggressor and to obscure
the fact that the Japanese were far more analogous to the Germans during
the war than to the Jews.... Understood as the equivalent of the Holocaust,
Hiroshima loses its unique historical meaning. It becomes a gimmick to
avoid confronting unpleasant reality. And that is unconscionable from both
the Japanese and the Jewish point of view.[42]

Japanese identification with Jewish victimization, Goodman and
Miyazawa argue, is manifest in other areas as well. The authors state, for
example, that *The Diary of Anne Frank* has also been misappropriated by the
Japanese. First published in Japan in 1952, more than four million copies
have been sold there, about the same number as in the United States. Indeed,
the *Diary* remains a popular text for young Japanese girls to this day. According to the authors, Frank's suffering is seldom utilized by the Japanese as an
opportunity to better understand racism and violence, either during World
War II or in the modern world. Instead, the lessons are oversimplified, with
Frank's fate portrayed merely as the tragic consequence of an incomprehensible war. As Goodman and Miyazawa point out, the forgiving nature of
young Anne Frank is often overemphasized, to the detriment of a more in-
depth understanding of crimes against humanity. The authors write, "In sum,
then, Anne Frank's *Diary* became a canonical text in Japan in large part
because it enabled the Japanese to relate to the Holocaust and World War II
without having to consider hard historical realities. It enabled them to feel
good about the war, to identify with a non-threatening, forgiving victim of a
conflict they had reformulated as a sort of natural disaster, and to get on with
the task of reconstruction."[43]

A side-by-side comparison of the covers on popular Japanese and Western editions of the *Diary* drives home this jarring disparity. As noted previously, the *Diary of Anne Frank* is published in Japan by Bungeishunju Ltd.,
the same company that published *Marco Polo* (and continues to publish

Bungei Shunju and *Shukan Bunshun* magazines). Whereas the Western Bantam edition features a black-and-white photograph of Anne Frank on its cover, Bungeishunju's Japanese edition features colorful cartoon characters on a soft-pink cover. The back-cover art, a drawing of an old European city, is strikingly reminiscent of the Disney Magic Castle, and a cartoonish sketch of children's stuffed animals adorns the spine. Thus, while the Bantam book's straightforward photograph of the author helps readers squarely face the reality of the journal, the Bungeishunju cover implies an almost fairy-tale quality. Indeed, this universally relevant piece of literature has been transformed by the designers at Bungeishunju Ltd. into a product specifically for girls.

The *Diary* has proved to be such a cash cow for Bungeishunju Ltd. over the years that some Japan observers have speculated that one reason the company moved so quickly to shut down *Marco Polo* was fear of losing its license to publish it.

Clearly, Bungeishunju Ltd. is far more concerned with profitability than with any consistency in its editorial content, for it is hard to imagine two more incongruent publications than the *Diary* and Bungeishunju Ltd.'s magazines. This underscores another strange aspect of the Japanese publishing world: that otherwise-respected book publishers readily stoop to producing magazines known primarily for muckraking, neonationalist politics. Shinchosha Ltd., also a substantial book publisher, similarly puts out *Shukan Shincho,* just as the powerful book publisher Kodan-sha Ltd. churns out the weekly newsmagazines *Shukan Gendai* and *Friday.*

Like Anne Frank's *Diary,* the story of Chiune Sugihara, "the Oskar Schindler of Japan," has been routinely misinterpreted by the Japanese media. This is not another instance of anti-Semitism, but simply of misinformation about Jews. As Rabbi Cooper has noted, Sugihara, the Japanese deputy consul in Lithuania during the Second World War, issued some 2,500 individual and family transit visas in 1940 to about 6,000 Polish Jews who sought refuge in Lithuania following the Nazi invasion of Poland, which Germany and the Soviet Union had partitioned in 1939. Sugihara issued the visas in spite of repeated demands, both by the Soviets and by his own foreign minister, Yosuke Matsuoka, that he desist.[44]

Yet NHK (Nihon Hoso Kyokai, or Japan Broadcasting Corporation) television's *Views and Opinions* program of April 29, 1998, which featured

In addition to publishing magazines such as *Shukan Bunshun, Bungei Shunju,* and *Shokun!*—magazines that are well known for their denials of Second World War atrocities—Bungeishunju Ltd. also publishes the Japanese-language edition of *The Diary of Anne Frank*. The book is widely read by preteen and teenage Japanese girls and is a standard teaching text for that age group. However, some writers have criticized the way the book is often presented in Japan. According to them, it is often taught simply as the tragic story of a girl who dies during the Second World War, with little discussion of the Nazi racism that led to her persecution. The design of the 2003 Bungeishunju edition is noteworthy for its cartoon-like presentation of the story. Pictured here in black and white, the background is actually a classic girlish soft pink, with the lettering in plum and the cartoon characters colored variously. The book is clearly designed to appeal to girls and young women. In contrast, Bantam Book's 1993 English-language edition presents the reader with a simple black-and-white photo of Anne Frank. It is obviously designed to appeal to a wide demographic.

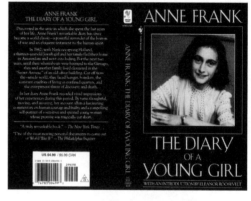

Sophia University professor and neonationalist Shoichi Watanabe, painted an astonishing revisionist assessment of the situation. According to Watanabe, Japan, unlike the United States and the United Kingdom, had disavowed the practice of racial discrimination and had adopted the most humanitarian of policies toward the Jewish people at the time. In this version of history, Sugihara had not heroically risked his job to save lives but was merely following the Japanese state policy of egalitarianism in assisting those in need during the war. Also remarkable was the timing of the broadcast—April 29, the birthday of Emperor Hirohito, who reigned throughout the war.

Although Japan did not actively persecute the Jews (as its German allies had requested), neither did it actively come to their aid, except, of course, in regard to the dubious "Fugu Plan." Sugihara deserves the highest recognition for his actions. His government, however, was anything but humanitarian, as evidenced by its murderous colonial policies in Korea, China, and other invaded countries, as well as by its postwar reprimand and premature "retirement" of Sugihara for his "insubordination." Indeed, Sugihara's de facto firing was such an impediment to the restoration of diplomatic relations between Lithuania and Japan in 1992 that the Japanese government formally apologized to Sugihara's family for its mistreatment of him.

That NHK would air a television show on such a propitious date, featuring Watanabe, is yet another sign of just how far Japanese false portrayals of history have infiltrated the mainstream media. Watanabe has been a board member of The Nippon Foundation, established by the late militarist and ultraright boss Ryoichi Sasagawa. He is also known for his denials of Japanese aggression during the war, including the Nanjing Massacre,[45] discussed in chapter 7.

Modern Japanese Anti-Semitism

Goodman and Miyazawa identify two separate influences in the 1970s and 1980s—on the Japanese political right and left, respectively—that sparked the explosion of anti-Semitic writing at that time: First, the marginalization of Communist and other leftist groups in Japan, which resulted from the LDP's virtual lock on power, gave Japanese on the left little hope of making significant inroads in their own country. With nothing to do at home, the authors argue, Japanese leftists looked abroad for "people's causes" to support. As a result, they came to identify closely with the Palestine Liberation Organization's, or PLO's, struggle against Israel. (Actually, whether the Japanese political left supported the PLO because they felt marginalized or for some other reason is beside the point. What matters is that there was a great deal of sympathy in Japan at that time for the Palestinians and thus negativity toward Israel.)

Almost simultaneously, from the time of the "oil crisis" of late 1973, Japanese conservative business elements began to feel the influence of Arab countries united in the Organization of Petroleum Exporting Countries (OPEC), whose control over oil prices could easily have derailed Japanese economic expansion. Many OPEC nations, of course, were and are identified closely with the PLO cause and have boycotted and imposed sanctions against Israel. Thus, Japanese conservatives—motivated by pragmatic rather than ideological concerns—threw in their lot against Israel. In this way, anti-Semitism became a common ground for the Japanese left and right, and thus an even more profitable topic for the media.

According to Goodman and Miyazawa, this confluence of concerns was reinforced with a rise in Japanese nationalism in the 1980s. As noted, Prime Minister Yasuhiro Nakasone, in office from 1982 to 1987, seized on this nationalism to make Japan a stronger international force. It was during this time that anti-Semitism in Japan began reaching its postwar peak and Japanese bookstores began featuring Jewish sections, well stocked with books on all sorts of Japanese-Jewish theories. Perhaps the most famous anti-Semitic Japanese writer is the prolific author Masami Uno. Two of Uno's hate-mongering works (the ridiculous titles of which are rendered into English as "If You Understand the Jews, You Will Understand the World" and "If You Understand the Jews, You Will Understand Japan"[46]) sold a total of 1.1 million copies between their publication dates in 1986 and the spring of 1987 alone.[47] Both are classic *Protocols of the Elders of Zion*–type conspiracy books, blaming the Jews for virtually everything wrong with the world and with Japan. Indeed, Uno has written more than twenty books with anti-Semitic content, and for some time during the 1980s and 1990s, he became a relatively respected Japanese public figure, even being invited to share his theories in an LDP lecture series. According to Goodman and Miyazawa, Uno is no mere aberration but comes out of a long tradition: "In sum, therefore, the recrudescence of Japanese anti-Semitism that began in the mid-1980s, epitomized by the work of Uno Masami, was not a novel or aberrant phenomenon but a logical product of Japanese history and the reiteration of longstanding Japanese images of Jews."

Pictured here are two books by Masami Uno, probably the most famous and one of the most vociferous anti-Semitic writers in Japan. Together, these two books sold about 1.1 million copies in 1986 and 1987 alone. They play upon an undercurrent in Japan of fear that there are forces in the world conspiring to destroy Japan. As improbable as it may seem to a Westerner, the titles of these books, translated into English, are "If You Understand the Jews, You Will Understand the World" and "If You Understand the Jews, You Will Understand Japan."

The afterword to the 2000 expanded edition of *Jews in the Japanese Mind* makes the argument that the paranoid, hateful cultural milieu engendered by anti-Semitic popular writers contributed significantly to the ideas espoused by the religious group Aum Shinrikyo. The cult, responsible for the sarin-gas attacks in Matsumoto and in the Tokyo subways, espoused anti-Semitism as a core aspect of its warped theology. Goodman and Miyazawa do not go so far as to blame the emergence of Aum Shinrikyo on the popularity of anti-Semitic writing in Japan, but they do make the case that Aum Shinrikyo tapped into this rich vein of anger and fear to put forward its own campaign. For example, in January 1995, two months before the Tokyo subway poison-gas attack, a blatantly anti-Semitic tract entitled "Manual of Fear: The Jewish Ambition—Total World Conquest" was published in the Aum Shinrikyo journal *Vajrayana Sacca*.[48]

According to Ely Karmon, writing in the annual report *Anti-Semitism Worldwide: 1998/1999*, "The publication of vitriolic material such as Aum's was possible because the Japanese government had never considered the circulation of anti-Semitic materials as harmful. Their unrestricted availability is accepted by Japanese at all levels because the right of freedom of expression in post-war Japan is absolute."[49]

As indirect as it may seem, this connection between Aum Shinrikyo and the acceptance of Japanese anti-Semitic writing in the mainstream Japanese press represents yet one more way that Yoshiyuki Kono was victimized by his country's media. Not only was Kono wrongly vilified by the news media, but the group that actually poisoned him and his family had benefited from the hateful ideas long encouraged and accepted by that selfsame media.

Anti-Semitism and Japanese Journalism

Philip Brasor wrote an opinion piece in the influential English-language Japanese newspaper *Japan Times* offering some trenchant insights into the issue of contemporary anti-Semitic writing in that country. In his article entitled "Ripple Effects of Sleazebag Journalism," he argues that Japanese anti-Semitism has less to do with actual hatred toward Jews than with Japanese journalism. "The root of the problem has less to do with creeping racism," he writes, "than with an ill-defined and poorly managed structure of journalistic ethics."[50] Brasor has a point. Japan is certainly not teeming with Jew-haters. Again, few Japanese have even met a Jew. According to Brasor, the root cause that has allowed anti-Semitic theories to flourish in Japan is the news media:

> Since the legitimate newspapers and national TV networks have close ties with government and financial leaders, it is left to the independent weeklies and tabloid dailies to perform the kind of investigative reporting you usually find in a working democracy. But the weeklies and tabloids are as likely to cover the trends in the sex industry as they are to find out who is to blame for a failing financial institution, and they use the same standard. What will grab the reader's attention. If that's your main criterion then stretching facts and making connections that don't exist can become everyday practices.[51]

As Rabbi Cooper discovered in his Japan work, greed combined with a dearth of journalistic ethics and a reliance on sensationalism were the fundamental motivating forces behind Bungeishunju Ltd.'s *Marco Polo* Holocaust denial.

Brasor's point that readers often look to newsmagazines for alternative perspectives is also important. Indeed, the *Shukan Post* article, ostensibly about a Jewish financial scheme to dominate the Japanese, claimed to have "uncovered the reality behind the takeover that you won't find in your daily newspaper." Similarly, the author of the *Marco Polo* article went to great lengths to insist that his "research" served as a counterpoint to the corrupt establishment media of Japan, the United States, and the world.

Thus, in many ways Jewish-conspiracy theories are a perfect subject for Japanese newsmagazines. Such theories are clearly "alternative" to the standard fare presented in the staid material of big papers and on the television and radio news. They tend to be based on the kind of unsubstantiated claims that unethical writers and publishers don't mind printing; and they also tend toward the truly sensational, appealing directly to one of humanity's basest fears: the fear of the unknown "other."

Jews in the Japanese Mind castigates Japanese intellectuals for failing to counter their country's anti-Semitism. Even though the authors acknowledge the substantial and continuously growing body of Japanese scholarship on Jews and Judaism, they still blame the Japanese intellectual community for not countering anti-Semitism forcefully enough. This may be a fair criticism, but Japanese journalists and the news-media industry as a whole are arguably even more culpable than the country's intellectual community.

At least some intellectuals have taken action for justice and accuracy. But while hateful hacks capitalize on the selling power of anti-Semitism, most Japanese journalists either sit silently by or, worse, actively contribute to the problem. Indeed, for all their research, neither Goodman nor Miyazawa could find an editorial piece roundly condemning Japanese anti-Semitism.[52]

Why have Japanese journalists remained so determinedly uninvolved on this issue? If most are not anti-Semites—as must obviously be the case—why have they not spoken out loudly against such unmistakable hate mongering? Why the silence?

Some Conclusions

Fear and dislike of the outsider, or "other," has roots many centuries old in Japan. Even its more recent incarnation, epitomized in the Japanese conception of the Jew, goes back at least a century and a half. Moreover, throughout its modern history, Japanese xenophobia has been manipulated to galvanize national unity. In the Second World War, for example, it dominated the popular consciousness. Even though the Japanese militarists did not join their Nazi allies in implementing the "Final Solution" to annihilate the Jews, they certainly embraced and espoused anti-Semitic rhetoric in order to unify the nation's hatred against its "Anglo-American-Jewish enemy."

This is the very same anti-Semitism that resurfaced so conspicuously in the last decades of the twentieth century, as part of a resurgence of Japanese nationalism. Goodman and Miyazawa write about this continuity:

> Japanese anti-Semitism is an eruption of the darkness in modern Japanese history. It is a malign version of the basic patterns of Japanese culture. It derives from the virulent political obscurantism of Japanese xenophobes, who pandered paranoid fantasies throughout the modern period to assuage their feelings of insecurity and anomie. It is an integral component of the ideology that, in the 1930s, assumed control of Japan and precipitated World War II. It is the hidden grotesque face of the wartime chauvinism that survived, transformed, after the war. To deny the historical roots of Japanese anti-Semitism is to ignore the historical legacy of Japanese ethnic nationalism and to deny the historical continuity of Japan.[53]

The problem is not that any specific person or people in the Japanese news media publish anti-Semitic information out of a desire to enslave the Japanese people or purposely undermine democracy. The main reason it is published is because it sells. No one is planting anti-Semitic stories or books in the popular press or hushing up those who would speak out against it. Some Japanese are simply drawn to stories that feature anti-Semitism. And, although the mainstream papers do not regularly run blatantly anti-Semitic content, they have supported anti-Semitic weeklies and books both by running their advertisements and by remaining obdurately silent. This reveals a profound negligence by Japanese mainstream journalists.

Many members of the Japanese establishment view anti-Semitism, like other forms of xenophobia and racism, as generally benign. The uniting of members of one group in their distrust of another group is as old as human politics. It is a key aspect of nationalism of all sorts and the sworn enemy of democratic principles. Ultimately, the Japanese establishment, including the news media, tolerates such bigotry because it is generally supportive of the Japanese system of governance.

Japanese journalists, accustomed to a mentality that emphasizes harmony and de-emphasizes individual initiative, and unaccustomed to journalistic ethical concepts that demand that they speak out, choose to ignore their anti-Semitic colleagues. Also, articles in defense of Jews are not in particular demand: they are unlikely to increase circulation figures and may even draw unwanted negative attention to their authors. Denouncing anti-Semitism in Japan offers only one reward: the knowledge that one is writing what is correct. Unfortunately, this reward does not seem to be enough.

Ultimately, both Jews and Japanese suffer. Both are misled and given a skewed vision of the other. The twentieth century offers far too many examples of unchecked racism leading to profound suffering on a terrible scale. This is why the works of Rabbi Cooper, Sandberg, and others are so important. Japanese anti-Semitism is an international issue—one that will no doubt remain until enough Japanese stand against it.

Unfortunately, bigotry, in all its many forms, is also an issue for the news media in many Western democracies. As with anti-Semitic writings in Japan, sensationalized hate language touches a chord in the human psyche that can result in huge profit for publishers. It is also easy to pillory those who look different from a majority population or who ascribe to a different religion or worldview. Ultimately, it is up to those in the mainstream of a culture to stay on guard against such lapses and to challenge them wherever they are found.

CHAPTER SIX

SMEARING A BUDDHIST LEADER

It should be said that matters seriously lacking factual foundation, as in this case, and of such scandalous content should not have been reported in the media so frivolously.

—from the conclusion of the Tokyo District Court ruling on the false charges brought by Junko and Nobuko Nobuhira against Daisaku Ikeda.[1]

An Extreme Case

On June 26, 2001, the Supreme Court of Japan ended a five-year saga that represented one of the most extreme cases of the abuse of freedom of the press in postwar Japan. In this case, *Shukan Shincho* not only exploited unfounded rape charges—later deemed by the courts to have "no factual basis" and to have been lodged for disingenuous reasons—but actually participated in the development, articulation, and leveling of those false charges. The case involves Daisaku Ikeda, one of Japan's most intriguing figures and the leader of the Soka Gakkai (Value Creation Society), the largest Buddhist sect in Japan. The Soka Gakkai is also a major political force in the country because its membership provides the bulk of support for the New Komei Party, one of Japan's most influential political organizations.

As in virtually all the other examples in this book, *Shukan Shincho*'s primary motivation appears to have been financial, although its coverage also helped to maintain some of the least democratic aspects of the Japanese system of governance, as described in chapter 1. Moreover, it is a prime example of the perfidious dangers posed by a national news media not grounded by clear ethical guidelines. In this case, the magazine-generated false scandal not only distracted the public's attention from more serious issues, it also served to damage the growing influence of the Soka Gakkai and, with it, the political clout of the Komei Party. When the magazine began covering its trumped-up scandal, the Komei Party was one of the principal threats to the political establishment in Japan. Because Ikeda is both the founder of the party and the honorary president of the Buddhist group, *Shukan Shincho*'s gratuitous exploitation of the false charges against him had the effect of dampening the party's influence.

Again, *shukanshi* do not, as a rule, help to maintain the Japanese system of governance out of any conscious effort by their writers or editors. But the fact remains that they regularly do support the country's elite bureaucratic, political, legal, and business institutions.

Just as in the tragic account of Yoshiyuki Kono, the Daisaku Ikeda case shows how vicious and personally damaging the *shukanshi* can be. This time, however, *Shukan Shincho*'s attack reached beyond the arena of law enforcement to exert a massive influence on public discourse and politics. This case study also illustrates the ways that the broader Japanese news media regularly support and condone blatantly immoral journalism, not only by assisting in the dissemination of false information but by ignoring gross ethical breaches.

The case is especially enlightening given the intense centralization of media power globally and the resultant difficulties that individuals around the world increasingly face when challenging malicious media lies. Although many aspects of this case are particular to Japanese culture, politics, and media, certain others hold universal relevance.

The Case in Brief

The false rape charges against Daisaku Ikeda were filed by a former member and volunteer leader in the Soka Gakkai, Nobuko Nobuhira, and her husband, Junko Nobuhira. The Japanese courts not only deemed the Nobuhiras' claims specious but concluded that the two had "abused their legal right to sue"[2] by filing them in the first place. The strongly worded verdict underscores the false nature of the charges, since Japanese courts deliver such verdicts so very rarely: of all the court cases tried in Japan between 1965 and the turn of the century, there were fewer than twenty such verdicts.

The judgment of the Tokyo District Court (upheld by the Tokyo High Court and the Supreme Court of Japan) reads in part:

> The complaint in this case can be considered unlawful, because it abuses the rights of action. Continuing the hearing of this case is not only cruel to the defendant, but may potentially result in the Court contrarily siding with the wrongful undertakings of the plaintiff. Thus, terminating the hearing of this lawsuit at this time is reasonable.[3]

Despite the obviously false nature of the claims, as borne out by the court's findings, *Shukan Shincho* employees actively coached the Nobuhiras and encouraged them to make those claims public in the magazine. Indeed, editorial staff at the magazine even went so far as to advise the couple on how to inflict the most damage on Ikeda.

In the end, the magazine benefited significantly from the false accusations by featuring thirty-four sensational articles on the subject by March of 2001, most of which were (as with most of the other *shukanshi* articles throughout this book) heavily promoted in advertisements for the magazine, each of which was read by tens of millions (see chapter 3). As a result, a huge portion of the Japanese public were thoroughly inculcated with the false idea that the Nobuhiras were innocent victims of a terrible crime perpetrated by Ikeda—despite the fact that no credible evidence was ever provided that any such thing ever took place and despite a great deal of evidence that the Nobuhiras concocted their claims for immoral purposes.

Unfortunately, as events bear out again and again, Japanese legal and media institutions are so poor at enforcing accountability for members of the press that *Shukan Shincho* was able to exploit and misrepresent the case for years without consequence. Indeed, in many ways the case even enhanced the magazine's profile because the coverage appeared to uninformed observers to represent bold journalism. The case is a quintessential example of the way that the news media can manipulate national opinion regardless of the facts, all in the name of freedom of speech and "the public's right to know."

The Buddhist Group

To understand the case, some familiarity with the Soka Gakkai and the Soka Gakkai International (SGI) is helpful. The SGI is a private organization of Soka Gakkai–affiliated groups worldwide. It can be thought of as an umbrella organization, with its member organizations coming from some 188 countries and territories around the world. SGI consists of legally autonomous lay-Buddhist organizations such as SGI-Brazil, SGI-Korea, SGI-USA, SGI-UK, SGI-France, and so on, with about 1.5 million members outside Japan, according to the organization's figures. Far and away the largest SGI-affiliated organization is the Japan-based group, known simply as the Soka Gakkai. The Soka Gakkai currently claims some 10 million members. Although the precise membership figure is disputed by some, all agree that the group has a substantial membership.[4]

Like other major religious institutions, the Soka Gakkai and the SGI have given birth to numerous affiliated organizations. Some are quite substantial. The *Seikyo Shimbun*, for instance, Soka Gakkai's organ newspaper, is technically Japan's third-largest daily newspaper, with a circulation of more than 5.5 million, although it is often categorized separately from other newspapers as a religious publication.[5] The Soka Gakkai supports a fully accredited Japanese university, Soka University, with a student body of 8,800 students, offering undergraduate through doctoral degrees in a wide range of subjects. The Soka Gakkai recently funded Soka University of America, a nonreligious liberal-arts college in Orange County, California, that was opened in 2001. The Soka Gakkai has also founded various institutions such as the Tokyo Fuji Art Museum, the Toda Institute for Global Peace and Policy Research, the

Institute of Oriental Philosophy, the Min-On Concert Association, the Victor Hugo House of Literature (in France), and the Boston Research Center for the Twenty-First Century.

The Soka Gakkai follows its own interpretation of Nichiren Buddhism, which has a detailed theology and features the central tenet that chanting the mantra "Nam-myoho-renge-kyo" leads to enlightenment. One of the newer Nichiren Buddhist groups, it was founded in 1930 as the Soka Kyoiku Gakkai (Value Creation Educational Society), a name shortened to Soka Gakkai after World War II. During the postwar decades, it grew into the largest lay arm of the Nichiren Shoshu Buddhist sect. The Soka Gakkai and the Nichiren Shoshu priesthood supported each other for many years, with the priests performing rites and other clerical duties while the Soka Gakkai focused on propagation and outreach. In 1991, however, they officially split over ideological and other differences and have maintained a staunchly adversarial relationship ever since.

Background

Given Soka Gakkai's meteoric rise from almost complete obscurity at the start of the postwar period to being the largest Buddhist organization, and one of the most influential of any kind, in all Japan just a few decades later, it is not surprising that controversy should attend it. During the war, founder Tsunesaburo Makiguchi and the man who would succeed him as president, Josei Toda, were imprisoned for the "thought crime" of refusing to support either the militant national state Shinto religion or the war being waged under its banner. Thus, almost since its beginnings, the organization was branded as subversive by Japan's ruling powers. In 1944, at the age of seventy-three, Makiguchi died in prison, a martyr to his beliefs.

After the war, Toda took charge and rallied the few scattered individuals who were all that remained of the group. Like Makiguchi before him, Toda proved to be an outspoken leader, making a strong public stand against all atomic weapons as early as 1957. By the time of his death in 1958, he had built the organization to include more than 750,000 member households.[6]

During the early postwar years, the Soka Gakkai was criticized for its aggressive proselytizing, which included accosting people in the streets to tell them about the practice, as well as challenging practitioners of other religions to debates. Members pursued potential converts with a persistence described by some as excessive, even insisting that converts dispose of symbols of other religions in their homes. Given the predilection of many Japanese for accepting multiple religions, as well as the Japanese cultural tendency to avoid confrontation, it is no surprise that the Soka Gakkai's proselytizing was viewed negatively by much of mainstream Japanese society. Although the group had stopped this methodology by the 1980s and has focused ever since on "sharing Buddhism in natural, socially accepted ways,"[7] it has been unable to completely shake the negative images from these efforts. Also during its early years, the group attracted many impoverished Japanese, people who did not work for large companies or belong to national unions. This earned it the added reputation of being a "gathering of poor people." The label was used derisively, but the Soka Gakkai welcomed it as a slogan that reflected its philosophy of embracing all people, especially the poor and suffering. Although the current membership represents a broad cross section of Japanese society, the early taint of being outside the mainstream remains.

Its minority group status notwithstanding, Soka Gakkai has established its own place within Japanese society. As early as 1989, Karel van Wolferen, in his book *The Enigma of Japanese Power*, identified it as a mainstream fixture: "Some of these [new] religions have become fairly large, rich and powerful. The best-known among them, Soka Gakkai, is of political significance.... It is also the most successful among the *shinko shukyo* [new religions] that have set up shop abroad. In the 1960's it created a great deal of disquiet in the system with its militant proselytizing and active hostility towards other, rival new religions. But it has settled down now and, with its own schools, university, political party and publishing empire has become a successful, albeit still somewhat controversial, participant in the system."[8]

Similarly, former U.S. Vice President Walter Mondale, who served as ambassador to Japan from 1993 to 1996, shared his impression of the organization in a telephone interview for this book:

The Soka Gakkai, I believe, is one of the groups that suffered under the war years. As people who are martyred often do, they developed a very strong commitment that makes them a very powerful minority force in Japanese society. They have their own political party, the Komeito;[9] they tend to be more concerned with issues of civil liberty, freedom of religion, and about Japanese remilitarization. I also noticed in Japan several comments expressing objections or fears about them. Wherever they were found, it was almost always used as a point to attack whoever was working with them.[10]

The Komei Party

Perhaps Soka Gakkai's most controversial move ever was in the mid-1950s, when it put forth political candidates for local assembly elections. In 1961, it formalized its participation by establishing the Komei (Clean Government) Political League. In 1964, the movement transformed into an official Japanese political party, the Komei Party. Kunishige Maeda, a spokesperson for the Soka Gakkai, says that this move into politics was a natural outgrowth of the organization's "socially oriented" Buddhist philosophy, which, he says, "equally cherishes both the social sphere and the way of life of the individual practitioner."[11]

The Komei Party severed its legal ties with the Soka Gakkai in 1970, when it also officially adopted the idea of an "open party"—one that invited membership from people of all faiths. This change in legal status coincided with a media scandal that continues to dog the organization to this day. At that time, some Komei Party officers were widely denounced for having attempted to use their political positions to suppress *Soka Gakkai O Kiru* (I Denounce Soka Gakkai), a book that was critical of the organization and its participation in Japanese politics.[12] Speaking about this incident, Soka Gakkai spokesperson Maeda stated in an interview for this book that both organizations "deeply regret" and have apologized for the actions of the officials involved. He emphasized that more than thirty years have passed since the incident and insisted that it is "unfair" to keep bringing the case up when, according to him, both the political party and the religious group have "consistently proven to be staunchly supportive of free speech."

"We were a relatively young organization at that time, 1970," he said, "but we have quite matured socially since that time."[13]

Despite the legal separation of the party from the religious group, the party continues to receive substantial support from the Soka Gakkai. Party leaders regularly dialogue with Soka Gakkai leaders on a variety of issues, and the Buddhist group actively encourages its membership to support the party during election campaigns.

Some critics have claimed that the Soka Gakkai's influence on politics through the Komei Party is at odds with the spirit of the Japanese Constitution, which calls for the separation of church and state. Others, however, point out that the involvement of religious organizations in politics is a common occurrence in many Western industrialized democracies, citing various Christian parties in Europe, as well as important Christian and Jewish constituencies in the United States. Still others point out that the Komei Party has long been a vocal supporter of freedom of religion, as well as of the separation of church and state in the country. In point of fact, if any major political party in Japan is guilty of violating Article 20 of the Constitution, which stipulates that the state and its organizations shall refrain from religious education or any other religious activities, it is the decades-dominant LDP. As noted previously, since 1985, various LDP prime ministers have garnered worldwide attention for their public worship at Yasukuni Shrine, this despite various court conclusions, between 1991 and 2004, that such activities violate the Japanese Constitution.

At any rate, by the 1980s the Komei Party was a well-established opposition force in Japan. Indeed, rather than criticize it as an overzealous religious party, some had begun to disparage it for what they described as its bland, mainstream agenda. In 1993, the Komei Party became a part of the first Japanese administration in thirty-eight years that did not include the Liberal Democratic Party (LDP). The party served as an important member of the eight-party Morihiro Hosokawa coalition government and its immediate successor. Although these two coalitions were short-lived, surviving less than a year before a new LDP government returned to power, the event raised high hopes for reform across the country before petering out over the decade.

In December 1994, Komei politicians also played a leading role in the development of the New Frontier Party, essentially a coalition party formed to challenge the newly regained LDP rule. Although the New Frontier Party was unable to oust the LDP, it scored a number of victories at the ballot box and continued to threaten LDP rule until the New Frontier's dissolution in 1997.

If ever Komei politicians constituted a genuine threat to the status quo of Japanese politics, it was during this period of continually shifting party alignments from 1993 to 1997. And it was within this superheated political climate that the Nobuhiras' false claims were seized upon and trumpeted by *Shukan Shincho*, as well as by a number of anti–Komei Party political papers.

Most recently, at the end of 1999, the New Komei Party (formed in 1998, after the New Frontier Party's dissolution) took on an entirely new role within Japanese politics, transforming itself after a long history as an opposition party into a member of a ruling coalition. It was then that New Komei first joined forces with its longtime foe, the LDP. Indeed, at the time of the publication of this book in 2004, the New Komei Party continues as part of the LDP coalition.

While some of its supporters have expressed fears that the New Komei Party would be co-opted by the LDP, party leaders such as Secretary General Tetsuzo Fuyushiba and Lower House member Yoshio Urushibara (both of whom were interviewed for this book) insist that the New Komei Party stands by its own agenda and serves as a moderating influence over more conservative elements of the LDP.[14]

Whatever one's take on the party, four distinct stages of its development can be discerned. It first emerged as a controversial new component of the Japanese political scene in the 1960s and 1970s. But by the 1980s, it had established itself as what appeared to be a permanent fixture within the entrenched Japanese opposition.

The next stage came with the dramatic political changes of the early and mid-1990s, when the party took on the role of a key challenger to LDP power for a number of years. Finally, 1999 saw the party enter its most recent period when it joined in a coalition to become a part of the ruling government.

Daisaku Ikeda

Daisaku Ikeda, as the leader of an influential, politically active group for more than forty years, has been a lightning rod both for harsh criticism and high accolades. Although he is not especially well known in the West, he is a household name in Japan. A 1999 survey of Japanese placed him among the twenty favorite authors of those polled.[15] Twenty years earlier, a *Yomiuri Shimbun* survey included Ikeda as one of the twenty "most respected individuals in Japan." Of the five ahead of him on the list, the only other living person was the then-emperor, Hirohito.[16] Nothing seems unusual in the least about an outspoken leader of a powerful minority religious group being looked upon with suspicion. Nor is it surprising that some of Ikeda's enemies have painted him as power hungry and out for personal aggrandizement. But, his defenders, pointing to his long list of accomplishments, reply that controversy is the

Kunishige Maeda is a spokesperson for the Soka Gakkai.

bedfellow of high achievement, especially when the achievements involve encouraging those in need while challenging entrenched power holders. Soka Gakkai spokesperson Maeda argues that virtually all those who "stand up for justice throughout history" have been targets of "unfounded attacks and false controversies." Moreover, Maeda asserts, this problem is especially serious in his country. "At the root of Japan's national character, there is a so-called islander mentality from which petty jealousies and infighting arise," Maeda explains. "President Ikeda[17] is, in a sense, very unusual for a Japanese, because he successfully reaches out internationally while supporting those in need. He is respected internationally for his efforts for peace. For those who do not want to acknowledge this, or who are jealous of this, he often becomes a target of attack."[18]

Perhaps more than anything else, those who praise Ikeda emphasize his legacy of speaking up for ordinary people. A passage from one of Ikeda's speeches given in 1966, when he was still a relatively new leader of his organization, illustrates why he has not been favored by traditional power holders in Japan. Although it is one of Ikeda's stronger statements, it is hardly a misrepresentation of his approach: "I am always a friend of the ordinary people, especially the poor and unhappy. As president, I will devote myself to this cause. I do not in the least fear the prime minister or the Diet members. Since I became president for the purpose of realizing the happiness of people, I fear only their voices."[19] Echoing this is a statement Ikeda made nearly forty years later, in November of 2003: "It is imperative that we change the state of the world in which good-hearted ordinary people are oppressed and forced to suffer. This is an age of democracy, an age where the people are sovereign. Those in even the most powerful positions of authority are there solely to serve the people. It must never be the other way around."[20]

Ikeda's actions toward China and Russia in the late 1960s and early 1970s are also illustrative of his controversial nature. In 1968, for example, he was severely criticized in Japan for being the first major religious figure in the country to call publicly for the normalization of relations with China. This was a radical move at the time, given the previous century of bitter war and violence between the two nations, and it resulted in accusations that Ikeda was "befriending" an enemy nation. At the time, Ikeda said, "China's position in international society is most tenuous. She is not represented in the UN and maintains very shaky ties with most other nations. . . . The first step to obtaining the desired goal is officially to recognize the government of China. The second is to get China a seat at the UN, . . . the third, stimulate economic and cultural exchange. . . . I know that many Japanese are afraid of Chinese aggression and advocate rigid adherence to the U.S.-Japan Security treaty and feel it better to avoid close ties with China. I take a somewhat different view."[21]

It is easy to see how such words from a religious leader with growing political clout might stir controversy in Japan in 1968. Of course, U.S. President Richard Nixon's visit to China in 1972 and his call for normalization between the United States and China completely reframed the issue. Not long afterward, in 1974, Ikeda made journeys to both China and the Soviet Union, where he engaged in what he describes as a "people's diplomacy" with People's Republic of China Premier Zhou Enlai and Soviet Premier Alexei Kosygin. Ikeda advocated stronger ties between Japan, China, and the Soviet Union.

Indeed, despite his many detractors in Japan, it is well nigh impossible to come up with any hard facts that justify an indictment of Ikeda's character.

Irrespective of personal opinions on his Buddhist faith, the politics and policies of the New Komei Party, or even his personality, records clearly support the contention that Ikeda is, to echo the title of a recent Oxford University Press book on the Soka Gakkai, a "global citizen,"[22] dedicated to human rights and internationalism.

His efforts in support of numerous refugee causes have earned him the United Nations High Commission for Refugees Humanitarian Award. He has also been instrumental in supporting numerous traveling exhibitions on similar causes, including "Human Rights in Today's World," "War and Peace," and "The Courage to Remember—Anne Frank and the Holocaust,"[23] to name but three. Given the troubling anti-Semitic trends in Japan, this last exhibit is especially noteworthy. Ikeda has also strongly endorsed and supported other international causes such as the Earth Charter and movements for the abolition of nuclear weapons. In 1975, he submitted (on behalf of the Soka Gakkai) some ten million signatures of citizens calling for the eradication of nuclear weapons. He has written extensively on these and related issues in his lengthy and detailed "Peace Proposals," which he has submitted annually to the United Nations since 1983. His 1996 Peace Proposal, for example, addresses the importance of human rights: "When seeking to define human rights in the broadest sense, I believe that the right to live in a truly humane way can be said to constitute the essence of human security. Human rights are fundamental and must take priority over all else; without human rights, neither peace nor human happiness is possible. Because human rights represent the most sublime and inalienable value, endowing people with their distinctly human character, their violation cannot be permitted, whether by states or by any other force."[24]

Actually, outside of Japan Ikeda is simply not the controversial figure that he is within his home country. By the publication date of this book, in 2004, he had received a staggering 156 honorary degrees and professorships from colleges and universities around the world, including the University of Glasgow, the Chinese University of Hong Kong, Moscow State University, the University of Delhi, the University of Denver, the City University of New York, and Morehouse College, to name but a few. Ikeda has also been named an honorary citizen of some 353 municipalities worldwide and has received

Daisaku Ikeda is shown here meeting with U.S. civil-rights activist Rosa Parks in Los Angeles. Ikeda first met Parks in 1993. He received the Rosa Parks Humanitarian Award in 1994. *(Photo courtesy of Soka Gakkai.)*

dozens of international awards and citations, such as the United Nations Peace Award.

Ikeda is also a prolific writer. More than a hundred of his novels, essays, collections of poetry, and children's books have been published by a variety of publishers in books that include editions in more than twenty languages. A unifying theme in Ikeda's writing is the idea that every person has a "unique mission" and unlimited potential, activated through "human revolution," a process of inner improvement and transformation. This may not strike most Westerners as an unusual theme for a religious leader of any faith. In the context of postwar Japan, however, it does stand out—especially given the strict hierarchical nature of Japanese society, which has not, as a rule, encouraged individuals to transcend the circumstances they are born into. George David Miller, in his 2002 book *Peace, Value, and Wisdom: The Educational Philosophy of Daisaku Ikeda*, zeros in on this aspect of Ikeda's approach, which, he says, emphasizes the intrinsic value of all people, regardless of social or other status: "Contrary to models of learning that encourage students to bow before external authorities, Ikeda's model of education turns people inward to internal authority: [Miller quotes Ikeda] 'The time has come to take first priority away from exterior authority and give it to the revolution that must occur in the heart of each human being.'"[25] To quote Ikeda directly:

Quite simply, there can be no true democracy unless the citizens of a country realize that they are sovereign, that they are the main protagonists, and then with wisdom and a strong sense of responsibility take action based on that realization. Democracy cannot be successful in its mission unless the people rouse themselves to become more informed and involved, unless they unite, unless they establish an unshakable force for justice and keep a strict eye on the activities of the powerful.[26]

Ikeda has also held cross-cultural dialogues with world leaders from a variety of disciplines. Thirty of these discussions have appeared as books in several languages. These include discussions with U.S. writer and philosopher Norman Cousins, two-time Nobel Prize winner Linus Pauling, British historian Arnold Toynbee, and former Soviet President Mikhail Gorbachev. At the time of the publication of this book in 2004, he is engaged in a dialogue with economist John Kenneth Galbraith.

Gekkan Pen

It is worth noting that aside from Nobuko Nobuhira's false charges, there is no record of any woman ever lodging an accusation of sexual misconduct against Daisaku Ikeda. But, the Japanese news media being what it is, *Shukan Shincho* is not the first Japanese magazine to publish a false story along such lines.

In the 1970s, a little-known far-right monthly men's magazine called *Gekkan Pen* ran a series of articles accusing Ikeda of womanizing.[27] A police investigation concluded that the editor of the magazine, Taizo Kumabe, had no evidence to support the articles, and he was arrested for criminal defamation on May 21, 1976. The court held that they had been invented and were patently false, and Kumabe was later found guilty of criminal defamation.[28] This was an even more extraordinary verdict than that in the Nobuhira case because it is so exceedingly rare and difficult for a magazine writer or editor to be found guilty of criminal libel in Japan. In the case of *Gekkan Pen,* the editor intentionally published material that he knew to be false, and he was thus found guilty of a crime. Moreover, unlike the *Shukan Shincho* articles discussed in this chapter, the *Gekkan Pen* articles did not cite the testimony of a single woman. (Again, other than Nobuhira, no woman has ever made an accusation of sexual misconduct of any sort against Ikeda.) The *Gekkan Pen* situation was so extraordinary that, in spite of Japanese magazine writers' well-earned reputations for publishing false information, there has only been one other guilty verdict in a criminal libel case involving a magazine since then, when two individuals from the now-defunct magazine *Uwasa no Shinso* (Truth of Rumors) were given suspended prison sentences for criminal libel in March 2002.

Speaking at a Soka Gakkai youth meeting in July 2003, Ikeda addressed the treatment he has received by the media in Japan over the years, both from the establishment press and the weeklies. He stressed his view that the Japanese establishment media has consistently failed to write in a meaningful way about either the Soka Gakkai's accomplishments or his own—"a situation that can easily be corroborated," he added. According to Ikeda, the Japanese media have largely remained silent on the contributions of the Soka Gakkai, while simultaneously attacking the organization and him personally in an attempt to profit from sensationalism while mitigating the Soka Gakkai's efforts to reform Japanese society. Addressing the coverage of weekly newsmagazines in particular, he stated, "What has been printed is insanity. We should always ask, 'Is there a witness to what the tabloids claim? Can they prove it?' We need to have the wisdom to discern the truth for ourselves." Ikeda insisted: "I have done nothing wrong. The scandalous articles that have appeared about me are all lies.... Some may think I deserve this treatment, but I do not deserve it."[29]

The Nobuhiras

Nobuko Nobuhira and her husband, Junko Nobuhira, hail from the northern Japanese island of Hokkaido, where they joined the Soka Gakkai in 1956. The two were active in the organization for many years, taking volunteer leadership roles within the organization in their local area. In 1992, however, the Soka Gakkai received complaints that the couple had duped and coerced rank-and-file members into lending them substantial sums of money, which they never repaid. The organization's rules prohibit members from borrowing money from one another, so it took seriously the accusations that the

Nobuhiras had not only borrowed from their fellow members, but that they had used their volunteer position to swindle the very people they were entrusted to support.

After investigating, Soka Gakkai leaders asked the Nobuhiras to resign their leadership positions; when the couple refused, they were removed from those positions. Eventually, Junko Nobuhira was taken to court by his victims in eight different lawsuits for his illegal money-borrowing activities, eventually losing all eight cases and being ordered by the courts to return some ¥68.74 million (yen) (US$687,400) to the lenders.

After he and his wife were removed from their volunteer positions, Junko Nobuhira sued Ikeda over a cemetery plot that he had purchased from the group. But, the suit was dismissed by the courts as baseless, because Ikeda, though honorary president of the Soka Gakkai, had no direct involvement with the matter and was thus neither professionally nor personally responsible for cemetery plots sold by the organization.[30] Had Nobuhira sincerely wanted to resolve the case, he would have sued the Soka Gakkai organization from which he had purchased it. Instead, he went after Ikeda personally. This can be compared to suing the CEO of a large corporation over a product sold by one division of that company. Rather than being an earnest lawsuit over the cemetery plot, this was an obvious attempt by Nobuhira to cause trouble for Ikeda.

Having been removed from their positions in May 1992, the Nobuhiras formally resigned their membership in the group in December 1993. Two years later, in December of 1995, a story that was intensely critical of both the Soka Gakkai and the Komei Party appeared in a publication of one of the Komei Party's main political rivals: the Japan Communist Party organ newspaper, *Akahata*.[31] The article was credited to an "anonymous former Soka Gakkai Women's Division Leader," later revealed to be Nobuko Nobuhira.

These details provide an important context for the appearance of Nobuko Nobuhira's false memoir in *Shukan Shincho* entitled "A Former Women's Leader in Hokkaido Breaks Her Silence, 'I Was Raped by Daisaku Ikeda,'" which appeared in February 1996, just after the *Akahata* article.[32] The piece ran in the magazine just a few years after the Nobuhiras had lost their leadership positions in the Soka Gakkai, less than a year since the courts had summarily dismissed Junko Nobuhira's attempted lawsuit against Ikeda over the cemetery plot, and less than two months since the Japan Communist Party featured Nobuko Nobuhira's article critical of the Soka Gakkai and the Komei Party, an article that made no mention of her impending sexual allegations. Also, by the time the false memoir ran in *Shukan Shincho,* Junko Nobuhira had recently lost three costly lawsuits for his and his wife's illegal money-borrowing practices. He was about to lose a fourth similar case, and an additional four cases in subsequent years.

While this background does not in itself prove Nobuko Nobuhira's memoir false, it certainly indicates a distinct pattern of dubious, immoral, and illegal behavior on behalf of the couple, a pattern that, as the district court concluded, "does not accord with the human principle of trustworthiness." This unmistakable pattern should have raised a string of bright red flags for any journalist considering writing about the couple's charges against Ikeda. Yet, it did nothing to dampen *Shukan Shincho*'s enthusiasm not only to feature Nobuko Nobuhira's false claims but to work closely with her and her husband in articulating their allegations and even in encouraging the couple to initiate a civil action on the matter. Nor did it dissuade many mainstream Japanese journalists and foreign press members from uncritically reporting the Nobuhiras' accusations. Indeed, Japanese daily newspapers ran a variety of advertisements for *Shukan Shincho*'s thirty-four sensational articles on the topic.

The False Memoir

Nobuko Nobuhira's false memoir graphically detailing her trumped-up rape allegations first appeared in the February 22, 1996, issue of *Shukan Shincho,* which was available at newsstands on February 15th. Like most major articles in the magazine, it was also heavily promoted as part of the *Shukan Shincho* advertising campaign. Thus, as noted, an estimated ten to twenty million people were exposed to the false headline: "I Was Raped by Daisaku Ikeda," as they were to many of the subsequent thirty-three articles published by the magazine on the subject. A selection of these bogus *Shukan Shincho* headlines includes: "'I Will Sue Ikeda,' Mrs. Nobuko Nobuhira Holds a Press Conference Stating That She Was Raped by Daisaku Ikeda"; "A Victim of 'Ikeda's

Raping' Confesses the 'Insanity' of Gakkai's Election Which Has Gone Too Far"; "Press Corps Quail with the 'Rape Lawsuit' of Daisaku Ikeda"; and "'Ikeda Rape Incident' That Foreign Reporters Report to the World."[33]

In her "memoir," Nobuko Nobuhira claimed to have been assaulted three times by Ikeda. She alleged that the first incident occurred in June 1973, when she was forty-six and Ikeda was forty-five years of age; that it happened a second time ten years later, in August 1983, when she was fifty-six and he was fifty-five; and she claimed that the third event happened eight years later, in August 1991, when she was sixty-four and he was sixty-three.[34]

Filing the Charges in Court

On June 5, 1996, some four months after *Shukan Shincho* published the false memoir, the Nobuhiras filed civil charges against Ikeda at the Tokyo District Court, seeking ¥74.69 million (about US$746,900) for damages suffered. Interestingly, when the court finally ruled on the matter four years later, the judge noted that "the plaintiffs' activities in the lawsuit constitute quite abnormal prosecution behavior for persons truly seeking relief from suffering, and clearly cannot be said to abide by principles of good faith and trust."[35] Even putting all the Nobuhiras' recently failed lawsuits aside, something was clearly dubious about Nobuko Nobuhira writing both an anonymous article attacking the Soka Gakkai for the Japan Communist Party and a graphic "memoir" for a *shukanshi* known for its lurid stories some months *before* beginning to pursue legal recourse against Ikeda.

Another critical point is that the couple filed only a civil suit and did not attempt to file criminal charges against Ikeda. Although they claimed to be the victims of grave criminal behavior—multiple violent rapes—rather than seeking to have Ikeda jailed, they sought only remuneration through the courts and publicity through the press. Had the couple attempted to bring criminal charges, the case would have fallen immediately under the scrutiny of government prosecutors, who would have been required by law to decide whether there was enough credible evidence to proceed. Given the complete absence of supporting evidence, as well as the numerous inconsistencies of the claims, there is no doubt that prosecutors would have dismissed the Nobuhiras' claims outright.

Pictured here are a few of the nearly three dozen articles featured in *Shukan Shincho* in support of bogus rape charges against Daisaku Ikeda. The Japanese courts later rejected the Nobuhiras' claims as false. The court said that their having been filed represented an abuse of the Nobuhiras' legal right to sue and went so far as to say that they were made "contrary to conduct in good faith and trust." The court ruling includes an admonishment of the Japanese press for having sensationalized and profited from such an unfounded charge.

Civil claims in Japan are a different matter. They are subject to no outside review and go directly to court, regardless of merit. Even in a case such as this, wherein the court eventually rejected the allegations as specious abuses of the right to sue, the plaintiffs are automatically entitled to two appeals to higher courts.

Thus, the Nobuhiras were automatically able to appeal their claims, rejected by the Tokyo District Court, to the Tokyo High Court and then to the Supreme Court of Japan. Moreover, because the Japanese court system is so infamously slow, the case dragged on for more than five years.

The Conclusions of the Court

The Nobuhiras had actually lodged six separate claims in the case, three on behalf of Nobuko and three on behalf of her husband, Junko. The Tokyo District Court dismissed all three of Nobuko's claims and one of Junko's claims due to time limits for suing in civil cases (something similar to the statute of limitations in the United States). The court then went on to reject the remaining two of Junko's claims as an abuse of his right to sue.

Nobuko Nobuhira had sought financial compensation for each of the alleged rapes, one in 1973, one in 1983, and one in 1991. Her husband lodged his own separate set of three claims for financial compensation related to each of these three alleged incidents. Japanese law allows husbands to sue alleged perpetrators accused of raping their wives. In these cases, husbands usually sue for having their "right to enjoy married life infringed upon," as Nobuhira did.

In Japan, alleged victims are required to sue for damages related to rape within three years of the alleged event. Therefore, when the Nobuhiras lodged their claims in 1996, all three of Nobuko Nobuhira's claims were dismissed because even the most recent of her claims was alleged to have occurred in 1991. But, only one of Junko Nobuhira's claims was dismissed for reasons related to the passage of time. Because Junko Nobuhira claimed to have only learned of the supposed rapes from his wife in 1995, the lodging of his claims in 1996 was deemed to be within the relevant three-year period.

A second legal issue related to time was, however, also applied to Junko Nobuhira's claims. This law requires a claim for an alleged incident involving assault on one's wife to be filed within twenty years of the date of the alleged incident. As a result, Junko Nobuhira's claim regarding the supposed 1973 incident was also dismissed. However, his remaining two claims, related to the supposed 1983 and 1991 incidents, were within the twenty-year period and were not dismissed. As noted, these last two claims were later rejected by the court as constituting an "abuse of the legal right to sue."

The unambiguous findings of the Tokyo District Court could not contrast any more sharply with *Shukan Shincho*'s coverage of the case. The court's conclusion reads in part, "Filing the suit does not sincerely aim to fulfill any substantive rights of the plaintiff or to resolve the lawsuit, and instead the complaint in this case has its purpose in imposing on the defendant the burden of responding to the suit and other losses." A second important point is that the court concluded Nobuko Nobuhira's statements to be "quite abnormal with respect to the statements describing the process of recollection." The court noted many different areas where her statements were inconsistent and concluded that the "reasons given for [her] confused memory are also very irrational without any convincing points, and lack credibility." The most extreme instance of the incredible nature of Nobuko's testimony came when—more than three years into the proceedings—she inexplicably increased the number of times she said she had been raped. The court wrote:

Consistently thus far, the defendant's wrongdoings allegedly occurred three times; however, according to the allegation after the change noted at the right, the wrongdoings occurred four times. This involves the basic framework of Nobuko's complaint, and from that perspective, the change in allegations should certainly have convincing reasons. Nonetheless, as examined below, as far as what the plaintiff states as reasons leading to the transition in plaintiff's allegations, none can be said to be sufficiently convincing.

The court also noted that despite the reportedly violent nature of the rapes, the Nobuhiras could point to no physical evidence or records of physical evidence, or to any witnesses or other evidence whatsoever that supported their claims in any way.[36] Indeed, compelling evidence overwhelmingly contradicted those claims.

For example, Nobuko Nobuhira said the alleged 1983 assault occurred in a specific prefabricated building at a Soka Gakkai facility, where she had been in charge of operating a coffee shop. Yet, not only did the coffee shop not exist in 1983, the entire building did not exist. It had been dismantled the previous year, a fact corroborated by aerial land-survey photographs taken by the Japanese government's forestry agency.

Regarding the supposed 1991 incident, Nobuko Nobuhira claimed in her *Shukan Shincho* memoir to have been raped in the early morning hours, outdoors, in such a violent manner that her clothes were left "in tatters" and that her "body was covered with bruises and scratches."[37] Yet, the location she gave (near an entrance gate to an SGI Soka Gakkai facility) was in plain sight of a security building that was manned at the time, and there were many people on the facility grounds. Yet none of the security staff, nor anyone else, had seen or heard any such event. Moreover, photographs taken of her on the day that she claimed to have been assaulted revealed no scratches or bruises on her face. In fact, contrary to her claim in *Shukan Shincho* that she could not participate in Japanese "radio exercises," or calisthenics, she was photographed doing just that. Indeed, Nobuko Nobuhira could not name or point to anyone who witnessed an altercation of any sort between her and Ikeda, nor could anyone corroborate any injuries, damaged clothes, or even any visible emotional upset during any of the hours and days that followed any of the dates she identified.

To rehash the minutiae of the court's proceedings would only give the Nobuhiras' fabricated claims more credence than they deserve; however, it seems worthwhile to quote a key section from the Summation (see appendix E for the complete Summation) of the actual court conclusion, as written by the presiding judge and upheld by both the high court and supreme court:

In advancing this case under the explanation that the factual foundation is severely lacking in each incident of this case, it may be inevitably assumed that the plaintiffs repeatedly performed the prohibited acts of lending and borrowing money between Soka Gakkai members by using their positions as senior leaders in that organization; that they became disgruntled with the organization because of their dismissals from their leadership positions within the Soka Gakkai, which resulted from their having caused troubles for the members; that they demanded but failed to obtain the return of cemetery plot monies after leaving the Soka Gakkai, and that they thus repeatedly made extortion-like phone calls to the Soka Gakkai headquarters, which still failed to produce any results; and that, as revenge, they publicly trumpeted the written narrative of Nobuko through the mass media; and that, as an extension to the foregoing, they filed the complaints in this case for the purpose of providing tangible and intangible losses to the defendant within and outside of the lawsuit.

Hence, the filing of this suit does not sincerely aim to fulfill any substantive rights of the plaintiff or to resolve the lawsuit, and instead the complaint in this case was made with the purpose of imposing on the defendant the burden of responding to the suit and of other losses. Moreover, the complaints alleged by the plaintiff lack factual foundation, and fall short of the requirement for protection. The complaint in this case, therefore, must be recognized as a legal action that severely lacks relevance with respect to the intentions and purposes of the civil litigation system, and is contrary to conduct in good faith and trust. Consequently, the complaint in this case can be considered unlawful, because it abuses the right of legal action. Continuing the hearing of this case is not only cruel to the defendant, but may potentially result in the Court contrarily siding with the wrongful undertakings of the plaintiff. Thus, terminating the hearing of this lawsuit at this time is reasonable.[38]

Shukan Shincho and the Soka Gakkai

The longtime adversarial relationship between *Shukan Shincho* and the Soka Gakkai is well known in Japan. By its own admission, *Shukan Shincho* has run almost exclusively negative coverage of the religious organization for decades. In response, Soka Gakkai publications have carried various articles denouncing *Shukan Shincho* as disreputable, and the organization has successfully sued the magazine on two occasions.

Yet, it would be a misrepresentation to describe the relationship between the magazine and the Buddhist group as one between mutually aggressive antagonists. The relationship is much more akin to that between Katsuichi Honda and *Shukan Bunshun*, described in the next chapter. In both cases, a *shukanshi* and its publisher singled out a victim for attack, implementing a campaign of false scandals and misinformation in order to benefit financially from the resultant controversies while damaging the reputation of the individual being attacked.

A search of the Oya Soichi Bunko magazine library shows that in the 770 issues published from 1987 (the earliest date available for computerized search) to July 24, 2003, *Shukan Shincho* published some 342 articles with the words "Soka Gakkai," "Ikeda," or "Komei" in the headline. (Specifically, there were 190 articles with "Soka Gakkai" in the headline, 82 with "Ikeda," and 77 with "Komei.") Overall, 44 percent of the issues of *Shukan Shincho* published during these fifteen years have featured negative stories about the organization, its leader, or the Komei political party with one or the other in the headline. This, of course, does not include articles that are about the Soka Gakkai, Ikeda, or Komei, but which do not include the three previously listed key words in their headlines. Given that such articles are in no short supply, it is certainly safe to say that well over half of all *Shukan Shincho* magazines published during the period included negative coverage of the topics in question and that this composes a standard and substantial part of the magazine's editorial approach. Although the coverage varies significantly from publication to publication, it is also safe to say that no other prominent news provider has written negatively of the Soka Gakkai, Ikeda, or the Komei Party nearly as intensively or regularly as has *Shukan Shincho*.

By contrast, a search of all major Soka Gakkai–related magazines during the same period for headlines containing the words *Shukan Shincho* yielded no articles whatsoever. Although Soka Gakkai–related publications have carried a number of articles critical of *Shukan Shincho*, particularly in recent years (2002–2003), such articles have not appeared often enough to come close to reciprocal coverage of *Shukan Shincho* by Soka Gakkai publications.

Of course, *Shukan Shincho* has had much more to gain in its negative coverage of the Soka Gakkai than vice versa. Because the Soka Gakkai is such a large and prominent organization, and Daisaku Ikeda has been so well known for so long, contentious articles about the group and its leader can yield huge sales for *Shukan Shincho*. With literally millions of active and inactive domestic Soka Gakkai members to draw from, *Shukan Shincho* (which has an average readership of less than half a million) need only sell additional copies to a tiny share of the group's followers and detractors to enjoy a serious boost in weekly sales figures.

Soka Gakkai publications, on the other hand, are not likely to receive any added sales by printing articles (negative or positive) about Japanese weekly newsmagazines. Their readers are mainly interested in Buddhism and are hardly drawn to articles about *shukanshi*. Moreover, every time the Soka Gakkai addresses scandals appearing in *Shukan Shincho*, it risks calling more attention to the magazines and their articles.

Legal History

As noted, the Soka Gakkai has taken *Shukan Shincho* to court twice, winning both lawsuits. According to spokesperson Kunishige Maeda, the organization could have brought and won many more cases against the magazine, but the Soka Gakkai purposely ignored the vast majority of defamatory articles: "The articles are written, in part, to damage our reputation, so responding to them is just rising to their bait."[39]

This fits with the common wisdom in Japan, which presumes that legal actions against the news media tend to be close to useless and, in fact, often provide media members with new ammunition to use in follow-up articles on the legal proceedings. Indeed, this court case is a prime example of this situation: the Nobuhiras' court case against the Soka Gakkai provided *Shukan*

Shincho with the opportunity to run thirty-four stories, each repeating the couple's bogus allegations against Ikeda.

Had the Nobuhiras not taken Ikeda to court, the magazine could not have justified running more than a handful of stories on the topic. And if the Soka Gakkai had countersued the Nobuhiras, that "issue" may well have been in the courts even longer and could have provided still more fodder for the magazine.

It is impossible to calculate how much *Shukan Shincho* profited from its coverage of the Nobuhiras' false allegations, but given the lurid nature of the subject, combined with one of the most-famous living Japanese, it must have been a lot.

Maeda speculates that had it all happened in the United States or Great Britain, his organization would have been able to sue the magazine successfully for huge sums as compensation for damages. But, in Japan, even had the Soka Gakkai been entirely successful, in both a countersuit against the Nobuhiras and a defamation suit against *Shukan Shincho,* the courts would not have required either to pay more than a pittance—perhaps not even enough to cover legal expenses. "Victories" in such cases result in meaningless punishment to the magazines, especially when the upside for the magazines in running defamatory articles can be so lucrative.

Editorial Rationale

Asked why his magazine has covered the Buddhist group and Ikeda so negatively over the years, Hiroshi Matsuda, who was editor in chief of *Shukan Shincho* from 1990 to 1998, said that it had nothing to do with the Soka Gakkai being a minority group or with the Komei Party being a challenge to the status quo in Japan. While he freely admitted that selling magazines is the top priority at *Shukan Shincho,* he insisted that his magazine has been "fighting for justice" for years, and that this has naturally meant writing critically about the Soka Gakkai, which he says is "not a true religion"[40] but a "subversive group."[41]

Matsuda contends that his magazine has gained a reputation for bravely standing up to the Soka Gakkai's "damaging influence" on Japanese society. "You know, when it comes to *Shukan Shincho* and the Soka Gakkai, I am not the first to fire a shot across their bow," he explained in an interview for this book. "*Shukan Shincho* has been providing critical coverage of the Soka

Gakkai on a continuous basis for more than twenty years. And essentially, the magazine started out with this when the Soka Gakkai was doing their missionary work, going out and getting converts.... The mainline press was essentially very weak in the way that they portrayed this problem. But *Shukan Shincho* came out with stern coverage."[42]

According to Matsuda, *Shukan Shincho* has a reputation for challenging the Soka Gakkai on many issues and thus has attracted more critics of the group than any other news media outlet: "Our critical coverage in turn caused *Shukan Shincho* to become a big collecting basket of sources about the Soka Gakkai. All those who were bullied or ostracized or thrown out of the organization or somehow maltreated by the Soka Gakkai started serving as sources for us. Shinchosha became like *the* place for people to bring their grievances with the Soka Gakkai so they could be exposed. So, basically, it's no miracle that we end up with most of the information about the Soka Gakkai compared to other members of the press. We have a lot more information than others that we feel compelled to release."[43]

Jun Kamei, a former *Shukan Shincho* staff reporter and assistant editor with twenty years' experience there, has a completely different take on *Shukan Shincho*'s coverage of the organization. Kamei, who worked with Matsuda at *Shukan Shincho*, left his job in disgust over what he describes as "consistently unethical" journalistic practices there. He argues that the magazine's coverage of the Soka Gakkai, like most of its coverage, has been driven almost purely by commercialism. According to Kamei, "The idea that *Shukan Shincho* fights for truth is absurd." He insists that the primary reason that Japanese weeklies, and especially *Shukan Shincho*, feature sensational articles about the Soka Gakkai is that they know that "those articles sell magazines."[44]

Kamei says that *Shukan Shincho*'s coverage of the Buddhist group has a special appeal to the magazine's particular readership. According to him, the key aspect of *Shukan Shincho*'s success is its ability to provide its readers with a "false sense of superiority." For this reason, he says, *Shukan Shincho* focuses intensively and negatively on Japanese minority groups: Koreans and other foreigner residents of Japan, women, poor people, human-rights organizations, and religious minorities such as the Soka Gakkai.

According to Kamei, *Shukan Shincho*'s readers receive special gratification from articles that portray minority religious groups in an ugly light:

> Religion is fairly secularized here in Japan, you know. There isn't much of it, really, outside of ceremonial events and the like. The Soka Gakkai, however, is an organization grounded in Buddhism. It is a big group with principles and prayer, a lot of prayer. And that activity of praying is quite odd from the perspective of the average Japanese.
>
> Even with Christian and Islamic praying, if it's devout and intense it tends to be derided by mainstream Japanese, who are primarily a secular people. It's not just that it makes people feel uncomfortable. It is that, but there's more to it actually. Pure, spiritual matters tend to make Japanese worried. Since all the ugliness and defeat of World War II, many Japanese feel that they need to have some sort of faith. But most of us don't have any real faith.
>
> Then there's the Soka Gakkai, with their intense praying, causing the rest of us Japanese to worry about whether or not we, too, should have faith in something. People are deeply concerned about what they should be doing. But then here comes a magazine like *Shukan Shincho* saying that the Soka Gakkai is just stupid, stupid, that they are crazy. That type of writing makes people feel much more comfortable. It's a relief to have someone feeding them lines like that. After reading *Shukan Shincho*'s advertised headlines and articles, they don't worry about not having faith anymore. Again, *Shukan Shincho* sells superiority, solace.[45]

Kamei emphasized that his understanding of *Shukan Shincho*'s editorial approach is not theoretical or speculative, but based on his long career there as a writer and assistant editor—jobs that required that he fully understand what appealed most to his magazine's readers. If he is correct, then it is not unreasonable to compare *Shukan Shincho*'s ongoing negative coverage of the Soka Gakkai with the negative coverage of Jews by the Japanese media in general. In the case of anti-Semitism, the weekly media are exploiting fears and confusion about a foreign religious minority. In the case of the Soka Gakkai, *Shukan Shincho* is exploiting those same fears and confusions about a domestic religious minority.

Jun Kamei is a former editor of *Shukan Shincho* who has since come out strongly against Japanese newsmagazine writing. He is holding his book *Shukanshi no Yomikata* (How to Read *Shukanshi*), a cutting exposé on the industry.

Maeda offered a similar take on the matter. When he was asked about *Shukan Shincho's* negative articles on the Soka Gakkai, Maeda focused less on the idea that the magazine's readers do not appreciate prayer and religion, and put forward the idea that the conflict is a matter of colliding worldviews. According to Maeda, those who regularly purchase Japanese weekly newsmagazines like *Shukan Shincho* are not likely to appreciate the idealistic sentiments espoused by the Soka Gakkai. He pointed to a famous statement by the late Juichi Saito, one of the founding forces behind *Shukan Shincho*. According to the magazine *Aera*, Saito asserted that "every human being at their core is uncivilized. Once you peel off their superficial appearance, they have a taste for love, money, women and fame. I am also extremely uncivilized. Although it is impossible for me [to physically have relations with women at my late age], I am still fond of them. I am also greedy. I wanted to write about these things in *Shukan Shincho* and I still have this desire."[46] According to Maeda, this perspective served as the foundation of *Shukan Shincho*: "Mr. Saito built an editorial policy on this idea, and delivered it in the format of a weekly journal, *Shukan Shincho*. Mr. Saito and those who buy into his philosophy as readers of these kinds of magazines may find it difficult to relate to the motivations of Soka Gakkai members who work hard to promote the common good with a positive sense of self-identity."[47]

Even if one does not agree with Kamei or Matsuda on the motivation and appeal to some readers of *Shukan Shincho's* attacks against the Soka Gakkai, it is impossible to deny that the magazine regularly singles out minority groups and unusual individuals for attack. Although the Soka Gakkai has in many ways established itself as a legitimate and respected part of Japanese society, as pointed out by Walter Mondale, it nevertheless remains a minority. And its leader, Ikeda, has long been an outspoken nonconformist. In relentlessly portraying the Soka Gakkai and Ikeda in negative ways, *Shukan Shincho* helps to moderate their influence, clearly buttressing the Japanese status quo.

Dr. Lawrence Carter, dean of the Martin Luther King Jr. Chapel at Morehouse College in Atlanta and an ordained Baptist minister, has worked with the SGI-USA and Daisaku Ikeda for many years. Morehouse College bestowed an honorary doctorate on Ikeda, and Dean Carter has initiated an annual award called the "Ghandi, King, Ikeda Community Builders Prize," and a traveling exhibit entitled "Gandhi, King, Ikeda: A Legacy of Building Peace." The award is cosponsored by the Martin Luther King Jr. Chapel at Morehouse College and the SGI-USA. According to Carter, he came up with the idea for the award, not to compare the three men for whom it is named, but as a way of extolling those whose actions for peace have cut across cultural and religious boundaries. Recipients to date include Prince El Hassan bin Talal of Jordan, president of the Club of Rome; Dr. Michael Nobel, board chair of the Nobel Family Society and the Nonviolence Project; and Nobel Peace Prize laureate Betty Williams. When the Ghandi, King, Ikeda Community Builders Prize became the subject of a critical 2003 *Shukan Shincho* article, Carter wrote a lengthy letter of protest to the magazine. In it, he states:

> "Controversy" is an inevitable partner of greatness. No one who challenges the established order is free of it. Gandhi had his detractors, as did Dr. King. Dr. Ikeda is no exception. Controversy camouflages the intense resistance of entrenched authority to conceding their special status and privilege. "Insults" are the weapons of the morally weak; "slander" is the tool of the spiritually bereft. Controversy is testament to the noble work of these three individuals in their respective societies.[48]

Carter's point zeros in on the penchant of *Shukan Shincho* and other Japanese weeklies to attack nonconformists and reformers. While *Shukan Shincho* no doubt ran its story primarily to sell copies, it also defamed Ikeda, an individual praised by Dean Carter and many others as a Japanese reformer. Unfortunately, outspoken individuals who challenge those in power in Japan are prime targets for *shukanshi*.

Shukan Shincho and the Nobuhiras

In 2000, after the Japanese Supreme Court confirmed the district court's rejection of the Nobuhiras' claims, Eiichi Yamamoto, a retired senior member of the editorial staff of *Yomiuri Shimbun* and a lecturer at Gakushuin University, wrote a book whose title can be translated as "Media Terrorism"[49] that deals with the Nobuhiras' charges. In the course of his research, Yamamoto, who is a practicing member of the Soka Gakkai, uncovered seventeen audio recordings of conversations that took place in early 1996 among the Nobuhiras, a *Shukan Shincho* writer named Mamoru Kadowaki, and others. The conversations occurred just a few weeks before Nobuko Nobuhira's "memoir" appeared in *Shukan Shincho* and included extensive discussions about what *Shukan Shincho* might publish on behalf of the Nobuhiras.

At the time of the discussions, Kadowaki was himself actively involved in a legal action involving a Soka Gakkai member and *Shukan Shincho*. The Soka Gakkai member had sued the magazine for defamation, focusing on material written by Kadowaki. In the end, the magazine was forced to pay ¥1.1 million, or about US$11,000, to the Soka Gakkai member. This was, at the time, about the average award given to a victorious plaintiff in a Japanese libel case. Of course, Junko Nobuhira had already lost his spurious cemetery-plot case, and the Nobuhiras together had lost three of their eight losing cases for their illegal money-borrowing practices. Although the recordings do not constitute a "smoking gun" or include unequivocal statements from Kadowaki or the Nobuhiras that they specifically intended to publish false information, they do include a number of provocative exchanges. For instance, Kadowaki repeatedly explains to the Nobuhiras that allegations of "sexual harassment" would not be sufficient to seriously damage the Soka Gakkai but that full-fledged rape charges would be required: "The court has to be convinced, and of course, people in general also have to be convinced. I, of course, understand your anger, Mr. Nobuhira. That's why I'm listening to your story now, to understand how far the facts go, and how we can deliver the maximum punch with them."[50]

Kadowaki states that if the harassment was "just something light, like an embrace, it would be no good."[51] Eventually, Junko Nobuhira responds to

Kadowaki's prodding and suggests that his wife up her charges. "What about rape, not merely attempted rape?" he asks.[52]

The recordings also include detailed discussions about the most effective way to hold press conferences, which type of lawsuit might be the most successful (criminal or civil), and plans for sharing the allegations with other media outlets and political rivals of the Komei Party.

Also recorded is the voice of a lawyer called in for consultation, as well as the voices of some lay leaders of Nichiren Shoshu, the Buddhist sect with which the Soka Gakkai had previously been affiliated, but from which it had split just a few years previously in 1991. According to Yamamoto, these recordings reached him via an anonymous member of Nichiren Shoshu who was outraged at their scheming.

On December 27, 2001, *Shukan Shincho* attacked Yamamoto's book in an article.[53] In the piece, the magazine claims that its staff also had copies of the recordings to which Yamamoto refers. The article does not question the accuracy of the statements on the recordings, as quoted by Yamamoto, including those noted above, but instead merely accuses Yamamoto of quoting the recordings too selectively. The magazine claims that Yamamoto failed to quote parts of the tape that "expose secrets" that prove that Nobuko Nobuhira truly was raped. But *Shukan Shincho* itself fails to identify what these "secrets" are. Needless to say, if anything on the recordings substantively supported her claims, it surely would have been used in court, and the Nobuhiras' case would not have been so strongly rejected.

The recordings show that the Nobuhiras, *Shukan Shincho,* and Nichiren Shoshu worked together to develop allegations and a course of action that would damage Ikeda and the Soka Gakkai while promoting their own agendas. In fact, in his interview for this book, Hiroshi Matsuda freely admitted that his staff at *Shukan Shincho* had worked closely with the Nobuhiras: "We spent about three weeks going over Mrs. Nobuhira's testimony. I was editor in chief at the time. At the beginning, she didn't want to admit what happened, and I think she was very hesitant because she was with her husband and she didn't want to talk about it. But as our reporter worked to convince her that it was important to talk about it, she was able to make the decision to do so in a natural fashion."[54]

Matsuda did not see any problem with his staff's decision to essentially become part of the story by working so intimately with the Nobuhiras for three weeks on the development of their accusations and court case. In discussing his magazine's coverage of the case, Matsuda, who has been with *Shukan Shincho* for more than thirty-five years, repeatedly invoked the old *shukanshi* shibboleth of literary-narrative journalism. He explained that Japanese *shukanshi* represent a special type of news source, "a very unique model in the world. They are unlike the weeklies in any other country. So this characteristic Japanese publication needs be considered like that. People need to clearly understand its uniqueness."

Matsuda said that while *shukanshi* writers strive to keep their material as accurate as possible and to avoid lawsuits, their readerships expect them to put their articles into a narrative form and to add a certain amount of "emotional expression":

> Whatever we do is based on hearsay, right, if you think about it. I mean, we are gathering impressions from as many people as possible at the time, so if those people give their impressions and exaggerate, there's always the possibility that the exaggerations seep through.
>
> We are in a world, though, where we have to be very careful about invasion of people's privacy and especially defamation issues. So, what we try to do is to eliminate as much as possible any of that. At the same time, we are in a business where we have to sell these publications. So the headlines, I think it's fair to say, have slight exaggerations in them. At the same time, without these exaggerations, it's almost like, you know, we're dead. It's like dead journalism. There's nothing exciting about it. In order for it to be alive and kicking, you know, you have to appeal to the emotions of the reader. It has to grab the person and say, "Hey, this is interesting." We define this as the metaphor tool. But it's very difficult for people to understand what we are trying to do.

According to Matsuda, the court conclusions in the Nobuhira case were not relevant to *Shukan Shincho*'s coverage:

> What it boils down to is that we hear what people have to say, and we write about it. I mean, in that sense, the facts are not necessarily going to be

completely in alignment with each other. There's going to be little, you know, degrees of error. Now, the truth is an entirely separate matter. So when we are sued, we constantly make certain that we get across the point that what we are trying to do is to present the truth. So, when you talk about Mrs. Nobuhira's rape and Daisaku Ikeda, you have to remember it was a long time ago. There was a significant lapse of time.[55] So, you know, of course, Mrs. Nobuhira's memory may have played tricks on her that caused things to be different. What I'm trying to say is that we discerned truth in what she had to say. And that is what was important, it's not the technical details or the lawsuit being lost and thrown out on technical merits.[56]

Matsuda's explanation that he and his editors "discerned truth" in a manner that differed from that of the court is revealing. As noted, in Japan there is a long tradition whereby "social truth" often takes precedence over facts; and while this tradition is by no means all-pervasive, it plays a big part in *shukanshi* reporting and has serious repercussions throughout the industry. Such a cultural attitude can even lend the veneer of respectability to the former editor of *Shukan Bunshun* and *Marco Polo* magazines, Kazuyoshi Hanada, when he asserts that public debate of whether the Nazis actually perpetrated the Holocaust ought to be acceptable. Hanada says this even after acknowledging the massive body of data that proves beyond any doubt the reality of that horrific slaughter. For Hanada, the fact that some individuals deny the Holocaust is enough to validate serious public debate on the subject. And just as there are those who, against all logic, dismiss as fiction the genocide of Europe's Jews, a vocal parade of so-called experts has stepped forward in Japan to claim that the infamous Nanjing Massacre never happened. As a result, active public debate on that subject exists today in Japan, again despite a mountain of irrefutable evidence to the contrary.

Hiroshi Matsuda was editor in chief of *Shukan Shincho* magazine from 1990 to 1998, during which time he oversaw the publication of many of the most extreme articles highlighted in this book.

In Japan, where the emphasis on "social truths" can override logic, science, and historical fact, reporters and publishers often feel completely free to regurgitate the claims of questionable sources (such as the Nobuhiras) without confirming the validity of their claims, sometimes even in the face of contradictory data. Thus, as Matsuda explains above, even though Nobuko Nobuhira's claims were unsupported by the evidence and were proven in court to contradict reality (e.g., her claim to have been assaulted in a building that did not exist at that time), *Shukan Shincho* "discerned truth" in what she said, and that is what mattered to them. In other words, according to Matsuda, the "social truth" of what he and his staff perceived superceded measurable, concrete evidence and logic.

Actually, it seems very likely that Matsuda and his staff discerned no truth whatsoever, social or otherwise, in the Nobuhiras' charges. As shown by the audio recordings, *Shukan Shincho* either helped to concoct the Nobuhiras' charges or at the very least encouraged the couple to invent and go public with them.

Still, that Matsuda could justify his magazine's libelous coverage with the argument that his staff "discerned the truth" of the Nobuhiras' claims, evidence to the contrary notwithstanding, is fundamental. Such a claim by Matsuda—formerly one of the most influential editors in his industry—goes right to the heart of Japanese newsmagazine reporting. It shows how *shukanshi* regularly subordinate accuracy to the overriding need to come up with sensational material. Although the same thing is done, to varying degrees, by tabloid journalists the world over, it is a special problem in Japan. The editorial philosophy of literary-narrative journalism provides editors and reporters with a powerful rhetorical tool—one that, when combined with the argument that "the public has the right to know," can justify writing and publishing just about anything.

The Wider Response of the System

Shukan Shincho's role in the Nobuhiras' false allegations did not occur in a vacuum. A number of publications and other players also exploited the malicious claims for their own ends.

As we have seen, the Soka Gakkai, by its very existence, can be perceived as a threat to the Japanese power holders in a number of ways. On a very basic level, the mere fact that it constitutes a distinct minority group within a nation where many pride themselves on their physical and cultural homogeneity is problematic in itself. But, as Jun Kamei has noted, the Soka Gakkai's intense spirituality may add to the discomfort felt by the dominant secular Japanese. Perhaps most important, however, is the religious group's support for a political party that has steadily gained in power and influence over the past forty-plus years.

Political events in the 1990s made the Komei Party a major player in the first real threat to the way the Japanese system had operated for decades. The LDP had dominated Japanese politics since the party's inception in 1955. So strong was the LDP's hold that many observers began describing the country as a single-party state.

So when the "LDP-free" Morihiro Hosokawa coalition took control of the government during parts of 1993 and 1994, it was a major milestone in postwar Japanese politics. During this brief period, the Komei Party played a critical role in the coalition. And although the LDP regained power in 1994, the many elections held over the next several years were contentious, to say the least.

It was in this political environment that the Nobuhiras' allegations were promoted in *Shukan Shincho*. As the Komei Party's founder and the leader of the organization that had provided it with the bulk of its electoral base, Daisaku Ikeda had been closely identified with the party throughout its history. A serious scandal involving him had the potential to create real trouble for the Komei Party, and it soon became clear that the party's many rivals were ready to capitalize on just such an opportunity.

Nobuko Nobuhira's false memoir first appeared in the February 22 issue of *Shukan Shincho*, which would have gone on sale around February 15, 1996. Interestingly, on February 19—just four days later—LDP politician Takashi Fukaya officially requested at the Lower House Budget Committee directors' meeting that Ikeda be summoned to the Diet to testify about the article.

Parliamentary summonses are standard practice in Japan, widely used to humiliate those being summoned. Fukaya even timed his request to coincide with televised Diet proceedings, a move that dealt a damaging blow to the Komei Party while giving *Shukan Shincho* great publicity. A month later, in April, Katsuhiko Shirakawa, another LDP politician, also tried to summon Ikeda before the Diet and for the same reason. And the next month, yet another LDP Diet member repeated the call. Although all three attempts were stymied, and Ikeda was never required to appear, they bolstered the legitimacy of the Nobuhiras' claims and contributed significantly to rumormongering on the matter.

And that was not all. *Jiyu Shimpo,* the LDP's organ paper at the time,[57] and *Akahata,* the Japan Communist Party's paper, also featured sensational coverage on the matter. Moreover, pamphlets reiterating the "memoir" were printed and distributed throughout Japan as part of anti-Komei election campaigns by both the LDP and Nichiren Shoshu. The Nichiren Shoshu magazine *Emyo* also publicized and supported Nobuko Nobuhira's false accusations. Like sharks circling an easy meal, the various rival groups closed in.

In the deluge of nearly three-dozen *Shukan Shincho* articles and the advertisements for each of those articles, election-related pamphlets featuring the accusations, summonses by LDP politicians, sensational articles that appeared in *Jiyu Shimpo, Akahata,* and *Emyo,* as well as the smaller pieces in the mainstream press, it is safe to say that the Japanese public was thoroughly informed that a woman claimed to have been raped by Daisaku Ikeda. Moreover, virtually all these reports presented the claims as true or likely to be true when precisely the opposite was the case.

This continued until 1998, when court proceedings on the matter began to make clear, to even the most casual observers of the case, that the Nobuhiras' charges were patently false and had been lodged for unscrupulous reasons. That year, the LDP

In 1998 Prime Minister Ryutaro Hashimoto apologized for the Liberal Democratic Party's exploitation of the incorrect reporting on the Nobuhiras' false allegations. *(Photo courtesy of AP/Wide World Photos.)*

issued two separate apologies to the Soka Gakkai for its role in exploiting the matter, including an apology from then–Prime Minister Ryutaro Hashimoto himself. Unfortunately, and all too typically, both apologies were largely ignored by the Japanese press. Moreover, the other publications, such as *Shukan Shincho, Akahata,* and *Emyo,* did not follow suit and have not apologized to this day.

Mainstream Coverage of the Nobuhiras' Charges

That for the most part mainstream newspapers and broadcasters in Japan merely noted Nobuko Nobuhira's charges with brief pieces on the topic or avoided reporting on it altogether does not absolve them from serious culpability in abetting the scandal.

On February 23, 1996, the Nobuhiras held the first press conference regarding her memoir in *Shukan Shincho.* A few months later, on June 24, the couple held a second press conference, this time at the Foreign Press Club of Japan, to publicize their having filed civil charges against Ikeda at the Tokyo District Court. While the first press conference was sparsely attended (as it dealt only with the publishing of the claims), many major commercial television stations, including TV Asahi's News Station and TBS's NEWS 23, covered the second conference concerning the filing of the claims in court. Of the broadcasters present, only the state-run station Nihon Hoso Kyokai (the Japan Broadcasting Corporation or NHK) refrained from putting something about the press conference on the air. The press conference was also noted in small news pieces that appeared in the back pages of many papers, although the *Yomiuri Shimbun* and the *Asahi Shimbun* withheld mention of it. The English-language *Japan Times,* for example, ran a short piece simply stating that Nobuko Nobuhira had appeared at the Foreign Press Club and giving the nature of her claims.

On the surface, this kind of reporting does not seem unreasonable or inappropriate. A closer look, however, reveals how frighteningly dangerous it can be, not only to those who are misrepresented—in this case, Ikeda—but also to the general public, which is grossly misled by such shoddy journalism. If every civil charge lodged in Japan were reported in such a sensational and irresponsible manner, there would be no newspaper space or airtime for actual news.

While most notices of the allegations were short and purely factual, not one of them contextualized those charges within the couple's serious ongoing legal and other problems or questioned the legitimacy of the charges in any way. Given the many reasons the courts listed for dismissing the couple's allegations, any diligent reporter would have had serious doubts about repeating those allegations on air or in print. Yet the Japanese establishment press failed to rise to the occasion. Not a single story ran in the leading papers, on television, or on the radio challenging, questioning, or otherwise properly contextualizing the couple's allegations made at the press conference.

This culpability does not end at mere sins of omission either, for headlines of *Shukan Shincho*'s libelous stories appeared in the advertisements promoting each week's issue of *Shukan Shincho* in many of the country's leading dailies. It is understandable for mainstream journalists in any country to ignore sensational charges that appear in an alternative magazine. How often, for example, does the *New York Times* or the *Times* in Great Britain bother to refute a scandalous article in less prestigious publications? Obviously, it seldom happens. However, Western tabloids do not regularly buy advertising space in top prestigious newspapers, where they brandish their headlines. In this case, however, Japan's mainstream journalists ignored such a blatant fabrication, even as it was being published on their own pages, via such advertisements. Moreover, the allegations did not just concern the dalliances of another celebrity, or even a midlevel politician, but graphically smeared one of the most famous and influential individuals in the country for the past several decades. Given the severity of the charges, the stature of their target, the fact that they appeared literally everywhere, and the way the LDP and Communist Party alike latched onto them (including on the Diet floor), one would expect at least one mainstream Japanese journalist to investigate their legitimacy in some meaningful way, either to champion them or refute them. Yet silence reigned.

Even when in 2000 the Supreme Court confirmed the district court's rejection of the Nobuhiras' claims as an abuse of the right to sue, the issue received scant attention in the mainstream press. Thus, while the initial false claims and proceedings of the court case were heralded across the country, the results were barely noted.

Hajime Kitamura, former editor in chief of *Sunday Mainichi,* former head of the Japan Federation of Press Workers' Unions, and current head of public relations for the *Mainichi Shimbun,* summed up the situation:

> The Soka Gakkai is a large and powerful religious organization in Japan. So if a weekly writes a critical article about this organization, that magazine is going to sell. Such articles are tasty morsels for them. Also, within the traditional political power structures of Japan, there has long been a strong anti–Komei Party view. Thus, from an objective perspective, it's not hard to see that there have been some political forces working hard to discredit the Soka Gakkai as a supporter of the Komei Party. Thus there have been lots of articles opposing the Soka Gakkai. . . . Because the Soka Gakkai is a considerably powerful organization, there are naturally a large number of people who don't like it. These people, of course, enjoy watching these fights in the media, and they buy the publications. However, those in our industry need to reflect on certain facts that have come out in recent years. Certain court cases have run their courses, and certain conclusions are unavoidable. It has become very clear that some of the negative coverage of the Soka Gakkai has been excessive to say the least. Some of it has been completely erroneous. It's been borne out by the facts. We really need to self-reflect.[58]

Lasting Impressions

This case shows how a magazine such as *Shukan Shincho* can drum up a false scandal that influences Japanese public opinion in deep and critical ways. Anecdotal evidence clearly indicates that a substantial portion of the Japanese public still remembers the Nobuhiras' accusations against Ikeda and still believes that there was some truth to them. Only a tiny portion of the Japanese public seems to be aware of the conclusion of the courts that the accusations were fabricated and that they had been lodged for unethical reasons.

The Nobuhiras' charges continue to mar the reputation of the Soka Gakkai, the New Komei Party, and Ikeda. In November 2003, for instance, an international paper with a reputation for reliability no less than the *Financial Times* brought up the claims without any reasonable contextualization or explanation. The English-language Japan edition of the paper included an article entitled "Japan's LDP Puts Faith in Religious Partner: New Komeito, a Party Backed by Buddhists, Is a Key Element of the Coalition's Re-Election Strategy." In the article, journalist Michiyo Nakamoto questions the long-term viability of the coalition. Emphasizing that in recent elections Komeito played a linch-pin role in keeping the coalition in power, the article notes that LDP supporters "seemed unconcerned about media claims of sexual harassment and even rape against Daisaku Ikeda, the spiritual leader of Soka Gakkai."[59]

Sadly, the elite, international readers of the paper are very likely to assume that there must be some substance behind such "media claims" of sexual harassment and rape against Ikeda—after all, these claims are being referenced in a serious political article in the staid and respectable *Financial Times*. No mention is made in the piece that only one woman (Nobuhira) has *ever* made a claim of sexual misconduct against Ikeda or that her claims were rejected by Japanese courts to be so "seriously lacking factual foundation" that they constituted an "abuse of the right to sue." Nor is there any note of the unreliable reputation of the "media" that initiated coverage of the claims and that are responsible for the vast majority of the coverage of those claims, namely, Japan's infamous *shukanshi*.

This instance highlights the often-underestimated influence of *shukanshi*, not just in Japan but throughout the world. In this case, *Shukan Shincho* was able to exploit fabricated claims—without fear of any serious legal repercussions—to the point that more than six and half years after its initial coverage and more than two years after they were judged by the Supreme Court as false, they are still referred to without qualification in a powerful Western newspaper.[60]

This example also raises the question of just how easy and effective it might be to intentionally plant similarly inaccurate stories in the Japanese news media—or, for that matter, how easily one might stir up similar scandals in other modern democratic nations. Indeed, the Nobuhiras' false accusations are also still commonly put forth as fact on the Internet in Japanese as well as in English and other languages—another illustration of what Richard Jewell's lawyer, L. Lin Wood, described as "the shout of guilty and the whisper of innocent."

This case study should raise serious alarms about the accuracy of information coming out of Japan. It is certainly not the only case of a Japanese citizen or group being unfairly persecuted by the Japanese news media. Given Japan's extraordinarily weak libel laws, its media is especially ripe for such abuses, but such abuses certainly can and do occur in other liberal democracies. All that is needed, really, is a highly commercialized press with a weak culture of journalistic ethics; a legal system heavily weighted toward large and powerful media corporations; unscrupulous media members willing to capitalize on sensational claims; a group or individuals with an axe to grind; and a complacent mainstream that is uninterested, unwilling, or unable to challenge such abuse.

Chapter Seven

Whitewashing the Nanjing Massacre and Attacking a Genuine Journalist

The prolonged and constant suppression of the truth and the secrecy over Japan's past deeds have been no accidental flaw in an otherwise open society. Make no mistake. These have served the interests of the men who derailed the train of democracy for their own greater good, as well as for the good of their patrons, clients and numerous sycophants. It has been crucial for them to keep Japanese people in the dark about what was done during the war. Were the truth to come out and be recognized by a wide public here, the entire leadership of this country, the leadership that has ruled over the past half century, would be readily delegitimized and thrown out of power.

—Roger Pulvers, *Japan Times*, December 2000[1]

One of the Most Important Stories of the Twentieth Century

The story of the Nanjing Massacre may well reveal more about Japanese power, Japanese journalism, and the Japanese system of governance than any other story of the twentieth century. The size and brutality of the massacre make it one of the most important stories of the century, not simply for the Japanese or the Chinese but for all people. It represents one of the most horrendous examples of human barbarity ever recorded.

Moreover, the struggle between those who would forget or deny the massacre and those who demand that it be remembered is one of the most contentious conflicts over language and history in the modern era. On one hand, it is the story of Japanese censorship, coercion, and propaganda; on the other, the story of at least some brave Japanese selflessly dedicated to revealing the historical truth, no matter how painful or personally risky it may prove to be. These uncompromising Japanese journalists, factory workers, teachers, academics, and even former soldiers have been on the forefront of documenting and disseminating information on the Nanjing Massacre despite the continuing denials and distortions from their fellow citizens. One of the foremost among them is the Japanese journalist Katsuichi Honda.

Although Honda is reviled by some in Japan and labeled anti-Japanese for criticizing the establishment in his country, time may well prove him one of his nation's finest patriots. The Japanese-language book *Media Yogo o Manabu Hito no Tameni* (Encyclopedia of Media and Communication Studies) has identified Honda as one of the two greatest Japanese journalists of the postwar period,[2] along with Oya Soichi (for whom, by the way, the best Japanese-language-magazine library is named: Oya Soichi Bunko). After working a notable career as a star reporter for *Asahi Shimbun* newspaper, Honda recently founded the small subscription-only weekly magazine, *Shukan Kinyobi* (Weekly Friday). *Shukan Kinyobi* has received harsh criticism for being "radically" critical of the Japanese power establishment, exposing war crimes, and vehemently defending the country's no-war constitution. Naturally, both Honda and *Shukan Kinyobi* have also been critical at times of Japan's often truckling relationship toward the United States, as well as of the United States itself and of other Western powers. Some of the criticism against Honda is not easily dismissed, because his unwavering stance has been known to exacerbate the polarization of Japanese domestic debate between the left and right. Still, it is difficult to describe his scholarship or integrity as anything but unimpeachable.

It would also be a mistake for Americans to assume that, because Honda and those like him have often disagreed with U.S. international policies, that he or those like him are in any way unsupportive of democracy in Japan.

Indeed, it would be a mistake to assume that the alignment of liberals and conservatives in Japan matches that of a country like the United States. Although, for instance, those on the right in Japan are often supportive of U.S. international policies, they are sometimes the least democratically minded domestically. Indeed, those on the right in Japan are often much closer in philosophy to the prewar militarists than most are aware. Ivan P. Hall, himself a strong and vocal advocate of American causes in Japan, has pointed out that many of those on the left in Japan are among the staunchest supporters of democracy in the country:

> Indeed, in postwar Japan, it has been the left that has most consistently defended the peace constitution; has at least tried to resist the gradual erosion of some of the democratic reforms of the occupation (for example, in education of workers' rights); has done the most to deplore the racist-chauvinist rhetoric of right-wing politicians; has fought the hardest for justice in what we call individual human rights cases; has put itself out for the rights of minorities and foreigners in Japan; and has—at the level of its professed ideals, at least—shown itself the most willing to contemplate a Japan open to the world, eschewing military adventurism, and refocusing its economic energies on the improvement of the daily life of its own people.[3]

At any rate, as far as this chapter is concerned, Honda's political positions are less important than his journalistic integrity and especially his groundbreaking role in understanding the Nanjing Massacre. Immediately following the massacre, the imperial authorities imposed a blackout in Japan of all mass-media information on the matter. The news blackout lasted the better part of a decade—until the war-crimes trials held after the country's defeat in the Second World War. This meant that few Japanese nationals, on the home front or elsewhere, had any idea of the horrors their military had perpetrated. Since then, and right up until today, Japanese apologists, strongly supported by far-right publishers such as Bungeishunju Ltd. and Shinchosha Ltd., and including many top-ruling Liberal Democratic Party (LDP) officials, have salted the deep wounds of Nanjing with justifications, double-talk, and bald-faced denials. These patent attempts to rewrite history amount to yet another crime against the victims.

Most educated Japanese are generally aware that the Japanese army did take Nanjing and that a massacre allegedly happened in the process. The problem is that nationalistic publishers, pundits, and politicians have managed to twist the facts until the indisputable, documented reality of the massacre has become a subject for legitimate debate.

So many fundamental aspects of the event are well established—by unequivocal documentation and reliable eyewitness accounts—that no rational person can doubt its authenticity. No matter how much the revisionists wish it would go away, the ugly fact remains that at the end of 1937 and the start of 1938, Japanese imperial soldiers in and around Nanjing senselessly slaughtered many tens of thousands of civilians and unarmed soldiers, and raped and tortured massive numbers of women and girls.

The Nanjing Campaign

Most historians view the Manchurian Incident (also known as the Mukden Incident) of September 18, 1931, as the initiation of Sino-Japanese military violence, which, in part, brought the Second World War to the Pacific theater. On this date, the Japanese Imperial Army exploded one of its own railways in Manchuria, blamed the event on China, and then seized upon the event as a pretext for occupying Manchuria. Japan subsequently installed its own puppet government, renaming the country Manchukuo.

Hostilities, including the intensive bombing of Chinese cities, continued during the next five to six years, when the famous Marco Polo Bridge Incident (also known as the China Incident) of July 7, 1937, finally led to the Japanese invasion of China proper. The incident was nothing more than a small skirmish, in which a few shots were exchanged between Chinese and Japanese forces. But Japan, knowing it had a military advantage over China, used it as an excuse to intensify hostilities. By the end of August 1937, the Japanese had secured the city of Peking (Beijing).

A month later, the Japanese Imperial Army opened up a second front in Shanghai, where a better-prepared Chinese army presented stronger resistance. Also, by August 15, the Japanese began bombing raids on Nanjing,

China's capital at the time. In November, the same month that Shanghai finally fell, the Japanese began a massive invasion of China, with the ultimate aim of taking the capital. The Japanese had hoped that an overwhelming victory over Nanjing would lead to a quick defeat of the entire country.

Japanese troops landed at Hangzhou Bay, Shanghai, and the Yangtze River area, with instructions to fight their way inland to Nanjing. Along their way to the capital, they made quick work of the Chinese resistance they encountered, and for the most part the Chinese troops were overrun or retreated toward Nanjing. In their absence, Japanese troops were largely free to do as they wished with the tens of thousands of Chinese civilian peasants and villagers they encountered. Sadly, the soldiers indulged in a campaign of mass murder, rape, torture, and exploitation.

A number of reasons exist for the Japanese soldiers' decision to pursue this violent course rather than simply pass by the civilians on their way toward the capital. Racial prejudice, for one, played a basic role in the military's actions. According to the Japanese theory of "proper place" then in vogue, each racial group on earth was thought to have a "natural role" to play in the human "social hierarchy" that would be achieved once the Japanese Empire dominated the world. Needless to say, the Japanese were at the top of this purportedly benign hierarchy, as a result of their "purity" and "virtue."

In his superb book *War without Mercy*, John Dower has clearly exposed the racism that existed on both the Allied and the Japanese sides during the Second World War. In the book, Dower points to Bungeishunju Ltd.'s flagship magazine as a source of the rhetoric that went with the Japanese concepts of "proper place":

In the January 1942 issue of *Bungei Shunju*, one of Japan's most popular middle-class monthlies, war with the Allied powers was greeted in racial terms that relied on much of the same sort of abstract and color-suffused language. The outbreak of the war, it was stated in an article entitled "Establishing a Japanese Racial Worldview,"[4] had clarified the Japanese character whose basic traits were brightness, strength, and uprighteousness. These qualities made the Japanese "the most superior race in the world," and it followed that all the other countries and peoples of Asia should be assimilated into the Greater East Asia Co-Prosperity Sphere in accordance with their particular abilities. Under no circumstances was it appropriate to think in terms of "formal equality," since no one else could equal the "bright and strong" moral superiority of the Japanese. Thus, the legalistic liberal worldview of the European and American powers had to be replaced by a racial worldview emanating from Japan. And the foundation for this racial worldview, in turn, would necessarily be a level of "spiritual and physical purity" that the Japanese alone were capable of attaining.

This was the rhetoric of "proper place" that runs like a deep current through all Japanese discussions of their role as the "leading race," but the *Bungei Shunju* article was unusually zealous in defining the metaphors which linked race, status, morality, purity, and color in the Japanese worldview.[5]

On the military field, of course, a much simpler racism took the lead, with many Japanese soldiers inculcated to think of their Chinese adversaries as less human, sometimes even equating them with animals. Indeed, a common epithet of Japanese soldiers for the Chinese was *buta*, meaning "pigs."

Another major factor for the brutality against the Chinese civilians was the extraordinarily strict, hierarchical nature of the Japanese military. It was not uncommon for superiors to beat and otherwise abuse their subordinates. The term "transfer of aggression" is commonly used to describe the way such brutality made its way down the ranks. The foot soldiers, the last in line, often took their aggressions out in horrific ways on enemy civilians and prisoners, the only classes of people they were likely to come into contact with who were "below" them in the hierarchy of the Japanese emperor ideology.

Other factors further set the stage for the violence at Nanjing. The Japanese military considered this attack to be fitting revenge against the Chinese, whose strong resistance at Shanghai had infuriated them. Also, the Japanese commanders had not set up proper food supply lines for their infantrymen, but ordered them to live off the land on their way to Nanjing. This meant that soldiers were not simply given permission to exploit local peasants and villages, but were under explicit orders to extract food and other supplies from them. And finally, there was the Japanese policy of "take no prisoners," because taking prisoners would have slowed their advance toward the capital.

Given this disastrous mix of circumstances, the potential for atrocities is easy to imagine: an army ruled by a brutal racist philosophy was ordered to fight its way across an enemy countryside, under orders to exploit the local population for food and supplies, while taking no prisoners.

Mark Eykholt, in an essay entitled "Aggression, Victimization, and Chinese Historiography of the Nanjing Massacre," gives this account: "Commanders pushed their units toward Nanjing, quickly outpacing supply lines and telling their men to survive on what they could scavenge. Soldiers robbed villages they passed through and Chinese they came across. Peasants were forced to carry equipment and goods for the Japanese troops, and villages were razed in order to efficiently end any threat of resistance. Brutalities were excused in the name of war and capturing Nanjing, and conquering the capital grew in importance with each new atrocity. These troops knew their job was to kill the enemy, and barely acceptable conditions of frontline warfare grew worse, thereby amplifying the animal natures of these soldiers as they marched toward Nanjing. To further encourage their men, officers promised women and plunder."[6]

Japanese troops descended in early December 1937, by which time most Nanjing residents with means to do so had abandoned the city. Thus, when the capital fell, the population was composed almost solely of poor people and deserting Chinese troops, many of whom had disposed of their weapons and uniforms in an attempt to blend in with the civilian population. In this respect, the Chinese military has been rightly criticized for making an already dire situation worse. The failure of the Chinese commanding officer, General Tang Shengzhi, to bring about an orderly retreat or surrender played a large part in the mass desertions by his troops. The presence of so many former Chinese soldiers mixed in with the civilian population provided the Japanese with yet another motivation for attacking civilians: they did not know which male Chinese were legitimate civilians and which were out-of-uniform enemy soldiers. Although this by no means justifies the wholesale slaughter of unarmed Chinese or the raping of women, the failures of the Chinese military certainly contributed to the escalation of the violence.

After Nanjing fell, on December 13, 1937, the Japanese military ran amok in the city and surrounding areas until February 1938, when relief garrison forces finally relieved the frontline fighters. Until that time, the soldiers continued with acts of arson, torture, murder, and rape on a scale that has few parallels in history. Buildings were looted and burned. Tens of thousands of presumed Chinese soldiers were rounded up and summarily executed. Civilians of all ages were tortured and executed. Women were raped by the thousands.

Robert Wilson's Diary and the Nanjing Massacre

The best-known American eyewitness account of the Nanjing Massacre is that of physician Robert Wilson, who described the city during the event as a "modern Dante's Inferno, written in huge letters with blood and rape. Murder by the wholesale and rape by the thousands of cases."[7]

Wilson was living in Nanjing at the time and was one of twenty-seven Westerners who courageously elected to remain in the city throughout the violent siege.[8] These Westerners banded together to create the "International Committee for Nanking Safety Zone," taking on the task of defining and attempting to support a refugee zone of sorts in Nanjing, within which noncombatants could ostensibly reside during the conflict without being attacked.

Although the zone made an incalculable difference, saving untold lives, it was not entirely successful. One problem was the thousands of deserting Chinese soldiers who posed as civilians in order to hide within its boundaries, providing the Japanese with justification not to honor the zone. Another problem was that many Japanese soldiers were simply out for blood and were unwilling to honor the zone.

Wilson's "Family Letters," printed in the book *Documents on the Rape of Nanking*, offer some understanding of the nature of the Nanjing Massacre, as well as indisputable documentary evidence. In the following excerpt, Wilson mentions the role of the Japanese news agency, Domei, which the Allies restructured after the war to form what are today the behemoth Japanese advertising agency Dentsu and the Kyodo and Jiji news services, the latter two being roughly comparable to the Associated Press and Reuters in the West. Wilson's letter of December 21, 1937, is a firsthand account of the atrocities that occurred in Nanjing:

Tuesday, December 21

This is the shortest day in the year but it still contains twenty-four hours of this hell on earth. We heard yesterday that the Japanese news agency, Domei, reported the population returning to their homes, business going on as usual and the population welcoming their Japanese visitors, or words to that effect. If that is all the news that is going out of the city it is due for a big shake up when the real news breaks.

Huge fires are set in every business section. Our bunch has actually seen them set the fires in several instances. Yesterday before going home to supper I counted twelve fires. Tonight at the same time I counted eight. Several of them include whole blocks of buildings. Most of the shops of our vicinity have been burned. The populace is crowding into the refugee camps even from the private residences within the zone as the degree of safety is slightly greater though there is no guarantee anywhere. If it were not for the way the Committee had gathered rice beforehand and done what they could to protect the population there would be a first class famine already and the slaughter would have been considerably greater.

Several more stories of the slaughter keep coming in. One man came to [Reverend John] Magee today with the tale of what happened to one thousand men led away from a place of supposed safety within the zone. The bunch contained perhaps one hundred ex-soldiers that had given up their arms and donned civilian clothes. The thousand were marched to the banks of the Yangtze, lined up two deep and then machine-gunned. He was in the back row, fell with the rest and played dead until, several hours later, the Japs had gone and he sneaked back to the city.

As we have seen a good many similar round-ups in this part of the city with no returns we presume the same has happened to all of them.

Yesterday a seventeen year old girl came to the hospital in the morning with her baby. She had been raped by Japanese soldiers the night before at seven-thirty, the labor pains had begun at nine o'clock, and the baby, her first, was born at twelve. Naturally at night she dared not come out to the hospital so she came in the morning with the baby who miraculously seemed to be safe and healthy.

This afternoon I put a cast on a lovely little girl of 13. When the Japanese came to the city on the 13th she and her father and mother were standing at the entrance of their dugout watching them approach. A soldier stepped up, bayoneted the father, shot the mother and slashed open the elbow of the little girl giving her a compound fracture. She has no relatives and was not brought to the hospital for a week. She is already wondering what to do when she has to leave. Both the father and mother were killed.

Day before yesterday at Hillcrest a young girl of nineteen who was six and a half months pregnant attempted to resist rape by two Japanese soldiers. She received eighteen cuts about the face, several in the legs and a deep gash in the abdomen. This morning at the hospital I could not hear the fetal heart and she will probably have an abortion. (Next morning: she died last night at midnight. Technically, a miscarriage.)[9]

Wilson's letter goes on to describe a number of other atrocities. Of course, neither Wilson nor anyone else in the city had an accurate bird's-eye view of the events then unfolding. Wilson could only judge the siege based on his personal experience and the information provided him by those around him. This factor—the difficulty for on-the-ground witnesses to understand fully any large-scale event—has been seized upon by the revisionists, who have attacked all eyewitness accounts of the massacre.

The Good Man of Nanjing[10]

John Rabe was a German member of the Nazi Party who actually spent a good deal of his adult life outside of Germany, in China, as a businessman. In 1937, when the Japanese marched into Nanjing, Rabe, like Robert Wilson, elected to stay in Nanjing. Again, this was a most amazing act on behalf of those who stayed, as other foreign nationals and most of the wealthier Chinese abandoned the city to its fate. Rabe was the lead figure behind the international safety zone for refugees in the city. Indeed, the survival of it depended largely upon his status as a German member of the Nazi Party and an official ally of the Japanese. Rabe is said to have used his status to great effect against Japanese soldiers and officials. Sadly, when he returned to Germany in 1938 and wrote to Hitler about the atrocities he had witnessed, he was arrested by the Gestapo. Rabe's diary, which he prepared for his family only, is an incredible document and even includes a number of photographs of victims of the massacre. Three brief 1937 excerpts from his diary follow:

December 13

It is not until we tour the city that we learn the extent of the destruction. We come across corpses every 100 to 200 yards. The bodies of civilians that I examined had bullet holes in their backs. These people had presumably been fleeing and were shot from behind.

The Japanese march through the city in groups of ten to twenty soldiers and loot the shops.... Of the perhaps one thousand disarmed soldiers that we had quartered at the Ministry of Justice, between 400 and 500 were driven from it with their hands tied. We assumed they were shot since we later heard several salvos of machine-gun fire. These events have left us frozen with horror.

We may no longer enter the Foreign Ministry, where we took wounded soldiers. Chinese doctors and nursing personnel are not allowed into the building, either.

We manage quickly to find lodging in some vacant buildings for a group of 125 Chinese refugees, before they fall into the hands of the Japanese military. Mr. Han says that three young girls of about 14 or 15 have been dragged from a house in our neighborhood. Doctor Bates reports that even in the Safety Zone refugees in various houses have been robbed of their few paltry possessions. At various times troops of Japanese soldiers enter my private residence as well, but when I arrive and hold my swastika armband under their noses, they leave. There's no love for the American flag. A car belonging to Mr. Sone, one of our committee members, had its American Flag ripped off and was then stolen.[11]

December 16

I've just heard that hundreds more disarmed Chinese soldiers have been led out of our Zone to be shot, including 50 of our police who are to be executed for letting soldiers in.

The road to Hsiakwan is nothing but a field of corpses strewn with the remains of military equipment. The Communications Ministry was torched by the Chinese, the Ychang Men Gate has been shelled. There are piles of corpses outside the gate. The Japanese aren't lifting a hand to clear them away, and the Red Swastika Society associated with us has been forbidden to do so.

It may be that the disarmed Chinese will be forced to do the job before they're killed. We Europeans are all paralyzed with horror. There are executions everywhere, some are being carried out with machine guns outside the War Ministry.[12]

December 17

In one of the houses in the narrow street behind my garden wall, a woman was raped, and then wounded in the neck with a bayonet. I manage to get an ambulance so we can take her to Kulou Hospital. There are about 200 refugees in the garden now. They fall to their knees when you walk by, even though in all this misery we barely know up from down ourselves. One of the Americans put it this way: "The Safety Zone has turned into a public house for the Japanese soldiers."

That's very close to the truth. Last night up to 1,000 women and girls are said to have been raped, about 100 girls at Ginling Girls College alone. You hear of nothing but rape. If husbands or brothers intervene, they're shot. What you hear and see on all sides is the brutality and bestiality of the Japanese soldiery.

Herr Hatz, our Austrian auto mechanic, gets into an argument with a Japanese soldier, who reaches for his sidearm but is immediately floored by a well-placed hook to the chin, whereupon he and his two Japanese comrades, all armed to the teeth, take off.

The Japanese consul general, Katsuo Okazaki, demanded yesterday that the refugees leave the Zone for their homes and open their shops again as soon as possible. The Japanese soldiers have saved them the trouble of opening their shops. There's hardly a shop in the city that has not been broken into and looted.[13]

This photo, from Mainichi Photo Bank, carries the following caption: "Nanjing Massacre Dead Bodies Piled up along the Yangtze River, December 1937." *(Photo courtesy of Mainichi Photo Bank.)*

Katsuichi Honda's Journey to China

Honda first became known for traveling to China in 1971 (before postwar diplomatic relations between China and Japan had been reestablished). While there, he interviewed surviving victims of the Japanese military aggression. The dispatches he sent back were serialized in *Asahi* newspaper, causing a tremendous stir in Japan. His detailed accounts of Japanese atrocities were often so gruesome that many readers found it difficult to believe that any human being—let alone their own countrymen—could have committed such deeds a mere three-and-a-half decades before. This was the first time since the end of occupation that the Nanjing war crimes were so widely and graphically publicized in Japan. At the time, many Japanese viewed them-selves as victims of the war that had ended in such grave defeat, and especially of the two atom bombs dropped by the United States.

Many, having bought into the militarist propaganda during the war, had not considered their country a cruel aggressor responsible for the deaths of twenty million of its Asian neighbors. Indeed, to this day a substantial por-tion of the Japanese population does not think of the war in terms of Japan-ese military aggression. For them, the war was just an unavoidable event—like a natural disaster—for which no one is accountable.

Honda was certainly not the first to recount the Japanese aggression toward China. Information was, of course, revealed and disseminated during the war-crimes trials. Also, Tomio Hora, a university professor, had published a number of books on the matter.[14] Honda, however, was the first to do so in such a public way—in *Asahi,* Japan's second-largest and most prestigious newspaper. Honda's series, which did not focus on the Nanjing Massacre in particular but on Japanese aggression in general, was compiled into a book entitled *Chugoku no tabi* (A Journey to China) the following year.[15]

Immediately, Honda's work came under vicious attack by right-wing apologists, in particular by writers working for the publisher Bungeishunju Ltd. Thus began the public debate over the Nanjing Massacre that continues to this day.

Nobukatsu Fujioka, one of the most popular contemporary right-wing apologists, said, in an interview for this book, "if you look at the postwar history, you can see that these issues became more prevalent after the 1970s. Honda and the *Asahi Shimbun* went to China in the early seventies and supposedly gathered up the information at the time. But they are simply verbatim accounts. They don't have any value."[16] According to Fujioka and those in his camp, Honda was misled by the Communist Chinese government, which supposedly provided him with hand-picked individuals, all previously coerced and duped into inventing lies about the Japanese military's behavior.

Honda, however, does not believe that those he interviewed were in any way prompted to lie to him or that he was unduly misled by the Chinese government at the time. He also counters the common charge against him, that he has illogically overemphasized the testimony of Chinese victims while de-emphasizing the accounts provided by Japanese officials and soldiers. Honda says that while he does recognize the official Japanese view of the event, his emphasis on the perspective of the victims is entirely justified. According to him, the voices of the surviving victims of the massacre have been muffled for so long that they deserve his attention. He further asserts that it should be the job of journalists to present the voices of common people, especially those who are disempowered and who don't have influence otherwise. He says that journalists need to counter the predilection of the news media in most countries to showcase only the views of those in power.

Although some of Honda's books focus on the stories of victims, as the selections below show, he hardly ignores the Japanese military's official position on the massacre. Indeed, his work includes many detailed discussions of the positions and viewpoints put forth by those in positions of great power.

What is perhaps most remarkable about Honda's writing is its authenticity, based on his painstaking research and extensive interviews of those who were present during the massacre. His reporting is full of human details and subtle nuances that put the reader face to face with each subject. No matter how horrifying, Honda insists on ensuring that the victims' tales are told.

A few selections of Honda's extensive work on the Nanjing Massacre, which spans more than thirty years, is quoted here. The first excerpt recounts the testimony of a victim. It comes from his English-language book *The Nanjing Massacre: A Japanese Journalist Confronts Japan's National Shame*, published in 1999.[17] The book is a dense compilation of superb research, containing more than 350 pages of testimony, hundreds of photographs, maps, newspaper stories, military accounts, and other evidence of the massacre. Honda's accounts include information from both Japanese and Chinese soldiers, as well as civilians such as Xia Shujin, whose story he recounts here:

> Xia Shujin (57) was seven years old at the time, one of five daughters. She lived in a nine-person household with her father (40), who was a laborer; her mother (40); two older sisters (15 and 13); two younger sisters (one four years old and the other just a few months), and her maternal grandparents (both 60). They lived near Xinlukou with six or seven other families in a compound surrounded by a wall.... Inside the common entrance gate was a T-shaped courtyard, with rooms rented by the various families lined up on either side.
>
> However, by the time the Japanese arrived in Nanjing, only the Xia family and one other family of four persons remained in the compound. An uncle and his wife had been living with the family, but by that time, they, too had left. Xia Shujin, who was only seven years old then, does not know why her family failed to evacuate, but she imagines that they found it awkward to move with old people and so many children.
>
> At about nine o'clock on the morning of December 12, 1937, the Xia family had just finished breakfast and were starting on their household chores.

Xia Shujin had nothing in particular to do, so she went out into the central courtyard.

Suddenly she heard someone pounding vigorously at the main gate. The old man who lived next door ran toward it, and he tried to undo the bolt. Xia's father also came running and headed toward the gate. The next instant, the bolt came undone, the door swung open, and some Japanese soldiers burst in, saying something in Japanese. Not understanding what they wanted, the old man simply stood there flustered, and the soldiers shot him down. Seeing this, Xia's father panicked, but as he turned to flee, the soldiers killed him with a shot in the back.

Horrified, Xia ran into the innermost of the family's rooms, and she and all her sisters, except the baby, crawled into a bed and covered themselves with a quilt and the mosquito net that the family typically kept hanging from the ceiling even during the winter.

Soon, they were aware of a large mob of soldiers rushing into the house— in her excitement, Xia had forgotten to shut the door. They heard the sound of boots tramping on the floor and a murmur of voices, and then, almost at the same time, gunshots. Being under the quilts, they could not see what was happening, but their grandfather, who was near the door, was being killed.

Just after that, the quilt was torn away from them with the tip of a soldier's bayonet. The large room was packed with Japanese soldiers. Xia's grandmother stood in front of the bed, trying to protect the four girls huddled there, but someone shot her with a pistol, and whitish bits of her brains flew through the air.

Then the soldiers grabbed the two older sisters to take them away. Terrified, Xia Shujin began screaming, and at that instant, she was stabbed with a bayonet and lost consciousness, so she did not see what happened after that. She did not realize it at the time, but she had been stabbed in three places: the left shoulder, the left side, and the back.

She does not know how long she was unconscious, but she became aware of her four-year-old sister, who lay by uninjured crying, under the quilt, which was wadded up against the wall. When the Japanese had ripped the quilt and mosquito net off the bed, they had evidently thrown them on top of her. At this point, there was no sign of the Japanese, and all was strangely quiet, but the room was filled with an eerie light. Their thirteen-year-old sister lay dead at the other end of the bed, naked below the waist, her legs trailing on the floor. In front of the bed, was their grandmother's body. Just inside the door was their grandfather's body. Against the opposite wall was a desk, and their fifteen-year-old sister lay dead on top of it, also naked from the waist down with her legs trailing on the floor. Xia could not tell whether her sisters had been stabbed or shot to death. There was no sign of their mother or the baby.

She crept out into the courtyard with her younger sister walking beside her. She was so stunned that she hardly felt any pain, despite her serious wounds. The two of them made their way into the makeshift air-raid shelter in their landlord's inner court. This was not the typical air-raid shelter dug into the ground, rather, four sturdy desks had been lined up together, with door panels on top and straw spread beneath. Because of the indiscriminate bombing attacks, the children had learned to take refuge there whenever they heard the buzzing roar of the Japanese planes.

The bodies of their mother and baby sister were right in front of the shelter. Their mother lay stretched out, her trousers pulled off, and the baby lay at her side. The two little girls crawled into the straw in the shelter, covered themselves with a quilt that they had brought from the house to protect themselves from the cold, and there they stayed for nearly two weeks.

Since they were afraid to go out during the day, they hardly ever left the shelter; but at night, they went back to the house to look for food. In their grandparents' room was a large iron pot containing a thick layer of burned rice. This rice had been deliberately overcooked to make a type of food known as guoba, which remains edible for a long time and is therefore useful for refugees or during emergencies. (Judging from the fact that they had cooked up some guoba, the family may have been preparing to leave.) The two children brought the pot to their shelter and ate from it. There was water in a large jar in the common cookhouse, but since they were too small to reach the water's surface, they took a box and used it as a step.

After about two weeks, an old woman from the neighborhood found them. She was a stranger, but she took the children to the old people's home in Jianxiaoxiang. Several days later, the uncle who had fled the city came to the old people's home looking for them, and he took them back with him to the evacuation zone.

"I don't know what happened to the bodies of my family members. My parents don't even have graves, so I can't pay my respects, and when I think about that, I feel very bereft, even now." Xia Shujin also told me that the four people who lived next door, the parents and two children, were killed.

"Ordinary" rapes, if not pitiful incidents like Xia Shujin's story, came to be no more than everyday occurrences.[18]

Honda's books are filled with such painful recollections, and Xia Shujin's may be especially pathetic, but within the body of Honda's research, it is by no means unusual. He has compiled many dozens of similar testimonies. Of course, Honda does not ignore the "official" version of the events of the day, either. In *The Nanjing Massacre*, he juxtaposes Xia Shujin's testimony with that of the Japanese *Library of War History* to great effect. Honda's quotation from the *Library of War History* includes events occurring in the same general vicinity, leading up to December 12, 1937, the day Xia Shujin's family was slaughtered:

In the 10th Army, the 114th and 6th Divisions attacked jointly in the direction of Yuhuatai, and on the 8th, they captured the enemy's forward positions. On the 9th, they broke through the second line positions, and beginning on the 10th, they attacked the third line positions at Yuhuatai and retrenchment positions. Breaking through stubborn enemy resistance, they captured one position after another, and on the 12th, the two divisions occupied part of the city walls.[19]

The differences between Xia Shujin's personal version of the attack on Nanjing and the official one of the *Library of War History* couldn't be starker.

The following day, December 13, was marked by the fall of Nanjing into Japanese hands. December 13 is also the day of the first of the three entries from John Rabe's diary quoted previously. Again Honda contrasts the testimonies of survivors such as Xia Shujin with Japanese newspaper accounts of the day. He writes, "to celebrate the fall of Nanjing on December 13, the *Asahi Shimbun* printed an extra edition consisting mostly of photographs. The

Yomiuri Shimbun put out a 'second evening edition' on the same day, with headlines such as, 'Complete Power of Life and Death over Nanjing' and 'War of Annihilation Spreads Throughout the City.' "[20] The accompanying article, reprinted by Honda, reads as follows:

> On the walls of Nanjing, December 13, special dispatch from Correspondent Ukishima: Thanks to the left flank units' crossing of the Yangtze and occupation of Pukou and to the main units' capture of all the gates in the walls of Nanjing, fifty thousand enemy soldiers, everyone from the General Tang Shengshi on down, are now completely surrounded by our forces. Valiant street-to-street fighting crowns the end of the coming offensive on Nanjing, and a war of annihilation has developed. The Guangxi and Guangdong armies, under the command of Bai Zhongxi in the eastern part of the city, and the 88th Army, directly under the command of Chiang Kai-shek, in all the southern areas of the city, are continuing their frenzied defense, but our troops, who have begun an all-out offensive, secured the greater part of the city by 11:00 a.m., and they have occupied every important facility. All that remains is the northern part of the city. In every part of the city flames rise to the heavens. Our troops are showing the utmost bravery amidst random shots and random attacks, and the sound is providing the most incomparably thrilling score for the fall of a city ever known in the Far East since the dawn of history is being played. The fate of Nanjing is completely within the hands of our troops, and this is deemed to be a major turning point in the course of the war.[21]

Once again, these selections represent only a tiny fraction of Honda's impressive body of research and writing. He further documents, for example, that Japanese "magazines vied with one another to carry articles glorifying the invasion and war. In addition to *Bungei Shunju, Hanashi* and *Genchi Hokoku* also published special issues and dispatched novelists and essayists to report from the front. Writers such as Hideo Kobayashi wrote many articles for *Bungei Shunju* as special correspondents."[22] Perhaps what makes his work most powerful is his ability to let the facts speak for themselves. For example, he quotes extensively from the field diaries of Japanese soldiers, who made notes such as this one by a soldier named Shogo Miyamoto: "In the evening, we finally returned, and we soon helped dispose of the prisoners and left. It was over 20,000. In the end, there was a great fiasco. We ended up wounding and killing a number of friendly troops. Our company suffered one dead, two wounded."[23] Honda quotes another Japanese soldier, Takaaki Endo, who noted, "I was tired. In the evening, I sent five men to punish more than 10,000 prisoners."[24] He quotes another soldier, Yoshio Sugeno, who wrote, "I joined in gunning down the remaining 10,000 or more prisoners."[25] And he quotes yet another, Tomiharu Meguro, who wrote in his field diary, "I was put to work shooting about 13,000 enemy soldiers. Over two days, the Yamada Unit shot nearly 20,000. It seems that all the prisoners of every unit are to be shot."[26]

Iris Chang's "Forgotten Holocaust"

Although some of Honda's work on the massacre has been translated into English, the event is probably best known to the broader English-speaking public through the influential book *The Rape of Nanking: The Forgotten Holocaust of World War II*,[27] a 1997 *New York Times* best seller by Iris Chang. Chang has received much-deserved accolades for widely publicizing both the massacre and the various attempts to ignore it—not only by the Japanese but also by the U.S. and Chinese governments. She has also been rightly commended for locating the diary of an important Western witness to the massacre, the German Nazi Party member John Rabe, who, despite his party affiliations, behaved heroically throughout the crisis, dedicating himself to protecting Nanjing civilians.

Like Honda's, Chang's work has not gone without its share of controversy. Most of the criticism of Chang's work comes from Japanese apologists who have labored to pick tiny holes in an attempt to dismiss her entire book, and with it the massacre. One of Chang's most severe critics is Nobukatsu Fujioka, who has sold literally millions of books in Japan, many of which explicitly defend Japanese wartime aggression.

Fujioka, who was interviewed for this book, is a particularly interesting person to discuss Japanese history with, because his intense passion for his subjects almost overwhelms. Unfortunately, his logic is severely lacking and his research is often fundamentally flawed on multiple levels. It would be easy to dismiss him outright as a crank were he not a professor at Japan's most prestigious institution of higher leaning, Tokyo University, as well as a prolific and best-selling author of literally millions of books. He is not a historian by training, but a professor of education.

One of Fujioka's most intriguing books is *Za Reipu obu Nankin no Kenkyu—Chugoku ni okeru Johosen no Teguchi to Senryaku*, which can be translated into English as "A Study of [Iris Chang's] *The Rape of Nanking*—Methods and Strategy of the 'Propaganda War' in China."[28] It features the cover of Chang's book on its own cover, and is chock-full of polemic indictments against it. His conclusions that Chang is completely off base and that the Nanjing Massacre never happened are both utterly nonsensical.

Nobukatsu Fujioka is a best-selling Japanese writer known for his avid denials of Second World War Japanese war crimes and atrocities. He is shown here holding one of his many books. The title translates as "A Study of [Iris Chang's] *The Rape of Nanking*—Methods and Strategy of the 'Propaganda War' in China," his attempt to refute U.S. author Iris Chang's best seller *The Rape of Nanking*. Fujioka's book features Chang's book on its cover.

And while much of the negative backlash against Chang's work was to be expected—given the extreme emotions surrounding the subject, the existence of a whole movement of Japanese historical revisionists fighting to deny the massacre, and Chang's staunch condemnation of the event—some minor criticisms of the book may not be completely specious. For example, some credible reviewers have raised questions on some minor points.[29] The accuracy and validity of these are beyond the scope of this work to explore properly. Still, it ought to be emphasized that the vast preponderance of measured assessments of Chang's book balance any minor criticisms with an acknowledgment of the validity and value of her work and her overall thesis: that the Nanjing Massacre represents one of the most extreme cases of barbarous violence in recorded history and that it has been sadly overlooked and underemphasized, in both the West and the East, for a host of unjust, often political reasons.

Chang's subtitle, *The Forgotten Holocaust of World War II*, which compares the Nanjing Massacre with the Holocaust of the Jews in Europe, is also a contentious issue to some. Even the highest credible estimate of those killed in the massacre (more than 300,000) is only a fraction of the 6 million Jews murdered by the Nazis. Even taking into account Chang's point that the Holocaust occurred over a number of years, whereas the Nanjing Massacre happened in just a matter of weeks, the two atrocities hardly compare in scale.

Moreover, to compare one group's victimization and suffering with another's is a dubious task, and one bound to spark controversy. Perhaps, though, it is unavoidable that such comparisons be made with the Holocaust, which has been enshrined in world consciousness as an ultimate example of systemized mass murder and genocide. Charles S. Maier, coeditor of *The Nanjing Massacre in History and Historiography,* gives the following example: "The Nanjing rampage seems all the more atrocious in that it involved not what has seemed so horrifying about the Holocaust—its bureaucratized planning and mechanized execution—but the often gleeful killing of perhaps hundreds of thousands of civilians by individual soldiers using sword and bayonet as well as bullet. The killings were all the more appalling in that they were unnecessary for the military objective, continued after the victory was secured, and apparently involved such joyful or at least indifferent murder. The accompanying rape and brutality short of murder—as in Bosnia more recently—served purposes of degradation and dehumanization as well as, possibly, sexual release."[30]

Still, however one tries, such unimaginably tragic events tend to defy any description or quantification, never mind comparisons. Chang's description of the Nanjing Massacre as a "holocaust" may serve at least one very important purpose, though. The comparison, not of the suffering and deaths of the victims or of the cruelty of the perpetrators, but of the politicization, or the symbolic uses, of the two atrocities seems perfectly appropriate and correct. Just as the Holocaust is the prime symbol of the brutal nature of the German Nazi aggression that led to the deaths of some six million Jews in Europe, the Nanjing Massacre has in many ways become a primary symbol of Japanese military aggression, which led to the deaths of some twenty-four million in Asia (twenty million non-Japanese and four million Japanese). Indeed, they share at least two important characteristics: they occurred *after* the victims had already surrendered, and the mass violence directed against them was because of *who* they were, not what they were doing or had done. More often than not, denials of these well-documented atrocities amount to crude attempts to defend the perverse worldviews of the murderous regimes that hatched them. In denials of the Jewish Holocaust, the defended philosophy is Nazi racism. In denials of the Nanjing Massacre, the defended philosophy is the racial superiority of the Japanese. In this way, at least, Chang's comparison seems right on target.

The Numbers Game

At least since the controversy erupted over Honda's reporting of the Nanjing Massacre, those who would try to deny the event have turned the debate into one of numbers. Those who would seek to mitigate Japanese responsibility inevitably argue that so few people were killed in Nanjing that it did not represent an extraordinary event. This can be a useful stance for Japanese international negotiators when the Chinese bring up the massacre during trade, diplomatic, and other discussions. Many Japanese also prefer this version of events because, of course, it is much easier to see one's national history in an idealized fictitious light than to struggle with a horrific legacy in broad daylight.

The revisionist stance is also most important to Japanese nationalists, who have correctly concluded that the Nanjing Massacre is the foremost symbol of moral bankruptcy of the Japanese militarism and emperor worship of the Second World War. To diminish the brutal nature of the Nanjing Massacre is to diminish the brutal nature of that militarism, as well as its oppressive philosophical underpinnings, which continue to reverberate in Japanese culture to this day.

The numerical games surrounding this event inevitably devolve into esoteric points of contention that have filled shelves of books. They amount to nothing, however, for *all* credible historians agree

This May 26, 1994, *Shukan Bunshun* article is typical of the Japanese focus on the number of those killed in Nanjing. The title here reads "REGARDING THE 'NUMBERS' OF THE NANJING MASSACRE INCIDENT." The writing that appears as part of the soldier sketch says "Nanjing History of War."

that a hellish atrocity of truly massive proportions took place at Nanjing and that a massive number of defenseless people were killed there.[31]

The Tokyo war-crimes trials, or International Military Tribunal for the Far East (which was sponsored by the Allies after the war), concluded that the total number of people killed in and around Nanjing was more than 200,000. Honda stated in an interview for this book that he also believes that "quite near to 200,000" were killed. While some respectable researchers have put the number as low as 100,000, the Chinese government maintains that 300,000 or more were killed. This last figure was even enshrined on the wall at the government-sponsored memorial to the massacre in Nanjing.[32]

The unfortunate truth is that a precise figure can never be known. No one kept a body count at the time. Many of the bodies were burned or dumped into the Yangtze River. The Chinese have not been especially open in letting researchers into their country. Moreover, huge volumes of Japanese documentation were destroyed at the end of the war as part of efforts to cover up such atrocities.

A Killing Contest

As noted, when Honda's book *Chugoku no tabi* (A Journey to China) was published in 1972, it created a terrific uproar. In response, such publishers as Shinchosha Ltd. and Bungeishunju Ltd., among others, became the venues for nationalist attacks on Honda and for assertions that the Japanese never massacred anyone in Nanjing. These companies published articles and books written by what are known in Japan as *yojinboteki chishikijin*, or "henchman-intellectuals"—individuals who are happy to concoct whatever stories are necessary to defend Japanese wartime aggression. Although Honda did receive some support for his work, in an interview for this book he describes the nature of the negative responses he faced:

> Only one chapter of my book *A Journey to China* focuses on Nanjing; the rest is about Shanghai and other things. Out of the whole book, they really only seriously criticized one story within one chapter of the book. In fact, that story didn't even fill a complete page in the book. Yet they tried to discredit all my work, based on their claim that part of one page of my book was wrong.

What I wrote about was just one event that one person at the Nanjing City Office told me about, as an example of what had gone on there. I quoted this person and said that there were two Japanese soldiers who were going to Nanjing who had decided to have a competition to see how many people they could decapitate with their swords. They were betting on who would be the first to kill one hundred people. This was just an episode that I heard and that I reported in the book the way I heard it. So, Bungeishunju started attacking me, saying that this example is a complete lie. This publisher essentially argued that if this one example is false, the entire massacre did not happen.

Honda noted that many revisionists have argued that the "killing contest" that he reported could not have happened. They claim that Honda was either a liar or a substandard journalist for having reported such an incredible story. Some have asserted that the swords of the lieutenant could not have stood up to such repeated use and that therefore the report is false. Others have called the report ridiculous, given that many Chinese soldiers were armed with guns and would not have been likely to succumb to sword attacks. At least one revisionist, Shichihei Yamamoto, calculated the number of beheadings that would have to have occurred per mile of the journey, and argued that it would have been physically impossible for anyone to perform such a feat.[33] Thus, the numbers game surrounding the Nanjing Massacre was launched from the very outset.

In point of fact, Honda's research later revealed that the "killing contest" was not mere oral folklore of China. In fact, it was first reported in a series of articles published by the wartime Japanese newspaper *Tokyo Nichinichi Shimbun* on November 30, 1937—before the fall of Nanjing—as part of the coverage of the campaign toward the city. The story of the contest was just another aspect of the pro-war Japanese propaganda of the time that portrayed Japanese soldiers as superhuman heroes. According to these articles, a pair of "heroic" second lieutenants beheaded one Chinese after another with their swords in the heat of battle. A paragraph from one of the Japanese *Tokyo Nichinichi* articles, republished by Honda, reads:

Second Lieutenant N killed nine at Henglinzhen, six at Weiguanzhen, and six at Changzhou Station on the twenty-ninth, for a total of twenty-five. Second Lieutenant M thereupon killed four in the vicinity of Changzhou Station, and when we reporters went to the station, we came upon the two of them conferring near there. Second Lieutenant M said, "With things going like this, I'll probably cut down a hundred by the time we reached Danyang, never mind Nanjing. You're going to lose. My sword has killed fifty-five, and it's only got one little nick on it." Second Lieutenant N responded, "Neither of us is killing people who run away. Since I'm serving as a _____, I'm not winning any points, but by the time we're in Danyang, I'll show you what kind of record I can rack up."[34]

Honda has reprinted a number of these articles in his recent book *The Nanjing Massacre,* along with the testimony of many eyewitnesses who saw Japanese soldiers decapitating helpless, unarmed Chinese prisoners. He has even tracked down a recollection of the killing contest as imparted by the infamous Lieutenant N himself, who was later executed as a war criminal. According to Honda, after having returned to Japan from the war front, Lieutenant N explained to some schoolchildren that he had not actually killed such a large number of people. Honda quotes Shishime Akira, who heard Lieutenant N speak to the children and wrote it up as follows in the December 1971 issue of the monthly magazine *Chugoku* (China). Lieutenant N is quoted in the magazine as saying: "Actually, I didn't kill more than four or five people in hand-to-hand combat. . . . We'd face an enemy trench that we'd captured, and when we called out "Ni, lai-lai!" (You, come on!), the Chinese soldiers were so stupid, they'd rush toward us all at once. Then we'd line them up and cut them down, from one end of the line to the other. I was praised for having killed a hundred people, but actually, almost all of them were killed in this way."[35]

Thus, according to Honda, the apologists who initially criticized him for having printed the story of the contest had a point: brave Japanese lieutenants never did race each other through dangerous battlefields to see who could behead a hundred Chinese in combat. Just as the apologists suspected, such a competition was an utter fabrication. However, the contest had been dreamed up neither by Honda nor by the Chinese to make the Japanese military seem unduly cruel—it had been reported by the Japanese militarist news media in a propaganda effort to make Japanese soldiers appear brave and heroic. Ironically, if Akira's account of Lieutentant N's statements to the schoolchildren is accurate, the truth was far more brutal than Honda had initially portrayed it. Rather than a competition between fierce warriors, it was most likely just a pitiful game between mass executioners, slaying unarmed men who (according to the international rules of war) should have been treated as prisoners of war.[36]

Although Honda and a number of other journalists like him have spoken out about the massacre, most Japanese journalists have refrained from standing up for the truth of the matter, thus permitting nationalist publishers such as Shinchosha Ltd. and Bungeishunju Ltd. to champion the revisionist cause. The negative articles against Honda appeared primarily in books and in monthly magazines such as *Bungei Shunju* and *Shokun!,* but they also appeared in a variety of weeklies such as *Shukan Shincho.*

Again, the result of the ongoing campaign waged by these publishers, and by the writers and so-called experts associated with them, is that significant portions of the Japanese public today believe that the "question" of whether the Nanjing Massacre took place is a legitimate issue of scholarly debate. This situation, for example, might be compared to a significant portion of educated U.S. citizens believing that the fact of the atom bombs detonated on Hiroshima and Nagasaki is debatable or to a sizable number of Germans believing that the mass murders at Auschwitz are a serious point of contention.

In an interview for this book, Kengo Tanaka, former president and CEO of Bungeishunju Ltd., said that he believed "the Nanjing Massacre, like the issue of the comfort women, is still an unresolved issue. We may not know what happened in our lifetimes."[37] Similarly, Akira Nakamura, a professor at Dokkyo University and the president of the Showa-shi Kenkyu-jo, or "Showa History Institute," and a contributor to the weeklies, has argued that those killed in the Nanjing Massacre are only a "tiny fraction" of those claimed by the Chinese and that "anti-Japanese" forces have seized upon it in order to disrupt the unity of the nation.[38] Best-selling Japanese author Nobukatsu Fujioka, an established contributor to Bungeishunju Ltd. and Shinchosha Ltd. magazines, reiterated his stance on the massacre in an interview for this book. "The conclusion of the Nanjing Incident that I reached is that it was just part of a propaganda machine put in place during the war by the enemies of Japan," he explained. "What really happened at Nanjing was very close to what happened in Paris between the Germans and the French. It was essentially a bloodless takeover of the city.... War-crimes types of killings were infinitely close to zero in Nanjing."[39]

Of course, not only staunch revisionists such as Tanaka, Nakamura, and Fujioka take these positions. Many Japanese, in all walks of life, still have either little or no awareness of the event, or they believe that the case has been unfairly overblown and that the Japanese imperial military was not as violent as claimed by the individuals Honda quotes. In fact, a number of Japanese reporters and editors, including those from major newspapers who were interviewed for this book, said they had "serious doubts" about these issues.

This October 22, 1992, *Shukan Shincho* article reads "Arguments Over the Number of Victims (Ranging from to 200 to 300,000) in Nanjing Massacre Temporarily Halted As Emperor's Visit to China Nears."

Indeed, the numbers games presented by the revisionists have gone quite a way toward justifying institutions, such as the Yasukuni War Memorial Museum in Tokyo, which glorifies Japanese military exploits in Nanjing and throughout Asia. Special attention is given at the museum to kamikaze pilots and other suicidal World War II forces, all of whom are touted as great, selfless heroes. Indeed, the museum presents a step-by-step explanation of the mid-twentieth-century campaigns, including the march toward and capture of Nanjing. Sadly, though, nothing is mentioned about the Nanjing Massacre; only the taking of the city is recounted. According to various displays at the museum, the Japanese Empire was not responsible for any particular military aggression but fought for the great good of mankind.

Revisionists' Efforts to Play the Numbers Game

Logically, Honda has made the convincing assertion that the Nanjing Massacre began with the arrival of invading troops along Hangzhou Bay on November 5, 1937, weeks before the actual battle for the city began. As explained earlier, these troops committed thousands of atrocities on their rampage toward the capital, and Honda logically concluded that those victims should be counted along with all other victims of the campaign. Honda also makes the sensible assertion that the massacre did not end until February 1938, weeks after the fall of the city, when garrison troops were brought in to replace the conquering soldiers, thus putting an end to the slaughter.

The most common method employed by Japanese apologists is to define an incident in the most restrictive terms possible, thereby limiting the death count to as small a figure as possible. Thus, whereas Honda and his allies logically define the Nanjing Massacre as having occurred throughout the military campaign to take the city and through the initial part of the occupation, those who would seek to deny or mitigate the horrors of what happened attempt to reduce the time frame and geographic area as much as possible. In contrast to Honda's sensible rationale, many revisionists have attempted to reduce the seriousness of the massacre by limiting its duration to that of the relatively short-lived battle for the city. They also have often tried to constrain the geographic location to that of the official city boundaries. Such a definition not only eliminates the many atrocities that occurred from Hangzhou Bay to Nanjing, it even eliminates the many mass executions and rapes that occurred in adjacent suburbs. According to the more extreme revisionists, even Xia Shujin's story might be discounted because it occurred just outside the city gates.

A good example of an article that attempts to play the numbers game appeared in *Shukan Shincho*. It is entitled "Arguments over the Number of Victims (Ranging from 200 to 300,000) in Nanjing Massacre Temporarily Halted as Emperor's Visit to China Nears."[40] The article expresses deep frustration with those who continue to insist that the massacre was a profound atrocity that left hundreds of thousands dead. The piece calls the larger estimates into question, while advocating the simple view that it really just doesn't matter and that the whole Nanjing event should just be forgotten. Of course, Japanese revisionists also almost uniformly tell the story of the massacre from the perspective of the conquering Japanese, relying on official testimony, including that of the military and political leadership. Testimonies of victims are seldom noted. Honda comments on this situation, claiming, "Our study group actually presents the facts on the Nanjing Massacre. Those who would deny the massacre don't have any facts. They simply use indirect information, so it isn't a fair debate. It's not one at all. Bungeishunju's readers and the readers of the other publications are being betrayed by lies."[41]

Ivan P. Hall tells of his own experience with Japanese revisionism on Nanjing in his 2002 book, *Bamboozled,* as well as in a telephone interview for this book. After visiting Nanjing in 1998, he says that it was an uncanny experience for him to return to the Foreign Correspondents' Club of Japan soon afterward, where he witnessed Japanese academics "waving their blackboard pointers over maps of the same terrain I had just walked across in China on my own," parading their "evidence" that supposedly proved that no massacre occurred and that Japanese soldiers had in many ways befriended the Chinese in Nanjing in 1937: "For them it was all a numbers game, as if getting the dead down from three hundred thousand to thirty thousand really mattered much when the greater moral horror lay in the nature of those wanton, face-to-face killings of unarmed individuals that went on for weeks without any Japanese in authority seeking to stop it. As the Australian historian Gavan McCormack has pointed out, history for these activists of the intellectual right lacks intrinsic standards of truth or evidence and is 'subject to the ultimate moral imperative of whether or not it serves to inculcate a sense of pride in being Japanese.'"[42]

Again, this issue of "actual empirical truth" versus "social truth" emerges. Hall and McCormack get to the core of the Nanjing "debate" in Japan. As McCormack points out in the sentence quoted by Hall, the actual, measurable, logical truth of the Nanjing Massacre is not that important to a large number of nationalist Japanese intellectuals. In the face of the stacks of irrefutable evidence presented by the Tokyo war-crimes trials and by Honda, Chang, and hundreds of others, they blithely reach for unreliable evidence and illogical arguments.

The following excerpt from *Shukan Shincho* is fairly typical of revisionist claims. Indeed, the argument presented is similar to the "rational-man" approach made by Masanori Nishioka, author of the *Marco Polo* magazine piece denying the Holocaust: what happened might have been wrong, but it was not nearly as bad as some make it out to be.

The *Shukan Shincho* piece entitled "Won't Japan Fare Well if It Doesn't Admit It Committed the Nanking Massacre?" focuses on the statements of the former minister of justice, Shigeto Nagano of the LDP. Nagano had publicly denied the Nanjing Massacre, but then, under political pressure, apologized for his denial and resigned his position. The article, which takes the position that Nagano should have held his ground and stuck by his denial of the massacre, opens with the following lead: "The Former Minister of Justice, Mr. Shigeto Nagano's silliness makes us speechless. He openly professed, 'The Nanking Massacre was made up.' We thought he would defend himself by showing the basis of his assertion. But

This *Shukan Shincho* article sports the headline "WON'T JAPAN FARE WELL IF IT DOESN'T ADMIT IT COMMITTED THE NANJING MASSACRE?" (*Shukan Shincho*, May 19, 1994.)

what he actually did was retract his statement and apologize for it. He showed no conviction in his own opinion. He then resigned from his position."[43]

Note the use of the word "theory" above. Rather than deny the massacre outright, *Shukan Shincho* settles at the outset for relegating the idea that 300,000 died to "theory" and then addresses the minister's statement as perhaps being worthy of defending.

After this lead, the piece provides a rough sketch of the basic events surrounding the Japanese invasion, reiterating that there is a substantial amount of controversy over the massacre. This detail then leads up to the second half and conclusion of the article, excerpted below. The language used includes such terms as the "Battle in Nanjing." Many Japanese revisionists also refer to it as the "Nanjing Incident." Both phrases imply that what happened was other than a massacre.

Some might correctly point out that in contrast to the revisionists' terms used to downplay the Nanjing Massacre, those who insist that it be recognized often refer to it with the more inflammatory name "Rape of Nanjing" or as a "Grand Massacre" or even as a "great grand massacre" in order to emphasize

the horrific quality of the event. But whether one agrees that these intensify-
ing terms should be used or not, there is at least a legitimate justification for
doing so. What occurred at Nanjing was a vile atrocity of incomprehensible
proportions. There is no excuse for downplaying the event as a mere incident
or even as yet another battle.

The *Shukan Shincho* article continues under the subhead, "Actual Number
of Those Killed May Be One-Tenth of Reported Figure":

> It was Kaikosha, a voluntary organization of former army officers, which
> attempted to reveal what precisely happened during the massacre. This orga-
> nization originally started investigating the truth of the massacre to disprove
> the fallacy of many reports of the incident with the belief that it couldn't have
> happened as reported. In the process of its investigation, this group began to
> realize that there was actually a certain degree of a massacre in Nanjing. With
> this new awareness, the organization began a series in its organ publication,
> starting in 1984 and running through February 1985, under the theme "The
> History of the Battle in Nanking."
>
> This series was later published as a book under the same title. This book
> is basically a collection of testimonies by the officers who survived the war.
> This book minutely analyzes the military's internal documents, including
> detailed records of engaged battles, which the group successfully collected
> and compiled in a large-scale effort for further analysis. Their analysis was
> very particular in that it was made from the viewpoint of servicemen. It was
> also nicely done, especially in comparison with the information that the
> National Government disclosed.
>
> According to this report by Kaikosha, the number of the executed POWs,
> including those captured soldiers who had discarded their military uniforms
> to mingle with ordinary civilians, amounted to 16,000. The number of reg-
> ular citizens who were slaughtered was 15,000. A total of 31,000 seemed to
> have perished in this massacre in Nanking.[44]

In contrast to Honda's work, *Shukan Shincho* relies on the information
from Japanese army officers, without referring to or quoting a single
survivor's testimony. Needless to say, such articles almost always avoid graphic
descriptions of the suffering that took place.

The article continues by referring to a variety of unsubstantiated "numbers" relevant to the event, such as population estimates of the city, deserting Chinese army personnel, POWs, and so forth. Based on these figures, the article uses the "rational-man" argument, which does not deny there was an incident of some kind, but proposes a much smaller scale than others have made it out to be:

Taking into consideration such rough calculations and the figures that we can obtain from analyzing the data of the military's detailed accounts of battle reports, we come up with the number of 31,000 including both servicemen and civilians. Of course, this figure includes those citizens who were killed in the actual battles. Also included in this number are those Chinese soldiers who killed one another in their exodus from the city. But many of them were victims as a result of the Japanese army's barbarous acts that included violence, stealing, raping, and slaughtering of surrendering POWs. All these actions taken by the Japanese military were in violation of the international law. Even 31,000 people are a lot of people and cannot be overlooked. However, the alleged death toll of 300,000 is simply too much in every possible sense.[45]

After admitting that some misdeeds were done on both sides ("Chinese soldiers killed one another") and drastically reducing the total number of victims, *Shukan Shincho* actually reverses the roles of the Japanese and Chinese, arguing that the Japanese are victims of the Chinese who won't share information. The Chinese are portrayed as unfairly blaming the Japanese militarists for the massacre. Admittedly, the Chinese government has used the massacre for political ends for many years, bringing it up as a bargaining chip in trade and diplomatic negotiations. The Chinese government has also been reticent to share documents and information with Japanese and other scholars. Still, *Shukan Shincho*'s attempt to make the Japanese look like victims is nothing short of preposterous. The following excerpt appeared in the magazine under the subhead, "The Chinese Government Refuses to Share Information":

Mr. Suzuki, the nonfiction writer who was quoted earlier, says that it may take another 100 years for us to know the whole truth of the Nanking Massacre.

He further comments: "As a matter of fact, China hasn't disclosed its data about the Nanking Incident. A great deal of historical data were discovered in Japan and Taiwan. And they have been disclosed ever since. For instance, how local newspapers in various areas in China and Chinese political party's organs actually wrote about this incident is still unknown today."...

For instance, Mr. Tang Sheng-zhi, the commander-in-chief of the Nanking Defense Forces, later discarded the National Party and joined the Communist Party. The remarks and documents that have something to do with him and his men haven't been disclosed either.

[Suzuki continues:] "To tell the truth, it doesn't make sense to discuss an issue without sufficient data of it. If Japan and China advocate mutual friendship, they should willingly disclose all the data they have and work together to reveal the truth of the Nanking Massacre. China hasn't done anything along this line with a seeming intention to draw more interests from Japan while keeping the truth in the darkness forever."

In a nutshell, Japan is at the mercy of China when it comes to the issue of revealing the truth of the matter of the Nanking Incident.[46]

The average reader of this article would reasonably conclude that although the Japanese army did commit some illegal acts in Nanjing, the Chinese behaved terribly too, both during and after the war.

But whereas Honda actually traveled to China numerous times, interviewing and photographing victims and compiling other evidence as well as quoting contemporary and historical documents, *Shukan Shincho* bases its reporting solely on former Japanese military men and Japanese "experts." *Shukan Shincho* tosses around with ease the numbers of dead and does so without attaching them in any meaningful way to actual human suffering.

Japanese novelist and activist Makoto Oda, in an interview for this book, describes the difference in perspective between those who attack or invade and those who are attacked or invaded as the "doing side of war" versus the "downside of war." According to Oda, who was born in 1933 and was a child during the Second World War, Japan experienced the "downside of war" when the United States began bombing the Japanese home islands in 1944 and 1945. Holding in his hands a picture of bombs falling from a U.S.

warplane, taken from within the plane, Oda says, "I was here at this time." He points between the bombs, to the outlines of a city below:

> I was somewhere in this area when these very bombs were dropped. This is why I know what the downside of war is. I have experienced being bombed. The doing side of war is a very different perspective. It's like looking down from this plane while the bombs are falling. Before the war, we Japanese only knew the doing side of war. I remember going to the movies and seeing the news footage and cheering about Japanese victories. That's the doing side. Then, at the end of the Second World War, we experienced the downside of war. Today, however, most Japanese have forgotten what it's like to be on the downside of war. The U.S. has never really experienced the downside of war. Now that so many years have passed since the Second World War, most Japanese are like people in the U.S., we only think of the doing side of war any more. We have forgotten the downside.[47]

While Japanese revisionists such as those who write for *Shukan Shincho* and *Shukan Bunshun* try to keep their readers focused on a perverted version of the "doing side of war" during the events in Nanjing, individuals such as Chang and Honda work hard to balance that perspective with what the downside of war was like there. Of course, this dynamic between those who would demand an even portrayal of war by the mass media—one that places a fair and equal emphasis on both the downside perspective and the doing-side perspective— and those who would prefer to focus only on the doing side of war is one that exists in all democratic nations. And, it is almost needless to say, those countries with economic and military might are far more likely to emphasize the doing side than the downside, which is often relegated to the margins.

Recent Numbers Games

The summer of 2003 brought yet another denial of the massacre by a leading Japanese political official—Eto Takami, a seventy-eight-year-old, three-time cabinet minister who leads the third-largest faction in the ruling LDP: "To say 300,000 people were killed in the Rape of Nanking is a pure fabrication, a big lie," Eto said in a speech to a local party chapter on July 12, according to the *Asahi Shimbun* and other national dailies.[48]

Denials such as Eto's have become just as commonplace in Japan as statements in the press and even by some government officials who correct the denials. The year 2001 brought the most recent permutation of the Nanjing Massacre numbers game. Minoru Kitamura, another well-known Japanese revisionist writer seeking to prove that the event never happened, published a book called *Nankin Jiken no Tankyu: Sono Jitsuzo o Motomete* (Research on Nanjing Massacre: Search for Its Real Image)[49] with Bungeishunju Ltd., the publisher of *Shukan Bunshun* weekly newsmagazine. In this book, Kitamura accuses Harold Timperley, a deceased Australian correspondent in China during the 1930s for the English *Guardian* newspaper (then called the *Manchester Guardian*), of "creating" the "myth" of the Nanjing Massacre. Timperley, who was in Nanjing at the time, had chronicled the events in his dispatches and in a widely read book of the time, *The Japanese Terror in China*.[50] It was Timperley who first estimated the number massacred at three hundred thousand.

According to Kitamura, Timperley's estimate was absurdly inflated. Kitamura accuses Timperley of having been an "agent of the Chinese Kuomintang" (the nationalist party of China during the war), who invented the number as part of a plot to smear the Japanese army. Bungeishunju Ltd.'s magazine *Shokun!* went so far as to say that Timperley was part of a plan "to present Japan in the role of absolute evil."[51]

The headlines in this image may or may not be reliable.

This January 2002 Bungeishunju Ltd. magazine entitled *Shokun!* (Gentlemen!) includes the lead headline (in the largest type size, located to the left of the man's face): "EXCAVATION! NEW DATA PROVES THE FABRICATION OF THE NANJING MASSACRE."

In response to Kitamura's book, John Gittings, a correspondent to the *Guardian* in 2002, did some investigation into the matter. Gittings wrote an article published on October 4, 2002, entitled "Japanese Rewrite *Guardian* History: Nanjing Massacre Reports Were False, Revisionists Claim."

Gittings analyzed the *Guardian* archives in London and concluded that when, back in the 1930s, Timperley reported 300,000 massacred, he specifically made reference not only to those killed within the city limits but to those who were slaughtered in the surrounding Yangtze River delta as well. This is precisely the logic that Honda uses today.

According to Gittings, Timperley sent three cables back to England. In the first cable, dated January 16, 1938, Timperley reported that a "survey by one competent foreign observer indicates [that] in [the] Yangtze delta no less than 300,000 Chinese civilians [have been] slaughtered, [in] many cases [in] cold blood."[52]

According to Gittings, when the Japanese learned about the details of Timperley's telegram, they quickly dispatched their own telegrams to Japanese embassies around the world to counter the report. These messages warned Japanese diplomats that Timperley's article would soon appear in the *Manchester Guardian* and that it would wrongly claim that 300,000 people were massacred at Nanjing. These hastily prepared Japanese telegrams incorrectly quoted Timperley by omitting his reference to the Yangtze River delta. Thus, right from the start, the issue of where the massacre took place and how many were killed was framed incorrectly, not by Timperley but by the Japanese militarists themselves.

"Drenched in Politics"[53]

So far, we have focused mostly on the domestic controversy in Japan surrounding the Nanjing Massacre. But the massacre is an international issue. China describes not just a massacre but a "Grand Massacre." The event has come to symbolize both China's weakness and its strength. For many years after the war, the Chinese government remained quiet on the matter, not wanting to draw attention to what it considered a humiliating event.

In more recent years, however, the Chinese government has used the massacre to contrast contemporary China's strength with its former weakness. Today's China, its government claims, is a nation in which such a thing will never happen again. Moreover, the Chinese government uses the Nanjing Massacre as an example of the danger posed by Japan and other foreign powers. Mark Eykholt writes, "Three hundred thousand deaths is more than just a number over which scholars argue. It is a multilayered symbol that for [the] Chinese signifies the unjustified pain inflicted on China by Western and Japanese power, and those who try to lessen or deny this number are, by extension, attempting to deny imperialist aggression."[54] The issue has been a contentious one in Sino-Japanese relations for decades now. The Chinese government has used the massacre a number of times to strengthen its hand in various negotiations with the Japanese—a tactic Eykholt describes as "playing the victimization card."[55] Indeed, the Chinese government has contributed much to misunderstandings about the massacre throughout the past sixty years. China remained quiet on the matter for decades and still refuses to disclose many of the key documents—a point that the *Shukan Shincho* article was able to capitalize on to minimize the event.

Another important player in the politics surrounding the massacre is the United States. In recent years, many Americans with Chinese ancestry, including Iris Chang, have rallied around the event, exposing Japanese cover-ups and denials with righteous indignation. Their work has begun what amounts to a small school of English-language studies on the massacre.[56]

However, even though the Chinese and Japanese are clearly the key players in the issue, the U.S. government must also accept some blame for supporting those who have denied the massacre. After the war, the U.S. occupiers of Japan, as well as the Tokyo war-crimes trials, focused lopsidedly on the war as it was waged between Japan and the West, sorely neglecting Japan's aggression against China and other East Asian nations. Once China became Communist and the United States had solidified its cooperative arrangements with Japan, the United States lost virtually all interest in exposing Japanese war crimes, in China or elsewhere. For instance, as stated, few Americans are cognizant of the devastating fact that Japanese militarism up to and throughout World War II led to the deaths of twenty million non-Japanese Asians.

To this day, the United States has put little diplomatic pressure on Japan to own up to its wartime legacy or make equitable reparations to its victims. The official line is that this is not the responsibility of the United States and that Japan's relationships with its neighbors are its own concern. Yet the fact remains that U.S. aid to Japan, including critical diplomatic and military support, has been instrumental in allowing Japan to evade its wartime responsibilities.

Dutch author Ian Buruma, who has followed the controversy over the Nanjing Massacre closely for some years, has described it as being "drenched in politics." Buruma attended ceremonies in Nanjing marking the fifty-fourth anniversary of the massacre. He interacted with Chinese, Japanese, and other internationals interested in the subject and then wrote a poignant analysis of his experience in the *Far Eastern Economic Review*. What comes through most in Buruma's insightful piece is the way the massacre continues to be used in contemporary politics, at the expense of properly understanding the historical facts. He comments with typical insight, "What tends to be forgotten in the midst of rumours, politics and ceremonies is what happened in Nanjing 54 years ago. It is the fate of events which are turned into symbols."[57]

Japanese Nationalism

Within Japan, the controversy over the Nanjing Massacre is regularly described as a "debate"; however, this is ludicrous. The controversy between those who would cover up one of history's worst massacres and those who would squarely confront it is no more legitimate a debate than the controversy between those who recognize that the earth is not the center of the solar system and those who stubbornly insist that it is.

In an interview for this book, former *Shukan Shincho* writer and assistant editor Jun Kamei has described the situation as follows: "I was a child during World War II. I was born in 1935, so I actually recall, for instance, the Pearl Harbor event, and I feel that the media in Japan today are starting to become quite similar to what the media were before and during World War II. They are becoming more and more uniform. The criticism is not being leveled at the government, and neither are they criticizing the U.S. They are losing their edge.... Magazines such as *Shukan Shincho* and *Shukan Bunshun* clearly embody the tendency to beat the drum of nationalism."[58] Kamei is one of many in Japan who believe that people need to understand the historic consequences of nationalism and militarism in order to avoid going down that road again. Unfortunately, such advocacy is not for the faint of heart. Katsuichi Honda, whose work embodies this belief, has had his life threatened for speaking out against Japanese militarism. He explained the situation in an interview for this book:

> In the early 1970s, there was a publication that featured interviews with different people and asking their opinions about the emperor. I was interviewed

and I said something very radical. I said something about the fact that there are Japanese people living in South America, in places like Peru and Brazil. And among them there is a group that asserts that the Japanese were not defeated during World War II. I said that the emperor should go to South America and be raised by these people like cattle.

So, with that comment, many right-wing people started criticizing me. Some men came to my office to threaten me, but we [were] able to just send them away. However, then they went to my family home. I wasn't there when they came, but from that point onward I began taking actions to protect my family. I decided not to reveal where I was living. I stopped having my telephone listed in the phone book. At the time, my child was only in the second year of primary school; however, these people actually contacted my child. As a result, we decided to move.

Today, there is a different last name printed on the gate of my home. I can't put the name Honda there. Also, I always use fake pictures on my book jackets and things, so that people will not easily know what I look like. By doing this, it makes it more difficult for people to find and attack me and my family.

However, these people have still come to places where I give speeches, which I began to do regularly after I left *Asahi*. So what I had to do was to begin wearing a bulletproof vest in public, as well as a gray-haired wig and glasses, so people won't easily recognize me later. I have had various death threats and have had to have police at events where I am speaking.[59]

A Japanese Rushdie

Honda has suffered a fate not unlike that of Bombay-born author Salman Rushdie, who was placed under a *fatwa*, or religious death sentence, by Ayatollah Ruhollah Khomeini in 1989 for what the Iranian spiritual leader considered insults to Islam in Rushdie's book *The Satanic Verses*. It is true that the threats to Rushdie's life appear to have come from a more powerful source than those against Honda, and no spiritual leader in Japan is known to have publicly ordered Honda's death. Moreover, Rushdie's avoidance of the threats against him has been far more public and more widely covered by the media. The two cases, nevertheless, are similar. Both men are accomplished writers, known for their quests for truth. Both were targeted for "insulting" supposedly

One of Japan's best-known journalists, Katsuichi Honda, is shown here in a wig and glasses. Honda has been forced to wear disguises in public because of multiple death threats made by Japanese ultrarightists who have been outraged by his rigorous reporting of the Nanjing Massacre and by his outspoken views against both Japanese militarism during the Second World War and nationalism during the postwar period. *(Photo courtesy of Katsuichi Honda.)*

sacred things: in Rushdie's case, Islam; in Honda's, the Japanese emperor and, by extension, the neonationalists who still use the emperor as a rallying point for Japanese racism. Both writers came under attack by violent zealots. Both had to change their lifestyles and drastically increase security measures around them. And both men have continued to write in spite of their trials. One of the key differences between the cases, however, is that Rushdie was threatened by a leader in a nondemocratic developing country infamous for its fanatical leadership. Honda, on the other hand, was threatened within a supposedly first-ranking liberal democracy.

This speaks volumes about the state of free speech in Japan. For, in fact, the same human impulse that drove the attack against Rushdie drove the attack against Honda—that is, a violent religious fanaticism that leaves little room for rational dialogue, never mind for dissension. Japanese neonationalists usually are not categorized as religious zealots. But those who would threaten the life of a writer and his family for having criticized the emperor can accurately be thought of as such. The World War II rhetoric of Japanese nationalists defines the emperor as divine. For this reason, it is no stretch to categorize today's Japanese neonationalists along with other dangerous fanatics worldwide. The same blinding zealotry that drives terrorists in other parts of the world to censor and attack their opponents drives Japanese nationalists to threaten Honda and those Japanese like Honda. Unfortunately such nationalism is unequivocally on the rise in Japan and is routinely ignored and even condoned by Japanese power holders who benefit from its quelling effects on the population.

This is not by any means to say that everyone on the right side of the political spectrum in Japan fits this category. Those who have threatened Honda are obviously extremists. Actually, a prime example of this neonationalist threat is the sound trucks that so regularly patrol the streets of Tokyo, blasting songs in praise of the emperor and screaming speeches in support of Japanese militarism and against foreigners of all sorts. For those who have not encountered such a group, it should be clarified that their noise represents a kind of violence and is actually painful to be near. Their nationalist cant is not amplified simply in order to be heard from a distance; it is blasted maliciously to create serious discomfort for anyone near them. It is true that such ultrarightists are outside of the mainstream of Japanese society and that they do not command a major contingency of followers. Most Japanese, it would seem, tend to be generally annoyed by and ashamed of their presence on the streets. David McNeil, who has written a superb paper entitled "Media Intimidation in Japan," writes, "The best estimates are that there are more than 100,000 far-right members in Japan belonging to almost 1,000 groups throughout the country, 800 of which are affiliated through an organization called *Zennippon Aikokusha Dantai Kaigi*, or the National Conference of Patriotic Associations."[60] But their relatively small membership figures certainly do not mean that they should be dismissed as in any way inconsequential. It may be impossible to quantify the effects of the ultrarightists on free speech in Japan, but they are not insubstantial.

McNeil explains how he became interested in Japan's ultraright, thanks to his firsthand experience with them. According to McNeil, he is the only foreign media member in Japan that he is aware of to experience their intimidation directly. McNeil and his wife were hosting a radio talk show in Tokyo when they brought up the subject of the Nanjing Massacre, a topic they rightly assumed to be incontrovertibly well documented and thus fair game for discussion. According to McNeil, he and his wife said on the air that visiting the Nanjing Massacre site was an edifying experience for them and recommended that their listeners visit it. "Thirty minutes after the show was broadcast, three members of a local 'political group' arrived at the studio and asked to see the management." According to McNeil, their visit was very successful and led to his station director applying pressure on him and his wife to change the content of their show. "Two days later the senior station manager called a meeting. He apologized for taking our time and explained that from now on he would be very grateful if we would not discuss political issues on the radio. If someone sent a fax or email in giving their opinions, it was fine to read it out over the air but not to give our own opinions. He said we would need to apologize over the air for the Nanjing comment. If we didn't, the men and their friends would drive their *gaisensha*, or black sound trucks, outside our [advertising] sponsors (two *ramen*, or Chinese noodle, restaurants, a bar, and a couple of real estate agents) and harass them until they withdrew their support. Violence was unlikely, but he couldn't rule it out. He apologized again for asking us to apologize. He handed us a sheet of paper the station had prepared for us to read on the next show. It said that we *humbly* apologized for the 'inappropriate comments' [*futekisetsu na hyogen*] we had made the previous week."[61]

McNeil goes on in his paper to outline a serious list of media intimidation in Japan on behalf of the ultraright, including the famous shooting of the mayor of Nagasaki in 1991 for having suggested that Emperor Hirohito may have had some responsibility for Japanese involvement in World War II, as well as less famous events, such as the hounding of various professors and media members by sound trucks. He concludes, "Every large media institution in Japan, and many small ones, have experienced political harassment of some sort."[62]

McNeil also makes the important distinction between "hard nationalism" and "soft nationalism." Whereas direct forms of intimidation, such as that against Honda, clearly fit under the heading of hard nationalism, more subtle attacks that are sometimes less in line with emperor worship and more in line with keeping the status quo in place fit under the heading of soft nationalism. It would seem that the articles in *shukanshi* and other magazines are a part of this latter category.

It would be overly simplistic, to say the least, to portray Shinchosha Ltd., Bungeishunju Ltd., or any other publisher of a *shukanshi* merely as die-hard far-right publishers dedicated to supporting Japanese nationalism above all else, for their nationalism is profit driven. If a topic did not sell, it's pretty safe to say that they would not waste ink on it. But stories about the Nanjing Massacre do sell, and the more inflammatory, the better.

Former *Shukan Shincho* editor Jun Kamei insists that many of his former magazine's readers are insecure individuals who want to be more than they are. According to him, they buy *Shukan Shincho* and similar magazines because the magazines degrade others and thus help their readership to feel better about their own lives. Kamei asserts that in their coverage of international issues, *Shukan Shincho* and related magazines such as *Shukan Bunshun, Bungei Shunju,* and *Shokun!* capitalize on the racist tendencies of their readers. "After the loss of World War Two, Japan was labeled a loser and also an invader. This was the truth, and this was obviously the chorus from the outside nations," Kamei says. "This exposes some of the worst aspects of the Japanese people, but before even World War Two there was a sense of superiority over the Koreans, Taiwanese, and Chinese. And so the Japanese essentially claimed that the other nations were inferior or lesser. And then after the war, there was a similar feeling. But it can't be outspoken anymore. It's sort of muted. There are a lot of men who sort of have these beliefs, and it's obviously been passed on to the youth to some degree. It continues to appear in weekly newsmagazine articles such as in *Shukan Shincho*."[63]

By supporting this thinking today, these publishers have been able to carve out quite profitable market niches that keep them generally aligned with those in power in Japan.

Just as with Japanese anti-Semitism, the least democratic aspects of the Japanese system benefit considerably from nationalism and racism. The Japanese system of governance relies on false beliefs that the Japanese are a uniquely special race of people, harmoniously united and as much innocent victims of World War II as any other nationals.

Roger Pulvers, who has more than thirty years experience with Japan, addresses this very issue in a 2000 commentary published in the *Japan Times*, writing that:

> The prolonged and constant suppression of the truth and the secrecy over Japan's past deeds have been no accidental flaw in an otherwise open society. Make no mistake. These have served the interests of the men who derailed the train of democracy for their own greater good, as well as for the good of their patrons, clients and numerous sycophants. It has been crucial for them

to keep Japanese people in the dark about what was done during the war. Were the truth to come out and be recognized by a wide public here, the entire leadership of this country, the leadership that has ruled over the past half century, would be readily delegitimized and thrown out of power.[64]

Honda and his colleagues' research undermines the secrecy that Pulvers writes about, even while revisionist publishers, writers, and politicians feel compelled to challenge that research. The Japanese system of governance relies on nationalism for legitimacy and cannot bear to have that nationalism damaged by Honda and those like him, who logically expose its deadliest faults. In this light, *shukanshi* can be thought of as "social antibodies" within the Japanese system that naturally rally to attack any perceived threat. Though not their only function, certainly one of their functions is to serve as sound trucks of the news world, harassing and intimidating in print those who dare to expose the truth.

A good example of this is a December 14, 2000, *Shukan Shincho* article enti-
tled "The Real Identity of the Chinese Who Claimed That 'The Nanjing Massacre' Was Real."[65] This ridiculous piece of propaganda dressed up as journalism attacks a Chinese woman who has lodged a lawsuit against a Japanese author and publisher who said her testimonies about the Nanjing Massacre were false. The article takes the position that the woman lodged her lawsuit as part of a conspiracy of anti-Japanese forces in China, and perhaps even domestically.

An even worse example is a June 24, 1999, article titled "Hero in China: Former Japanese Soldier Who Cries Out 'Nanjing Massacre.'"[66] Note that, as with the previous article, the term Nanjing Massacre is placed in quotations to imply that no such thing ever happened. In this case, *Shukan*

The headline of this 2000 *Shukan Shincho* article proclaims "THE REAL IDENTITY OF THE CHINESE WHO CLAIMED THAT 'THE NANJING MASSACRE' WAS REAL." The piece paints her as part of an anti-Japanese plot. (*Shukan Shincho*, December 14, 2000.)

Shincho is attacking a former Japanese soldier, Shiro Azuma, who has bravely admitted to the atrocity. The article includes the pull quote, "His writings are complete lies." In his book, Azuma admits to having decapitated three Chinese with his sword, actions that have caused him great grief ever since. Among other things, he also witnessed the burning alive of other helpless Chinese. *Shukan Shincho* essentially tries to damn Azuma as a traitor because some Chinese have hailed him as upright and admirable for having confessed.

The plain truth of the matter is that the coverage of the Nanjing Massacre by Honda and his brave Japanese compatriots should not be controversial. They do not provide grounds for legitimate debate; they are factual records. They are only cast as "controversial" in Japan because they challenge the unhealthiest forms of nationalism and the dysfunctional system that it supports. Unfortunately, this situation is emblematic of similar situations in countries the world over, where national acts of injustice are defended, devalued, or denied by those who prefer that they just be forgotten.

Nationalism versus Patriotism

Karel van Wolferen has presented his views on the fundamental difference between unhealthy "nationalism" and a more healthy "patriotism":

> Nationalism is a political movement with an implicit ideology that portrays one's country as somehow superior to other counties, and as deserving of special privileges without regard for international concerns. Nationalism in history has frequently been a reaction to a threat from the external world.... Nationalism thrives on a sense of national insecurity. Nationalism is sometimes an inevitable necessity when a country is just being formed as the home of a nation that gains independence from foreign overlords. But in well-established countries it can easily lead to unhealthy excesses. It nurtures expansionist dreams among rulers. It can stir up people into belligerency and aggressive action against neighboring countries.
>
> Patriotism, by contrast, follows from genuine and reasonable emotions connected to a concern for the well-being of the country to which one belongs. Nationalism cannot be together with internationalism in the same person. But patriotism is perfectly compatible with internationalism. In fact, there may be

good reasons to conclude that patriots make good internationalists, since a mature love for their country makes them wish that their country can conduct itself responsibly on the international stage. Patriots do not generally have the tendency to blame foreigners for problems that are home-made.[67]

According to van Wolferen, Japan (like too many nations) suffers from a lack of healthy patriotism and an excess of destructive nationalism. Unscrupulous writers and publishers capitalize on this dangerous dichotomy and exploit it when they put profit before journalistic ethics.

Whereas patriots the world over have risked their lives to protect their countries against external threats, Katsuichi Honda has continued to risk his life in the face of dangerous and insidious *internal* threats. He is an example not only for his fellow Japanese, but for journalists and patriots everywhere. Honda comments on his motivations for his work on the subject: "Thus I wrote this book [*The Nanjing Massacre*] not as a means of apologizing to China but as a means of revealing the truth to the Japanese people. Having been a child at the time, I bear no responsibility for the actual massacre, but as a Japanese journalist, I bear some responsibility for leaving the story unreported for so long."[68]

This spirit generally seems to be the motivation of most of the Japanese dedicated to revealing the truth of what happened in Nanjing. They are individuals who, no matter how painful it might be—or even how dangerous for themselves and their families—are committed to the betterment of their nation and the ultimate happiness and prosperity of the Japanese people. They recognize that such noble goals can be accomplished only by establishing an accurate understanding of Japanese history. And that history includes a dark period of autocratic militarism, which was supported by a nationalism that, unfortunately, is still alive and well.

Relevance

As the extensive background information in this chapter illustrates, *shukanshi* and other magazines make up only a small fraction of the story of how the Nanjing Massacre has played out in the classic conflict between brave, altruistic Japanese writers and advocates such as Honda, and quack

This June 24, 1999, *Shukan Shincho* article reads "HERO IN CHINA: FORMER JAPANESE SOLDIER WHO CRIES OUT 'NANJING MASSACRE.'" A pull-out quote on the page announces, "His Descriptions Are Complete Lies." It is deeply critical of a former Japanese soldier, Shiro Azuma, who has testified to having participated in the Nanjing Massacre. Here, *Shukan Shincho* criticizes him for having been praised for his honesty by the Chinese.

fundamentalists and ultranationalists like Fujioka. At its heart, this is the story of what Oda describes as the conflict between those on the "doing side" and those on the "downside" of war. As such, the massacre serves as a supreme example of how those on the doing side can not only spin the news to fit certain agendas but can white-wash the most unambiguously heinous of atrocities—even in a democratic nation such as postwar Japan.

The U.S. professor of linguistics, Noam Chomsky, who participated in an e-mail interview for this book,[69] has compared the Japanese treatment of the Nanjing Massacre with that of the U.S. treatment of the Vietnam War. In a 2002 dialogue with Japanese professor Kenichi Asano, Chomsky put his thoughts on the matter this way: "It's very much like what you've been writing about the Nanjing Massacre in your country. We just won't write about our own atrocities.

Let's take Vietnam, the Vietnam War. Does anybody have any idea how many people were killed in Vietnam? I mean, we don't know within millions. And the reason is nobody cares. Nobody cares. You know, we were slaughtering millions of Vietnamese. Who cares?"[70] Whether or not one is in accord with Chomsky's comparison of the Nanjing Massacre with the Vietnam War, his key point is impossible to dismiss. The mainstream U.S. view of that war is often focused on the ramifications for the United States, with relatively little attention paid to the legacies on the other side.

As this book goes to print, the global "War on Terror" rages on and is expected to continue with no end in sight. On March 11, 2004, hundreds of civilians were killed and injured in Spain in terrorist bombings. Meanwhile, the U.S.-led coalition (which has included Spain) continues to grapple with guerrilla resistance to its occupation of Iraq, even as images of Iraqi prisoners being tortured by U.S. and British personnel are circulated around the world.

Regardless of one's feelings about actions in Iraq, it is impossible to dispute that media coverage (in the United States and in Great Britain, certainly) has been heavily tilted to the perspective of the coalition "doing side." Broadcast time and print space is consistently skewed in favor of military and other official, coalition sources—information given at press conferences and to embedded soldiers and the like—with far less attention paid to the daily plight of ordinary Iraqi civilians: the people who are being "liberated." The body counts and injury rates for Iraqi civilians are rarely forthcoming and seldom receive more than lip service. The "downside" perspective is clearly neglected.

Whether an individual is fully supportive of a given military action or dead set against it, the public of a democratic nation requires an accurate view of that military action in order to assess it. The story of the Japanese news media and the Nanjing Massacre is the story of a democracy deeply at odds with itself as to how to view one of its most consequential military actions. Sadly, the Japanese people were gravely misled about the nature of the event when it happened, and they continue to be misled to this day. This is also the story of how that event and its telling will affect that nation's present and future, both domestically and internationally.

It is a story well worth knowing, not only out of respect for its many victims in China, not only because of what it says about a betrayed Japanese public that continues to be deceived, but for the potential victims of present and future military actions worldwide.

CHAPTER EIGHT

ATTACKING FORMER SEX SLAVES: A SECOND RAPE

Every time I see the scars, I remember how they slashed me. How can they say there is no history of what they did to us when the evidence is on my body? To say that this did not happen, to deny history, this is the most wicked act.

—Ok Seon Lee, surviving sex slave of World War II Japanese military[1]

Ok Seon Lee's Testimony

The story of the Japanese military's "comfort women"—the estimated 80,000 to perhaps 200,000[2] girls and young women enslaved and forced to provide sex to the Japanese military during the Second World War—remains a highly emotional issue throughout much of East Asia and beyond. It has been a political football of sorts for more than a decade now, as the relatively few surviving comfort women strive to see justice served and their tragic cases duly acknowledged by the world, while many Japanese nationalists strive just as mightily to deny or diminish the reality of their sufferings. The case has also become important in the interactions between Japan and those countries from which comfort woman were taken during the war, such as today's

North and South Korea, Taiwan, the Philippines, Indonesia, Malaysia, and China. Meanwhile, despite at least a half-dozen English-language books in print verifying the story of the comfort women, it remains an often overlooked historical reality throughout much of the West.

One of the surviving former comfort women, Ok Seon Lee, spoke as a guest of the Korean-American Students Association of Brown University in the autumn of 2002. While in the United States, Lee also participated in an interview for this book. At that time, she was seventy-five years old. For the previous two years, she had been living in a charity home operated for surviving comfort women in South Korea. Before that, she lived in China, where she had resided for almost five decades after three years of enslavement as a Japanese military "comfort woman." Her story has never before been published.

Anyone familiar with the testimonies of other former comfort women will recognize Ok Seon Lee's experience as sadly typical. One of the most remarkable aspects of her story is simply that she lived so long and can tell it now. For reasons that will become clear, the great majority of the comfort women did not survive as long as she has. Her story is that of a peasant girl forced against her will into sexual slavery to a vast military machine:

> My name is Ok Seon Lee. I was born in the mountains in Korea. I grew up in a poor family until I was fifteen years old. From the age of seven to fifteen, I complained endlessly because I wanted to go to school and learn. But my family could not afford to send me to school. Eventually, my mother told me that if I became a foster child in another family, I would be able to go to school. I jumped for joy in excitement and agreed to become a foster child. However, when I got there, it was not what I expected. I wound up working for a family who ran a restaurant that sold udon noodles. They did not send me to school; instead, I had to do odd jobs all the time. When I asked when I would be able to go to school, they just put me off. Months went by like this. Finally, they told me that the only way I could go to school would be to earn lots of money for them. But how could I make money for them when I was basically just a servant to their family?
>
> I tried to run away a number of times but was always caught and punished. They told me that I did not work enough and that I didn't listen to

Ok Seon Lee gives her testimony at Brown University on November 16, 2002.

them. Without any consultation with me, and without the knowledge of my family, they sold me to another place in Ulsan. When I arrived in Ulsan, I realized that I had been sold to work at a bar. There I also had to do errands and odd jobs.

One day when I was out on an errand in the town, I was captured by a Japanese man. I tried to fight him off, but my resistance had no effect. He took me down the road and threw me into a truck. On the truck, there were five other girls— six including myself. We had all been captured and were held against our will.

At the time, I did not know if I was going to China, or the U.S., or Japan, or somewhere else. We did not know anything, except that the journey was long. Eventually, because we each began to fight and yell, demanding to be let go, they stuffed our mouths with cloth. I had actually arrived in China but did not know this until one year after my arrival. We arrived at a train station, and got off in what we later found out to be an area called Doe-moon. We spent a night there in a place that served as a prison. After that night, we woke up and were split apart. I do not know where four of the girls were sent, but another girl and I were placed on a train without any knowledge of what was to be done with us. We finally arrived at a place called Yun-gil, an airport. This airport was small, and Japanese soldiers were expanding it. There was a lot of construction going on, and we were assigned to pull weeds from the ground with shovels.

We had been given a tiny bit of food in the morning and began work in the afternoon. We were given no more food that day and were not allowed to stop until nightfall. The weather was bitterly cold, and since we had no decent clothes with us, we shivered terribly. Because it was so cold, and because we had so little food, it was difficult for us to work efficiently, so they kicked us and beat us and said that we were not good workers.

The only food we received were small balls of flour. How were we supposed to eat only that and work? The youngest girl there was fourteen years old. I was fifteen. The oldest was seventeen years old. The Japanese soldiers there had no mercy or compassion. They beat us all the time, until we bled, saying that we were bad workers. We would resist and try to fight back to the best of our abilities, telling them that we wanted to go home.

Eventually, the Japanese soldiers approached us and told us that we were changing locations. We got excited, thinking that we were finally being sent home to Korea. But they did not send us home. Instead, we were sent to a comfort station. When we arrived at the comfort station, they told us that in order for us to serve the soldiers, we needed to be clean. We did not have any decent clothes, though, and were filthy with dirt. We hadn't even been able to brush our hair since we had been captured.

At the comfort station, they washed us and gave us new clothes and wooden sandals. However, these clothes and other things came at a price. They were put on a tab as our debt. They told us that we needed to serve a lot of soldiers in order to make enough money to get rid of our debts. Only then would we be allowed to go home. All these young girls, fourteen-, fifteen-, sixteen-year-old girls, what did we know? There is probably no one listening to my testimony who is as young as fifteen years old. What did we know? They took in young girls who had no knowledge and fed them almost nothing besides the food they gave to the pigs, and they expected us to serve up to thirty or forty soldiers per day.

Usually on the weekdays there weren't that many soldiers, but on the weekends, because the soldiers had time off, there were so many that came to us. They lined up outside the comfort station. But how were we able to serve thirty to forty men per day?

They took one fourteen-year-old aside, saying that she had not yet matured and took a knife to cut her and slashed her so that she would bleed. We were all told that if we resisted we would be killed. When we resisted, they beat us until we bled. At times, we had blood all over our bodies.

Once a week, the military infirmary sent out people to give us physical examinations to see if we had been infected with any diseases. If we had any symptoms, they would tell the comfort station manager not to allow us to serve soldiers, and they gave us these injections called 606. This was an injection of mercury, which they believed would heal everything but was actually poisonous.

However, the managers at the comfort station didn't care for the doctors' warnings. Even though they knew some of the comfort women had sexually transmitted diseases, we were constantly forced to serve soldiers anyway. We had no other choice. Usually the lower-ranking soldiers heeded our cautions, but the officers never listened to us. Even though we asked them to use condoms, they refused. When we protested or fought back, they would beat us until we fell to the ground. No matter how badly we bled, they continued to beat us. When we fell to the ground, they would grab us and stand us up and slash our bodies with their knives and swords. Blood would sometimes be pouring all over us, but they continued to slash us. If we resisted, they stabbed us. Even now, I have many scars from being slashed with knives and swords.

When I see these scars still on my body today, I think, "How can I forget what these Japanese soldiers did?" Even until the day I die, I will never forget what they did to us. Every time I see the scars, I remember how they slashed me. How can they say there is no history of what they did to us when the evidence is on my body? To say that this did not happen, to deny history, this is the most wicked act.

I wanted to die. But there was no way for any of us to choose death. We did not have money to buy poison, and there were no trees to hang from. We could not even run away, because we were not allowed to go out.

However, we felt we either had to run away or die. So we often ran away. After a terrible beating once, I decided I had to run away. But in a moment I was captured and was forced to live in the comfort station. Still, I decided that I would rather die than stay there living like that. One day when they opened the front gates, because a lot of soldiers were coming, I ran away from the comfort station. I had actually succeeded in escaping out of the comfort station, but I had nowhere to go. I knew I was in China, but I had no idea which road would lead to Korea. Even if I did know which direction to go, I had no money. In no time I was recaptured and forcefully brought back and beaten again.

From then on, I was not left alone. They kept asking me if I was going to run away. And because I kept saying that I would, they continued to beat me. When I kept resisting, and they tired of beating me, they brought in soldiers who took over for them and beat me as well. They did not hit me and beat me to teach me a lesson; they beat me so that I would die. After a beating like this, I felt like there was no hope. I could not run away. I could not die. I couldn't do anything. I lived like this—in hell—for three years. I lived in hell for three years and did not even know when Korea had won its independence. Even when planes flew above us and dropped bombs, we just thought that a war was going on.

One day, the soldiers and the manager came to us and told us we had to relocate and migrate to another place. We followed them on foot for three days and ended up deep in the mountains. We left the roads and were surrounded by lots of big trees. By this time we had not eaten for two days. The soldiers then said to us, "You must be hungry. Why don't we go and get some food for you?"

But in reality the soldiers did not care about us. They had lied to us, saying that they would bring back food. But this was just a part of their ploy to abandon us. So all the soldiers left, leaving us behind in the mountains. There were about ten of us. What were we to do? We knew if we stayed in the mountains we would die. So we tried to escape. Eventually we wound up on our knees, crawling down the mountain like dogs until we ended up on a narrow road that led us into the city of Yun-gil. We were starving, so we asked people to give us food, but most of the people in the city had migrated there from somewhere else, and the area was very poor. Many people hid during the day and only came out to eat and travel by night.

Because there were so many of us comfort women, we decided that we would have a better chance of survival if we split up. Some of us eventually met men and were lucky enough to be asked to live with them. This is how we survived after the war. I wanted to return back home to Korea, but I had no money and no idea how to even get there. A lot of people ended up just living harsh lives, never being able to return back home.[3]

After being taken in by a Chinese man, whose family she helped raise, Ok Seon Lee remained in China for about fifty years. She eventually returned to South Korea, where she now lives with other surviving former comfort women. She says she is "fairly happy now" and that she is "well cared for." However, in addition to the many scars on her body, she continues to suffer from a number of emotional and physical problems that stem from her ordeal.

Japanese Military Comfort Stations

As Ok Seon Lee's testimony makes clear, Japanese military comfort stations were places where soldiers had sex with teenage girls and young women. But, despite the claims of some Japanese historical-revisionist writers, comfort stations were not brothels, and the teenagers and young women who lived in the stations were not prostitutes. The word "prostitute" implies some degree of choice on the part of a person who accepts payment in exchange for sexual services. Irrefutable evidence clearly proved that the girls and young women such as Lee were there against their will.[4] Moreover, these girls and young women never received significant compensation and usually none to speak of.[5] According to Lee, for example, the only compensation she was ever given in exchange for sex were "tickets" handed to her by the soldiers, which she was required to pass on to the comfort-station managers. Although some girls and young women did receive financial "tips" and most were theoretically (according to Japanese military regulations) supposed to receive pay, few survivors managed to hold onto any money. Like Lee, they were all required to pay their captors, who were infamous for charging huge sums for their clothes, food, and other necessities. Even if a comfort woman could have saved something, it would likely be useless in the ravaged postwar economies that she faced upon release, where currencies often changed and where savings accounts were not always honored.

Approximately 80 percent of the sex slaves were Korean; most of the rest came from other countries occupied by Japan such as Taiwan, China, and the Philippines. The vast majority were teenagers. By one approximation, 80 percent were between the ages of fourteen and eighteen.[6] George Hicks, in his *The Comfort Women: Japan's Brutal Regime of Enforced Prostitution in the Second World War,* refers to statistical data on the comfort women derived from

telephone hotlines set up in 1992 in Japan and South Korea to collect information about comfort stations and comfort women who had been "duped,
abducted or coerced into sexual slavery."[7] Sangmie Choi Schellsted's indescribably poignant book *Comfort Women Speak: Testimony by Sex Slaves of the
Japanese Military* includes plainspoken, graphic testimony from nineteen surviving former sex slaves, seventeen of whom gave their ages at the time of
their abductions, the average of which was 15.74. Similarly, Keith Howard's
heart-wrenching book *True Stories of Comfort Women* includes the testimony
of surviving victims. Of these, the average age at abduction was 16.8 years.
See table 8.a for a breakdown of the ages at which these girls and young
women were abducted. It might be noted here that prostitution was legal in
both Korea and Japan at the time. The legal age for licensed prostitutes in
Japan was eighteen. The average age in Korea was seventeen. One 1940 document left by a Japanese army unit in China indicates that comfort women
were supposed to be at least sixteen years old.[8]

Table 8.a. Average Age at Abduction of Comfort Women Whose Stories Are Recounted in Schellsted and Howard

AGE	NUMBER OF WOMEN IN SCHELLSTED	NUMBER OF WOMEN IN HOWARD
22	0	1
21	1	1
19	0	2
18	2	2
17	1	4
16	6	5
15	4	2
14	2	1
13	1	0
11	0	1
Average age of abduction	**15.74**	**16.8**

Source: Compiled from Sangmie Choi Schellsted, ed. *Comfort Women Speak: Testimony by Sex Slaves of
the Japanese Military* (New York: Holmes and Meier, 2000) and Keith Howard, ed. *True Stories of the
Korean Comfort Women* (London: Cassell, 1995).

While the average ages of abduction of the women in these two books does not prove anything scientifically about the demographics of all comfort women, they are at least consistent with what is known about the women: namely, that a great number of them were not women by modern standards at all, but teenage girls. In fact, a substantial number of them were not old enough to work as legal prostitutes, according to either Japanese or Korean standards. Of course, and it cannot be emphasized enough, Japanese military comfort women were not prostitutes, as they were neither being compensated nor were they acting on their own volition. Indeed, the case was just the opposite. Thus, the term "comfort women" is doubly a misnomer, since it implies not only that these females provided mere "comfort" (as opposed to being forced into sex), but also that they were mainly women (i.e., adults), when in reality they were predominantly teenagers.

Although the girls and young women in Japanese comfort stations were raped daily, often by dozens of soldiers, this does not simply represent

This photograph, courtesy of the U.S. National Archives, is accompanied by a caption from the archives that reads, in part, "In the Sittang area, where the Japanese twenty-eighth Army was cut-off and annihilated in its attempts to break out from Burma into Siam.... Many prisoners were taken. With them were found a small party of Chinese girls forcibly employed by the [Japanese] in their 'Comfort Corps.' Picture shows: ———, one of the Chinese girls, supplies information to a British officer at Rangoon. August, 1945."

another case of an invading army committing rape—a circumstance all too common in the history of warfare. Indeed, most scholars, including an international panel of judges who held a mock trial on the matter,[9] as well as the United Nations Commission on Human Rights,[10] have concluded that between the early 1930s and the end of the war, the Japanese military planned and implemented the sexual enslavement of as many as 200,000 teenagers and young women—a case that truly is "unique in world history."[11]

Japanese Recruitment Methods

By the start of the 1940s, whenever the Japanese military conquered an area, it "recruited" girls and young women from cities, villages, and the surrounding countryside. Procedures for the recruitment process do not seem to have been uniform throughout the empire. Eyewitness testimony (from Japanese soldiers and medical professionals, civilians of various nationalities, and surviving former sex slaves such as Lee) shows that the military authorities used whatever methods were most expedient. Sometimes they employed civilian "subcontractors"; at other times, they used uniformed soldiers. Recruitment included the appropriation of existing brothels and prostitutes in conquered lands, but demand far exceeded that source and required targeting ordinary women and girls.

These four young women were discovered by the Chinese army on Sung Shan Mill on the Burma Road after the army had driven the Japanese out of the village in September of 1944. The soldier at left is unidentified. (*Photo courtesy of the U.S. National Archives.*)

Again, it ought to be emphasized that while some small number of women who served in the comfort system had been prostitutes previously, once they became comfort women, they lived their lives as sex slaves of the Japanese military. Moreover, while some Japanese women did work as legal prostitutes during the war, both in Japan and elsewhere, these prostitutes were not comfort women. The

This August 14, 1944, image, courtesy of the U.S. National Archives, is marked with the caption: "... in charge of prisoners of war at Myitkyina Burma with the captured 'Comfort Girls' of the Japanese garrison at Myitkyina."

term comfort women, as used here, is meant to refer only to those women who were forced into sex slavery by the Japanese military machine.

The Japanese military naturally targeted the poorest and least educated girls and women, such as Lee, among conquered populations. The disappearance of these girls was least likely to cause problems with the local population, their families or guardians were more easily coerced into turning them over, and they were also more easily duped through false promises of steady employment. Such deception appears to have been the most common method of recruitment, although the tactic naturally became less effective as information about the comfort system spread among conquered populations. As a result, Japanese authorities relied increasingly on kidnapping—as in the case of Lee, who was grabbed off the street—as well as brutal slave raids on villages and towns. In such instances, soldiers simply stormed civilian homes, taking sisters, daughters, and wives by force. The many descriptions of these raids are strikingly consistent from one survivor to another. One description of such a raid, recounted by a Chinese woman (identified as "Madame X") who had lived in British Malaya (now Malaysia) at the time, appears in

George Hicks's groundbreaking 1994 book, *The Comfort Women: Japan's Brutal Regime of Enforced Prostitution in the Second World War*. A selection from Madame X's testimony is included here:

> Sometime in January 1942, the Japanese occupied Kuala Lumpur—but all that seemed remote to us. We were safe in our little village. No Japanese would bother us there. Then one day in February 1942, two lorries full of Japanese soldiers came into our village. I remember it was February because it was on my mother's birthday. How did the Japanese find our village? They were led there by a thirty-year-old traitor. How could he do such a thing, directing the Japanese soldiers to our village?
>
> I was cooking at the time and was unable to escape. The armed soldiers moved quickly through our village, cutting off all hope of escape. Three soldiers with rifles came to our house while the rest fanned out through the village. They burst in and grabbed me. My parents tried to rescue me but my father was kicked in the head. Blood went everywhere. I struggled as hard as I could, but I got kicked in the head too. I still have that scar. See? Then my panties were ripped off and one of the soldiers undid the front of his trousers. While the other held me down, he stuck his thing into me. I had no idea what he was trying to do. I knew nothing about the facts of life. I was only fifteen and hadn't even had my first period.
>
> It was agonizing. Blood came out. They did it on the kitchen floor, right in front of my parents and brother. Three soldiers did it to me in turns, and then they took me out and put me in one of the lorries along with some other girls from my village. My brother was put in the other lorry and taken away. We never saw him again. As I was being put in the truck, my parents rushed out to try and rescue me. My father was trailing blood from his wound. For the next three years, I was constantly haunted by that last vision of my parents, especially my father's blood on the ground.[12]

To do justice to the vast scale of the atrocities would require many such accounts. The above passage, along with Lee's, has been selected to provide some balance to passages printed later in this chapter, which deny the truth of these girls' and young women's experience.

Reasons for Establishing the Comfort-Station System

The targeting of nonprostitutes and young women was also considered more desirable for the comfort-station system because venereal diseases were less prominent among local civilians than among experienced prostitutes. One of the key reasons the system was established was to prevent the spread of debilitating venereal diseases among Japanese soldiers. Outbreaks of such diseases could be costly and had already led to the loss of whole battalions of men. Yuki Tanaka explains the severity of the problem for the Japanese military (and for other nations) in his book *Japan's Comfort Women*:

> The Japanese commanders in [the post–World War I expedition in] Siberia were also troubled by the high VD rate amongst their troops. According to the official record, 1,109 soldiers were treated as VD patients between August 1918 and October 1920. The true figure was probably much higher. Even when the official figures are compared with 1,399 deaths and 1,528 casualties during the same period, one realizes how seriously VD affected the combat strength of the troops.[13]

But the desire to control outbreaks of venereal disease among the troops was not the only motivation for developing the comfort-women system. Ok Cha Soh, the president of the Washington Coalition for Comfort Women Issues, an advocacy group based in Washington, D.C., gave an interview for this book. According to Soh, there were a number of other motivations for the development of the Japanese military comfort system:

- The simple satisfaction of soldiers' sexual desires that were not being met through other healthy means, such as the granting of leave, wherein soldiers could return home. This was particularly true as the war intensified and soldiers were dispatched farther from Japan and the demands of the war made the granting of such leaves impossible.
- The "raising" of soldiers' spirits or morale, which was often difficult to keep high, given the stresses of war and the well-documented brutal conditions under which Japanese soldiers served.

- The prevention of mass rapes of civilians, which led to great difficulties in controlling local populations once they were conquered. The tens of thousands of rapes of the women of Nanjing were a key factor in motivating military leaders to institutionalize comfort stations on such a large scale.
- The superstition among the Japanese military that sexually sated soldiers fought better and had increased fortunes on the battlefield. In keeping with this, there was a belief that soldiers who had not had sex for some time were more prone to accidents.
- To reduce dangers from so-called pillow talk with traditional prostitutes, who could serve as enemy spies.
- The severe racist and sexist attitudes in the Japanese military, which helped such a system to develop.
- Finally, the brutal, hierarchical nature of the Japanese military, which contributed to the development of the system. Not only were leaders able to implement the system without protest from subordinates, but many soldiers found it "natural" for non-Japanese young women to be placed under their domination.[14]

Conditions at the Comfort Stations

Once captured, victims such as Lee and Madame X were soon incarcerated in comfort stations. They were usually each assigned a tiny room just large enough to fit a mat, where they lived as sex slaves. Like Lee, many surviving comfort women commonly testify to "serving" twenty to forty soldiers per day, although numbers obviously differed according to circumstances.

Comfort stations were of three different types: those owned and operated entirely by the Japanese army; those ostensibly privately owned, but in reality tightly controlled by the military and only for use by the military; and those owned and frequented by civilians but under an agreement with the army to provide "special services" for military personnel. In making these distinctions, it must be noted that there was far less difference between "military" and "civilian" personnel within the Japanese Empire than the dichotomy implies today in the West. Under its "total-militarization" policy, all Japanese

Mainichi Photo Bank identifies this photograph as being taken in January 1938, in Shanghai, and depicting the first comfort-woman station directly operated by the military and housing 120 women. *(Photo courtesy of Mainichi Photo Bank.)*

subjects were required to fulfill the needs of the state. Thus, although not all the managerial functions of the comfort-women system were handled by uniformed military personnel, these "civilian functions" were still sanctioned, sponsored, and controlled by the state. According to Hicks, "Administration was generally similar for both categories, being described in terms applied to most enterprises under wartime conditions, as 'officially controlled and privately managed.'"[15]

As Lee experienced, doctors regularly inspected the women and girls in an effort to stem the spread of venereal diseases. But, as she also has noted, not all soldiers followed the rules, and condoms were not always available. In most cases, the girls and women were also subjected to regular beatings, both from station operators and from soldiers, and most of the survivors, like Lee, still bear scars.[16]

In less favorable situations, they were allowed only short, sporadic sleeping times and near-starvation rations, had to serve in combat zones (even on the actual front lines), and were even forced to join the troops on difficult marches and other perilous military movements. Most Japanese military records were systematically destroyed at the end of the war, but in those that remain, the girls and women are usually referenced as "war supplies"— another indication that they were not fully recognized as human beings. Indeed, they were often shipped to the front lines in trucks right along with ammunition. Comfort women such as Lee were often referred to by Japanese soldiers as *pi* (pronounced "pea"), a Chinese term literally meaning "goods" or "articles," but which is also slang for female genitals.

As Lee also relates, it was common for these so-called *pi* to bleed to death from rapes and beatings, or to die from diseases, miscarriages, and other consequences of their servitude. Understandably, many also committed suicide. Toward the end of the war, in particular, they were abandoned, as in the case of Ok Seon Lee, or even summarily executed when they became difficult for a unit to maintain.[17] Mortality rates have been estimated to be as high as 75 percent.[18] Many survivors, of course, also suffered, and continue to suffer, from acute psychological illnesses.

Psychological Aftermath

Those who initially survived the war returned, destitute, to their respective war-ravaged countries, or else (like Lee) attempted to assimilate themselves into the foreign country where they had been enslaved. Although a tiny percentage of Dutch and Polish women were among their ranks, most were Asians, members of cultures where victims of rape have traditionally been spurned and persecuted. Scholar Keith Howard described the psychological trauma of these women:

> Many women subsequently found they were barren, and many still suffer from ailments, from womb infections, high blood pressure, stomach trouble, heart trouble, nervous breakdowns, mental illness and so on. The psychological aftermath is far more serious than the physical suffering endured in the comfort stations. Apart from nervous breakdowns or mental disorders, the effects of which can be noticed externally, the minds of former comfort women are haunted by delusions of persecution, shame and inferiority. They want to avoid contact with other human beings. Taken together, all of these make it difficult for the women to carry on any normal social life. The prejudice and discrimination heaped on them by society makes them feel particularly wretched. People around the women tend to despise them, guessing even if never told, that they were sexually victimized while abroad.[19]

Of those who managed to live to old age, only a relatively small number have had the desire, courage, and opportunity to step forward and testify publicly. It is no surprise that most survivors have kept the stories of abuse and humiliation to themselves, often taking them to their graves. Until the end of the 1980s, these women had absolutely nothing to gain by speaking out, yet everything to lose. It was only by that time, when old age left many of them with little reason to keep their secrets—and a grassroots

This August 1945 image, courtesy of the U.S. National Archives, is accompanied by the following words from its original caption: "British Rescue 'Comfort Corps.'"

movement on their behalf began to draw them out—that some of the women began to step forward publicly.

Compensation

Official recognition and financial and other assistance for the survivors has been sorely inadequate in Japan. In contrast to the many memorials, museums, and monuments to the victims of, for example, the Holocaust in Germany, not a single national site exists in Japan dedicated to the comfort women. And although a number of Japanese prime ministers have offered variously worded apologies to the comfort women,[20] no apology has been ratified by the Diet as a statement on behalf of the government, and the government itself refuses to pay compensation directly to survivors. It must be stated that a number of admirable Japanese legislators have advocated on behalf of the surviving women, but the Japanese government nevertheless maintains that all war reparations were accounted for in various postwar treaties; yet these treaties make no mention of the comfort women.

The Japanese government has chosen instead to support a nongovernmental organization, innocuously named the "Asian Women's Fund,"[21] which has paid some compensation to 285 women in Asia and 79 women in the Netherlands as of September 2002, and has announced the conclusion of the collections of funds. Although these payments were accompanied by copies of an acknowledgment of their suffering by the prime minister at the time, neither the payments nor the apologies were made on behalf of the Japanese government. Subsequently, most of those who support the cause of the comfort women consider the Asian Women's Fund to be little more than a public-relations shield for the Japanese government and an attempt by the government to buy its way out of a moral challenge.

Indeed, it would appear that the fund has itself misled the public in weekly newsmagazines. In this case, however, it is not a *shukanshi* but an English-language issue of *Newsweek* that is involved. The fund's Web site[22] featured a link, labeled: "This is a reproduction of an article that appeared in the April 7, 2003, issue of *Newsweek*." The link, which was up from April 2003 through April 2004, allowed visitors to download the page of information that ran in *Newsweek*. The page was entitled "Atonement Projects for Former 'Comfort Women'" and was graphically designed like a news article. The page itself also included the headline, "This is a reproduction of an article that appeared in the April 7, 2003, issue of *Newsweek*," and it featured a question-and-answer section between an unnamed "interviewer" and an advocate of the fund. The "article" touted the fund as a valuable organization dedicated to assisting the victims of the comfort-women system and supporting women throughout Asia. However, there is a key difference between the "article" featured on the fund's Web site and the page that actually appeared in *Newsweek:* What actually appeared in *Newsweek* was not an article at all. It was a paid advertisement. In fact, the actual published piece in *Newsweek* featured the unmistakable headline across its top: "ADVERTISEMENT." On the fund's Web site, however, this label was missing, and in its stead appeared the contradictory and false statement: "This is a reproduction of an article that appeared in the April 7, 2003, issue of *Newsweek*."

When questioned via telephone in April 2004, Asian Women's Fund Program Director Mizuho Matsuda said that this was a "mistake" that occurred when the Web site was built. It was pointed out to Matsuda that it seemed dubious that such a mistake would be made. This seemed especially so, given that the Web site's English-language homepage featured so little information. It also seemed strange, even if one overlooks the mislabeling of the advertisement as an article, that any organization would feature an advertisement

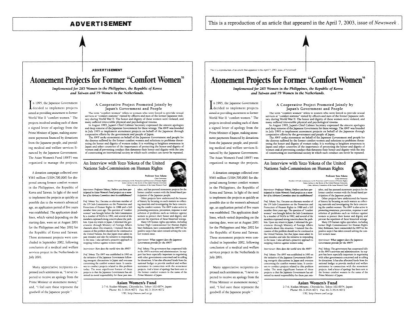

Although the two pages above are almost identical, the one on the left is clearly labeled with the heading "ADVERTISEMENT." This is an actual page taken out of a copy of the April 7, 2003, edition of *Newsweek*. The image on the right, however, is labeled, "This is a reproduction of an article that appeared in the April 7, 2003, issue of *Newsweek*." This is how it was featured on the Asian Women's Fund Web site from April 2003 until April 2004, when the fund was questioned on this matter as part of the research for this book. According to the program director, the mislabeling was a mistake. The page has since been removed entirely from the Web site.

in such a way. Matsuda, however, did not offer any further explanation. Indeed, almost immediately after being contacted about this issue, the fund removed all reference to the advertisement from their site. It would appear that the fund no longer found it useful to feature a copy of the page once it was correctly labeled as an advertisement.

At any rate, that the fund would label its advertisement in *Newsweek* an "article" and feature it on its Web site as validation of its work is intriguing, especially given the intense role of *shukanshi* in shouting down the comfort women and in validating those who would deny them. It underscores the reality that the very real physical torture that so many girls and young women were subject to during the war has devolved into a petty game of semantics on behalf of those who would whitewash the atrocity. Those who deny and seek to downplay the state-sponsored sex slavery desperately seek to legitimize their

false views of history. It would seem that that they have found a good deal of
legitimization for their cause in the weekly magazine sector of Japan and that
they continue to seek out such legitimization elsewhere. Unfortunately, the
issues at stake—the well-being of the elderly survivors who no doubt will not
be with us much longer, as well as the reputation of the Japanese nation—are
no petty matters. Both deserve to have the truth be known and acknowledged
so that they can move forward in a peaceful and productive manner.

Unfortunately, the Japanese government continues to dodge legal responsibility and to fight court challenges to its stance. Indeed, as noted, many survivors such as Lee have refused to accept anything whatsoever from the fund,
despite facing issues of severe poverty, illness, and old age. When asked in an
interview about her stance on this matter, Lee replied, "Recently, we were
asked to accept some Japanese private funds as compensation. By offering this
kind of money, the Japanese government hopes that comfort women will stop

Shown here (left) is Ok Cha Soh, president of the Washington Coalition for Comfort Women
(WCCW), with President George W. Bush. Soh and her colleagues have been lobbying the U.S.
government for years for support of the comfort women's situation. The WCCW would like
surviving comfort women to receive the same kind of recognition that Jewish survivors of the
Holocaust have received from the United States. They promote research and education pertaining to crimes against comfort women and would also like the United States to pressure
Japan to officially admit responsibility, to issue an unqualified apology on behalf of the nation,
and to provide compensation to the few survivors still living.

speaking out and go away. However, we refused to accept it. We request the Japanese government to acknowledge and compensate us at the governmental level. I never received anything from the Japanese government. I want an official apology from the Japanese government as a whole. It did this to me. It should provide compensation to me."[23]

Ok Cha Soh says that despite their often impoverished situations, the majority of the comfort women have taken the same stance as Lee. "Time is of the essence," she insists. "We are all praying that the Japanese government will accept responsibility before it's too late and all of these women are gone."[24]

This view of the Asian Women's Fund has been confirmed by a major United Nations (UN) study on the matter. The "special rapporteur," Mrs. Radhika Coomaraswamy, who investigated the plight of the women from all sides, concluded in her report to the UN that, first and foremost, what surviving comfort women want is an official apology from the Japanese government, which they ultimately hold responsible for their fates.[25] Coomaraswamy writes, "the Special Rapporteur sees the Fund as created, as an expression of the Japanese Government's moral concern for the fate of 'comfort women.' However, it is a clear statement denying any legal responsibility for the situation of these women ... it must be understood that it does not vindicate the legal claims of 'comfort women' under public international law."[26]

Ignoring the Comfort Women

Immediately after the war, the victorious Allies, under the auspices of the Supreme Command of Allied Powers (SCAP) and the Tokyo war-crimes trials, failed to pursue justice on behalf of the comfort women. More recently, it is only fair to note, the United States and other Western governments have worked diligently to ensure justice for surviving victims of the Holocaust, but still little action has been taken to assist surviving comfort women. One can only speculate how different the situation might have been had more Western women been abused as *jyugun ianfu*. (In Japanese, the phrase *jyugun ianfu*, which means "comfort women following the army," is used for "military comfort women." The common term for "comfort women" has become simply *ianfu*.)

Although the Japanese leadership has fought tooth and nail to avoid direct responsibility for the comfort women on behalf of the government, a number of Japanese citizens have taken major risks and made admirable sacrifices to assist the surviving comfort women, as well as to help people face the realities of their nation's frightful wartime legacy. These include Japanese activists, reporters, writers, broadcasters, filmmakers, lawyers, and even a number of prominent politicians. *Asahi* newspaper, for example, has done much to legitimize the comfort women's cause in Japan.

Still, anecdotal evidence indicates that surprisingly few Japanese are fully aware that their government and military perpetrated this massive crime just over a half century ago. Even among those who are aware of the "issue," there remains much confusion about the historical reality. Similar to the Nanjing Massacre, this is in large part the result of continued efforts by pro-establishment, conservative forces and individuals who have downplayed, distorted, and denied the comfort women's plight, going so far as to make outrageous counteraccusations against the survivors. The most unconscionable even accuse all surviving victims, such as Lee, of having been prostitutes by choice during the war and of being opportunists today. As a result, whereas virtually everyone outside Japan who has studied the situation acknowledges the historical truth of the comfort women's plight, many highly educated Japanese continue to think of it as an unresolved, controversial issue, the truth of which remains unknown.

Historical Revisionism by the Weekly Newsmagazines

Not surprisingly, one of the leading publications to have attacked the former comfort women is the weekly newsmagazine *Shukan Shincho*. The following representative article appeared in *Shukan Shincho* in 1992, soon after the *Asahi Shimbun* covered an international hearing on the comfort-women situation. The article opens:

> The International Hearing Regarding Japan's Postwar Compensations was just held and reported in the mass media with an atmosphere that this event was conducted as if it were under the auspices of the United Nations. However, the fact was that a committee was first formed with funds, which were contributed by civil organizations in Tokyo and Osaka, to hold this meeting

for the sake of "investigating how much Japan violated the human rights of the people in the Asian countries and gave them financial damages during World War II."

To show a leading example of Japan's violation of human rights, the committee had located, in various Asian countries, the so-called comfort women who served the Japanese military during the war to satisfy the soldiers' sexual needs. The committee invited them to the meeting mentioned earlier to accuse Japan through their firsthand testimonies. The committee mainly consisted of the lawyers who served as members of the Japanese Lawyers Association to Protect Human Rights. This association includes scholars who are college professors and activist women who belong to civic organizations.

As you know, each of the six women, who were from Korea, the Philippines, North Korea, Holland, China, and Taiwan, testified how cruel and barbarous the Japanese military was during the war. (A participant from Holland actually resides in Australia.) The Chinese representative got so excited in her speech that she actually fainted, shouting, "I hate the Japanese."[27]

This is obviously a thoughtfully composed piece of writing addressed to a politically aware audience, and not a mere "tabloid article" that can easily be dismissed as irrelevant. Like the revisionist anti-Semitic and Nanjing Massacre articles discussed earlier, it is presented as a serious news article. It opens with an ostensibly unbiased, fact-oriented perspective that nevertheless puts its Japanese readers on the defensive. For how else would the average Japanese react to an account that focuses not on any substantive facts but on an elderly Chinese woman hysterically shouting, "I hate the Japanese"?

After reemphasizing the presence of international media members at the event and criticizing the *Asahi Shimbun* for what it describes as biased, anti-Japanese coverage of the issue, the *Shukan Shincho* article continues with the following subheading and text:

Did Japan Commit a Sin in View of the International Common Law?

In short, here we see a strange formula in which some Japanese are revitalizing the old issue in conjunction with the past behavior of the Japanese military in order to attack their own current government. It is perhaps correct to say that the former Korean comfort women are being used in this context to help fulfill their strange cause. Mr. Akira Nakamura, a professor at Dokkyo University states:

"If you claim that the Japanese government should pay some compensations to those women who served as comfort women during the war, you have to investigate well what actually happened to them. It is said that some Japanese went to Korea to instigate Koreans by saying they might get some compensations through the comfort women's issue. Of course, as Japanese mass media reported, these women must have been through hellish experiences during the war, but surely, not all of them, I should say. I interviewed those who were involved in setting up entertainment centers in the Japanese military camps and those who were close to some comfort women, even though I didn't have any chance to talk directly to any comfort woman. As a result, I found out that the military's entertainment centers were no different from ordinary prostitutes' quarters that legally existed in Japan before the war. The so-called comfort women usually worked for two or three years at these entertainment centers in the Japanese military bases. And some of them made so much money that it was enough to build a house.

"Of course, some of the women may have been forcefully mobilized to become comfort women. Also, some may have been cheated by prostitution brokers to become prostitutes. These women may deserve some compensation, but they are limited in number. The majority of these women began to serve as comfort women on their own. Or they became prostitutes to pay back their parents' debt. Those were the days when even in Japan women in poor families were sold to prostitution houses. I think it is too much to hold the Japanese military, alone, responsible for what happened to these women and ask the current Japanese government to pay further compensation for that."

Note that these are not crude denials of the comfort-women system as much as insidious distortions. *Shukan Shincho* does not simply come out and say that the surviving comfort women are liars and Japan bashers. Instead, it employs rhetorical tricks: implications, omissions, non sequiturs, innuendo, and quotations from so-called authorities and experts. The question, posed in the subheading, of whether Japan broke international law is avoided and replaced through the implication of new questions, such as "Are certain Japanese citizens abusing the issue to damage the country from within?" and "Are the Koreans motivated by the prospect of financial compensation from the Japanese government?"

Note also that the article focuses on the Korean comfort women while ignoring the presence at the compensation hearing of comfort women from the Philippines, China, Taiwan, and Holland. Japan has a long history of difficult relations with North and South Korea, both of which have used the comfort women's plight to gain leverage in negotiations with the Japanese over a variety of issues. Rather than seriously investigate the comfort women's claims by actually interviewing any of them or other eyewitnesses, *Shukan Shincho* capitalizes on the politics of the situation by emphasizing their Korean connections.

Another sentence from the selection convolutes the truth still further, through the use of false relativism: "Those were the days when even in Japan women in poor families were sold to prostitution houses." Nakamura implies that the Second World War comfort-women situation is being judged outside of its proper historical context, as if to say that the times were so different during the war (which had ended forty-eight years before the publication of the article) that contemporary 1990s moral standards regarding prostitution and sexual slavery cannot be applied.

Price list and regulations posted at a Japanese military comfort station. (*Photo courtesy of Mainichi Photo Bank.*)

Nakamura asserts, "As a result, I found out that the military's entertainment centers were no different from ordinary prostitutes' quarters that legally existed in Japan before the war." Here, he plainly equates the comfort women with prostitutes. Note his use of the term "entertainment centers" rather than "comfort stations" or even "brothels."

Akira Nakamura

Akira Nakamura was interviewed at some length for this book. Since the publication of the *Shukan Shincho* article quoted previously, Nakamura has

founded the so-called Showa-shi Kenkyu-jo, or "Research Institute of Showa History," located in the Ginza, an exclusive area in Tokyo reputed to have some of the most expensive real estate in the world. Although Nakamura refused to divulge his institute's funding sources, he explained that its purpose is to "pursue accuracy in Japanese history," particularly surrounding topics such as the comfort women and the Nanjing Massacre. According to Nakamura, a wide variety of anti-Japanese forces have been conspiring to destroy the "unity of the nation by spreading false claims about the history of the Japanese Empire." These forces, he says, include members of every major Japanese political party, with the exception of factions of the Conservative Party and factions of the Liberal Democratic Party (LDP).

Akira Nakamura is a professor of history at Dokkyo University and the head of the Research Institute of Showa History. A regular contributor to Japanese magazines, he is a staunch defender of Japan's World War II legacy and denies the claims of surviving comfort women.

When asked about the comfort women's claims, Nakamura produced a notebook with hundreds of pages of documentation—all organized with dozens of color-coded bookmarks—that he insisted proves that the Japanese military never institutionalized sexual slavery and that comfort women such as Lee were really just common prostitutes. Most of the information in the notebook provided was culled from Nakamura's own Research Institute of

Showa History monthly newsletter, *Showa-shi Kenkyu-jo Kaiho*.[28] Included in the notebook were the transcripts of interviews of a few "comfort women" by American soldiers immediately after the war. Because, in the course of the interviews, none of these few women recorded by these specific transcripts had complained to the Americans about having been sex slaves, Nakamura cites this as "proof" that there were no comfort stations or comfort women. "If they had been mistreated, why didn't they tell the Americans?" He also has a number of testimonies by former Japanese soldiers who say that there were no comfort stations, as well as testimony from other "experts," including himself.

Nakamura says he is convinced that not only were there no such things as comfort stations, but that the Japanese Imperial Army "protected and defended the prostitutes" from the managers of brothels and "others who might have tried to exploit them."

It should be noted that Nakamura was only a boy during the war and thus has no firsthand knowledge of the situation in Korea or elsewhere at that time. Moreover, when asked if, in the course of his extensive research, he has ever interviewed, listened to, spoken with, or otherwise interacted with a former comfort woman, Nakamura says that he has not. Although hundreds of surviving comfort women such as Lee have offered their testimony in public places in Japan and around the world, Nakamura says that it has been "impossible" for him to interview one directly.

And, when asked if he has ever spoken to, or heard of, a Second World War prostitute who served the Japanese military and who claims that she was treated well by the Japanese, he also says no. In point of fact, he has had no direct communication with any woman who provided sex to the Japanese military during the war. "I can't get that," he says. "The women who were Japanese refuse to open their mouths. But the women who are Koreans . . . they won't talk, either. The Japanese women believed it was their mission to serve the country in that way, so they feel there is no reason to complain."[29]

Nakamura has even gone so far as to proclaim that many comfort women were paid vast amounts of money and were extremely well treated for their service. According to information widely disseminated by Nakamura on the Internet, in his newsletter, and elsewhere (in English and in Japanese), at least one comfort woman earned about twice the annual salary of the highest-paid Japanese military officer, General Tojo![30] "Many of them earned enough to buy their parents a house after the war," he says. "The supply-and-demand ratio was so out of whack." Needless to say, it is absolutely ridiculous to imply in any way that the many tens of thousands of girls and young woman who were violently forced to serve as sex slaves for the Japanese military were in any way significantly compensated for the unspeakable sufferings they underwent. All credible research on this matter makes this point of fact incontrovertibly clear.[31]

When pressed on the matter of his never having met a former comfort woman, Nakamura pointed to a piece of testimony that his "research" has yielded, although its vague nature says more about the quality of Nakamura's "scholarship" than about the comfort-women issue. Nakamura explained that he once received a telephone call from an elderly Japanese woman who had served as a nurse in Korea. According to him, this nurse (whose name he no longer remembers) told him that she had once met a Japanese prostitute who had worked in Korea during the war. This prostitute had told the nurse that she had spoken with some Korean elementary schoolchildren during the war and that many of these children had told her that they wanted to grow up to be Korean comfort women so that they could get rich. Astoundingly enough, Nakamura actually presented this story in his interview for this book as if it were proof that comfort women were well paid.

Many of the preposterous claims that Nakamura offered in the course of his interview for this book would be almost comical if they did not consist of disparaging material against tragic victims, such as Lee, whose lives were turned into living hells as a result of the system, or if they had not been foisted upon the Japanese public as "expert testimony" in publications such as *Shukan Shincho*. For example, when asked why so many hundreds of elderly women would pretend to have been sex slaves in their youth, Nakamura replied, tellingly, "It's a difficult issue, but by and large, Koreans don't like Japanese. They continuously try to denigrate Japanese. And, of course, they want money, so they seek compensation."

When confronted with Lee's specific story, Nakamura's response was similar: "She is a liar, and I can prove it," he said. He explained that the reason he "knew"

Lee is a liar is that "tens of thousands of comfort women could not have been taken" by the Japanese military from Korea. "Now, let's say that they were all taken off the street. If this were the case, you'd have a huge number of witnesses," Nakamura asserts. "But no one in Korea has witnessed these abductions. Not a single Korean. Why? Very strange. Let's say eighty thousand were forcibly abducted. These are all people individually claiming to be abducted, but no one saw anything. There were thirty million people at the time in Korea."[32]

Of course, despite Nakamura's claims, there actually are witnesses to what happened to the comfort women. Indeed, these witnesses include Japanese soldiers themselves. There exist a number of soldier-testimony compilations, including *Jugun Ianfu—Moto Heishitachi no Shogen* (Wartime Comfort Women—The Testimonies of Former Soldiers) and *Sei to Shinryaku—Guntai ianjo 84 kasho Moto Nihonhei kara no Shogen* (Sex and Invasion: Eighty-Four Comfort Stations in Testimonies of Former Japanese Soldiers).[33]

One of the most important of the former soldiers to step forward is Seiji Yoshida, who published two books admitting his work as a "recruit manager"

Akira Nakamura is proud to have appeared in a strip produced by the best-selling neonationalist cartoonist Yoshinori Kobayashi. In this cartoon, Kobayashi's lead character—an idealized version of himself—discovers Nakamura in a tent adjacent to Yasukuni Shrine during a nationalist event. Kobayashi strongly praises Nakamura for his writings and kindness. (*From Yoshinori Kobayashi, "Gomanizumu Sengen Extra—Dai Yon Sho: Dai-Toua Senso—Sofu Tachi no Monogatari" ["'Arrogance-ism' Manifesto—Extra. Chapter 4: Greater East Asia War—Grandfather's Tale"].*)

who led the violent roundup raids. Yoshida is mentioned in the *Shukan Shincho* article quoted in this chapter. He is the author of two books about the slave-raid expeditions in which he participated in Korea, during the war, "My War Crimes: The Forced Draft of Koreans" and "Korean Comfort Women and the Japanese: The Memories of a Shimonoseki Labor Recruit Manager."[34] Part of his testimony includes the following:

> In 1943 to 1944, I worked as an official for Japan's labor recruitment organization coordinating approximately one thousand young "comfort women" into such labor.... Korea was a colony of Japan and we forcibly recruited young married women from... Korea as most young unmarried women were already mobilized to munitions factories. These married women were recruited in [an] inhuman way. A group of wartime policemen entered into rural corners of Korea, surrounded entire villages, and seized well-proportioned women. The policemen and followers grabbed screaming infants from the young women's arms and passed the infants to the remaining old women before forcing the young women into trucks.[35]

Another fact showing the absurdity of Nakamura's statements is that no one has ever claimed that the comfort women were rounded up en masse in urban areas. Japanese military comfort women were gathered up over a period of years through a variety of means and in multiple war-torn countries that covered huge landmasses.

Despite his prestigious-sounding Research Institute of Showa History, located in Tokyo's Ginza district, and despite his title of professor, Nakamura presents theories that do not even merit serious consideration, except perhaps to illustrate the sort of racist charlatan and mountebank who is able to pose as an expert in Japanese newsmagazines. It is difficult to believe that any competent reporter could interview Nakamura without recognizing him as a source of phony, illogical propaganda were there not such a great and growing number of such individuals in the country.

Indeed, Nakamura's stance on the case of the comfort women is reminiscent of Nobukatsu Fujioka's testimony regarding the Nanjing Massacre. While both are passionate professors with seemingly impressive credentials, their logic and scholarship are embarrassingly flimsy.

Again we see how the idea of "truth" in Japanese society can be different from that in the West. The idea of "social truth," or truth that is agreed upon by social groups independent of observable reality, has strong roots and is often seized upon by people desperate to reconcile their personal beliefs with the larger world. In this case, Nakamura and Fujioka seem desperate to cling to a worldview that supports Japanese neonationalism, regardless of the facts. Both have obviously benefited tremendously from championing their causes, but neither appears to be purely an opportunist. Instead, they seem to fervently believe that the Nanjing Massacre was a nonevent and that the Japanese military never kept sex slaves. For them, the most important "truth" of all seems to be that Japan is a great nation that could not have committed such atrocities. In-depth discussions with each man seem to confirm that they are both genuinely dedicated to their beliefs.

John Nathan, in his superb 2004 book, *Japan Unbound*,[36] includes many thoughtful and detailed interviews, some with Japanese nationalists, many of whom are well established within the country's mainstream power structure, including the popular Tokyo governor Shintaro Ishihara. Nathan successfully puts forth the theory that a good deal of the success of such individuals is the desperate search in Japan for a sense of identity. Nathan argues that Japan at the turn of the millennium is going through especially volatile social changes and that one result of this quest for a renewed sense of identity is an upsurge in nationalism. This may well be the case; but it in no way justifies the outright lies that Nakamura and those like him perpetrate against the few surviving comfort women.

Back to *Shukan Shincho*

Let us return to *Shukan Shincho*'s 1992 article, which vehemently attacks Seiji Yoshida while strongly supporting Nakamura's claim that anti-Japanese forces are plotting against the country:

A PLOT MAY EXIST BEHIND THE ESCALATION
OF THIS COMFORT WOMEN ISSUE

Here is another individual who is said to be the ultimate instigator of this comfort women's issue. His name is Seiji Yoshida, a 79-year-old man. Mr.

Yoshida published two books based upon his experience during the war, entitled *Korean Comfort Women and the Japanese* and *My War Crimes: The Forced Draft of Koreans*. In these books he explicitly confesses how he was involved in operations to hunt Korean women with the cooperation from the military and police, then send them to the entertainment centers in the Japanese military bases. He also vividly depicts how the Japanese soldiers raped the Korean comfort women one after another.... [These books] are being read in Korea as a Japanese's confession of the past Japanese military's ugly behaviors. Those who take interest in tackling the comfort women's issue must first read these books. Dreadfully enough, these books definitely compel their readers to hate the Japanese.

Recently, however, Mr. Kunihiko Shin, professor of Takushoku University, and Mr. Yoshiaki Itakura, a researcher of the Showa history of Japan, individually made a report claiming that some parts of Mr. Yoshida's books may have been made up. Their new contention has been shaking the footing of those who take issue with the past mobilization of the comfort women by the Japanese military.

In fact, to investigate the truth of the matter, Professor Shin went to Cheju Island, where Mr. Yoshida alleges he hunted Korean women to put them in the entertainment centers in the Japanese military bases. In his visit to Cheju, Professor Shin interviewed local people and examined written documents to find out the truth of what happened during the war concerning the alleged institutionalized Korean comfort women. According to him, the unanimous response he received over there was, "The idea of the institutionalized comfort women is a farce. It is far from the truth." There are a number of statements in Mr. Yoshida's books that can't help but be regarded as fabrications. His descriptions of his birthplace and academic history are also suspected as cases of fabrications.[37]

The article concludes with the following line: "More than a few people are sensing a plot mapped out by North Korea behind the commencement of the current uproar over the issue of the institutionalized comfort women."

It is fascinating to see how *Shukan Shincho* is able to entirely disregard two published books by Yoshida describing his personal experience as an abductor of comfort women. Relying instead on the testimony of "experts" who, like Nakamura, have no direct experience whatsoever with the subject, the article offers no specific arguments against Yoshida. It simply states, "There are a number of statements in Mr. Yoshida's books that can't help but be regarded as fabrications," without explaining what those statements are or why they should be regarded as false. When asked about Yoshida for this book, Nakamura responded similarly: "Yoshida is a liar. This has already been proven."[38] Needless to say, Nakamura didn't offer any specific proof of this outside of the ridiculous arguments already noted above.

In deference to Yoshida, who bravely and publicly admitted to having personally participated in the abduction of an estimated one thousand comfort women, we quote his words as recorded by the acclaimed filmmaker Dai Sil Kim-Gibson: "You know some people are skeptical regarding what I had said about my helping to forcibly draft Korean women on Cheju Island, providing trucks and soldiers from Army headquarters. But I want you to know that I stand by what I said. Even now, my life is threatened by some Japanese; they think I betrayed my motherland, Japan. Under the circumstances, why would I make up a story? When the Japanese mass media sided with my accusers without hearing my side of the story, I was so disappointed."[39]

A sampling of similar articles on the comfort women in *Shukan Shincho* includes the following:

- "A STRANGE JAPANESE WHO MAKES UP STORIES OF THE MOBILIZA-TION OF COMFORT WOMEN" (January 5, 1995)[40]
  This article states that publications revealing the reality of the comfort women are "all fabricated," and quotes an "expert" who states that most of the comfort women were sold into prostitution by their parents. It is especially critical of Yoshida.
- "A GRAND FICTIONAL REPORT BY *ASAHI SHIMBUN*'S SEOUL CORRE-SPONDENT ON INSTITUTIONALIZED COMFORT WOMEN" (August 10, 1995)[41]
  In this article, *Shukan Shincho* attacks *Asahi Shimbun*'s Seoul correspondent and expresses its

belief that *Asahi Shimbun* has been masterminding a campaign to make the Japanese government look bad and force it to take responsibility over the issue of comfort women.

• "THE ORIGIN OF THE FALSEHOODS OF THE FORCED MOBILIZATION OF COMFORT WOMEN" (May 2 and 9, 1996, combined issue)[42] This article claims that a landmark United Nations human-rights document supporting comfort women's claims is false. It goes on to impute Seiji Yoshida's contentions.

• "KANAGAWA HUMAN RIGHTS CENTER STOPS YOSHIKO SAKURAI'S SCHEDULED LECTURE, A CASE OF OPPRESSION OF FREEDOM OF SPEECH" (February 13, 1997)[43] This supports Yoshiko Sakurai, a free journalist, who does not believe that the Japanese military was involved with the forced rounding up of sex slaves during the war.

• "*ASAHI SHIMBUN*'S 'HYPOCRITICAL' REPORTAGE DENYING THE FALSEHOOD OF FORCED MOBILIZATION OF COMFORT WOMEN" (April 17, 1997)[44] This is yet another *Asahi Shimbun*–bashing article from *Shukan Shincho* over the comfort women. To its credit, *Asahi* has performed superb

The pull-out quote on the left reads "Reporter Uemura's 'Intentional' False Reporting."

journalistic work on this topic. But *Shukan Shincho* insists upon throwing up a screen against the victims' claims.

Again, it is important to remember that the headlines for these articles were widely advertised throughout Japan, so that while perhaps only hundreds of thousands read the actual articles, millions saw the headlines.

How the Stories Work

Given the magnitude of the atrocity so vehemently denied by *Shukan Shincho* and given that the denials have been based on spurious research and the flimsiest logic, it is worth considering the magazine's motivations.

As always, financial incentive comes in first for *Shukan Shincho*. The comfort-women issue fits right in with *Shukan Shincho*'s commercial aims in a number of ways. First, in posturing as an alternative viewpoint to the establishment press, the magazine often takes a strong stance that contradicts one or more of the national daily newspapers; more often than not, this is the *Asahi Shimbun*. By attacking *Asahi*, the magazine can create a stir and thereby catch the eye of both those who might dislike *Asahi*'s politics and those who subscribe to the paper. After all, *Asahi* is the world's second-largest daily newspaper, with more than eight million readers of its morning edition alone. This strategy is not unlike the weekly magazine's attacks on the Soka Gakkai. As with the Buddhist group's membership, *Shukan Shincho* needs only to tap into a small percentage of *Asahi*'s circulation to see a significant increase in its own.

Another attraction is the nature of the story itself. Hiroshi Matsuda, editor of *Shukan Shincho* throughout much of the 1990s when the previously noted articles ran, commented in an interview for this book that the magazine is famous for featuring articles on "the seamy sides of things . . . like scandals and women."[45] While this issue is obviously about much more profound issues than "the seamy sides of things," as Matsuda puts it, at first glance at least, it is custom-made for *Shukan Shincho*'s readership. In a manner of speaking, the plight of the comfort women could be described as the biggest sex scandal of all times.

A third motive for publishing the comfort-women articles is the relative lack of effort needed to write them. Rather than delve into any serious investigation or analysis of evidence, the writers of many of these stories had only to describe *Asahi*'s coverage of the story and then interview some "experts," or "intellectual henchmen," whose outlandish statements on the matter were assured.

A fourth, subtler draw of the issue involves that of *Shukan Shincho*'s appeal to its audience. To quote Jun Kamei again, "They are selling this euphoric aura of superiority."[46] According to the former writer and assistant editor of the magazine, *Shukan Shincho* intentionally runs articles that exploit the suffering of others. In this case, readers get to look down on the comfort women for supposedly having been prostitutes during the war and behaving like opportunists today, and on Koreans and other "anti-Japanese" forces who are plotting to damage the nation, as well as on Seiji Yoshida, whom *Shukan Shincho* portrays as a liar.

Supporting the System

As with the other case studies in this book, the misrepresentation of comfort women in the Japanese news media supports the least democratic aspects of the Japanese system of governance. In essence, these articles defend the Japanese imperial military. As with the Nanjing Massacre discussed in the previous chapter, by defending the empire's actions, *Shukan Shincho* appeals to a growing neonationalist sentiment that the aims and actions of the empire were in many ways legitimate. This book has already addressed the fact that many of today's contemporary Japanese leaders—in big business, the bureaucracy, and the LDP—are the direct inheritors of power from the country's Second World War militarists. To admit the reality of an institution as abominable as the comfort-women system would be to admit to the moral bankruptcy of the prewar and wartime Japanese government. This is essentially why the Japanese government has failed to pass a Diet resolution apologizing to the country's former sex slaves. To do so would not simply make amends for past mistakes, it would undermine many of the ways that things are done in Japan today.

By denying the heinous nature of the comfort-women system, Japanese nationalists can uphold the false myths that prop up the least democratic aspects of modern Japanese society. The most reliable strategy is to frame the issue as just another instance of the Japanese being unfairly attacked by foreigners—thereby increasing negative feelings against non-Japanese. Since all the "comfort women" are of non-Japanese descent, it is easy to portray them simply as anti-Japanese foreigners. This helps to reinforce the feeling held by many Japanese that Japan is but a "small island nation" surrounded by many larger, hostile countries that threaten its welfare. Fostering such a mind-set makes it easier to unite the Japanese against these perceived common enemies and behind current leaders. In this respect, anti-comfort-women articles are eerily like the anti-Semitic articles discussed in chapter 5. Whether it be a worldwide conspiracy of Jews bent on destroying Japan, or a Korean-based conspiracy of "anti-Japanese forces" (as Nakamura calls them) strategizing to hurt the country through comfort women, the message is the same: Japan is unjustly under fire. Again, *Shukan Shincho* can be seen as a Japanese extremist sound truck of the media, rushing to intimidate and scream down anyone identified as a threat against their worldviews.

Misogyny

Attacks against the comfort women and their cause can also be accurately viewed as vestiges of the violent sexism so prevalent in prewar and wartime Japan. While the comfort-women system certainly represented a terrible abuse of human rights in general, more specifically, it was an extreme manifestation of a vile, misogynous current that ran through Japanese culture at that time. This is not to imply that the maltreatment of women has not been or is not a serious, universal, worldwide problem. The fact remains, however, that wartime Japan had an especially strict hierarchical society, within which women were not highly valued. In the previous chapter, the Japanese concept of "proper place" was discussed, wherein each race of people around the globe was designated as less "pure" than the Japanese race. This was the case even more for non-Japanese women. If non-Japanese men could be treated as subhuman (as the residents of Nanjing were in the winter of 1937–1938) the young girls and teenagers within the comfort-women system were treated even worse. At the core of the Japanese comfort system was the belief that females, and especially non-Japanese females, were inherently less valuable, even less human, than Japanese males.

Women's rights have come a long way since the Second World War in Japan. Unfortunately, and despite the Diet's passage, in 1999, of the Basic Law for a Gender-Equal Society, sexism remains a core characteristic of Japanese society, as it is of most societies, actually. Sexism in Japan plays a pivotal part within the relatively rigid social hierarchies that support the country's power structure, which tends to relegate certain classes of people to certain fixed social roles. Indeed, a variety of comments from major political leaders continue to show that sexism remains alive and well within Japanese leadership circles.

On June 26, 2003, for example, two top LDP members uttered public state-ments that simply would not be tolerated in mainstream Western European and North American society. At a panel discussion in Kagoshima held for the benefit of kindergarten operators and mothers of kindergarten-age children, former Japanese Prime Minister Yoshiro Mori asserted that Japanese women are duty-bound to their country to give birth and raise children, just as he disparaged those women who do not.

"Welfare is supposed to take care of and reward those women who have lots of children," Mori said. "It is truly strange to say we have to use tax money to take care of women who don't even give birth once, who grow old living their lives selfishly and singing the praises of freedom."[47]

But the former prime minister's comments were nothing compared to his panel colleague, lawmaker and former cabinet minister Seiichi Ota, who found something praiseworthy in the act of gang rape. Criticizing the younger gen-eration of Japanese men as "lacking the courage" to propose marriage, he com-mented that "at least gang rapists are still vigorous. Isn't that at least closer to normal?" According to reports of the event, after a nervous burst of laughter from the audience, he chuckled, "I'll get in trouble for saying this."[48]

Should these examples not reveal enough about the mind-set of certain LDP leaders, just a few days after the panel discussion, the weekly magazine *Shukan Bunshun* quoted Yasuo Fukuda, a key lieutenant of Prime Minister Junichiro Koizumi and the then–minister in charge of gender equality(!).

This December 19, 2002, *Shukan Shincho* book review sports the headline "THE SHOCKING IMPACT OF A BOOK WRITTEN BY A KOREAN WRITER 'IN FAVOR OF JAPAN,' GLORIFYING COMFORT WOMEN." The article is a positive review of a Korean writer's book, the improbable title of which translates into English as "A Theory of Prostitutes: Every Woman Is a Prostitute." The book argues that the Japanese military comfort-woman system was nothing more than a system of prostitution, with no sex slavery involved. It states that Korean comfort women were treated by the Japanese just as they have been treated in the strictly patriarchal Korean society for many years. Although the book was almost banned in Korea, the article says it is a best seller in Japan.

Fukuda, who spoke with reporters at an off-the-record briefing, said that women are often themselves responsible for being gang raped. "The problem is that there are lots of women dressed provocatively," he said.[49] Although Fukuda later denied the statement, saying, "I meant something completely different," other reporters who were present confirmed the *Shukan Bunshun* quote as accurate.

In this case, a *Shukan Bunshun* reporter was responsible for publicizing Fukuda's "off-the-record" sexist comments (although they appeared in a different magazine first), but the Japanese weeklies are almost universally acknowledged to be crudely sexist publications. As already noted, most of them sport photos of young women on their covers and feature soft pornography, puerile cartoons, and the like throughout. Although magazines like *Shukan Shincho* and *Shukan Bunshun* de-emphasize pictorial pornography, they usually carry sexist erotica as well as lascivious jokes and illustrations that degrade women. Articles such as those against the comfort women discussed in this chapter fit perfectly in this milieu of devaluing women. They combine with other xenophobic and nationalistic pieces to engender a general feeling among the *shukanshi* readership that powerful "anti-Japanese" forces are always lurking in the shadows ready to attack. True, the primary reason that such articles are run is that they sell magazines, but a critical corollary effect is that they are supportive of the Japanese status quo.

Because in Japan there is so little incentive to support the comfort women's cause, there has been no groundswell of Japanese scholars or journalists united to refute the baseless articles put out by publications such as *Shukan Shincho* or their associated "intellectual henchmen" like Fujioka and Nakamura. Thus, for want of champions, the history of the comfort women, like the history of the Nanjing Massacre, has been transformed into a false "controversy." Again, it is not just magazines and their allies that are to blame. Too many Japanese journalists, scholars, and others have failed to stand up against the magazines' attacks against comfort women and thus bear responsibility as well.

Victims of a Second Crime

The comfort women and the others who are unfairly attacked by Japanese weekly newsmagazines are not the only victims. Those who purchase and read the stories are also victims, as are the vast majority of the Japanese public who see them advertised, and as are all of us who are influenced by public opinion in the world's second-largest economy.

As with the Nanjing Massacre, a number of respected Japanese journalists and others interviewed for this book said that they have serious doubts about the claims of former comfort women such as Ok Seon Lee. Anecdotal evidence indicates that substantial portions of the Japanese public either are unaware of the existence of the comfort-women system during the war or believe that the facts of the matter are an issue for serious scholarly debate. Certainly not many in the West know anything about this immense crime that occurred throughout East Asia just half a century ago.

Journalist Katsuichi Honda has written at length on the matter of accountability. According to him, Japanese who were children during the war or who were born after the war carry no guilt for what their forefathers did. But he does see it as the duty of all Japanese to recognize their country's past for what it is. To Honda, those who willfully forget or purposely distort the past commit a second crime against the original victims. "The third postwar generation in Japan is going abroad in a manner unimaginable in Japan a few years back. It is common for young Japanese people to visit nearby Asian countries. However," Honda explains, "in these countries there are people who detest our national anthem and flag. How many Japanese youth are ignorant [of Japanese war crimes] and merely enjoy the high value of the yen? This is the result of our second crime."[50]

Honda, like others, believes that in order to create genuine democracy, where lesser crimes are not tolerated and greater crimes will not recur, the Japanese must confront the reality of the Japanese military comfort women.

Japanese author Yuki Tanaka, in his book *Hidden Horrors: Japanese War Crimes of World War II*, makes the point:

What is needed is a clear indication that the extraordinary atrocities and crimes in wartime have a closer connection with the everyday life of ordinary people than we might want to acknowledge. It is also necessary to help Japanese people understand that by failing to acknowledge that they were deceived and dragged into the war by the military leaders, citizens at large eventually *supported* the war and as such bear responsibility. . . . If ordinary people are unable to examine their past unequivocally, I believe such people are also incapable of the clear self-analysis needed to grasp and confront current political and social problems.[51]

Perhaps the most powerful aspect of Tanaka's assertion is its universality, because it points out the hidden "collateral damage" of the war crimes. The "second crime" of forgetting or denying the suffering of the comfort women reaches far beyond the original victims. The general public, hoodwinked into believing false, sanitized versions of history, become unknowing victims as well, for they are the ones who ultimately suffer the effects of a dysfunctional democratic processes. A corollary of this, of course, is that the lack of historical awareness has obviously left plenty of intellectual room for current LDP leaders and others to disparage women and to publicly joke about abominations such as gang rape. One may only speculate how differently women might be treated in Japanese society were the not-so-distant history of the "comfort stations" widely known and accurately recognized.

Sex Slavery Here and Now

In September 2003, U.S. President George W. Bush addressed the UN General Assembly and named trafficking of sex slaves in the world today "a special evil." If ever Bush's invocation of the word "evil" was appropriate, it was in this context. For even while the Japanese government dodges its responsibilities to its few surviving sex slaves—and while that responsibility is obscured behind a smokescreen of deception and lies—the practice of sex slavery becomes increasingly common worldwide, especially in wealthy, developed countries such as the United States.

In a powerful exposé entitled "The Girls Next Door," in the January 25, 2004, *New York Times Magazine*, journalist Peter Landesman paints a picture that is, like Ok Seon Lee's and Madam X's testimony, painful to read and difficult to process. One of the tamer passages in the piece reads:

> What the police found were four girls between the ages of 14 and 17. They were all Mexican nationals without documentation. But they weren't prostitutes; they were sex slaves. The distinction is important: these girls weren't

working for profit or a paycheck. They were captives to the traffickers and keepers who controlled their every move.... The police found a squalid, land-based equivalent of a 19th-century slave ship, with rancid, doorless bathrooms; bare, putrid mattresses; and a stash of penicillin, "morning after" pills and misoprostol, an antiulcer medication that can induce abortion. The girls were pale, exhausted and malnourished.

It turned out that 1212 ½ West Front Street was one of what law-enforcement officials say are dozens of active stash houses and apartments in the New York metropolitan area—mirroring hundreds more in other major cities like Los Angeles, Atlanta and Chicago—where under-age girls and young women from dozens of countries are trafficked and held captive. Most of them— whether they started out in Eastern Europe or Latin America—are taken to the United States through Mexico. Some of them have been baited by promises of legitimate jobs and a better life in America; many have been abducted; others have been bought from or abandoned by their impoverished families.[52]

According to Landesman, in 2003 the CIA estimated that between 18,000 and 20,000 people are trafficked annually into the United States. But, experts at both the U.S. State Department and at nongovernmental organizations say that the CIA's figures are probably low. There may be as many as 30,000 to 50,000 sex slaves in captivity in the United States at any given time.

Landesman takes his readers into brothels that are eerily similar to comfort stations, with men lined up to take their turns in squalid stalls with girls and young women who are forced (via brutal abuse and death threats against them and their families) to have sex with "20 to 30 men per day." From the impoverished countries around the world that give birth to them, to the U.S.-Mexican border, to the backs of vans and dark corners of basements in the United States, Landesman makes a detailed study of the mechanisms of North American sexual slavery in the twenty-first century.

Landesman introduces us to a U.S. sex slave survivor named "Andrea":

Andrea told me she was transported to Juarez dozens of times. During one visit, when she was about 7 years old, the trafficker took her to the Radisson Casa Grande Hotel, where there was a john waiting in a room. The john was an older American man, and he read Bible passages to her before and after having sex with her. Andrea described other rooms she remembered in other hotels in Mexico: the Howard Johnson in Leon, the Crowne Plaza in Guadalajara. She remembers most of all the ceiling patterns.[53]

And while this is not a case of government-sponsored sexual slavery, as in the Japanese military during the Second World War, it would be a mistake to assert that law-enforcement and other officials in many countries are not complicit in the maintenance of modern sex trafficking. When contemporary Westerners consider the methods of the Japanese military comfort system, it is all too easy to fall into the trap of thinking that it was an atrocity from another time, another place, and another culture.

Bush's statements and Landesman's article stand out as much for being well worded as for their being out of the ordinary. That U.S. government officials estimate that tens of thousands of individuals are held as sex slaves and that there is little-to-no public discourse on this actively committed crime against humanity—in the news media or elsewhere—is truly astonishing. Seen in this light, the media treatment of Japanese military comfort women becomes all the more relevant.

CHAPTER NINE

THE SUN ALSO RISES

This is a completely fascinating time in Japan. It's fascinating because Japan has reached a complete dead end in field after field after field. And there's no place to turn now. Of course, you can go on propping up the system for a long time, and that's what is being done now.

—Alex Kerr[1]

A Dire Situation

While the case studies in this book may represent extreme examples, they are the results of extreme corruption. They have been selected because they illustrate, in such unambiguous terms, the failures of the Japanese news media to support its citizenry. The industry's power is tightly concentrated and is especially dangerous given the country's ineffectual libel laws. The industry demonstrates appallingly low professional standards of truth and journalistic ethics—a situation exacerbated by a culture of conformism that tends to suppress serious analysis of the power structure. Also, the sharp split between the establishment, or press club, news providers and the so-called alternative press does not support the citizenry's right to be well informed. This destructive dichotomy throws what might be described as the Japanese news media's one-two punch against democracy. The Japanese establishment news media jabs away at the public with its relentlessly authoritative "official" news product, which *shukanshi* follow up periodically with their ugly roundhouses of untrustworthy sensationalism. Meanwhile, the potential of the news media to support civil sovereignty and the democratic process is further beaten back by the steady march of Japanese nationalism, which continues to grow decade after decade since the end of the Second World War. Finally, by engaging in what has been called "media *ijime*," or media bullying, Japanese journalists (especially those who work for *shukanshi*) often function as enforcers of the status quo, attacking nonconformists, minorities, and foreigners—whoever is deemed a misfit or a threat.

As long as the Japanese news media continues to dodge its responsibility to provide fair and accurate information and analysis, it will likely be impossible to reform the Japanese system of governance as it currently stands. Because the situation with the Japanese news media is so dire, analyzing and confronting it can be especially helpful in understanding similar media issues in other "advanced" democratic nations. Many of its cultural, ethical, and structural shortcomings can be found in news media around the globe. Consequently, many of the same prescriptions for reform in Japan will work just as well elsewhere—even in countries where the problems do not appear as acute.

Characteristics of the Japanese News Media

The case studies in this book illustrate at least four main problems with the Japanese news media. These problems have crippled it, ensuring that even its finest journalists and publishers are unable to effect change.

Highly Concentrated Industry

The high concentration of media power in Japan has facilitated intensely collusive relationships between media, government, and big business. As noted previously, a mere six companies currently dominate the Japanese national daily press and broadcast news—coincidentally, the same number of companies that dominate the U.S. news-media market.[2] Those who would

dismiss the problem often argue that the Internet has substantially diversi-
fied the sources of news available to the public in recent years and that the
concentration of media power is hence not a problem. They are mistaken.
Despite the explosion in the number of Internet users worldwide, especially
in wealthier countries such as Japan, and in spite of the mass proliferation of
Web sites purporting to present the news, most people still get their news
from the same source companies that provided it to them before the advent
of the Web. The fact is that the same companies that dominate traditional
media have supremacy online as well, if only because they have deep pockets
and well-established news-gathering networks. And even though today's
major Japanese companies tend to produce impressive varieties of news
resources (publications, television and radio shows, and online offerings),
these still come from the small number of companies that produced the news
in the past; and therefore, they naturally offer only a limited spectrum of
information and perspectives.

One need only go back to the second and third decades of the twentieth
century to see how diverse the Japanese media landscape once was. Unfortunately, nearly all these papers were systematically driven out of business
by the militarists, leaving a highly concentrated, easily manipulated news
industry that they used to rally the public behind their plans for world
domination. During just a few years in the late 1930s and early 1940s, Japan
lost an astounding 1,400 daily newspapers,[3] a loss the consequences of
which are impossible to fathom. The contemporary Japanese news-media
structure is a direct result of this legacy. The situation is reflected in the
infamously bland, uniform, and uncritical coverage provided by the establishment press. In the case of the Matsumoto sarin-gas incident, for example, law-enforcement authorities had no trouble spoon-feeding the
establishment news media bogus information about an innocent man who
was in fact a victim of that attack. The media swallowed the police's allegations against Yoshiyuki Kono hook, line, and sinker, barely raising an eye-
brow at the flimsy evidence provided, and passed the "news" on to a public
that deserves far better.

The lack of diversity in the news media also has contributed to anti-
Semitism, since virtually no mainstream Japanese reporters or editors have

seriously protested such blatant racism. Similarly, the monolithic Japanese establishment press failed utterly to question the bogus rape charges against Soka Gakkai leader Daisaku Ikeda or even to report properly on the outcome of the court cases that decisively vindicated him.

If the Japanese establishment press were willing to step outside the narrow boundaries of official-source news and authority-based perspectives, and get serious about investigating and analyzing the real news related to how the country is actually run—or even merely present the news in a significantly more interesting way—*shukanshi* would see their sales plummet.

The vast size and dominance of the major news companies in Japan also contribute to the mind-set among establishment journalists that they need not confront the *shukanshi's* transgressions. It is as if the establishment press considers itself too elite, too highbrow and important, to deign to engage the vulgar weeklies. As with journalists in other countries, Japanese journalists are often highly privileged and very well paid, and thus naturally view themselves as members of an "elite class." Rather than identifying with everyday people, they too often view and treat regular citizens with disdain and thus produce a "news product" that is equally disdainful of the general public.

One consequence of this elitism is that many people both inside and outside Japan mistakenly dismiss *shukanshi* as insignificant, when precisely the opposite is true. As this book shows, *shukanshi* are serious influencers of public opinion. Yet instead of challenging nationalistic, misogynistic, and xenophobic *shukanshi* articles, the establishment press tacitly condones them with silence and even actively promotes them by permitting advertisements with *shukanshi* headlines to run in their pages unchallenged. Just like Japanese schoolteachers, though aware that *ijime*, or bullying, is present, they choose to look away.

Low Professional Standards of Truth and Journalistic Ethics

Related to the lack of diversity of media power in Japan is the abysmal lack of journalistic ethics throughout the industry. In a country where loyalty to the company takes precedence over commitment to one's profession, and where companies wield vast power over the lives of their employees, it is not surprising that many find it far easier simply to go along than to stand up or stand out. As the old Japanese adage goes, "the nail that sticks up gets pounded down." In the establishment press, this mentality is exacerbated by the vast *kisha* club system, which institutionalizes and enforces close cooperation—and collusion—between journalists and their sources. This absence of principles creates a situation wherein most establishment journalists simply do not feel duty-bound to report injustices, either with aggressive investigative reporting or with editorials. A lack of professional standards of truth is, of course, especially problematic in the realm of *shukanshi,* particularly given the popular editorial approach of literary-narrative journalism, pioneered by *Shukan Shincho* in the 1950s. Schooled on the job in this dubious tradition as most *shukanshi* reporters and editors are, few recognize anything wrong with the routine embellishment and exaggeration of facts to make them more saleable. In fact, many of these so-called journalists feel duty-bound to fill in missing details, stretch facts, exaggerate circumstances, and even sometimes invent stories.

In example after example, *shukanshi* journalists take the approach that objective truth is subservient to "social truth" and social circumstance. Nor is this considered in any way an illegitimate practice. It is the industry-accepted approach to covering the news.

Commercialism and Sensationalism

Unlike the establishment news media, which bases profits on maintaining large broadcast audiences and gigantic subscriber bases, Japanese weekly newsmagazines rely on newsstand sales for more than 90 percent of their circulation. Thus, the immediacy of their appeal is everything. While issues such as nationalism and politics, editorial leanings, and current fashions certainly help to determine what gets covered and how, what ultimately matters most is what sells.

This, of course, is not to say that free-market competition in the news business is a bad thing. It is often responsible for the maintenance of a robust and vital news product. The reason commercialism yields a poorer result in the Japanese weekly newsmagazine industry than in news-media sectors of other industrialized, democratic countries is that *shukanshi* commercialism is so unrestrained. While in other nations, journalistic guidelines and ethical traditions usually work together with libel laws to curb the most scurrilous digressions, this simply is not the case for Japanese weekly newsmagazines. As a result, tens of millions of Japanese are exposed each week to advertisements and articles touting gross exaggerations and bald-faced lies.

The questions, then, are these: Why do Japanese cultural, civic, and business leaders permit *shukanshi* to publish and run advertisements for such infamously unreliable material in such an unregulated environment? Why, in a country as socially sophisticated and well ordered as Japan, is the weekly newsmagazine industry allowed to spew such inaccuracies at the public with such little regard for consequence? Why are legal repercussions not implemented more fiercely? And why are the magazines not widely denounced for the media atrocities enumerated in this book?

The simple answer is that the *shukanshi*'s lawlessness is not a serious threat to the way things are run in Japan. Indeed, quite the contrary. A comparison has been drawn in this book between the *shukanshi* and the Japanese neonationalist sound trucks that have become such a regular feature of Japanese urban life. The comparison is worth revisiting. By any reasonable standards, the thugs that drive around in sound trucks, blasting their absurd nationalist cant at Japanese citizens, are criminals and outlaws. Rather than simply exercising their right to free speech, they create noise hazards at the very least and in some circumstances commit a form of assault with their sound blasts. Many of these trucks are truly physically painful to be near.

It certainly would not take much for Japanese politicians, bureaucrats, and police to pass and enforce laws and regulations against such disturbances, or to have the sound-truck people fined or tossed in jail. Few would argue with the observation that most Japanese would like to see some reasonable limits placed on them. Yet nothing is done. The question is, why not? And the answer is that the sound trucks are supportive of the powerful Japanese neonationalists. They are a most-effective intimidation tool, used to shout down anyone who speaks out against the false myths that legitimize the Japanese system of governance.

It is sometimes said in Japan that top politicians and other power brokers have direct connections with these groups and that they can dispatch sound trucks as they desire. There may or may not be any truth to this. The fact is,

Shown here are a number of ultrarightist sound trucks blasting their emperor-worship rhetoric.

however, that they don't usually need to be dispatched. The sound-truck personnel do their jobs quite well, and apparently without much instruction.

Shukanshi often play a similar function in Japanese society. They are happy to attack and intimidate those individuals and groups who get out of line. Their methods are, as shown in this book, often clearly immoral. Moreover, it wouldn't take a lot of effort for Japanese power holders to implement serious libel laws that would quickly put an end to the worst of the *shukanshi*. Given that the same political party has been in power for nearly half a century, it is absurd to suppose that the ethical lapses of *shukanshi* could not be reined in with ease, were it so desired. Yet, just like the sound-truck teams, they support the status quo by attacking nonconformists and other perceived upstarts.

Ultranationalism

Japanese politics of the past few decades have been compared to a car with its steering out of alignment—always veering to the right. The left in Japan has been in decline for so many years now that many consider it to be hardly a factor anymore. The results of this gradual but steady shift is manifest in many areas, from membership in the left-wing political parties to the content of school textbooks, from the mandatory reinstatement of the national anthem and rising-sun flag in public schools to the general tenor of political discourse.

Although some do worry that contemporary Japanese neonationalism could lead to a resurgence in militarism of the sort that led to the Second World War, this is a distinctly minority viewpoint. International business interests, American military might, an increasingly powerful China, a nuclear North Korea, and a host of other geopolitical and cultural factors make the specter of a dangerously militaristic Japan an unlikely prospect, certainly in the near future. What concerns most observers is the effect that Japanese nationalism has domestically on an already weak democratic process and internationally on tensions in Southeast Asia and beyond. Given its behemoth economic power, as well as the legacy of distrust between Japan and its neighbors, the continued growth of Japanese nationalism can only destabilize the region by retarding trade, impeding cultural exchanges, and slowing the spread of democracy.

In March of 2004, Japan got a small taste of just how costly its virulent neonationalism can be. According to a *Wall Street Journal* front-page article, China had been planning on giving to a Japanese consortium a whopping $15 billion contract for the building of a Beijing–Shanghai bullet train. However, when a small group of young professional Chinese heard about the contract, they became outraged that their government might award such a lucrative deal to a Japanese group, even while the Japanese continue to deny the reality of its Second World War brutality. The group set up a Web site to protest the contract and to solicit signatures on their petition that their government withhold the contract from the Japanese. They had set a goal of collecting 10,000 online signatures, but they apparently tapped into a widespread sentiment in China, for they collected 87,320 signatures in just 10 days. In a relatively rare example of grassroots Chinese activism, the petition apparently made a difference too. "That helped persuade the Railway Ministry to derail the Japanese bid and to reconsider German and French offers for the $15 billion project," wrote the *Wall Street Journal,* citing ministry advisors.[4] As China continues to grow and challenge Japanese interests in the region, the situation is likely to get uglier, especially if mainstream Japanese publications like *shukanshi* continue to spout their absurd and offensive historical revisionism.

One reason that *shukanshi* often carry nationalistic pieces has to do with their need for sensational articles that differ from the coverage of the daily press. Because the Japanese daily press is already very conservative, weekly newsmagazines have the choice of moving either to the left of that conservatism (toward the more liberal side) or to the right of it (toward the neonationalistic side). Given the weeklies' conservative readers and big-business sponsors, the choice is usually an easy one. As the old saying goes, "he who pays the piper chooses the tune." Neither the big-business establishment that buys advertising in the magazines nor the relatively well-off and predominantly male readership that buys the magazines are likely to want to support publications that seriously challenge the social system of which they are a part. By choosing an editorial position that is more nationalistic than the establishment media, *shukanshi* appear bold and outspoken (and thus controversial) while avoiding alienating their support bases.

Reform

Author Alex Kerr, who has resided in Japan for much of his life and is one of the staunchest critics of the way the country is run, holds some very real hope for Japanese reform today. He says that despite the steady increase in nationalism and the many horrendous failures of the media, he has begun to see emerging some admirable grassroots movements for reform. According to Kerr, the country's worst problems have finally led to movements for change. He describes the situation in an interview for this book:

> Today there is an increasing sense of crisis and an increasing sense of anger here. The Japanese leadership and the American academics may feel that Japan is just fine, but the Japanese people don't feel that way. They are rather upset about the way things are—at least a large part of the population is upset about it. And so Japan may finally be entering a time when it achieves a more genuine democracy than it has ever had before. I actually think this is a completely fascinating time in Japan. It's fascinating because Japan has reached a complete dead end in field after field after field. And there's no

place to turn now. Of course, you can go on propping up the system for a long time, and that's what is being done now.[5]

Kerr says that while the Japanese system of governance continues to be maintained through various superficial fixes—such as borrowing money, passing blame, stalling for time, and distracting attention away from the real problems—it continues to fail the citizenry. Kerr's thoughts accord with those of a number of leading Japanese thinkers, including Akio Mikuni, head of Japan's leading bond-rating agency: "Japan is still mired in feudalistic thinking and social structures," Mikuni explains. "No social revolution has occurred to create full-fledged Japanese citizens, a political system, or a market economy. The policy elite will thwart any serious challenge as long as it can maintain its instruments of control over the economy, suppress consumption, maximize savings, and rely upon external rather than internally generated demand to keep the Japanese industrial machine going."[6]

Yet Kerr feels that Japan's current problems contain within them the seeds of hope. According to him, an increasing sense of the desperate state of the nation has prompted a significant minority of Japanese to begin agitating for change:

Japan is now becoming more open to foreigners than it has ever been since I was a child. It's easier to open your own company. Japanese are now letting foreigners do some things here. Maverick governors are also appearing and doing things differently. You are also getting an explosive growth in NPOs [nonprofit organizations]. Until a few years ago it was essentially impossible to start an NPO in Japan unless you were the government or had enormous funds. But it has become much easier, and now these NPOs are cropping up everywhere. And that's because people have essentially given up on the center and started doing things themselves. That attitude, when you give up on the center and start doing it yourself, that attitude is democracy. So yes, I do have optimism for Japan.[7]

Unfortunately, few mainstream Japanese journalists appear willing or able to portray these grassroots movements for change accurately. Instead, the establishment news media tends to keep its focus on the views and opinions of its powerful information sources, just as *shukanshi* continue either to beat the drums of nationalism or to keep their readers distracted with meaningless sensationalism, pornography, and the like.

It would seem to some that announcements of "change on the horizon" in Japan—such as that offered by Kerr—have been a part of the Japanese landscape for nearly half a century now, although little substantial change ever really seems to take place. However, it may well be that Kerr is onto something here at the start of the twenty-first century. It is certainly getting difficult to see how the Liberal Democratic Party (LDP) can retain the hegemony over Japanese politics that it has held for nearly a century, especially as its control over Diet seats continues to dwindle from election to election. But without a more robust free press, it is still difficult to imagine profound reform, even if the LDP were to finally be ousted for a substantial period.

Longtime Japanese resident Alex Kerr is a vocal advocate for reform in the country. He is the author of the English-language books *Lost Japan* and *Dogs and Demons: Tales from the Dark Side of Japan*. He is also an award-winning writer in Japanese.

Moreover, even as the Japanese economy appears to be regaining its feet in 2004 after more than a decade-long recession, it is almost impossible to imagine the Japanese economy growing again as it did in the first few decades of the postwar period. The fact is that reforms, such as those pointed to by Kerr, are desperately needed in a country that is undergoing very real social shifts—in a "Japan Unbound," as author John Nathan has described it in his thus-titled book.[8]

External Pressure to Open Markets

It is often said that dramatic change does not occur in Japan without strong influence from outside the country. This view reflects the common wisdom that the ruling elites tend to be so fully in control that it is all but impossible for those out of power within the country to challenge them. Certainly, the two most dramatic changes to have occurred in Japan during the past century and a half—the Meiji Restoration of 1868 and the post–World War II reforms—both resulted from overwhelming external pressure.

Still, the country's growing grassroots movements can potentially yield powerful results, with or without external pressures assisting them. Indeed, as Kerr points out, true democracy is the result of grassroots movements and may, by definition, be impossible to impose from outside. That said, the importance of external pressures should not be discounted. Even if they are not the source of change, they can often serve as vital catalysts.

Ivan P. Hall, in his 2002 book *Bamboozled!*, makes a powerful case for the need for U.S. and other Western policymakers to be more proactive with Japan. While Hall approaches the issue primarily from a perspective of U.S. economic and political interests with respect to Japan rather than simply advocating reform for reform's sake, his arguments are relevant all the same. Hall documents Japanese investment of tens of millions of dollars each year into political lobbying efforts in foreign countries. He reveals the intensive support and encouragement the Japanese have provided to pro-Japan academics in foreign countries, and he further exposes a variety of other Japanese international programs and schemes created ostensibly for "improved understanding" between Japan and other countries but that function primarily to influence foreign nations to support Japanese goals. Author Pat Choate wrote of this before Hall did, in his 1990 book, *Agents of Influence: How Japan's Lobbyists in the United States Manipulate America's Political System*. Choate goes so far as to liken Japan to a third political party in the United States, noting the "at least $100 million" that the country spends each year to hire Washington lobbyists and other influencers.[9] Hall concludes that Japanese corporate and governmental involvement in the United States represents "the most extraordinary attempt in history by one nation—in aggressive pursuit of its national interest—to influence the entire intellectual system of a peacetime ally."[10] Hall outlines the many ways that Japanese markets have generally remained well insulated from international competition, a fact that many believe has led to the deterioration of the Japanese domestic economy. Thus, despite superficial changes resulting from the trade friction of the 1980s, Japan has never fairly reciprocated the access it has received to many U.S., European, and other markets. While Japan is certainly more open today than it has been in previous decades, it is time that serious efforts be made, especially through multilateral trade bodies and in concert with other countries, to force the Japanese to open up their domestic markets to fair competition in all fields.

A Japanese news media that is more open to foreign competition would result in a greater awareness by the international community of gratuitous attacks on human rights by Japanese newsmagazines and others. It is hard to imagine that the media atrocities outlined in this book could continue unabated in a thoroughly internationally integrated Japanese domestic economy: one where foreign-owned media companies and journalists compete freely, where a substantial number of foreign academics live and work, where many international lawyers practice, and where the existence of domestic and international nonprofit organizations such as those described by Kerr are firmly established. The way foreign advertisers were able to force rapid change in Bungeishunju Ltd. over its *Marco Polo* Holocaust denial is a case in point. While the international community tends to maintain a hands-off approach to Japanese domestic concerns (an approach that is greatly encouraged by the Japanese), the *Marco Polo* case proves that international businesses have real clout in Japan.

This does not mean that Japan should simply remove all trade and structural barriers or otherwise subject its domestic companies to unfair or unrestrained competition. As many in the so-called antiglobalization movement have successfully pointed out, unrestricted trade is no panacea for society's woes. Japan, however, has been afforded far greater access to a number of other countries, such as the United States, than it has ever provided in return. Given the close relationship between Japan and the United States on security matters, U.S. leverage might be just as effective in the realm of security as in the economic sphere—especially because the end of the cold war has meant that the United States no longer relies on Japan's strategic location in the way it once did. An effective short-term strategy, for example, might be to let the Japanese establishment know (preferably in a discreet but persuasive manner) that continued U.S. cooperation on defense depends on Japan's being seen to acknowledge rather than deny its historical misdeeds and on having a media that supports rather than violates human rights.

Such moves would very likely spur reforms of Japan's news media. While Japan will surely continue to resist such efforts, and there will certainly be uncomfortable backlashes against any pressure in this direction, the country's leaders will undoubtedly take action if it means maintaining harmonious international relations with its closest allies.

Dismantling the Press Club System

The Japanese press club system is one of the key factors contributing to the corruption of the Japanese news media. It not only institutionalizes and enforces collusive relationships between Japanese journalists and their establishment-news sources; it also encourages self-censorship, contributes to the boring and unhelpful nature of the establishment news, provides reporters with an inflated sense of privilege and elitism, and discourages independent work and investigative reporting.

Japanese press clubs are the key cause of the destructive dichotomy between the establishment news media and the "alternative" press. Regardless of what its defenders might say, the Japanese press club system is an embarrassment to Japanese journalists and an insult to the public it betrays.

Unfortunately, even among those who recognize press clubs for the corrupt institutions they are, some do not call for their elimination. Dismantling of the press club system will not stop collusion between the news media and Japanese establishment, they say. And even a cursory look at news-media industries around the world shows that a press club system is no prerequisite for collusive and corrupt reporting. Many have pointed out that the national news media in the United States and Europe often serve as mouthpieces for big corporate interests, big government, and other elite institutions.

Still, the abolition of the press clubs in Japan would go a long way toward opening up the world of Japanese public discourse. As the press clubs currently function, collusion between journalists and their sources is not only tolerated but actively enforced. Without the clubs, these codified, institutionalized collaborations might well begin to dissolve over time, leaving room for healthier, arm's-length relationships.

Although the press club system continues with little prospect for serious change on the horizon, the elimination of the system could conceivably come through a number of different avenues. The best route would be through calls for elimination of the system by either the Japanese public or Japanese journalists themselves.

Unfortunately, Japanese reporters regularly abuse the powers afforded them through the press club system by failing to properly scrutinize their sources. Even nonestablishment journalists, such as magazine writers who are banned from the press clubs, benefit from them. Without the clubs, the Japanese establishment news media would likely become less uniform in the way it covers the news and thus far more interesting. Such a change would subsequently leave the *shukanshi* less room to claim that they cover the "real" or "unofficial" news in Japan and leave them scrambling for a new raison d'être. Were magazine journalists allowed the same access to news sources as that currently provided to press club journalists, the magazines would no longer have an establishment press to counter. Who knows? Given direct, unfettered access to press conferences and to the politicians, bureaucrats, and businesspeople who hold them, Japanese newsmagazine journalists might even be transformed into admirable news sources.

One can only wonder what the result would be if the Japanese public fully understood that government bureaucrats and politicians, from the local to the national level, all working in public buildings and drawing salaries from public coffers, are required by private media companies to allow only certain people (representatives of those private media companies) to attend their "public" press conferences. What would the public's response be if it really knew that most Japanese government press releases and briefings, given by public officials about the workings of public institutions, are usually only shared with the members of privately operated clubs?

Unfortunately, and in spite of the efforts of the European Union to demand change, real reform of the clubs is unlikely to occur anytime in the near future. Still, it ought to remain a primary goal, no matter how long-term, of everyone seriously interested in a just Japanese society.

Freedom-of-Information Law

Along with the eventual elimination of the press clubs, Japanese media reformers often call for a freedom-of-information law such as that in the

United States. As it now stands, Japanese bureaucrats and politicians keep vast amounts of government information to themselves or allow access only to press club journalists. Were a legitimate freedom-of-information law in place, Japanese citizens might finally be given direct access to the information required to make truly informed electoral and other decisions. The Liaison Committee on Human Rights and Mass Media Conduct (JIMPOREN) Web site quotes Kazue Suzuki, a member of JIMPOREN and an *Asahi Evening News* feature editor, who believes that should "a law guaranteeing access to government information be enacted [so that] both journalist and general public can obtain the same information available to press club members today then the system will naturally self-destruct."[11]

Judicial Reform

One of the most straightforward methods for reforming Japanese journalism would be to strengthen Japanese libel laws. While there was improvement in this area during the years 2002 and 2003, awards should be raised much higher. Moreover, there should be greater parity between libel victims so that the system does not discriminate against average, everyday citizens, who should be compensated for unfair libel attacks at just as high a rate as celebrities, politicians, and other powerful figures. This does not mean that Japanese courts should simply start awarding unreasonably large sums to victims, as United States courts are reputed to have done. Libel laws—and even tort law in general—could easily be reformed to start providing awards and punishments that are appropriate to the offenses committed. The harsh reality is that the Japanese judiciary has consistently failed throughout the postwar period to serve justice in Japanese libel cases.

Japan's two-track libel-law system, which differentiates between criminal and civil libel charges, has long neglected individual human rights while permitting large and powerful media companies to break, with minor consequences, both the spirit and the letter of the law. For years, awards in civil libel cases have averaged a mere ¥1 million (about US$10,000)—less than the expense of bringing such a lawsuit! Fortunately, between about 2002 and 2003, that average began to rise, so that the average award today is probably within the ¥1 million to ¥5 million range (US$10,000 to US$50,000), with some judg-ments in the ¥5 million to ¥8 million range (US$50,000 to US$80,000). As noted in chapter 3, a 2001 Tokyo District Court study panel of five judges released a report saying compensation for defaming a publicly known figure should be set between ¥4 million and ¥5 million (about US$40,000 to US$50,000), and time will tell how this recommendation and others like it will be met. An especially good sign is that in October 2003, the largest single award in a Japanese libel suit was given—¥19.8 million (US$198,000). Japan needs more large judgments like this one, and much greater ones as well. The reality is that for major corporations like Bungeishunju Ltd., Shinchosha Ltd., Kodan-sha Ltd., and the like, ¥5 million (US$50,000) is simply not a signifi-cant amount of money—and even ¥19.8 million (US$198,000) barely affects their financials. Indeed, when it comes to Japan's mammoth media members, such as NHK, Yomiuri, and Asahi, ¥19.8 million is laughable. Such awards may well prove to be enough to put micropublishers and very small publishers out of business, but they are only just enough to begin influencing the editorial rooms of the big media players.

Again, such moves need not put a chill on serious reporting. What is pro-posed here is simply for malicious writers, editors, and publishers to be held accountable for their crimes and for their victims to be compensated fairly.

Education

Ultimately, the only way for the news media in any country to improve is for journalists to improve their understanding of the importance of their role in a democracy. Regardless of legal, business, or social issues, the news media can only be as good as its journalists.

One obvious way to improve the Japanese news media is to create more schools of journalism. They are all but nonexistent in Japan today. It is true that schools of journalism bring their own sets of problems. Instead of encouraging genuinely diverse ideas and dissension, such schools can some-times merely work to weed out nonconformism and reward orthodoxy. Indeed, even if more schools were established in Japan, there is no guarantee that the industry would hire its graduates.

There is no silver bullet. Still, that many Japanese journalists lack an understanding of the more social and democratic mission of their profession is a problem that must be addressed. Whether through the establishment of more schools of journalism or through other mechanisms, such as industry-wide training, professional organizations, reporters' unions, interactions with quality journalists from abroad, or grassroots movements within the industry, there needs to be a fundamental shift in the mind-sets of individual Japanese journalists if the profession is ever to develop beyond its current, stunted state.

Relativism

No doubt some readers will be tempted to dismiss all or parts of the criticism presented here against the Japanese news media, believing perhaps that the industry may have "some problems" but that the same is true for the news media of many other similar countries. It is easy to point to other nations, such as Russia, where independent journalism has been retarded to the point that Russian journalists today are almost never allowed to question their president directly. And, of course, dictatorships abound, where journalists are routinely punished for speech and thought crimes. When compared to the standards of these countries, the Japanese news media does not look so bad after all. In fact, the many fine journalists noted throughout this book are testaments to the superb quality of reporting that can occur in Japan. But, when compared with the news media of the world's major democracies, the institutional structures and professional standards of the Japanese news media can only be described as especially untrustworthy.

Many in the international community will no doubt point an accusatory finger at the United States, whose news media (many say) has taken a sharp turn for the worse since September 11, 2001, in its failure to seriously challenge American leaders and their moves to war in Afghanistan, Iraq, and on various fronts of the "War on Terror." Still others will criticize the U.S. news media for its elitist, liberal, and corporate biases. Why criticize the Japanese, some might question, when Western journalists so often fail to counter their own ruling institutions and power holders, when they are owned and operated by privileged elite who are so removed from average everyday citizens, when commercialism and sensationalism run rampant, when there is an across-the-board dumbing down of discourse, and when media consolidation continues unabated?

But the shortcomings of journalism outside Japan excuse nothing. The Japanese news media does deserve special attention. It offers profound lessons. Like perhaps no other news media on earth, the Japanese model presents the appearance of freedom and independence while actually being co-opted, collusive, and corrupt.

Until serious reforms are implemented, readers everywhere should be keenly conscious of the fact that news reports prepared by Japanese journalists—whether in Japanese or translated into other languages—go through a substantially different preparation process than the news reports coming out of most Western democracies. The vast majority of the material that comes from the Japanese establishment media—the main newspapers, broadcasters, and news services—derive from within the closed doors and cloistered rooms of the country's infamous *kisha* clubs, where they are written up by reporters who have intimate ties to their sources and who have been inculcated with a professional ethic vastly different from their Western counterparts. While all this certainly does not mean that every story to make its way out of the Japanese establishment news media is false (quite the contrary, they are usually factually accurate, as far as they go), they do tend to come from a very specific viewpoint and to have been wrung through an airtight control apparatus. Japanese stories and information that come from the *shukanshi* sector of the country's news media ought to be scrutinized even more intently. Fact and fiction are mixed with a unique creativity that makes sorting the wheat from the chaff all but impossible. They also deserve to be read, followed, and studied by policymakers, academics, and everyone else seriously interested in keeping a finger on the pulse of contemporary Japanese culture and public opinion.

Continuing Down the Same Old Road

This chapter presents a smattering of ideas and thoughts for media reform in Japan from a variety of sources. Realistically speaking, there is not a great likelihood that many of these will be implemented in the near future. The power relationships surrounding the media tend to be deeply entrenched, and there is little incentive for individuals or groups to cede their advantages. This brings up a simple but critical question: What if things do not change? What if reforms are not implemented?

As has been established by the preceding case studies, the Japanese news media is currently capable of running unsubstantiated, yet extremely successful, smear campaigns with few repercussions to themselves. Moreover, that same media is equally capable of raising real questions and even of inventing serious debates over otherwise thoroughly documented historical facts. If the Japanese news media can pull the wool over the public's eye today, as it has with such success in the previously mentioned cases, what will it be capable of ten, twenty, or thirty years into the future, assuming reforms are not implemented?

The future of a Japan that continues on its current political and economic trajectories, with the same, unreformed news-media sources outlined in this book, presages neither a flourishing of democracy nor a flourishing of Japanese culture. John Nathan's 2004 book *Japan Unbound,* subtitled "A Volatile Nation's Quest for Pride and Purpose," paints the unmistakable picture of a turmoil-filled Japan desperately struggling to regain its feet after years of social instability. In his thoughtful book, Nathan presents at least one series of statistics that are impossible to overlook. "In 1998, Japan's suicide rate abruptly jumped 35 percent to more than 30,000 deaths for the first time in postwar history," he writes. "This number is twice as many suicides per capita as occur annually in the United States. Suicides increased again in 1999 to 35,000, and have remained above 30,000 ever since." Nathan points out that these statistics may even be misleadingly low because they only include those who die within twenty-four hours of attempting suicide.[12]

For a wealthy, democratic country, the people of Japan seem surprisingly troubled. Given the extreme natures of the case studies in this book, one must wonder just how the current Japanese news media contributes to this stark reality—and how that news media may contribute to an even more dire future if no reform or other changes occur.

One of the recurring themes in this book is the relevance of Japanese news-media models to those in other countries. Western news organizations increasingly face the same kind of institutional, structural, and (to varying degrees) even cultural challenges that the Japanese news media faces.

Thus, if it is reasonable to say that Japanese democracy, and by extension the happiness of the Japanese people, is undermined by the news media, then in light of similar media trends and factors in the West, it is not much of a stretch to conclude that democracy and the well-being of all people worldwide are also facing serious challenges in this area. Democracy cannot prevail without the healthy flow of accurate information. One need only look back a number of decades at events such as the Holocaust, the Nanjing Massacre, and the enslavement of Japanese military comfort women to see what can happen to nations with collusive, co-opted, and corrupt news media.

Misinformation, exaggerations, and lies in the mass media are often at the roots of mass violence. In the 1930s and 1940s, the atrocities noted here were all born of misinformation and propaganda. That such fallacies were allowed to circulate was the direct result of complacent citizens and subjects who failed to take decisive action when lies became "news." Today, those same atrocities are being lied about, distorted, and denied anew, in Japan and beyond. Moreover, various terrorist campaigns and major military actions are fueled by the same kind of "news reporting" that led to the atrocities explored here.

It is one thing to say that the future of journalism and democracy is up to each nation, each journalist, each citizen. But it is something entirely different to consider the modern news media in light of the experiences of people like Ok Seon Lee, Madame X, Xia Shujin, Yoshiyuki Kono, Richard Jewell, Daisaku Ikeda, Katsuichi Honda, John Rabe, Harold Timperley, Seiji Yoshida, and the American sex slave "Andrea." The particulars of news reporting may sometimes seem obtuse and abstract, but they translate directly into human experience.

ACKNOWLEDGMENTS

The year was 1864, and it was a capital offense for a Japanese subject to leave the country. But impelled by a burning desire to improve himself, the twenty-one-year-old Shimeta Neesima (or Jo Niijima) risked it all by secreting himself in the hold of a Western brig on its way to China. Eventually, through a combination of pluck and luck, Neesima found his way to Boston, Massachusetts, aboard the apt-named vessel *Wild Rover*. It was skippered by a man from Cape Cod, Massachusetts, by the name of Horace Taylor. *Wild Rover*, in fact, was owned by another Cape Codder, Alpheus Hardy.

Neesima and Hardy quickly developed a close relationship, and the Japanese was soon adopted by the American. Hardy was so taken with Neesima that he sponsored a Western education for him, sending him first to Phillips Andover Academy and later to Amherst College. During this time, Neesima made regular summer sojourns to North Chatham on Cape Cod to visit his friend Captain Taylor. In just a few years, Neesima became the first Japanese in history to receive a college degree in a Western country. He later returned to Japan, where he founded Doshisha University in Kyoto, an important university with a strong tradition of intellectual independence.

Neesima, Hardy, and Taylor created a bridge of friendship and scholarship between Cape Cod and Kyoto that has been crossed yet again in the making of this book, some 140 years after Neesima's brave journey. This time around, however, the Cape Codder is the student of the Kyoto-ite. I am deeply grateful for the assistance of my coauthor, Professor Takesato Watanabe, who has taught at Doshisha University for more than 15 years.

As with all such collaborations, there has been a division of labor, so that while I performed the interviews and actually physically wrote this book, Professor Watanabe served as guide, teacher, advisor, and translator throughout. During the process, he taught me not only about the Japanese news media, but about the news media in general, about democracy, and—most importantly—about being a magnanimous mentor, comrade, and collaborator.

The list of other individuals who deserve acknowledgment is not short. First and foremost are Susan Bouse and Michael Carr, both of whom participated in the editing and made this book far better than it ever could have been without them. Bouse, of Bouse Editorial in Denver, Colorado, also provided invaluable guidance on many publishing and other technical issues. I am deeply appreciative of her wisdom and professionalism. I would also like to acknowledge researcher and translator Andy Nagashima, whose creativity and initiative are matched only by his thoroughness.

Seth A. Reames, of SARJAM Communications (http://www.sarjam.com), performed the majority of the interpreting for interviews and also accomplished a substantial amount of the translating. He is a gifted linguist, equally able to convey ideas as emotions. Nancy Salada is also a one-of-a-kind translator and interpreter who helped in innumerable ways.

Special thanks also goes to authors and professors Kenichi Asano of Doshisha University; Ivan P. Hall, currently at Remin University in Beijing; and Ellis S. Krauss of the University of California at San Diego, each of whom gave inspiring and cogent feedback on many critical details. I am a genuine fan of each of them. Their students are very lucky to have them as teachers. Karel van Wolferen of the University of Amsterdam was also exceptionally hospitable, warmly sharing his formidable reservoir of knowledge. Also, Laurie Anne Freeman of the University of California at Santa Barbara, Bonnie Oh of Georgetown University, and L. Lin Wood, attorney at law, provided superb feedback and other important help.

Special thanks also goes to Ok Cha Soh of Washington Bible College, president of the Washington Coalition for Comfort Women, not only for her continued assistance in this project, but also for her admirable dedication to an important cause.

I would like to thank former publisher Al Regnery and current publisher Marji Ross, of Regnery Publishing, for believing in this book.

Finally, I am honored to acknowledge Anna Mitsu, David Cummings, Mary Powers, Nathan Braund, Betty Gamble, Don Baker III, Don and Judy Baker, Constance Hughes, Bill Steere, Alan Brown, Janette Day, Gary Lamb, Gretchen Putonen, Mark Jasper, Mike Tougias, Ed Simms, Roger Tanner, Dan Welles, Stephen Seay, Vick Martin, and George Waugh for their various contributions and support. Also, and especially, Leslie Steere Gamble, for both her invaluable help and her wonderful example.

—Adam Gamble
Cape Cod, Massachusetts

INFORMAL, UNSCIENTIFIC SURVEY CONDUCTED FOR THIS BOOK

Methodology

- Interviews were conducted July 16, 17, and 18, 2003 by Adam Gamble with a male Japanese/English interpreter.
- Pedestrians were approached and asked to participate in a survey conducted for an American publication.
- Pedestrians were approached in greater Tokyo metropolitan areas of Shinjuku, Tokyo, and Ginza.
- Each question was phrased similarly each time it was asked.

Gender:

21 women, 79 men

Question 1

What age range are you in?

Responses:

AGE RANGE	NUMBER OF RESPONDENTS
18–25	20
26–35	16
36–45	22
46–55	26
56–65	14
more than 65	2

Question 2
What is your occupation?

Responses: Greatly varied, with about 42 different occupations given.

Question 3
What is the difference between the way that Japanese weekly newsmagazines cover the news and the way that Japanese daily national newspapers cover the news?

Responses: As this was an open-ended question, with no choices offered to respondents, this question served mainly as an ice-breaker, and the responses varied tremendously. While a few respondents answered this question at great length, most gave short, vague replies. Some pointed out the frequency of publication (the dailies being daily, the weeklies being weekly), some pointed to the delivery methods (home delivery versus newsstand sales), others said one or the other was more reliable (of these, most felt that the daily papers were more reliable, but a couple respondents thought the magazines were). Many individuals also noted that the magazines offer more-detailed coverage of stories and more opinions, while the daily papers presented shorter, less-detailed articles that are more fact-based. Some were unsure how to describe the differences.

Question 4
Which is more truthful, daily newspapers or weekly newsmagazines?

Responses:
Newspapers: 83
Weekly magazines: 4
They are equally truthful: 10
No answer: 3

Question 5
Do you read weekly newsmagazines?

Responses:
Yes: 54
No: 46

Note: Of 21 women asked, 9 said "yes," they do read weekly newsmagazines. Thus 42.9 percent of women say they read weekly newsmagazines. Of 79 men asked, 45 said yes. Thus 57 percent of men said that they read weekly newsmagazines.

Note: No differentiation was made in the question between those who read weekly newsmagazines occasionally or regularly.

Question 6
Which weekly newsmagazines do you read?

WEEKLY NEWSMAGAZINE	NUMBER OF RESPONDENTS WHO READ
Friday	4
Shukan Bunshun	9
Flash	1
Yomiuri Weekly	2
Shukan Shincho	7
Focus	1
Weekly Asahi	4
Shukan Gendai	6
Aera	3
Shukan Post	4
Weekly Mainichi	1
Newsweek	1
Playboy	1
All	3
Depends	7

Question 7
Do you read the ads for weekly newsmagazines in subways, trains, and/or in newspapers?

Responses:
Yes: 99
No: 1
Note: The one person who replied that he doesn't read shukanshi *advertisements said that the reason is that he has vision problems and can't see them clearly. He added, without being asked, that he probably would read them if he could.*

Question 8
Are you influenced by the ads for weekly newsmagazines?

Responses:
Not influenced: 24
Somewhat influenced: 18
Influenced: 48
Very influenced: 10
Note: By their own admission, 77 percent of those surveyed are influenced by the advertising in the magazines.

Question 9
How trustworthy do you think Japanese weekly newsmagazines are?

Responses:
Very trustworthy: 36
Somewhat trustworthy: 37
Somewhat untrustworthy: 9
Very untrustworthy: 12
Unwilling or unable to quantify: 6

Question 10
What percentage of the information in weekly newsmagazines is true or accurate?

Responses:
Average answer: 46 percent
Note: Three people did not answer the question.

Question 11
What percentage of the information in Japanese daily newspapers is true or accurate?

Responses:
Average answer: 73 percent
Note: This question was only posed to 50 people, of which 4 would not or could not give a figure.

Question 12
How happy are you with the way Japan is governed?

Responses:
Unhappy: 28 (56 percent)
Somewhat unhappy: 12 (24 percent)
Happy: 4 (8 percent)
Very happy: 1 (2 percent)
No answer: 5 (10 percent)

Question 13
How would you rate the degree of your happiness with Japanese governance?

Responses:
Average answer: 38 percent happy
Note: This question was only posed to 50 people, of which 6 would not would not or could not give a figure.

ANATOMY OF *SHUKANSHI*

For those English-language-only readers interested in a deeper look at the genre, this appendix highlights one issue from each of four different Japanese weekly news-magazines. All four magazines come from the same week at the end of October and beginning of November 2003. Those selected are among the best-selling in the industry: *Shukan Post, Shukan Gendai, Shukan Bunshun,* and *Shukan Shincho.* None are owned by newspaper-publishing companies, and they all are generally considered news "alternatives" to the mainstream press and broadcast sector. For *Shukan Post* and *Shukan Gendai,* translations are given of the cover headlines. For *Shukan Bunshun* and *Shukan Shincho,* translations of the tables of contents are provided, since their covers have no headlines.

Of special note in each issue is the extraordinarily wide variety of material presented. Clearly, there is something in each magazine for virtually anyone: news, entertainment, sports, book reviews, comic strips, pictorials, puzzles, gossip, and so on. If they are nothing else, these magazines are intriguing.

It is somewhat unfortunate that the covers of the *Shukan Post* and *Shukan Gendai* are reproduced here in black and white only, for each headline is actually colored with differing bright colors, making the covers truly something to behold. Many of the punctuation marks and font styles have also been dropped in the translations, to avoid undue confusion. Of course, Japanese weekly newsmagazines deal with a tremendous amount of Japan-oriented material and other topics that only regular readers are likely to immediately recognize. As a result, bracketed notes have been added immediately below many of the headlines, both to explain certain details and to comment on them.

Shukanshi headlines present a variety of challenges to translators. Too literal a rendering often yields little more than gobbledygook in English. However, if translators take too much license in making the headlines fit English-language sensibilities, they often lose their original flavor and even much of their original meaning. Indeed, it's no exaggeration to compare the difficulties of translating *shukanshi* headlines with those of translating haiku or other poetry. The headlines may not represent high art, but they are certainly crafted with high artifice. They also often include a considerable amount of ambiguity, so that it is not uncommon for native Japanese speakers to be confused about their meanings.

Another challenge that arose in translating this material has little to do with linguistics but everything to do with ethics. If a single point is made in this book, it is that *shukanshi* headlines are exceedingly unreliable and should never be taken at face value. In rendering the covers and tables of contents, the question must be asked: are the authors of this book contributing to the dissemination of weekly newsmagazine stories? Unfortunately, the answer is, at least to some degree, yes. However, we feel that in order to properly show the real nature of these publications, at least some small portion of the material they put out needs to be presented, if only to properly educate readers. In translating the Japanese into English, the names of many of the individuals connected with dubious assertions, accusations, and insults have been replaced with a set of initials. The prime exception to this is high-ranking government officials.

At the expense of belaboring a point, please do not accept as true any of the information provided by the headlines and tables of contents of these magazines. As the case studies in this book demonstrate, these magazines are parts of an industry that has denied incontrovertible historical atrocities and perpetuated all manner of other lies at the expense not only of their victims but of the public in general. Even the most pedestrian statements should be doubted.

Shukan Post 10/03/03

1. Sixty-Eight Color Pages. Bikini-Clad Mayumi Ono Performs Spread Eagle. Noriko Aota's Knock-Out Body

2. *Shukan Post* 10/31/03 340 yen

3. Bright Naked Bodies, Energetic at Night Too

4. Rhythmic Gymnastics Beauty Spreads Legs on Water

5. Otoha and Sayuri Anzu

6. Ramen Intense Competition Zones
   [Note: Ramen-noodle restaurants are a popular, inexpensive type of eatery in Japan.]

7. Men's Weekend in Asia
   [Note: A serialized color section for entertainment destinations in Asia, primarily for men.]

8. Super Expanded Edition: Sensual Color Pictorials and Gift Giveaways

9. Revealing Koizumi's 3 Trillion Yen of Highway Pork
   [Note: Koizumi is the current prime minister of Japan. See chapter 1 for a discussion of the pork-driven nature of government operations in Japan.]

10. Full Investigative Scoop: President Fujii, Makiko, Muneo in Full Counterattack
    [Note: Haruho Fujii is the former president of the Japan Public Highway Corporation. A member of the Lower House of the Diet and the daughter of late Prime Minister Kakuei Tanaka, Makiko Tanaka resigned from the LDP amidst political fallout concerning hiring practices of secretaries. Formerly an influential Diet member hailing from Hokkaido, Muneo Suzuki has faced charges of bribery.]

11. World's Top Sacrifice Hitter Masahiro Kawai's Confessional! "Good-bye, Giants"
    [Note: The Giants are the Yomuiri Giants professional baseball team.]

12. Lawyer Toru Hashimoto; New Series "Honest Match!"
    [Note: This lawyers is starting a new, serialized opinion section in the magazine beginning with this issue.]

13. Announcer AT's First Admissions about Daytime Drinking and KT
    [Note: AT is an announcer and program host for Fuji TV. Typical of the shukanshi's predilection for hyperbole, the actual interview reveals that her daytime drinking is a glass of champagne for lunch.]

14. Shocks Running through Sony's 30-Year-Olds' Early Retirement Program

15. "Batsu Ichi" Comic-Strip Character "Manager Mitamura" Teaches Readers How to Get Women Off
    [Note: "Batsu Ichi" (translated as "Once Divorced") is an adult comic strip. The lead character of the comic strip is divorcé Manager Mitamura, who possesses great lovemaking skills.]

16. Hitoshi Tanimura: New Sure-Win Methods for New Autumn Pachinko Machine Models
    [Note: Pachinko is a very popular form of machine gambling, somewhat akin to slot machines.]

17. Kazuhisa Kimura: Nightclub-Hopping Heaven

18. Ai Miyazato: 30-Yard Swing Provides Steady Improvement
    [Note: Turning pro while still a high-school student, Ai Miyazato is a women's golf phenomenon in Japan.]

19. Katsuya Nomura Critiques Horiuchi and Ochiai
    [Note: Nomura, Horiuchi, and Ochiai are former professional baseball stars. Horiuchi and Ochiai are managers of the Yomiuri Giants and Chunichi Dragons respectively for the 2004 season. Nomura managed the Hanshin Tigers through the 2002 season.]

20. "Forget-to-Receive-Your-Pension" Trap of the Health and Labor Ministry

Shukan Gendai 11/01/03

1. Insider Exposé: "Dear Bloodless, Heartless Yomiuri Giants Team"
   [Note: The Yomiuri Giants are the winningest, wealthiest Japanese professional baseball team, not dissimilar to the New York Yankees in the United States.]

2. *Shukan Gendai* 11/1/03 Special Price 350 yen

3. Color Section: Autumn Ramen, Round No. 2
   [Note: Ramen-noodle restaurants are a popular, inexpensive type of eatery in Japan. "Round No. 2" indicates that this is the second installment in a series about these restaurants.]

4. Wildly Tasty! 30 Famous Eateries Under the Tracks from East to West
   [Note: "Under the tracks" indicates a common situation of many "no-fuss" Japanese restaurants that are literally housed under train overpasses. "From East to West" indicates that the thirty establishments discussed in the article are from "all across the country."]

5. Super Special Edition: Kyoko Fukada / Son-Ha Yoon / Ayana Sakai
   [Note: These are young female celebrities showcased in a color pictorial section.]

6. Scoop Exposé: Let's Get Our Pensions Back from the Shameless Bureaucrats!

7. Extreme Pictures: Pension-Fund Bureaucrats Enjoy Salacious Entertainment
   [Note: This article was written by Tatsuya Iwase, who was interviewed for this book. Iwase authored The Reason Why Newspapers Are Boring. *Together with photos, the piece details the entertaining of a deputy director of the Social Insurance Agency by senior bureaucrats of the Saitama Social Insurance Bureau. The entertaining consisted of dinner at an exclusive restaurant with two young women "companions" attending. The event was allegedly designed to give thanks for increases in the Saitama bureau's budget. The article accuses the officials of wasting citizens' pension funds and theorizes that the entertainment could be deemed bribery, based on the amounts spent.]*

8. Fujii Bomb: Corrupt "Highway Pork" LDP Diet Members
   [Note: Ousted by the current government led by Prime Minister Koizumi, Haruho Fujii is the former president of the Japan Public Highway Corporation, which has been under intense scrutiny for its lax accounting practices since 2003.]

9. Even Yasuo Tanaka! This is the Kan-Ozawa Cabinet Member List
   [Note: Kan and Ozawa lead the Democratic Party of Japan, the main political opposition at the time of the publication of these magazines against the LDP (Liberal Democratic Party) ruling coalition. Tanaka is the progressive governor of Nagano Prefecture. (See chapter 2 for information on Tanaka's radical stance on Japanese press clubs.) He is famous for winning a recall election initiated by his conservative prefectural assembly members.]

10. Must See: RH's Beautiful Breasts Fondled Galore in Alluring Acting Scene
    [Note: This former teen idol is now an actress in her twenties and has plenty of notoriety.]

11. Reality Right Here Now: Are Your Preparations O.K. for Deposit Lockup?
    [Note: "Reality Right Here Now" is an expression common to shukanshi *headlines.* Deposit Lockup *is the title of a book written by Takahiko Soejima. The article describes a scheme mandated by the government to discontinue and invalidate existing currency notes and thus force the public to exchange them for new notes at banks. However, those individuals who attempt to trade in large sums of the old currency find that some of their money is "locked up" and not available for immediate withdrawal from the banks.]*

12. Color Section, Women Undress: Heroine from "Masked Rider" Show; Chairwoman from Comic Book *Damen's Walker;* Actress Who Played Starring Role Takara Jenne of Takarazuka Revue
    [Note: These are the descriptions of women posing in nude and seminude color photo spreads]

13. Battle of Women: Makiko / "Watermelon Cups" / Ko Yong-Hee / A Baseball Star's Beautiful Wife, Others
    [Note: Makiko Tanaka is a Diet member and the daughter of the former Prime Minister Kakuei Tanaka (see chapter 2 for information on Kakuei Tanaka); "Watermelon Cups" is the derogatory nickname of a regional newscaster; Ko Yong-Hee is one of the wives of Kim Jong Il, leader of North Korea.]

14. Big Breakthrough Exposé Features:

15. Obviously Pathetic Schools / Some Good Schools at Standard Deviation 40
    [Note: Japanese students vie to attend academically prestigious high schools by advancing their percentiles under statistical standard deviation, since the schools rank by percentile ranges. In terms of academics graded by exam papers, students must belong to the requisite percentile or higher for the school they desire to enter.]

16. Fifty Recommended Private High Schools by Standard Deviation

17. Reform School for Bad Kids

18. Naming Names: Failing Schools, Flourishing Schools

19. The Real Inside Situation at Famous Private High Schools

20. Gulf Widens with *Yutori* Education
    [Note: Yutori education refers to an initiative begun over a decade ago in which educators suggested that yutori or "laxness" was needed to counterbalance the long-standing Japanese tendency toward tsumekomi or "cramming" of academic trivia.]

21. Public High Schools Worthy of Attending

Shukan Shincho 10/30/03 © Shinchosha 2003

[VERTICAL TYPE FROM RIGHT]

26   Don't Put on That Good-Guy Face! The Truly Filthy Face Exposed by a
     Construction Vendor: "President Fujii Matter-of-Factly Accepted a Picture
     Worth 10 Million Yen"
     *[Note: Haruho Fujii is the former president of Japan Public Highway Corporation. He is
     accused in this article of accepting valuable artwork as a bribe. The article includes a pho-
     tograph of Fujii smiling and is typical of the intensely aggressive and negative tone of
     shukanshi.]*

51   Exposé of a Serving Postmaster: Even with All of These Problems, the Spe-
     cial Post Offices Are Not Going to be Eliminated!
     *[Note: This article is very critical of the postal system and is backing a proposal to priva-
     tize it.]*

46   Secrets of Women in the Celebrity World
     [Note: This article is a standard Shukan Shincho *negative attack piece.]*

     KS: Refuses Popular Drama Casting for Unheard-of Reasons

     HY: Turned into an Advertising Beacon of the Soka Gakkai
     *[Note: This piece criticizes HY for her membership in a Buddhist organization. See chap-
     ter 6 for more information on the Soka Gakkai.]*

     MN: Such a Beautiful Woman, But with Terrible Drinking Habits

     RH: The Reason She Quit University Was That She Played Around with Boys
     *[Note: This article accuses RH of having dropped out of university as the result of being
     a "party girl."]*

     AM: Definitely a Number-One Skinflint

54   People Whose Lives Were Thrown into Chaos when Muneo Suzuki Abandoned His Election Run
[Note: Suzuki was a Diet member from a district in Kushiro, Hokkaido, and has been arrested and accused of pocketing public funds in a political scandal.]

148 Special Reading: 60 Years Since 100,000 Students Were Sent off to War
[Note: This article covers a reunion of former World War II Japanese soldiers. It focuses on the more sensational remembrances of the participants, including their recollections of kamikaze and other suicide units. While the piece does not explicitly support Japanese World War II war aims, it also notably avoids the topic of Japanese war aggression or of responsibility for the war.]

145 Curse of Hoshino Befalls Hanshin Tigers
[Note: As general manager, Sen'ichi Hoshino led the Hanshin Tigers pro baseball team to win the league pennant in 2003. Citing health reasons, Hoshino subsequently retired.]

42   Diary of Crimes Found at the Lair of the Sniper Who Shot Police Agency Director General Kunimatsu
[Note: Takaji Kunimatsu was the top law-enforcement officer of Japan when he was shot leaving his condominium to go to work on March 30, 1995.]

[HORIZONTAL TYPE; LEFT SIDE]

32   Tempo

[L] The Two-Faced Nature of the Government Exposed by SDF Dispatch to Iraq
[Note: SDF is an abbreviation for Self Defense Forces, essentially the Japanese military.]

[B] LDP or DPJ? Whose Situation Is Improving?
[Note: LDP is the Liberal Democratic Party; DPJ is the Democratic Party of Japan. The two were vying for power at the time these magazines were published.]

[I] Man Bought Masumi Hayashi Site at Devil's Price of 6.66 Million Yen
[Note: Hayashi has been convicted of murdering people in her community by introducing arsenic into a stewed curry shared at a neighborhood event. Her home burned down, but the lot has sold to the man noted in this article. Hayashi is currently appealing her conviction.]

[Sp] Koji Uehara Stalked by the Yankees
[Note: Uehara is a star baseball player in Japan who is being courted by the New York Yankees, according to the article.]

[S] Improbable Reasons for Movement to Maintain Nikkatsu Studio

[A] Profitability of Late-Night Art Museum at Roppongi Hills

[Sc] Why the Emperor's Prostate Gland Numbers Rose

136 Tempo [Part Two]

[P] *Kyogen* Teruko Nagaoka (Fifty-First Hiroshi Kikuchi Award, Actress), Others
*[Note: This award is named after Hiroshi Kikuchi, founder and first president of
Bungeishunju Ltd. He was a staunch supporter of the Japanese Second World War militarists. In the 1930s and 1940s, he helped to organize the so-called Pen Corps, a team
of propagandists and co-opted journalists under the auspices of a Japanese military-
intelligence unit.]*

[Bo] Tatsuro Dekune Reviewing the Book *Natsuhiko no Kageboshi*

[TV] Viewer Ratings of *Shiroi Kyotou* Laugh Off Drama Woes

[To] Real-Estate Appraisers' Political Organization Nixed

58   The World Incident
[Note: Section on sensational current events from around the world.]

NOVEL SERIALS

110	*Nichiginken 11*	Main Koda
94	*Sakura Densetsu 41*	Rei Nakanishi
82	*Second Virgin 60*	Yoshinaga Fujita
117	*Kuroi Hokokusho*	Kenji Fujii

REGULAR COLUMNS AND ESSAYS

60	Super Retirement Methods 18	Yukio Noguchi
64	My Weekly Food Diary 306	Yuriko Ishida
68	Hisaya Morishige's Testaments 73	Teruhiko Kuze
126	Kazuya Fukuda's Fighting Criticism 74	Kazuya Fukuda
128	My Golf 41	Isao Aoki
154	Japan Renaissance 90	Yoshiko Sakurai
70	Oh! Edo Story 18	Takehiko Noguchi
72	Yoshizumi Ishihara's Dressing-Room Window 25	Yoshizumi Ishihara

*[Note: Yoshizumi Ishihara is the second son of Shitaro Ishihara, the maverick, nationalist
governor of Tokyo.]*

81	Life Advice: Men Worry Too 41	Jakucho Setouchi
109	Smart Dying 26	Masako Ikeda
125	Nonwatcher's Guide to TV Gossip 74	Misao Hayashi
130	Secret Flower Garden 74	Mihoko Yamada
132	Blaaah Mornings, Romantic Nights 74	Yuka Saitoh
136	Freestyle Odd Views 74	Masayuki Takayama

[REGULAR SMALL FEATURES]

PHOTO-SPREAD SERIES

Shukan Bunshun 10/30/03 © 2003

[VERTICAL TYPE FROM RIGHT TO LEFT; UPPER SECTION]

26   Exclusive Confessions, Installment 2!

Full Counteroffensive Exposé, All Real Names

Public Highway Corporation President Haruho Fujii

Mikio Aoki, Prime Minister Koizumi, Secretary Iijima
[Note: Aoki is a former chief cabinet secretary, Secretary Iijima is Koizumi's first secretary.]

The Inside Story of Politicians' Intervention in Executive Policy

Interview Write-Up by Takahide Kaga

138 House of Commons Election Predictions: Elected vs. Lost, Right before General Elections

Complete Data on Election Districts and Proportional Districts, Full Effort Across 20 Pages
[Note: This is an extensive and impressive article outlining predictions for an upcoming Lower House Diet election. The analysis presented by the author is most engaging.]

Democratic Party of Japan Leaps Forward, Government and Opposition Parties Neck and Neck, Potential for Change in Government

The Theory Is Floated That Koizumi Will Be Held Responsible if the LDP Gets 215 Seats or Less
[Note: Koizumi is the prime minister of Japan.]

Democrats Near 200 Seats

LDP Big Fish in Tough Battles:

Taku Yamazaki, Kenzo Muraoka, Hideyuki Aizawa, Sei'ichi Ota

Kunio Hatoyama Fiercely Catching up with Naoto Kan
[Note: Fighting for a seat in Tokyo District 18, incumbent Hatoyama of the LDP, and Kan, president of the Democratic Party of Japan, were in a fierce election war.]

Kaifu and Takako Doi also on Election Threshold
[Note: Kaifu is a former prime minister, and Takako Doi is the former president of the Socialist Party.]

Takami Eto, Masaharu Nakayama, Naoto Kan: Junior Politicians All Failing
[Note: According to the article Eto, Nakayama, and Kan are nurturing their next generation of successors from within their own families.]

Mini Spread for Malcontents

38 TV Station with the Worst Ethics Taking Sides with Murderous Teacher
[Note: Over 500 people are apparently suing this teacher, who reportedly abused a particular pupil.]

39 More Celebrities Emerging from Nightclubs: YS, KI, SK

41 Daiwa Bank NY Branch Colossal Loss Case; Superior of Formerly Imprisoned Ryo Inokuchi is Promoted
[Note: Iguchi worked for Daiwa Bank in New York in the 1990s and covered up trading losses amounting to $1.1 billion. He was criminally charged and sentenced to prison.]

41 Secretary General's Car-Grabbing Case: Taku Yamazaki Throws His Weight Around and Shinzo Abe Finds It Tough to Stand Up against Him
[Note: According to the article, Yamazaki, former secretary general of the LDP, refused to give up his use of a car provisioned for the post of secretary general when he lost the position to Abe, the new secretary general. Now Abe does not have the car that he is supposed to receive as a benefit of being secretary general.]

158 Public Officials' Lives Are Too Juicy

One Trillion Yen Worth of Consumption Tax Disappears into Faked Work-time

161 Game-Brain Research to Prevent Children from Becoming Criminals, by Atsuko Kusanagi

Video-Game Ratings in the U.S. Stricter than in Japan

THIS WEEK
[Section on sensational, international current events]

[Note: The article raises questions about a recent North Korean defector.]

Movies: First-Place Movie Holding Back *Zatoichi*
[Note: Zatoichi is a classic story about a blind samurai with amazing swordsmanship. Kitano Takeshi directed and starred in this recent feature-length movie.]

New Products: Fashionable Assembly Eyeglasses

Health: Sports Doctor Association

Opinion on Articles Discussing Newspaper Mistrust and Economics

PHOTO SPREADS

Rich Colored Beauty Illustrated   Chiaki Kuriyama

Special Project: Fun Place Names, Can You Read Them?

Special Project: "Crimson Foliage" Kyoto, Photography by Katsuhiko Mizuno

[Note: Matsui is Japan's baseball hero who plays for the New York Yankees.]

Comprehensive Feature: Sudden Resignation of GM Hoshino
[Note: An ace pitcher in his playing days, Hoshino led the often-last-place Hanshin Tigers pro baseball team to win the league pennant in 2003.]

[Note: Kuman is the owner of the Hanshin Tigers and chairman of the Hanshin Group.]

[Note: Nomura was the manager of the Hanshin Tigers immediately prior to Hoshino.]

[Note: Tanka is a specialized Japanese style of poetry, made up of thirty-one syllables. The more widely known style of Haiku is seventeen syllables.]

[Note: Reprints of erotic or lurid letters sent in by readers to women's magazines.]

[LOWER COLUMN OF VERTICAL TYPE]

82	Shinjuku Red Cape	Makoto Shiina	[column]
90	No Makeup Spirit	Shigeru Muroi	[column]
102	Thank you, But	Toshio Takashima	[column]
68	The Answerer	Kumiko Takeuchi	[column]
78	Famous Orators	Takashi Saitoh	[column]
77	Oranku no Ike	Ichiriki Yamamoto	[column]
81	Shopping Queen	Usagi Nakamura	[column]
101	A Windfall Philosophy	Kenji Tsuchiya	[column]
58	Life Starts at 51	Nobuhiko Kobayashi	[column]
118	Wild Rose	Mariko Hayashi	[novel]
104	Operation Rose Dust	Harutoshi Fukui	[novel]
136	Work to Help People	Shoko Egawa	[column]
133	Come On! Yoshikatsu	Yoshikatsu Kawaguchi	[column]
61	MLB Fan Column	Kaechoong Lee	[column]
92	Sen-chan's Floating and Sinking	Manabu Senzaki	[column]
72	Hits to Consider	Haruo Chikada	[pop music]
71	Horii Investigations	Ken'ichiro Horii	[column]
124	Biography of a House	Yasushi Akimoto	[column]
62	Interview with Mariko Koike	Sawako Agawa	[interview]
134	News Archaeology	Naoki Inose	[analysis]

BUNSHUN LIBRARY
[book reviews and commentary]

47	Toshimitsu Kishi	*Kurofune*
	Ken Sakamura	*Senso no Kagaku*
	Kazuhiro Fujiwara	*Sembetsu Shugi wo Koete*
	Zhan Jing	My Reading Diary
	Tsubasa Yamaguchi	Sixty Minutes with the Writer
	Yuzo Tsubouchi	Target Paperbacks
	Tetsuya Miyazaki	New Century Learning Class
	Fumio Yamaguchi	Can I be of Assistance?
	Fumiro Kayama	Mystery Reviews

THIS WEEK'S NEW RELEASES

THINGS TO SEE AND LISTEN TO

COMICS

APPENDIX C

Faxed letter of January 19, 1995, from Rabbi Abraham Cooper, associate dean of the Simon Wiesenthal Center, to Ferdinand Piech, chairman of Volkswagen. Cooper sent similar letters to the heads of a number of corporate advertisers in *Marco Polo*.

January 19, 1995

Ferdinand Piech
Chairman
VOLKSWAGEN
Berliner Ring 2
38436 Wolfsburg

VIA FAX: (495) 361 92 8282

Dear Mr. Piech:

VOLKSWAGEN ran an advertisement in the February 1995 issue of the Japanese magazine <u>Marco Polo</u>. Please be advised that the editors of this publication chose to commemorate the 50th anniversary of the liberation of Auschwitz by running a ten-page story in this issue (enclosed) which denies any Jews were gassed there. I enclose also a translation of their magazine editorial lead-in and the entire Japanese text.

On behalf of the 385,000 constituent families of the Simon Wiesenthal Center, on behalf of the Holocaust survivors everywhere and in the name of historic truth and human decency, I urge VOLKSWAGEN to immediately decide to stop all future advertising in <u>Marco Polo</u> a publication which sadly has chosen the path of hate mongering.

Please advise us of your company's decision as soon as possible.

Sincerely,

Rabbi Abraham Cooper
Associate Dean

RAC:sg

cc: Simon Wiesenthal

APPENDIX D

Letter of October 25, 2001, from Masao Asano, director, Public Relations Department, Asahi National Broadcasting Co., Ltd., to Rabbi Cooper, associate dean of the Simon Wiesenthal Center.

October 25, 2001

Rabbi Abraham Cooper
Associate Dean, Simon Wiesenthal Center
1399 South Roxbury Drive
Los Angeles, California 90035-4709

Dear Rabbi Cooper,

Thank you for your letter of October 22nd, 2001. We have been discussing the matter with the officials at the Israeli Embassy in Tokyo and we have decided to take the following measures regarding the situation:

**On measures to be taken by TV Asahi
regarding Mr. Kawamura's comments made in "Super Morning"**

The comments made by the commentator, Kouji Kawamura, in TV Asahi's morning show "Super Morning" on October 15th and 17th 2001 have been pointed out as being incorrect by the Israeli Embassy in Japan, the Simon Wiesenthal Center and the Committee Against Anti-Semitism in Japan.

There is no doubt that the program nor Kawamura himself did not have a slightest anti-Semitic intention. However, it is extremely regrettable that his comments had caused misunderstandings among our viewers and the relevant parties, and we consider it necessary for us to correct such misunderstandings.

Based on the above consideration, we will take specific measures within the program to seek understanding of the situation from as many people as possible.

Proposed Outline of the morning show; "Super Morning":

- The Program   "Super Morning"
- Duration of the corner   approximately 5 minutes
- Time and Date of Broadcast   As soon as our preparations for interviews, filming, etc. are ready.
- Format   Studio live and pre-recorded interviews

1-1-1 Roppongi, Minato-ku Tokyo 106-8001, Japan Tel: 81-3-3587-5470, Fax: 81-3-3505-3541

TV Asahi
Asahi National Broadcasting Co.,Ltd.

● Structure

1) Presentation of Mr. Kawamura's comment
2) Protests made against the comment
3) Regret expressed by Mr. Kawamura
4) Pre-recorded comment by Ambassador Yitzhak Lior, the Israeli Ambassador to Japan
5) Commentary made by Professor Gerald Curtis, Columbia University

We hope you would find the above to be an appropriate measure to solve the problem of misunderstandings.

Sincerely yours

Masao Asano

Masao Asano
Director
Public Relations Department
Asahi National Broadcasting Co.,Ltd.

cc. : The Committee Against Anti-Semitism in Japan
The Israeli Embassy in Japan

1-1-1 Roppongi, Minato-ku Tokyo 106-8001, Japan Tel:81-3-3587-5470, Fax:81-3-3505-3541

This is the summation section of the Tokyo District Court Judgment of May 30, 2000, written by the presiding judge, Shintaro Kato in *Nobuhira v. Ikeda*, Tokyo District Court Civil Section 28, Heisei 8 (Wa) ["Heisei 8" is the emperor's calendar year 8, which is 1996] Number 10485 Damage Compensation Claims Case, Judgment of First Instance. The judgment was upheld by the Tokyo High Court and the Supreme Court of Japan.

Summation [Starting on page 159 of the judgment]

1. The plaintiffs are senior citizens who have dropped out of a religious organization and have no authoritative power whatsoever, while the defendant is the honorary chairman of a prominent religious organization of this nation that guides a large number of believers.

Also, the detail of the complaint, if true, is a wretched event with the highest of shame for Nobuko, who is a woman. This type of complaint is made only when the plaintiff has first made a significant amount of resolve and includes cases where the weak can often score a point against the powerful and where the court must listen. Consequently, the court has considered it its duty to elucidate the facts in this case, since the plaintiff's claims were subject to adjudication, even though Nobuko's claims were legally hindered by the statute of limitation.

2. It goes without saying that everyone, even those with no social power, has equal recourse to the procedures of civil litigation and that nobody—no matter how endowed with wealth and empowered with title and authority—can avoid being questioned in a court open to the public if it is necessary for the elucidation of facts in the procedures of litigation. The court has kept these obvious principles in mind, envisioning the possibility of directly questioning, under certain circumstances, the plaintiff, witnesses, and the defendant. Further, the court has heard the case by reminding itself that the confidence in civil procedure could be damaged, and the authority of civil procedure lost, if facts exist that are not fully examined. The court has thus listened intently and with an open mind to the plaintiff's complaint and allegations, as well as to the refutations of the defendant, and has carefully examined the record by applying diligent study to all proofs and rebuttals submitted.

3. To the extent of the evidence viewed in this case, the conclusion is as previously indicated. In advancing this case under the explanation that the factual foundation is severely lacking in each incident of this case, it may be inevitably assumed that the plaintiffs repeatedly performed the prohibited acts of lending and borrowing money between Soka Gakkai members by using their positions as senior leaders in that organization; that they became disgruntled with the organization because of their dismissals from their leadership positions within the Soka Gakkai, which resulted from their having caused troubles for the members; that they demanded but failed to obtain the return of cemetery-plot monies after leaving the Soka Gakkai, and that they thus repeatedly made extortion-like phone calls to the Soka Gakkai headquarters, which still failed to produce any results; and that, as revenge, they publicly trumpeted the written narrative of Nobuko through the mass media; and that, as an extension to the foregoing, they filed the complaints in this case for the purpose of imposing tangible and intangible losses to the defendant within and outside of the lawsuit.

Hence, the filing of this suit does not sincerely aim to fulfill any substantive rights of the plaintiff or to resolve the lawsuit, and instead the complaint in this case was made with the purpose of imposing on the defendant the burden of responding to the suit and of other losses. Moreover, the complaints alleged by the plaintiff lack factual foundation and fall short of the requirement for protection. The complaint in this case, therefore, must be recognized as a legal action that severely lacks relevance with respect to the intentions and purposes of the civil litigation system and is contrary to conduct in good faith and trust. Consequently, the complaint in this case can be considered unlawful, because it abuses the right of legal action. Continuing the hearing of this case is not only cruel to the defendant, but may potentially result in the Court contrarily siding with the wrongful undertakings of the plaintiff. Thus, terminating the hearing of this lawsuit at this time is reasonable.

4. Conclusion

As discussed above, the present claim is dismissed as unlawful, because it abuses the right of legal action. The ruling shall stand according to the text.

Notes

Introduction

1. Karel van Wolferen, *The Enigma of Japanese Power: People and Politics in a Stateless Nation* (New York: Alfred A. Knopf, 1990), p. 231.
2. Under the authority of SCAP, the Supreme Command for Allied Powers.
3. United Nations Population Division, as of the year 2003, Japan, in "Table 1. Total Population by Sex and Sex Ratio, by Country, 2003," http://www.un.org/esa/population/publications/wpp2002/wpp2002annextables.PDF. In this table, the total population of Japan is listed as 127,654,000.
4. "Mega Cities," *National Geographic*, November 2002, pp. 76–77.

Chapter One

1. Herbert P. Bix, *Hirohito and the Making of Modern Japan* (New York: Perennial, 2000), pp. 578–579.
2. Chalmers Johnson, *Japan: Who Governs?: The Rise of the Developmental State* (New York: W. W. Norton, 1995), p. 319.
3. Alex Kerr, interview with Adam Gamble, June 16, 2003, Tokyo.
4. Kenichi Asano, interview with Adam Gamble, November 9–10, 2002, Boston and Yarmouth Port, MA.
5. Katsuichi Honda, interview with Adam Gamble, July 5, 2002, Tokyo.
6. Karel van Wolferen, *Naze Nihonjin wa Nihon o Aise nai no ka: Kono Fuko na Kuni no Yukue* [Why Can't the Japanese Love Japan], trans. Susumu Ohara (Tokyo: Mainichi Shimbunsha, 1988); Karel van Wolferen, *Nihon to Iu Kuni o Anata no Mono ni Suru Tameni* [Can Japanese Control Their Own Fate?], trans. Kiyomi Fujii (Tokyo: Kadokawa Shoten, 2001).
7. Karel van Wolferen, "Bourgeoisie—The Missing Element in Japanese Political Culture" (Unpublished English-language manuscript for *Ikare Nihon no Churyu Kaikyu*, trans. Chikara Suzuki [Tokyo: Mainichi Shimbunsha, 1999]).
8. Bruce S. Feiler, *Learning to Bow: Inside the Heart of Japan* (Boston: Houghton Mifflin, 1990), p. 237.
9. Alex Kerr, *Dogs and Demons: Tales from the Dark Side of Japan* (New York: Hill and Wang, 2001), p. 5.
10. See appendix A for details about this survey.
11. "*Mainichi Shimbun* Survey," *Mainichi Shimbun*, January 4, 2001.
12. "Poll: 82% of Voters Distrust Politicians, Politics," *Daily Yomiuri* (English edition), July 14, 2002.
13. Richard Katz, *Japan: The System That Soured: The Rise and Fall of the Japanese Economic Miracle* (Armonk, NY: M. E. Sharpe, 1998), p. 18.
14. Patrick Smith, *Japan: A Reinterpretation* (New York: Pantheon Books, 1997), p. 26.
15. Prime Minister Koizumi visited Yasukuni on New Year's Day, 2004.

C H A P T E R O N E, CONTINUED

16. Ivan P. Hall, *Bamboozled!: How America Loses the Intellectual Game with Japan and Its Implications for Our Future in Asia* (Armonk, NY: M. E. Sharpe, 2002), p. 67.

17. William Safire, "Remember 'Japan, Inc.'" *New York Times*, August 9, 1976, p. 17.

18. J. Mark Ramseyer and Frances McCall Rosenbluth, *Japan's Political Marketplace* (Cambridge, MA: Harvard University Press, 1993), p. 124.

19. Kerr, *Dogs and Demons*, p. 17.

20. Ibid., p. 19.

21. Ramseyer and Rosenbluth, *Japan's Political Marketplace*, p. 9.

22. John W. Dower, *Embracing Defeat: Japan in the Wake of World War II* (New York: W. W. Norton / The New Press, 1999).

23. Smith, *Japan: A Reinterpretation*, p. 28.

24. Tim Weiner, Stephen Engelberg, and James Sterngold, "C.I.A. Spent Millions to Support Japanese Right in 50's and 60's," *New York Times*, October 9, 1994, pp. 1, 14.

25. Smith, *Japan: A Reinterpretation*, pp. 16–17.

26. These views are expressed by Asano in an e-mail exchange with Adam Gamble, May 2, 2003.

27. In Norimitsu Onishi, "For Japan's Insider-Turned-Rebel, Decade-Old Revolution Is Still a Work in Progress," *New York Times*, January 18, 2004.

28. Ichiro Kamoshita, interview with Adam Gamble, July 3, 2002, Tokyo.

29. Walter Mondale, telephone interview with Adam Gamble, June 6, 2003, coauthor in Dennis, MA, interviewee in Minneapolis, MN.

30. Chalmers Johnson, *Japan: Who Governs?*, p. 13.

31. Ramseyer and Rosenbluth, *Japan's Political Marketplace*, p. 29.

32. Karel van Wolferen, *The Enigma of Japanese Power: People and Politics in a Stateless Nation* (New York: Alfred A. Knopf, 1990), p. 5.

33. Ibid.

34. John Owen Haley, *Authority without Power: Law and the Japanese Paradox* (New York: Oxford University Press, 1991), p. 14.

35. In the case of Supreme Court justices, the LDP has a record of making appointments at the very end of judges' careers, when they are in their mid-sixties, close to the mandatory retirement age of seventy. Thus, even if a Supreme Court justice were to begin acting contrary to the LDP's desires, the threat would only be short-lived.

36. Ramseyer and Rosenbluth, *Japan's Political Marketplace*, p. 158.

37. Ibid., p. 150. The authors note that "in 1989 Japanese citizens filed about 650,000 civil suits in the national district courts and 1,150,000 in national summary courts (there are no prefectural or municipal court systems). By contrast, in district courts they filed only 1,100 administrative suits, and in summary courts only 250 (Saiko, 1989, pp. 6–9)."

38. According to Alex Kerr, 95 percent of all cases brought against the government by Japanese citizens are lost. Kerr, *Dogs and Demons*, p. 57.

39. The police may keep a suspect for two days before notifying the prosecutors, who are then given one day to ask a judge for authorization for another ten days' detention, which can then be extended for a second ten-day detention.

40. Law scholars and others such as John Owen Haley (see Haley's book *Authority without Power*) have come to the defense of Japanese law enforcement's obsession with confessions, arguing that the system is on the whole notably lenient and generally successful in keeping order and in rehabilitating rather than punishing criminal defendants. However, one must wonder just how many innocent Japanese have suffered under the vast discretion of Japanese law-enforcement officers. The Japanese may be successful at using noncodified methodologies for achieving a relatively orderly society, but at what cost?

41. Murray Sayle, "Letter from Japan: Poison, Why a Puzzling Village Crime Has Unnerved a Nation," *New Yorker*, November 22, 1999.

42. "Two Paths to Justice," *Japan Times*, November 9, 2003.

43. Muhammad was arrested on October 24, 2002, and was sentenced to death just sixteen-and-one-half months later on March 9, 2004. Asahara was arrested on May 16, 1995, and sentenced to death on February 27, 2004, eight years and about nine-and-one-half months later.

44. Johnson, *Japan: Who Governs?*, p. 97.

45. Katz, *Japan: The System That Soured*, p. 17.

46. Karel van Wolferen, interview with Adam Gamble, July 20–21, 2002, near Amsterdam.

47. Katz, *The System That Soured*, p. 4.

48. Kerr, *Dogs and Demons*, p. 209.

49. Ibid., p. 354.

50. In Howard W. French, "Tired of News That Rocks the Boat? Visit Japan." *New York Times* News Service, February 16, 2000.

51. Jon Carter Covell and Alan Covell, *Japan's Hidden History: Korean Impact on Japanese Culture* (Elizabeth, NJ: Hollym International, 1984), dust-jacket flap.

52. "Religious Groups Condemn Mori's 'Divine Nation' Remark," *Japan Times*, Friday, May 18, 2000.

53. Karel van Wolferen, *The Enigma of Japanese Power: People and Politics in a Stateless Nation* (New York: Alfred A. Knopf, 1990), p. 14.

54. Feiler, *Learning to Bow*, p. 12.

55. Ruth Benedict, *The Chrysanthemum and the Sword: Patterns of Japanese Culture* (Boston: Houghton Mifflin, 1946).

56. Bix, *Hirohito and the Making of Modern Japan*, pp. 578–579.

CHAPTER TWO

1. Tatsuya Iwase, interview with Adam Gamble, December 19, 2002, Tokyo.

2. The top ten U.S. circulations as of March 2003 are by *USA Today* (2,162,454), *Wall Street Journal* (1,820,600), *New York Times* (1,130,740), *Los Angeles Times* (1,014,044), *Washington Post* (796,367), *New York Daily News* (737,030), *Chicago Tribune* (693,659), *New York Post* (620,080), *Newsday* (579,351), and *Houston Chronicle* (548,508). Numbers reflect Monday through Friday circulations except as follows: *Chicago Tribune* (Wednesday through Friday); *Los Angeles Times* (Thursday through Saturday). Audit Bureau of Circulations, FAS-FAX, March 2003.

3. Monthly average circulation from January to June 2002. Circulation figure is that reported to NSK (Nihon Shimbun Kyokai or Japan Newspaper Publishers and Editors Association) by *Yomiuri* and confirmed by NSK to be close to that published in the monthly "ABC Report" by the Japan Audit Bureau of Circulations, http://www.pressnet.or.jp/english/index.htm.

4. According to the World Association of Newspapers, 2003 (at http://www.wan-press.org/article2825.html), they are among the top ten. However, figures given include circulation figures for both the morning and the evening editions of Japan's newspapers. If one simply counts the circulation figures for the morning editions of Japan's papers, the largest four are still among the top ten in the world, with the *Sankei Shimbun* only among the top twenty largest in the world.

5. The precise figure is 1.09 newspapers per day as of 2002. See NSK Web site at http://www.pressnet.or.jp/english/data_e/01circulation.htm.

6. "The Japanese and Television, 2000," a survey conducted by Nihon Hoso Kyokai (NHK) and presented in a paper by Shuichi Kamimura, Chiho Ikoma, and Sachiko Nakano, "The Japanese and Television, 2000—The Current State of TV Viewing," Japan Media Review, Summer 2000, http://www.nhk.or.jp/bunken/bcri-fr/h13-f1.html.

CHAPTER TWO, CONTINUED

7. Susan J. Pharr and Ellis S. Krauss, eds., *Media and Politics in Japan* (Honolulu: University of Hawai'i Press, 1996), p. 5.

8. "Yomiuri Shimbun sha Yoron Chosa" ["Yomiuri-Shimbunsha Public Opinion Poll"], *Yomiuri Shimbun*, November 1, 2000, p. 36.

9. Howard W. French, "Tired of News That Rocks the Boat? Visit Japan," *New York Times* News Service, February 16, 2000.

10. Alex Kerr, interview with Adam Gamble, June 16, 2003, Tokyo.

11. In Laurie Anne Freeman, *Closing the Shop: Information Cartels and Japan's Mass Media* (Princeton, NJ: Princeton University Press, 2000), p. 102.

12. Katsuichi Honda, interview with Adam Gamble, July 5, 2002, Tokyo.

13. Tom Reid, Lecture on the topic of the role of media in democracy (Soka Gakkai International Lecture Series, March 31, 1997).

14. Tatsuya Iwase, *Shimbum ga omoshiroku nai ri yuu* [The Reason Why Newspapers Are Boring] (Tokyo: Kodan-sha, 2001).

15. In French, "Tired of News That Rocks the Boat? Visit Japan."

16. Gregory J. Kasza, *The State and the Mass Media in Japan, 1918–1945* (Berkeley and Los Angeles: University of California Press, 1988), p. 285.

17. John W. Dower, *Embracing Defeat: Japan in the Wake of World War II* (New York: W. W. Norton / New Press, 1999). See chapter 14, "Censored Democracy: Policing the New Taboos."

18. Ibid., p. 439.

19. Ibid., pp. 439–440.

20. Monthly average circulation from January to June 2002. Circulation figures are those reported to NSK by member newspapers. All those given are reported by NSK have been confirmed by the relevant monthly "ABC Report" of the Japan Audit Bureau of Circulations, http://www.pressnet.or.jp/english/index.htm.

21. Ben H. Bagdikian, *The Media Monopoly*, 6th ed. (Boston: Beacon Press, 2000), p. x.

22. Ibid., pp. xii–xiii.

23. Hajime Kitamura, interview with Adam Gamble, April 2, 2003, Tokyo.

24. *The Guardian Media Guide*, published by the *Guardian* newspaper, says that the BBC receives most of its income from license fees—£2.37 billion in 2000–2001. The remainder comes from BBC World Wide (£96 million) and the Foreign Office grant for the World Service (£205 million). Steve Peak and Paul Fisher, eds. *The Guardian Media Guide* (London: Guardian, 2001), p. 158.

25. Ellis S. Krauss, *Broadcasting Politics in Japan: NHK and Television News* (Ithaca: Cornell University Press, 2000), p. 241.

26. Karel van Wolferen, "Bourgeoisie—The Missing Element in Japanese Political Culture" (unpublished English-language manuscript for *Ikare Nihon no Churyu Kaikyu,* trans. Chikara Suzuki [Tokyo: Mainichi Shimbunsha, 1999]).

27. William De Lange, *A History of Japanese Journalism: Japan's Press Club as the Last Obstacle to a Mature Press* (Richmond, VA: Japan Library, 1997).

28. Ivan P. Hall, *Cartels of the Mind: Japan's Intellectual Closed Shop* (New York: W. W. Norton, 1998).

29. Kyodo News, "Nothing to Hide? Press Clubs Stymie Free Trade in Information: EU," *Japan Times*, November 7, 2002.

30. Kyodo News, "EU Again Calls for End to Press Clubs," *Japan Times*, December 12, 2003.

31. Iwase, interview with AG.

32. Ken Takeuchi, interview with Adam Gamble, May 19, 2002, Tokyo.

33. In Kenichi Asano, "Japanese Self-Imposed 'Kisha-Club' System Decays Investigative Journalism" (paper presented at Preconference of International Communication Association, Workshop 6, Democracy and Media in East Asia, Yonsei University, Seoul, Republic of Korea, July 14, 2002).

34. Ibid.

35. Ivan P. Hall, telephone interview with Adam Gamble, June 8, 2003, coauthor in Dennis, MA, interviewee in Honolulu, HI.

36. Kengo Tanaka, interview with Adam Gamble, December 19, 2002, Tokyo.

37. Takeuchi, interview with AG.

38. Maggie Farley, "Japan's Press and the Politics of Scandal," in *Media and Politics in Japan,* eds. Susan J. Pharr and Ellis S. Krauss, pp. 133–163 (Honolulu: University of Hawai'i Press, 1996), p. 145.

39. Terry MacDougall, "The Lockheed Scandal and the High Costs of Politics in Japan," in *The Politics of Scandal: Power and Process in Liberal Democracies,* ed. Andrei S. Markovits and Mark Silverstein (New York: Holmes and Meier, 1998), p. 223.

40. De Lange, *A History of Japanese Journalism,* p. xiv.

41. Freeman, *Closing the Shop,* p. 115.

42. Brian Covert, e-mail to Adam Gamble (in response to list of questions sent to interviewee), December 26, 2002.

43. This figure comes from Tatsuya Iwase, who identified and sent questionnaires to 800 clubs in the research for his book *Shimbum ga omoshiroku nai ri yuu* [The Reason Why Newspapers Are Boring].

44. Freeman, *Closing the Shop,* p. 82.

45. Asano, "Japanese Self-Imposed 'Kisha-Club' System Decays Investigative Journalism."

46. Freeman, *Closing the Shop,* p. 82.

47. While Iwase sent questionnaires to institutions that are technically "private" such as major unions, power companies, and economic federations, he kept his focus on governmental organizations and nongovernmental organizations that have a public-service orientation. Thus, he did not send to purely private companies such as Toyota, etc.

48. This does not include 7 replies Iwase received after having analyzed the data from the first 529 replies.

49. Asano, "Japanese Self-Imposed 'Kisha-Club' System Decays Investigative Journalism."

50. Kitamura, interview with AG.

51. Anne Garrels, *Naked in Baghdad: The Iraq War as Seen by NPR's Correspondent* (New York: Farrar, Straus and Giroux, 2003), pp. 16–17.

52. Reid's audio diary was broadcast during "Democracy in Iraq," *On Point,* NPR, March 19, 2004.

53. In Freeman, *Closing the Shop,* p. 114.

54. Leon V. Sigal, *Reporters and Officials: The Organization and Politics of Newsmaking* (Lexington, MA: D. C. Heath, 1973), p. 124, table 6.6.

55. Freeman, *Closing the Shop,* p. 63, where Freeman makes reference to Toshio Hara, "Happyo jaa-narizumu jidai e no teiko" ["Resisting Announcement Journalism"], *Shimbun Kenkyu,* December 1979, p. 21.

56. Bob Garfield, telephone interview with Adam Gamble, June 12, 2002, coauthor in Yarmouth Port, MA, interviewee in New York, NY.

57. Kenichi Asano, interview with Adam Gamble, November 9–10, 2002, Boston and Yarmouth Port, MA.

58. See "Journalism Schools in the United States," compiled in October 2002 by Edgar Huang and expanded substantially by Sheryl Larson, University of Southern Florida, St. Petersburg, Department of Journalism and Media Studies, http://www1.stpt.usf.edu/journalism/j-schools.html.

59. Masanori Yamaguchi, in JIMPOREN, "Mission Statement [11], V. Road to Reform, C. The Need for Systematic Reforms," Liaison Committee on Human Rights and Mass Media Conduct, http://www.jca.apc.org/~jimporen/mission11.html).

60. Honda Katsuichi, *The Impoverished Spirit in Contemporary Japan: Selected Essays of Honda Katsuichi,* ed. John Lie, trans. Eri Fujieda, Masayuki Hamazaki, and John Lie. (New York: Monthly Review Press, 1993), p. 215.

CHAPTER TWO, CONTINUED

61. Kiyoshi Takada, interview with Adam Gamble, April 4, 2002, Tokyo.

62. MacDougall, "The Lockheed Scandal and the High Costs of Politics in Japan," p. 223.

63. Covert, e-mail to AG, December 26, 2002.

64. Hall, telephone interview with AG.

65. Karel van Wolferen, "Why Can't the Japanese Love Japan?" (unpublished English-language manuscript for *Naze Nihonjin wa Nihon o Aise nai no ka: Kono Fuko na Kuni no Yukue*, trans. Susumu Ohara [Tokyo: Mainichi Shimbun-sha, 1988]).

66. Sam Jameson, "A Veteran American Journalist Looks at the Japanese Media," Japan Policy Research Institute, http://www.jpri.org/WPapers/wp40.html. *Asuteion*, Fall 1997.

CHAPTER THREE

1. Makoto Oda, interview with Adam Gamble, April 6, 2003, Kobe, Japan.

2. In Andrew A. Lipscomb and Albert Ellery Bergh, eds., *The Writings of Thomas Jefferson*, Memorial edition, Thomas Jefferson to Edward Carrington, 1787 (Washington, DC: Jefferson Memorial Association, 1903–1904), 6:57.

3. Walter Williams, "Journalist's Creed" is reprinted on the National Press Club's Web site, "About the Club: History and Ethics," http://www.press.org/abouttheclub/history-ethics.cfm.

4. NSK, "Guidance, Responsibility and Pride," Canon of Journalism, part 6, adopted June 21, 2000, Japan Newspaper Publishers and Editors Association, http://www.pressnet.or.jp/English/about/canon.htm.

5. Jay Rosen, *What Are Journalists For?* (New Haven, CT: Yale University Press, 1999), p. 1.

6. In Lipscomb and Bergh, eds., *The Writings of Thomas Jefferson*, Thomas Jefferson to John Norvell, 1807, 11:224.

7. Jim Hogshire, *Grossed-Out Surgeon Vomits Inside Patient!: An Insider's Look at the Supermarket Tabloids* (Venice, CA: Feral House, 1997); Bill Sloan, *I Watched a Wild Hog Eat My Baby!: A Colorful History of Tabloids and Their Cultural Impact* (Amherst, NY: Prometheus Books, 2001).

8. Sloan, *I Watched a Wild Hog Eat My Baby!*; S. Elizabeth Bird, *For Enquiring Minds: A Study of Supermarket Tabloids* (Knoxville: University of Tennessee Press, 1992); Hogshire, *Grossed-Out Surgeon Vomits Inside Patient!*

9. Ivan P. Hall, e-mail to Adam Gamble, October 16, 2003.

10. Jun Kamei, interview with Adam Gamble, December 18, 2002, Tokyo.

11. U.S. State Department, 18 Jun 52-Working Draft PSB-D-27 (1827) f PSB RE Draft Psychological Strategy Plan for the Pro-US Orientation of Japan-CD385 (Psy. Warfare), National Archives; and U.S. State Department, 29 Dec 52-Memo (01770) f PSB t DSD RE National Psychology Program for Japan-CD385(Psy. Warfare), National Archives.

12. Hajime Kitamura, interview with Adam Gamble, April 2, 2002, Tokyo.

13. This figure excludes tabloid "sports newspapers."

14. Teruo Shimomura, "Various Publishing Distributions" in "Book Making Q and A," http://www.syuppan.net/ mura_HP/hon/hon_305.html. Shimomura's data are based on sources from Tetsudo Kousaikai, which manages news kiosks at JR Stations in Japan.

15. In Paul Baylis, "Despite Flaws, Vitality of Magazines and Tabloids Surprises and Entertains," *Asahi Shimbun* (English edition), October 9, 2002.

16. Alex Kerr, *Dogs and Demons: Tales from the Dark Side of Japan* (New York: Hill and Wang, 2001), p. 5.

17. In " 'Kisha Club' Tradition Dies Hard," *Japan Today*, January 30, 2003.

18. Kitamura, interview with AG.

19. Ellis S. Krauss, *Broadcasting Politics in Japan: NHK and Television News* (Ithaca: Cornell University Press, 2000), p. 75.

20. "'Kisha Club' Tradition Dies Hard."

21. Kengo Tanaka, interview with Adam Gamble, December 19, 2002, Tokyo.

22. Howard W. French, "Tired of News That Rocks the Boat? Visit Japan," *New York Times* News Service, February 16, 2000.

23. Jun Kamei, *Shukanshi no Yomikata* [How to Read *Shukanshi*] (Tokyo: Hanashi no Tokushu. 1985).

24. Kamei, interview with AG.

25. Tatsuya Iwase, interview with Adam Gamble, December 19, 2002, Tokyo.

26. In Hiroshi Matsubara, "Magazine Muckrakes where Major Media Won't Make Waves," *Japan Times*, November 10, 2002.

27. "'Doku-gasu Jiken' Hassei-gen no 'Kai-ki' Kakeizu" ["The Originator of Poisonous Gas and His Macabre Family Line"], *Shukan Shincho*, July 14, 1994, pp. 128–132.

28. In Baylis, "Despite Flaws, Vitality of Magazines and Tabloids Surprises and Entertains."

29. See Jeffrey A. Ourvan, "Damage Control: Why Japanese Courts Should Adopt a Regime of Larger Libel Awards," *New York Law School Journal of International and Comparative Law* 21, no. 2 (2002): p. 320, which contains a footnote reference to Masao Horibe and John Middleton, "Japan," in *International Media Liability: Civil Liability in the Information Age*, p. 235.

30. Kamei, interview with AG.

31. In Tom Brislin, "Anti-Semitic Articles and Books Not Uncommon in Japan," Japan Media Review, September 26, 2003, http://www.ojr.org/japan/media/1064022502.php.

32. Kensuke Nishioka, interview with Adam Gamble, April 2, 2003, Tokyo.

33. Kenichi Asano, interview with Adam Gamble, Boston and Yarmouth Port, MA, November 9–10, 2002.

34. *An Advertiser's Guide to Magazines in Japan 2002–2003, No. 14* (Tokyo: Japan Magazine Advertising Association, 2002), p. 12.

35. Ibid., p. 13.

36. Asano, interview with AG.

37. Tanaka, interview with AG.

38. Matsuda, interview with AG; Kamei, interview with AG.

39. Ian Buruma, *The Wages of Guilt: Memories of War in Germany and Japan* (London: Phoenix, 1994), p. 221.

40. Kamei, interview with AG.

41. Bruce S. Feiler, *Learning to Bow: Inside the Heart of Japan* (New York: Houghton Mifflin, 1990), p. 246.

42. Ibid., p. 247.

43. John Nathan, *Japan Unbound: A Volatile Nation's Quest for Pride and Purpose* (Boston: Houghton Mifflin, 2004), p. 28.

44. Kamei, interview with AG.

45. Ibid.

46. Ibid.

47. Kazuyoshi Hanada, interview with Adam Gamble, April 4, 2003, Tokyo.

48. Ibid.

49. Kamei, interview with AG.

50. Andrei S. Markovits and Mark Silverstein, eds., *The Politics of Scandal: Power and Process in Liberal Democracies* (New York: Holmes and Meier, 1998), pp. 2–3.

51. Karel van Wolferen, untitled unpublished English-language manuscript of "Sukyandaru ni yotte Nihon Kenryoku Kiko wa Ikinobiru" ["Scandals Maintain Japanese Power"], *Chuokoron*, September 1991.

52. Ibid.

53. French, "Tired of News That Rocks the Boat? Visit Japan."

54. Alex Kerr, interview with Adam Gamble, Tokyo, June 16, 2003.

CHAPTER THREE, CONTINUED

55. Kensuke Nishioka, *"Uwasa no shinso" Toppu ya kagyo -Scandal o Oe!* ["The Truth Behind the Rumor": Freelance Reporting—Catch the Scandal!] (Tokyo: Kodan-sha, 2001).

56. Nishioka, interview with AG.

57. Ibid.

58. Kiyoshi Takada, interview with Adam Gamble, April 4, 2003, Tokyo.

59. Ibid.

60. Oda, interview with AG.

61. Ibid.

62. Hiroshi Matsubara, "Libel Payouts Soar: Crackdown Has Publishers Running Scared," *Japan Times,* April 3, 2004.

63. Ibid.

64. Ibid.

65. Ibid.

66. Ourvan, "Damage Control," pp. 307–321.

CHAPTER FOUR

1. Yoshiyuki Kono, interview with Adam Gamble, May 19, 2002, Matsumoto, Nagano.

2. JIMPOREN, Mission Statement, Liaison Committee on Human Rights and Mass Media Conduct, http://www.jca.apc.org/~jimporen/mission01.html.

3. Kenichi Asano, interview with Adam Gamble, November 9–10, 2002, Boston and Yarmouth Port, MA.

4. Richard Jewell, interview by Mike Wallace, "Sixty Minutes II: Falsely Accused," CBSNEWS.com, January 2, 2002, http://www.cbsnews.com/stories/2002/01/02/60II/printable322892.shtml.

5. Kathy Scruggs and Ron Martz. "FBI Suspects 'Hero' Guard May Have Planted Bomb," *Atlanta Journal-Constitution,* July 30, 1996, p. 1.

6. Mary Brenner has noted in *Vanity Fair* that while Ray Cleere, then president of Piedmont College, had reported to police that Jewell was "a little erratic" and "almost too excitable," even this is hardly the same as "frustrated." Marie Brenner, "American Nightmare—The Ballad of Richard Jewell," *Vanity Fair,* February 1997, http://www.mariebrenner.com/articles/nightmare/jewell1.html.

7. Phil Kloer, "Centennial Park Bombing: Reruns of News Tapes Underscore Case Twist: TV to Capitalize on Interview Footage," *Atlanta Journal-Constitution,* July 31, 1996, p. A11.

8. Richard Jewell and Watson Bryant (one of Jewell's attorneys), interview with Kenichi Asano, transcript, Atlanta, October 14, 1997, http://www1.doshisha.ac.jp/~kasano/FEATURES/ATLANTA/atlanta-interview.html.

9. Dave Kindred, "A Long Wait in the Shadows after His Moment in the Sun," *Atlanta Journal-Constitution,* August 1, 1996, p. A14.

10. According to the Web site Journalism.org, "Brokaw would later say on CBS's '60 Minutes' that he had 'very high-ranking federal law enforcement officials in Washington and in Atlanta' who had confirmed the story. He also noted that the report included the qualification: 'Please, understand absolutely that he is only the focus of this investigation. He's not even a suspect yet.'" See "Case Study: Richard Jewell and the Olympic Bombing," http://www.journalism.org/resources/education/case_studies/jewell.asp.

11. See "Sixty Minutes II: Falsely Accused," CBSNEWS.com, June 26, 2002, http://www.cbsnews.com/stories/2002/01/02/60II/main322892.shtml.

12. In Brenner, "American Nightmare."

13. Ibid.

14. Richard Jewell, opening remarks before the United States House Subcommittee on Crime, Committee of the Judiciary, July 30, 1997, http://www.house.gov/judiciary/375.htm.

15. L. Lin Wood, interview with Adam Gamble, August 16, 2002, Atlanta, GA.

16. Ibid.

17. Ibid.

18. Wood, interview with AG; Jewell and Bryant, interview with Asano.

19. Wood, interview with AG.

20. Jewell and Bryant, interview with Asano.

21. On February 27, 2004, Shoko Asahara, the leader of Aum, was found guilty of the Tokyo sarin-gas attack and for directing the Matsumoto attack.

22. The description of the sarin-dissemination system comes from a paper entitled "Chemical Terrorism in Japan: The Matsumoto and Tokyo Incidents," Organization for the Prohibition of Chemical Weapons, http://www.opcw.org/resp/html/japan.html.

23. Kono, interview with AG.

24. *Tsuma yo! Waga Ai to Kibo to Tatakai no Hibi* [My Wife! Days of My Love, Hope, and Struggle] (Tokyo: Ushio Shuppansha, 1998).

25. In Eiichi Yamamoto, *Genron no Terorizumu: "Netsuzo Zasshi" Shukan Shincho o Kaibo suru* [Media Terrorism II: Anatomy of a "Fabricating Magazine," *Shukan Shincho*] (Tokyo: Ohtori Shoin, 2002).

26. John Nathan, *Japan Unbound: A Volatile Nation's Quest for Pride and Purpose* (Boston: Houghton Mifflin, 2004), p. 26.

27. In "Goiken ban Saito Juichi Komon Chokugeki Intabyu-Waga Shinchosha Shain ni Tsugu" ["Direct Interview to an Opinion Leader and Advisor Juichi Saito—Advice to You, Our Employees at "Shinchosha"], *Shukan Bunshun*, July 31, 1997, pp. 40–41.

28. Kazuyoshi Hanada, interview with Adam Gamble, April 4, 2003, Tokyo.

29. Jun Kamei, interview with Adam Gamble, December 18, 2002, Tokyo.

30. In JIMPOREN, "Mission Statement [7], V. Tabloid Horror, B. A History of Collusion and Abuse," Liaison Committee on Human Rights and Mass Media Conduct, http://www.jca.apc.org/~jimporen/mission07.html.

31. " 'Doku-gasu Jiken' Hassei-gen no 'Kai-ki' Kakeizu" ["The Originator of Poisonous Gas and His Macabre Family Line"], *Shukan Shincho*, July 14, 1994, pp. 128–132.

32. Kamei, interview with AG.

33. Hanada, interview with AG.

34. Ibid.

35. Ibid.

36. Hajime Kitamura, interview with Adam Gamble, April 2, 2003, Tokyo.

37. Ibid.

38. "Moudoku Sarin 'Seizohan' o Meguru 'Kai-joho' to Hitotsu shika nai Toppakou" ["Surreptitious Information of Criminal Who Produced Heinous Sarin Gas and the Only Conceivable Scenario That Can Enable a Breakthrough in Investigation"], *Shukan Shincho*, August 4, 1994, pp. 51–54.

39. "Sugata o Miseta 'Dai ichi Tsuho sha'—Matsumoto Dokugasu Jiken" ["First Person Who Reported Incident Reveals Himself: Matsumoto Toxic Gas Incident"], *Shukan Shincho*, August 11 and 18, 1994 (combined issue).

40. This is according to Eiichi Yamamoto, a former crime reporter and later an editor at *Yomiuri Shimbun*; and Kenichi Asano, himself a former Japanese crime reporter and the author of the best-selling book *Hanzai Hodo no Hanzai* [The Crime of Crime Reporting] (Tokyo: Gakuyoshobo, 1984).

41. Kono, interview with AG.

42. Ibid.

43. Laurie Anne Freeman, *Closing the Shop: Information Cartels and Japan's Mass Media* (Princeton, NJ: Princeton University Press, 2000), p. 110.

CHAPTER FOUR, CONTINUED

44. Kenichi Asano, interview with Adam Gamble, November 9–10, 2002, Boston and Yarmouth Port, MA.

45. Kono, interview with AG.

46. See chapter 3.

47. Kono, interview with AG.

48. Ibid.

49. Helen Hardacre, "Aum Shinrikyo and the Japanese Media," Japan Policy Research Institute, Working Paper No. 19, April 1996, http://www.jpri.org/publications/workingpapers/wp19.html.

50. As of the publication of this book the lawsuit between Jewell and the *Atlanta Journal-Constitution* remains pending, awaiting a trial date.

51. Asano, interview with AG.

CHAPTER FIVE

1. Abraham Cooper, interview with Adam Gamble, May 1, 2002, Los Angeles.

2. This figure was offered by Rabbi Abraham Cooper, associate dean of the Simon Wiesenthal Center, in an interview for this book. Authors David Goodman and Masanori Miyazawa estimate that there were only one thousand Jews in Japan in 1995. See their *Jews in the Japanese Mind: The History and Uses of a Cultural Stereotype,* Expanded edition (Lanham, MD: Lexington Books, 2000), p. 8.

3. Tom Brislin, "Anti-Semitic Articles and Books Not Uncommon in Japan," Japan Media Review, September 26, 2003, http://www.ojr.org/japan/media/1064022502.php.

4. Goodman and Miyazawa, *Jews in the Japanese Mind,* p. 10. The authors point out that whereas the anti-Semitism in a country such as Japan, which is all but bereft of Jews, is unusual, the case is not without precedent. England, for example, prohibited Jews from living within its borders for four hundred years, from 1290 to 1656, during which time many negative myths about Jews circulated.

5. Masanori Nishioka, "Sengo Sekaishi Saidai no Tabuu: Nachi 'Gasu shitsu' wa Nakatta" ["The Greatest Taboo in Post-War History: There Were No Nazi Gas Chambers"], *Marco Polo,* February 1995, pp. 170–179.

6. Ibid., pp. 171–173.

7. Kyle B. Olson, "Matsumoto Sarin Jiken wa Terorisuto no Hanko da: Bei Kagaku Heiki Ken Fukushocho ga Matsumoto de Tettei Kensho" ["The Matsumoto Sarin Incident Is a Terrorist's Crime: Associate Dean of the U.S. Chemical Weapon Research Institute Conducts a Thorough Verification in Matsumoto"], *Marco Polo,* February 1995, p. 156.

8. *An Advertiser's Guide to Magazines in Japan 1993–1994* (Tokyo: Japan Magazine Advertising Association, 1993).

9. Goodman and Miyazawa, *Jews in the Japanese Mind,* p. 273.

10. Brislin, "Anti-Semitic Articles and Books Not Uncommon."

11. Ibid.

12. Mitsuyoshi Okazaki, speech given at an event organized by *Asahi Shimbun* for members of the *Asahi Shimbun* Cultural Society, Tokyo, July 10, 1996; recounted in the now defunct magazine *I-Media* 152 (1996): pp. 43–45, published by *Asahi Shimbun.*

13. Kengo Tanaka, interview with Adam Gamble, December 19, 2002, Tokyo.

14. Kazuyoshi Hanada, interview with Adam Gamble, April 4, 2003, Tokyo.

15. Ibid.

16. David Lazarus, "Poorando ga Otoshita Kage: Aushubittsu ga Abunai" ["'Auschwitz Hangs by a Thread': The Shadow Created by Poland's Democratization"], *Marco Polo,* December 1992, pp. 142–150.

17. Hanada, interview with AG.

18. Kazuyoshi Hanada, interview with Associated Press, "Jewish Group Blasts Magazine for Denying Holocaust," *Daily Mainichi,* January 26, 1995, as cited by Tom Brislin, "Anti-Semitic Articles and Books Not Uncommon."

19. Tanaka, interview with AG.

20. In the now defunct magazine *Kane* 51 (1998): 20–23.

21. Neil Sandberg, telephone interview with Adam Gamble, January 16, 2003, coauthor in Yarmouth Port, MA, interviewee in Los Angeles.

22. Brislin, "Anti-Semitic Articles and Books Not Uncommon."

23. David Goodwin, "Anti-Bigotry Fight Starts with Information," *Asahi Evening News*, April 9, 1995, as cited by Tom Brislin, "Anti-Semitic Articles and Books Not Uncommon."

24. Takao Toshikawa, et al. "Chogin Warera ga ketsuzei 5-cho en o kuu Yudaya shihon jinmyaku tsui ni tsukanda!" ["Finally Unveiled! The Human Network of Jewish Capital That Devours Five Trillion Yen of Our Hard-Earned Taxes through the Long-Term Credit Bank of Japan"], *Shukan Post,* October 15, 1999, pp. 34–35. Note that although the author is listed as Takao Toshikawa, the article was changed so drastically that the magazine had to write him an apology.

25. Translation in Goodman and Miyazawa, *Jews in the Japanese Mind*, p. 276.

26. The *Oriental Economist,* http://www.orientaleconomist.com/index.html.

27. In Goodman and Miyazawa, *Jews in the Japanese Mind,* p. 277.

28. Koji Kawamura made his assertions on two *Super Morning* shows, on October 15 and October 17, 2001.

29. TV Asahi Web site, http://www.bs-asahi.co.jp/access/list.html.

30. Goodman and Miyazawa, *Jews in the Japanese Mind,* p. 12.

31. Ibid., p. 11.

32. Ibid., pp. 12–13.

33. Ibid., p. 33 n 52: "*Iwai Katsuhito, Benisu no shonin no shihonron* [The Theory of Capitalism in The Merchant of Venice], Iwanami shoten, 1985. The book had gone through six printings in its first six months. Iwai, who received his Ph.D. from MIT and taught at Yale from 1973 to 1979, is also the author of *Disequilibrium Dynamics* (New Haven: Yale University Press, 1981)."

34. For example, see "Israelites Came to Japan," at http://www5.ocn.ne.jp/~magi9/isracame.htm, http://www.geocities.com/athens/parthenon/1237/tmp.html, and http://www.pbs.org/wgbh/nova/israel/losttribes3.html#japan.

35. Victor E. Marsden, trans., *The Protocols of the Meetings of the Learned Elders of Zion*, translated from the Russian (Los Angeles, CA: Christian Nationalist Crusade, 1934). The first Japanese edition of this book was translated from the Russian by Ho Koushi under the pen name Norihiro Yasue as *Sekai Kakumei no Rimen* [Behind the World Revolution] (Tokyo: Niyusha, 1924).

36. Marvin Tokayer and Mary Swartz, *The Fugu Plan: The Untold Story of the Japanese and the Jews During World War II* (New York: Paddington Press, 1979).

37. John W. Dower, *War without Mercy: Race and Power in the Pacific War* (New York: Pantheon Books, 1986), p. 258.

38. Goodman and Miyazawa, *Jews in the Japanese Mind*, pp. 108–110.

39. Ian Buruma, *The Wages of Guilt: Memories of War in Germany and Japan* (London: Phoenix, 1994).

40. Richard Rubenstein, *The Cunning of History: The Holocaust and the American Future* (New York: Perenial, 1975), p. 7.

41. Ivan P. Hall, telephone interview with Adam Gamble, June 8, 2003, coauthor in Dennis, MA, interviewee in Honolulu, HI.

42. Goodman and Miyazawa, *Jews in the Japanese Mind*, pp. 178–179.

43. Ibid., p. 172.

CHAPTER FIVE, CONTINUED

44. In two separate telegraphs dispatched on August 14 and 16, 1940, Matsuoka rejected Sugihara's request for formal ministry approval to issue the transit visas. See Yukiko Sugihara, *Rokusen-nin no inochi no biza* [Visas for Six Thousand Lives] (Tokyo: Asahi Sonorama, 1990); and Hirrel Leven, *In Search of Sugihara* (New York: Free Press, 1996).

45. Shoichi Watanabe, *Kokueki no Tachiba kara* [From the Standpoint of National Interest] (Tokyo: Tokuma Shoten,1996).

46. Masami Uno, *Yudaya ga Wakaru to Sekai ga Miete Kuru: Sen Kyuhyaku Kyuju nen "Shumatsu Keizai Senso" he no Shinario* [If You Understand the Jews, You Will Understand the World: The Scenario Toward "Economic War Catastrophe" in 1990] (Tokyo: Tokuma Shoten, 1986); Masami Uno, *Yudaya ga Wakaru to Nihon ga Miete Kuru: "Kudo ka Nihon" o Yudaya ga Techu ni Surutoki* [If You Understand the Jews, You Will Understand Japan: When "Hollowing Out Japan" Fall Into the Hands of Jews] (Tokyo: Tokuma Shoten, 1986).

47. Goodman and Miyazawa, *Jews in the Japanese Mind*, pp. 1–2.

48. *Vajrayana Sacca*, January 25, 1995, p. 3. Although this volume was dated January, it was actually published in December 1994.

49. Ely Karmon, "The Anti-Semitism of Japan's Aum Shinrikyo: A Dangerous Revival," in *Anti-Semitism Worldwide: 1998/1999*, annual report by the Stephen Roth Institute for the Study of Contemporary Anti-Semitism and Racism at Tel Aviv University, Nebraska University Press, http://www.ict.org.il/articles/aum_antisemitism.htm.

50. Philip Brasor, "Ripple Effects of Sleazebag Journalism," *Japan Times*, November 4, 1999.

51. Ibid.

52. Goodman and Miyazawa, *Jews in the Japanese Mind*, p. 240.

53. Ibid., p. 260.

CHAPTER SIX

1. See appendix E for a Summation of this verdict, written by the presiding judge, Shintaro Kato. *Nobuhira v. Ikeda*, Tokyo District Court Judgment of May 30, 2000, Tokyo District Court Civil Section 28, Heisei 8 (Wa) No. 10485 Damage Compensation Claims Case, Judgment of First Instance. "Heisei 8" is the emperor's calendar year 8, which is 1996.

2. The court conclusion may also be translated as "abuse of the right of [legal] action." However, for clarity, the translation "abuse of the right to sue" is used here.

3. *Nobuhira v. Ikeda*, May 30, 2000.

4. The Japanese Ministry of Education and Science records the estimated number of members of each religious group in Japan, which, if totaled, yield a figure of about twice the total population of the entire country, showing that either the memberships of many religious groups in Japan are seriously overestimated or that many Japanese claim membership in multiple religions. Both seem likely. Another problem is the difficulty of accurately calculating the membership of any religious organization. For instance, how much time should pass after a member has attended an activity before he or she is dropped off the rolls? At any rate, it is safe to say that the Soka Gakkai's membership is substantial and highly influential in Japan.

5. Some question the accuracy of this figure, too, since some Soka Gakkai members have multiple subscriptions to the paper, thus perhaps inflating the number of actual readers. Again, however, no one questions that the *Seikyo Shimbun* has a massive readership numbering in the millions and that it is one of the largest daily newspapers in Japan and in the world.

6. The Soka Gakkai calculated its membership at the time by "households," not by individual members. Thus, whether one member or all of the members of a home belonged to the organization, that "household" was counted as one.

7. According to Soka Gakkai spokesperson Kunishige Maeda, in an interview with Adam Gamble, July 8, 2002, Tokyo.

8. Karel van Wolferen: *The Enigma of Japanese Power: People and Politics in a Stateless Nation* (New York: Alfred A. Knopf, 1990), pp. 275–276.

9. As noted elsewhere, the Soka Gakkai and the New Komei Party are legally separate organizations.

10. Walter Mondale, telephone interview with Adam Gamble, June 6, 2003, coauthor in Dennis, MA, interviewee in Minneapolis, MN.

11. Maeda, interview with AG.

12. *Soka Gakkai O Kiru* has been translated into English as: Hirotatsu Fujiwara, *I Denounce Soka Gakkai* (Tokyo: Nisshin Hodo, 1979).

13. Maeda, interview with AG.

14. Tetsuzo Fuyushiba, interview with Adam Gamble, July 5, 2002, Tokyo; Yoshio Urushibara, interview with Adam Gamble, July 5, 2002, Tokyo.

15. *Yomiuri Shimbun* Survey, *Yomiuri Shimbun*, November 7, 1999, p. 15.

16. *Yomiuri Shimbun* listed the top twenty results from a poll that asked "who are the Japanese you respect most?" Of them, Ikeda was sixth behind the former prime minister Shigeru Yoshida, the late medical doctor Hideyo Noguchi, the early nineteenth-century agronomist and so-called peasant sage Sontoku Ninomiya, the famous Meiji-period educator, Yukichi Fukuzawa, and the then-reigning Emperor Hirohito. "Honsha Gyarappu Seikatsu Ishiki Hatsuno Doji Chousa" ["Together for the First Time, *Yomiuri Shimbun* and the Gallup Organization Conducted a Survey of the Daily Life of the People"], *Yomiuri Shimbun*, May 3, 1979, p. 11.

17. Ikeda is the honorary president of the Soka Gakkai and the president of the SGI. Regardless of his titles, however, he is indisputably the spiritual leader of the organization.

18. Maeda, interview with AG.

19. Daisaku Ikeda, *Lectures on Buddhism* (Tokyo: Seikyo Press, 1970), p. 5:193.

20. At an SGI executive leaders conference held in Tokyo, November 25, 2003, as reported in an article entitled "The People Are Sovereign," *World Tribune* (weekly newspaper for SGI-USA), February 27, 2004.

21. From a speech entitled "The Key to World Peace" (eleventh general meeting of Soka Gakkai student division, Nihon University, September 8, 1968).

22. David Machacek and Bryan Wilson, eds. *Global Citizens: The Soka Gakkai Buddhist Movement in the World* (Oxford: Oxford University Press, 2000).

23. The exhibition "Human Rights in Today's World" was first shown in April 1993 at the United Nations University in Tokyo. The exhibit "War and Peace" has toured five countries and ten cities, including New York and Moscow. The exhibit "The Courage to Remember—Anne Frank and the Holocaust" was created with the cooperation of the Simon Wiesenthal Center. This exhibit has been shown at forty-six venues throughout Japan since its May 1994 Tokyo opening.

24. Daisaku Ikeda, *Faith into Action: Thoughts on Selected Topics by Daisaku Ikeda* (Santa Monica, CA: World Tribune Press), 1999, p. 275.

25. George David Miller, *Peace, Value, and Wisdom: The Educational Philosophy of Daisaku Ikeda* (Amsterdam: Rodopi, 2002), pp. 53–54.

26. Ikeda, *Faith into Action,* p. 262.

27. These articles appeared in a successive special-feature article entitled "Corrupted Soka Gakkai" ["Hokai Suru Soka Gakkai"] in the 1976 March and April issues of *Gekkan Pen*. See: "Shiju Goju no Taizai o Okasu Soka Gakkai" ["Soka Gakkai Commits Four to Fivefold Major Crimes"], *Gekkan Pen,* March, 1976 (sold in February), p. 80; "Gokuaku no Taizai Okasu Soka Gakkai no Jisso" ["Real Aspect of Soka Gakkai That Commits Atrocious Great Crimes"], *Gekkan Pen,* April 1976 (sold in March), p. 76.

CHAPTER SIX, CONTINUED

28. While *Gekkan Pen* editor Taizo Kumabe was found guilty of criminal defamation by the Tokyo District Court in 1983, a decision that was upheld by the Tokyo High Court the following year, he passed away during his appeal to the Supreme Court. Because Kumabe had died, the Supreme Court dismissed the prosecution against him and did not rule on the merits of the case.

29. Daisaku Ikeda, speech to Soka Gakkai youth meeting, Tokyo, July 16, 2003.

30. *Nobuhira v. Ikeda,* Tokyo District Court Judgment of May 30, 1996, Tokyo Distric Court Division 28, Heisei 8 (Wa) Number 10485, Case of claim for compensation of damages; Tokyo High Court Judgment of January 31, 2000, Tokyo High Court Division 11, Heisei 12 (Wa) Number 3364.

31. "Soka Gakkai wa Senkyo Kyodan Moto Fujinbu kanbu ga Kataru" ["'Soka Gakkai Is a Religious Organization for Election,' Remarks a Former Women's Division Leader"], *Akahata*, December 30, 1995.

32. Nobuko Nobuhira, "Chinmoku o Yabutta Hokkaido Moto Fujinbu-kanbu 'Watashi wa Ikeda Daisaku ni Reipu sareta'" ["A Former Women's Leader in Hokkaido Breaks Her Silence, 'I Was Raped by Daisaku Ikeda'"], *Shukan Shincho*, February 22, 1996, pp. 58–63.

33. "Ikeda o Uttae masu" (Photogravuer) ["'I Will Sue Ikeda' (Photogravuer)—Mrs. Nobuko Nobuhira Holds a Press Conference Stating That She Was Raped by Daisaku Ikeda"], *Shukan Shincho,* March 7, 1996, pp.12–13; "'Ikeda Reipu' Higaisha ga Buchimaketa Kokomade Yatta Gakkai—Senkyo no 'Kyouki'" ["A Victim of 'Ikeda's Raping' Confesses the 'Insanity' of Gakkai's Election Which Has Gone Too Far"], *Shukan Shincho*, March 7, 1996, pp. 46–50; "Ikeda Daisaku 'Reipu Sosho' de Ishuku suru 'Hodo-jin'" ["Press Corps Quail With the 'Rape Lawsuit' of Daisaku Ikeda"], *Shukan Shincho*, June 20, 1996, pp. 44–48; "Gaikokujin Kisha Tachiga Sekai ni Tsutaeru 'Ikeda Reipu Jiken'" ["'Ikeda Rape Incident' That Foreign Reporters Report to the World"], *Shukan Shincho*, July 4, 1996, p. 28.

34. Nobuhira, "I Was Raped by Daisaku Ikeda."

35. *Nobuhira v. Ikeda,* May 30, 2000.

36. Initially, in her *Shukan Shincho* "memoir," Nobuko Nobuhira claimed that after the alleged August 1983 incident she had gone to see a doctor and had kept the medical certificate issued by him. This was supposed to be "the" physical evidence of the rape. However, the certificate was dated October 19, 1983, two months after the time of the alleged rape. The prognosis written by the doctor certified that approximately three weeks of treatment was to be necessary from the date of the visit and that the injury was "Contusive Fractural Injury and Multi-Contusion."

The defense submitted as evidence the doctor's statement, in which he indicated that Nobuko Nobuhira's injuries, for which he treated her, had occurred sometime very close to her October 19, 1983, visit with him. He also stated that in laymen's terms the illness that he treated her for, "Contusive Fractural Injury and Multi-Contusion," was a scratch and bruises. He further added that prior to the filing of the lawsuit, Nobuhira and her lawyer visited him and that he had explained these same details to them at that time.

The defense also conducted an investigation about the injury and learned that Nobuko Nobuhira had been hit by a bicycle ridden by a young boy in mid-October of that year. Immediately after the accident, she went to a nearby hospital for treatment and took the boy, who was not injured, with her. However, since the boy left the hospital while she was being treated, her husband, Junko Nobuhira, protested to the hospital and accused them of letting the boy flee without giving his personal information and thus impeding the Nobuhiras from pursuing the boy for legal damages. These facts were substantiated by statements given by the owner of a grocery store near the site of the accident and by the president of the hospital where Nobuko Nobuhira was treated immediately after the accident. (This is not the same hospital from which she received the certificate.)

It was clear from all of the evidence presented that the Nobuhiras tried to manipulate the court by using a medical certificate obtained in relation to an incident that occurred two months after the alleged rape. The court found that the injury indicated in the certificate was suffered sometime close to the time of the diagnosis, that there was the possibility that it was caused by the bicycle accident, and that it could not be considered proof of her August 1983 rape allegation.

37. Nobuhira, "I Was Raped by Daisaku Ikeda."

38. The entire Summation of the District Court Conclusion in this case is reprinted in appendix E of this book.

39. Maeda, interview with AG.

40. In Hans Katayama, "*Shukan Shincho*: Victim—or Victimizer," *No. 1 Shimbun*, November 15, 1997, p. 4. *No. 1 Shimbun* is the paper published by and for the Foreign Correspondents' Club of Japan.

41. Hiroshi Matsuda, interview with Adam Gamble, December 19, 2002, Tokyo.

42. Ibid.

43. Ibid.

44. Jun Kamei, interview with Adam Gamble, December 18, 2002, Tokyo.

45. Ibid.

46. Shinichi Sano, "'Shuppan kai Saigo no Kaibutsu' no Shizuka naru Hibi. Saito Juichi" ["Quiet Days of the Last Monster in Publishing Circles: Juichi Saito"], *Aera*, March 15, 1999, pp. 60–64.

47. Maeda, interview with AG.

48. Lawrence Edward Carter Sr. to Kiyoshi Hayakawa, editor in chief of *Shukan Shincho*, June 2003.

49. Eiichi Yamamoto, *Genron no Terorizumu: Shukan Shincho "Netsuzo Hodo Jiken" no Tenmatsu* [Media Terrorism: Full Account of *Shukan Shincho*'s Fabricated Reporting Incident] (Tokyo: Ohtori Shoin, 2001).

50. In Yamamoto, *Genron no Terorizumu* [Media Terrorism], p. 157.

51. Ibid.

52. Ibid., p. 159.

53. "Honshi o 'Netsuzo Shukanshi'to Danjita Moto Yomiuri Kisha no Shotai" ["True Identity of Former Yomiuri Journalist Who Claimed Our Magazine Is a Fabricated Weekly Magazine"], *Shukan Shincho*, December 27, 2001, pp. 47–48.

54. Matsuda, interview with AG.

55. At the time that the Nobuhiras filed their claims in 1996, about five years had passed since the date of the most recent alleged incident, about thirteen years had passed since the previous alleged incident, and about twenty-three years had passed since the alleged first incident.

56. Matsuda, interview with AG.

57. *Jiyu Shimpo* was the name of the LDP's organ newspaper at the time of the scandal; however, the LDP changed the name to *Jiyu Minshu* in 1999 to avoid confusion with other similarly named political movements in Japan.

58. Hajime Kitamura, interview with Adam Gamble, April 2, 2003, Tokyo.

59. Michiyo Nakamoto, "Japan's LDP Puts Faith in Religious Partner: New Komeito, a Party Backed by Buddhists, Is a Key Element of the Coalition's Re-election Strategy," *Financial Times Limited*, Japan edition, November 6, 2003. Asia-Pacific sec., p. 2.

60. While the *Financial Times* did run a letter to the editor by SGI director of communications Rie Tsumura rebuffing the comment about "media claims," it failed to run an apology or a correction.

CHAPTER SEVEN

1. Roger Pulvers, "The Stage Is Set for Genuine Change," *Japan Times*, December 17, 2000.

2. Takesato Watanabe and Koji Yamaguchi, eds., *Media Yogo o Manabu Hito no Tameni* [Encyclopedia of Media and Communication Studies] (Tokyo: Sekaishiso-sha, 1999), pp. 310–311.

3. Ivan P. Hall, *Bamboozled!: How America Loses the Intellectual Game with Japan and Its Implications for Our Future in Asia* (Armonk, NY: M. E. Sharpe, 2002), p. 90.

CHAPTER SEVEN, CONTINUED

4. Ogushi Toyoo, "Nippon Minzoku Sekaikan no Kakuritsu" ["Establishing a Japanese Racial World-view"], *Bungei Shunju* 20, no. 1 (January 1942): 24–33.

5. John W. Dower, *War without Mercy: Race and Power in the Pacific War* (New York: Pantheon Books, 1986), pp. 211–212.

6. Mark Eykholt, "Aggression, Victimization, and Chinese Historiography of the Nanjing Massacre," in *The Nanjing Massacre in History and Historiography*, ed. Joshua A. Fogel and Charles S. Maier, pp. 11–69 (Berkeley and Los Angeles: University of California Press, 2000), pp. 17–18.

7. Robert Wilson, "The Family Letters of Dr. Robert Wilson," in *Documents on the Rape of Nanking*, ed. Timothy Brook, pp. 207–254 (Ann Arbor: University of Michigan Press, 1999), p. 214.

8. The twenty-seven Westerners who remained in Nanjing included seventeen Americans, six Germans, two Russians, one Australian, and one British. See Timothy Brook, Introduction, in *Documents on the Rape of Nanking*, p. 3.

9. Wilson, "The Family Letters of Dr. Robert Wilson," pp. 219–220.

10. John Rabe, *The Good Man of Nanking: The Diaries of John Rabe*, trans. John E. Woods (New York: Vintage Books, 1998).

11. Ibid., pp. 65–67.

12. Ibid., pp. 75–76.

13. Ibid., p. 77.

14. See bibliography for a selection of Hora's books.

15. Katsuichi Honda, *Chugoku no tabi* [A Journey to China] (Tokyo: Asahi Shimbunsha, 1972).

16. Nobukatsu Fujioka, interview with Adam Gamble, April 2, 2003, Tokyo.

17. Katsuichi Honda, *The Nanjing Massacre: A Japanese Journalist Confronts Japan's National Shame*, trans. Karen Sandness (Armonk, NY: M. E. Sharpe, 1999).

18. Ibid., p. 154–158.

19. Ibid., p. 144.

20. Ibid., pp. 165–166.

21. Ibid., p. 166.

22. Ibid., p. 257.

23. Ibid., p. 349.

24. Ibid.

25. Ibid.

26. Ibid.

27. Iris Chang, *The Rape of Nanking: The Forgotten Holocaust of World War II* (New York: Penguin Books, 1997).

28. Nobukatsu Fujioka and Shudo Higashinakano, *Za Reipu obu Nankin no Kenkyu—Chugoku ni okeru Johosen no Teguchi to Senryaku* [A Study of (Iris Chang's) *The Rape of Nanking*—Methods and Strategy of the "Propaganda War" in China] (Tokyo: Shodensha, 1999).

29. See Eykholt, "Aggression, Victimization, and Chinese Historiography," p. 56; Takashi Yoshida, "A Battle over History: The Nanjing Massacre in Japan," in *The Nanjing Massacre in History and Historiography*, pp. 117–118; Daquing Yang, "The Challenges of the Nanjing Massacre: Reflections on Historical Inquiry," also in *The Nanjing Massacre in History and Historiography*. pp. 161–162; and Robert Entenmann, "Review of Iris Chang, *The Rape of Nanking: The Forgotten Holocaust of World War II*," http://www.hartford-hwp.com/archives/55/481.html.

30. Charles S. Maier, Foreword, in *The Nanjing Massacre in History and Historiography*, pp. vii–viii.

31. One of the lowest figures—probably too low—came in a lecture on the matter by John Rabe, who stated, "We Europeans put the number at about 50,000 to 60,000. According to the Red Swastika Society, which had taken on the task of burying the bodies, but could not bury more than 200 a day,

there were about 30,000 bodies still lying unburied in the suburb of Hsiakwan on 22 February 1938, the date I left Nanking." However, Rabe clearly was not counting those killed by Japanese soldiers on their march inland to the city from the shore, which both Honda and Harold Timperley include in their estimates. Erwin Wickert, the editor of Rabe's diary, comments on Rabe's estimate, "It is likely that Rabe's estimate is too low, since he could not have had an overview of the entire municipal area during the period of the worst atrocities. Moreover, many troops of captured Chinese soldiers were led out of the city and down to the Yangtze, where they were summarily executed. But, as noted, no one actually counted the dead. See Rabe, *The Good Man of Nanking*, p. 212.

32. *Quin-Hua Rijun Nanjing datusha yunan tongbao jinianguan* (Memorial for Compatriot Victims of the Japanese Military's Nanjing Massacre).

33. In Yoshida, "A Battle over History," p. 81.

34. As reprinted in Honda, *The Nanjing Massacre*, p. 125.

35. Ibid., p. 126.

36. In April 2003, some of the now elderly children of both of the second lieutenants initiated lawsuits against *Mainichi Shimbun* (which used to be *Tokyo Nichinichi Shimbun*), *Asahi Shimbun*, the publisher Kashiwa Shobo, and Honda. The family members claim that no such contest ever occurred, that the lieutenants were wrongly exploited as heroes by the newspapers during the war, that they were wrongly convicted and executed as war criminals after the war, and that the postwar writing about them that states that they killed anyone illegally is also incorrect. They claim the lieutenants were simply innocent Japanese soldiers who did not victimize anyone, but who were themselves victims.

37. Kengo Tanaka, interview with Adam Gamble, December 19, 2002, Tokyo.

38. Akira Nakamura, interview with Adam Gamble, December 20, 2002, Tokyo.

39. Nobukatsu Fujioka, interview with Adam Gamble, April 2, 2003, Tokyo.

40. "Tenno Hochu de Ichiji Chudan Nankin Gyakusatsu no Sanjyu mannin kara Nihyaku nin" ["Arguments over the Number of Victims (Ranging from 200 to 300,000) in Nanjing Massacre Temporarily Halted as Emperor's Visit to China Nears"], *Shukan Shincho*, October 22, 1992.

41. Honda, interview with AG.

42. Hall, *Bamboozled!*, p. 51.

43. "Nankin Gyakusatsu Attato Iwanaito Nihon wa Toore nainoka" ["Won't Japan Fare Well if It Doesn't Admit It Committed the Nanking Massacre?"], *Shukan Shincho*, May 19, 1994, pp. 134–136.

44. Ibid.

45. Ibid.

46. Ibid.

47. Makoto Oda, interview with Adam Gamble, April 6, 2003, Kobe, Japan.

48. Takami Eto, "Fury at Nanking 'Lie' Claim," BBC News, July 13, 2003, http://news.bbc.co.uk/go/pr/fr//1/hi/world/asia-pacific/3062141.stm.

49. Minoru Kitamura, *Nankin Jiken no Tankyu: Sono Jitsuzo o Motomete* [Research on Nanjing Massacre: Search for Its Real Image] (Tokyo: Bungeishunju, 2001).

50. Harold Timperley, *The Japanese Terror in China* (New York: Modern Age Books, 1938).

51. See John Gittings, "Japanese Rewrite *Guardian* History: Nanjing Massacre Reports Were False, Revisionists Claim," *Guardian*, October 4, 2002, http://www.guardian.co.uk/international/story/0,3604,804169,00.html.

52. Ibid.

53. This phrase is taken from Ian Buruma, "China: Memories of the Nanjing Massacre Are Drenched in Politics: War and Remembrance," *Far Eastern Economic Review* 153, no. 36 (September 5, 1991).

54. Eykholt, "Aggression, Victimization, and Chinese Historiography," p. 49.

55. Ibid., p. 46.

CHAPTER SEVEN, CONTINUED

56. Actually, along these lines, it ought to be noted that at least two books by Japanese revisionists deny-
    ing the massacre have appeared in English, both published in the year 2000: *What Really Happened
    in Nanking: The Refutation of a Common Myth*, by Tanaka Masaaki, and *The Alleged "Nanking Mas-
    sacre": Japan's Rebuttal to China's Forged Claims*. Both books were published in Tokyo by Japanese
    publishers but are available to U.S. buyers through Internet bookstores. They are representative of
    the kinds of garbage scholarship to which Japanese readers are so regularly exposed to in *shukanshi*
    and elsewhere. Masaaki's book design even incorporates an absurd piece of Japanese propaganda
    published in the *Asahi Shimbun* of December 25, 1937, pp. 122–123. Originally titled, "Nanking
    Smiles; City Sketches," it features the picture of a Japanese soldier tending to a Chinese boy, along
    with other delighted Chinese children grinning ear to ear and playing games with the Japanese sol-
    diery. See Tanaka Masaaki, *What Really Happened in Nanking: The Refutation of a Common Myth*
    (Tokyo: Sekai Shuppan, 2000); Tadao Takamoto and Tasuo Ohara, *The Alleged "Nanking Massacre"*:
    Japan's Rebuttal to China's Forged Claims (Tokyo: Meisei-sha, 2000).
57. Buruma, "China: Memories of the Nanjing Massacre Are Drenched in Politics."
58. Jun Kamei, interview with Adam Gamble, December 18, 2002, Tokyo.
59. Honda, interview with AG.
60. David McNeil, "Media Intimidation in Japan," Discussion Paper 1, *Electronic Journal of Contempo-
    rary Japanese Studies*, March 27, 2001, http://www.japanesestudies.org.uk/discussionpapers/
    McNeill.html.
61. Ibid.
62. Ibid.
63. Kamei, interview with AG.
64. Pulvers, "The Stage Is Set for Genuine Change."
65. "Nankin Dai-Gyakusatsu wa Honto to Uttaeta Chugoku-jin no Shotai" ["The Real Identity of the
    Chinese Who Claimed That 'The Nanjing Massacre' Was Real"] *Shukan Shincho*, December 14, 2000,
    p. 49.
66. "Chugoku de Hiirou Nankin Dai Gyakusatsu o Sakebu Moto Nihonhei" ["Hero in China: Former
    Japanese Soldier Who Cries Out 'Nanjing Massacre'"] *Shukan Shincho*, June 24, 1999, p. 150.
67. Karel van Wolferen, "Why Can't the Japanese Love Japan?" (unpublished English-language manu-
    script for *Naze Nihonjin wa Nihon o Aise nai no ka: Kono Fuko na Kuni no Yukue*. trans. Susumu
    Ohara [Tokyo: Mainichi Shimbunsha, 1988]).
68. Honda, *The Nanjing Massacre*, p. xxvi.
69. Noam Chomsky, e-mail to Adam Gamble (in response to a list of questions provided to intervie-
    wee), October 16, 2002.
70. Kenichi Asano and Noam Chomsky, "Chomsky-Asano Talk: To Resist" (unpublished English-lan-
    guage manuscript for *Aragau Yuki Noomu Chomusuki Asano Kenichi Taidan* [Tokyo: Gendai Jin-
    bunsha, 2003]).

CHAPTER EIGHT

1. Ok Seon Lee, interview with Adam Gamble, November 17, 2002, Providence, RI.
2. Many estimates have placed the number of comfort women between 100,000 and even more than
   200,000. (The United Nations Commission on Human Rights agrees with this larger estimate. See
   the final report on item 6 of the commission's fiftieth session of its Sub-Commission on Prevention
   of Discrimination and Protection of Minorities ["Contemporary Forms of Slavery: Systematic,
   Rape, Sexual Slavery and Slavery-Like Practices during Armed Conflict"], submitted by Mrs. Gray
   J. McDougall, special rapporteur, entitled "An Analysis of the Legal Liability of the Government of
   Japan for 'Comfort Women Stations' Established during the Second World War." A copy of this doc-

ument is available in Sangmie Choi Schellsted, ed., *Comfort Women Speak: Testimony by Sex Slaves of the Japanese Military* [New York: Holmes and Meier, 2000], pp. 136–154.) However, the 80,000 to 100,000 number comes from one of the most meticulously researched books on the subject: Yuki Tanaka's *Japan's Comfort Women: Sexual Slavery and Prostitution During World War II and the U.S. Occupation* (New York: Routledge, 2002), p. 32.

3. Ok Seon Lee, "Personal Testimony" (presentation to the Korean American Students Association, Brown University, Providence, RI, November 16, 2002).

4. This basic point of fact has been thoroughly documented and is incontrovertible. See the testimony of surviving comfort women recounted in books such as Schellsted, *Comfort Women Speak*; Keith Howard, ed., *True Stories of the Korean Comfort Women* (London: Cassell, 1995); and George Hicks, *The Comfort Women: Japan's Brutal Regime of Enforced Prostitution in the Second World War* (New York: W. W. Norton, 1994), pp. 19–20. These testimonies make this fact abundantly clear. It is also substantiated by testimony from numerous Japanese soldiers, such as that of former Japanese military recruiter Seiji Yoshida, and by ample documentary evidence as well. See also Chin Sung Chung, "Korean Women Drafted for Military Sexual Slavery by Japan," in *True Stories of the Korean Comfort Women*, pp. 18–20; and Yoshimi Yoshiaki, *Comfort Women: Sexual Slavery in the Japanese Military During World War II* (New York: Columbia University Press, 1995), pp. 98–128.

5. See Howard, ed., *True Stories of the Korean Comfort Women*, p. 21, as well as the various testimonies in the book. See also the testimonies in Schellsted, ed., *Comfort Women Speak*; in Hicks, *The Comfort Women*, p. 92; in Yoshiaki, *Comfort Women*, pp. 142–144; in Dai Sil Kim-Gibson, *Silence Broken: Korean Comfort Women* (Parkersburg, IA: Mid-Prairie Books, 1999), pp. 53–55; and in Tanaka, *Japan's Comfort Women*, pp. 54–56.

6. See Hicks, *The Comfort Women*, p. 17.

7. Ibid., p. 20.

8. Howard, *True Stories of the Korean Comfort Women*, p. 17.

9. The Women's International War Crimes Tribunal on Japan's Military Sexual Slavery, held in Tokyo, December 8–12, 2000, was a well-publicized mock trial presided over by an international female panel of four judges: Carmen Argibay (Argentina), Christine Chinkins (United Kingdom), Willy Mutunga (Kenya), and presided over by Honorable Judge Gabrielle Kirk McDonald (United States).

10. See Mrs. Gray J. McDougall's final report entitled "An Analysis of the Legal Liability of the Government of Japan for 'Comfort Women Stations' Established during the Second World War," reprinted in Schellsted, ed., *Comfort Women Speak*, pp. 136–154.

11. This phrase is taken from Howard, *True Stories of the Korean Comfort Women*, p. 25.

12. In Hicks, *The Comfort Women*, p. 55.

13. Tanaka, *Japan's Comfort Women*, p. 11.

14. From Ok Cha Soh, "Presentation on Korean Comfort Women Issue" (presentation to the Korean American Students Association, Brown University, Providence, RI, November 16, 2002).

15. Hicks, *The Comfort Women*, p. 84.

16. Howard, *True Stories of the Korean Comfort Women*, p. 23.

17. Ibid.

18. Kim-Gibson, *Silence Broken*, p. 198.

19. Howard, *True Stories of the Korean Comfort Women*, p. 24.

20. See the Web site for the Asian Women's Fund at http://www.mofa.go.jp/policy/women/fund/, which includes the following pages: "The Contents of the Letter of the Foreign Minister Makiko Tanaka Sent to the Project Implementation Committee in the Netherlands (PICN) on July 6, 2001," "Letter from Prime Minister Koizumi to the Former Comfort Women (Year 2001)," and "Statement by Prime Minister Tomiichi Murayama (August 31, 1994)."

21. Asian Women's Fund, 4th Floor, Sogo Kudan-Minami Bldg. 2-7-6 Kudan-Minami Chiyoda-ku, Tokyo. Web site at http://www.awf.or.jp/english/index.html.

CHAPTER EIGHT, CONTINUED

22. Asian Women's Fund, http://www.awf.or.jp/english/index.html.

23. Lee, interview with AG.

24. Ok Cha Soh, interview with Adam Gamble, November 17, 2003, Providence, RI.

25. Mrs. Radhika Coomaraswamy, "Report of the Special Rapporteur on Violence against Women, Its Causes and Consequences on Human Rights Resolutions 199/45" and the addendum, "Report on the Mission to the Democratic People's Republic of Korea, the Republic of Korea and Japan on the Issue of Military Sexual Slavery in Wartime," United Nations Economics and Social Council Commission on Human Rights, Fifty-second session, January 1996. Section 61 deals with the issue of apology. The entire report is reprinted in Schellsted, ed., *Comfort Women Speak*, pp. 112–130. The specific quote regarding the desire for apology appears on page 119.

26. Ibid., p. 129 in Schellsted.

27. "Ianfu Mondai no Sendosha wa 'Kono Otoko' ni noru Sendosha" ["Agitators of the Comfort Women Issue Use 'This Individual' as Their Leverage"], *Shukan Shincho*, December 31, 1992, pp. 142–146.

28. The Web address of this newsletter is http://japanese.joins.com/html/2003/0103/20030103181728400.html.

29. Akira Nakamura, interview with Adam Gamble, December 20, 2002, Tokyo.

30. See Nakamura's claim at http://www.jiyuu-shikan.org/e/db2c.html.

31. See Howard, *True Stories of the Korean Comfort Women*, p. 21, as well as the various testimonies in the book and the testimonies in Schellsted, *Comfort Women Speak*. See also Hicks, *The Comfort Women*, p. 92; and Yoshiaki, *Comfort Women*, pp. 142–144.

32. Nakamura, interview with AG.

33. Rumiko Nishino, *Jugun Ianfu—Moto Heishitachi no Shogen* [Wartime Comfort Women: The Testimony of Former Soldiers] (Tokyo: Akashi Shoten, 1992); 1992 Kyoto "Oshietekudasai! 'Ianfu'Joho denwa" Hokokushu Henshu Iinkai [1992 Kyoto "Please teach me! 'Comfort Women' Information Calls" Editorial Committee for Collection of Reports], ed., *Sei to Shinryaku—Guntai ianjo 84 kasho Moto Nihonhei kara no Shogen* [Sex and Invasion: Eighty-Four Comfort Stations in Testimonies of Former Japanese Soldiers] (Tokyo: Shakai Hyoronsha, 1993).

34. Seiji Yoshida, *Watakushi no Senso Hanzai: Chosenjin Kyosei Renko* [My War Crimes: The Forced Draft of Koreans] (Tokyo: San-ichi Shobo, 1983); Seiji Yosida, *Chosenjin Ianfu to Nihonjin: Moto Shimonoseki Roho-doin-bucho no Shuki* [Korean Comfort Women and the Japanese: The Memories of a Former Shimonoseki Labor Recruit Manager] (Tokyo: Shin-Jinbutsu-Orai-sha, 1977).

35. Seiji Yoshida, "Request for Supporting 'Comfort Women,'" Transnational Foundation for Peace and Future Research, November 5, 1997, http://www.transnational.org/features/yoshida.html.

36. John Nathan, *Japan Unbound: A Volatile Nation's Quest for Pride and Purpose* (Boston: Houghton Mifflin, 2004).

37. "Ianfu Mondai no Sendosha wa 'Kono Otoko' ni noru Sendosha" ["Agitators of the Comfort Women Issue Use 'This Individual' as Their Leverage"], pp. 142–146.

38. Nakamura, interview with AG.

39. In Kim-Gibson, *Silence Broken*, p. 48.

40. "'Ianfu Kyosei Renko' Mondai o Decchi ageta Henna Nihonjin" ["A Strange Japanese Who Makes Up Stories of the Mobilization of Comfort Women"], *Shukan Shincho*, January 5, 1995, pp. 58–60.

41. "Asahi Shimbun Souru Tokuhain no 'Jugun Ianfu' Kiji no Dai-Kyokou" ["A Grand Fictional Report by *Asahi Shimbun*'s Seoul Correspondent on Institutionalized Comfort Women"], *Shukan Shincho*, August 10, 1995, pp. 138–141.

42. "Jyugun Ianfu Kyosei Renko 'Kyogi Repooto' no Genkyo" ["The Origin of the Falsehoods of the Forced Mobilization of Comfort Women"], *Shukan Shincho*, May 2 and 9 (combined issue), 1996, p. 164.

43. "Sakurai Yoshiko Koen o Chushi ni Oiyatta Kanagawa Jinken Sentaa no Genron Danatsu" ["Kana-gawa Human Rights Center Stops Yoshiko Sakurai's Scheduled Lecture, a Case of Oppression of Freedom of Speech"], *Shukan Shincho*, February 13, 1997, pp. 46–49.

44. "Jyugun Ianfu 'Kyosei Renko' no Uso o Mitomenai Asahi Shimbun no 'Gizen' Hodo" ["*Asahi Shimbun*'s 'Hypocritical' Reportage Denying the Falsehood of Forced Mobilization of Comfort Women"], *Shukan Shincho*, April 17, 1997, pp. 36–40.

45. Hiroshi Matsuda, interview with Adam Gamble, December 19, 2002, Tokyo.

46. Jun Kamei, interview with Adam Gamble, December 18, 2002, Tokyo.

47. Reported in "Fury over Japan Rape Gaffe," BBC News, World edition, June 27, 2003, http://news.bbc.co.uk/2/hi/asia-pacific/3025240.stm.

48. Ibid.

49. Ibid.

50. Katsuichi Honda, *The Impoverished Spirit in Contemporary Japan: Selected Essays of Honda Katsuichi*, ed. John Lie, trans. Eri Fujieda, Masayuki Hamazaki, and John Lie (New York: Monthly Review Press, 1993), p. 95.

51. Yuki Tanaka, *Hidden Horrors: Japanese War Crimes in World War II* (Boulder, CO: Westview Press, 1996), p. 215.

52. Peter Landesman, "The Girls Next Door," *New York Times Magazine*, January 25, 2004.

53. Ibid.

CHAPTER NINE

1. Alex Kerr, interview with Adam Gamble, June 16, 2003, Tokyo.

2. Ben H. Bagdikian, *The Media Monopoly*, 6th ed. (Boston: Beacon Press, 2000), p. x.

3. William De Lange, *A History of Japanese Journalism: Japan's Press Club as the Last Obstacle to a Mature Press* (Richmond, VA: Japan Library, 1997), p. xiv.

4. Charles Hutzler, "Yuppies in China Protest via the Web—And Get Away With It," *Wall Street Journal*, March 19, 2004, pp. A1–A8.

5. Kerr, interview with AG.

6. In Ivan P. Hall, *Bamboozled!: How America Loses the Intellectual Game with Japan and Its Implications for Our Future in Asia* (Armonk, NY: M. E. Sharpe, 2002), p. 27, where Hall footnotes the quote as coming from Mikuni, "The Mirage of Japanese Financial Reform," p. 1.

7. Kerr, interview with AG.

8. John Nathan, *Japan Unbound: A Volatile Nation's Quest for Pride and Purpose* (Boston: Houghton Mifflin Company, 2004).

9. Pat Choate, *Agents of Influence: How Japan's Lobbyists in the United States Manipulate America's Political System* (New York: Alfred A. Knopf, 1990), p. xi.

10. Hall, *Bamboozled!*, p. xxii.

11. See the Web site for the Liaison Committee on Human Rights and Mass Media Conduct, http://www.jca.apc.org/~jimporen/mission11.html.

12. Nathan, *Japan Unbound*, p. 28.

SELECTED BIBLIOGRAPHY

Print and Online Sources

An Advertiser's Guide to Magazines in Japan 2002–2003, No. 14. Tokyo: Japan Magazine Advertising Association, 2002.

"*Asahi Shimbun* Souru Tokuhain no 'Jugun Ianfu' Kiji no Dai-Kyokou" ["A False Report by *Asahi Shimbun*'s Seoul Correspondent on Institutionalized Comfort Women"]. *Shukan Shincho,* August 10, 1995. pp. 138–141.

Asano, Kenichi. *Hanzai Hodo no Hanzai* [The Crime of Crime Reporting]. Tokyo: Gakuyoshobo, 1984.

———. "Japanese Self-Imposed 'Kisha-Club' System Decays Investigative Journalism." Paper presented at Preconference of International Communication Association, Workshop 6. Democracy and Media in East Asia Conference, Yonsei University, Seoul, Republic of Korea, July 14, 2002.

Asano, Kenichi, and Noam Chomsky. "Chomsky-Asano Talk: To Resist." Unpublished English-language manuscript for *Aragau Yuki Noomu Chomusuki Asano Kenichi Taidan.* Tokyo: Gendai Jinbunsha, 2003.

Bagdikian, Ben H. *The Media Monopoly.* 6th ed. Boston: Beacon Press, 2000.

Benedict, Ruth. *The Chrysanthemum and the Sword: Patterns of Japanese Culture.* Boston: Houghton Mifflin, 1946.

Bix, Herbert P. *Hirohito and the Making of Modern Japan.* New York: Perennial, 2000.

Brasor, Philip. "Ripple Effects of Sleazebag Journalism." *Japan Times,* November 4, 1999.

Brenner, Marie. "American Nightmare—The Ballad of Richard Jewell." *Vanity Fair,* February 1997. http://www.mariebrenner.com/articles/nightmare/jewell1.html.

Brislin, Tom. "Anti-Semitic Articles and Books Not Uncommon in Japan." Japan Media Review. September 26, 2003. http://www.ojr.org/japan/media/1064022502.php.

Brook, Timothy, ed. *Documents on the Rape of Nanking.* Ann Arbor: University of Michigan Press, 1999.

Buruma, Ian. "China: Memories of the Nanjing Massacre Are Drenched in Politics: War and Remembrance." *Far Eastern Economic Review* 153, no. 36 (September 5, 1991).

———. *The Wages of Guilt: Memories of War in Germany and Japan.* London: Phoenix, 1994.

"Case Study: Richard Jewell and the Olympic Bombing." http://www.journalism.org/resources/education/case_studies/jewell.asp.

Chang, Iris. *The Rape of Nanking: The Forgotten Holocaust of World War II.* New York: Penguin, 1997.

Choate, Pat. *Agents of Influence: How Japan's Lobbyists in the United States Manipulate America's Political System.* New York: Alfred A. Knopf, 1990.

Covell, Jon Carter, and Alan Covell. *Japan's Hidden History: Korean Impact on Japanese Culture.* Elizabeth, NJ: Hollym International, 1984.

De Lange, William. *A History of Japanese Journalism: Japan's Press Club as the Last Obstacle to a Mature Press.* Richmond, VA: Japan Library, 1997.

"'Doku-gasu Jiken' Hassei-gen no 'Kai-ki' Kakeizu" ["The Originator of Poisonous Gas and His Macabre Family Line"]. *Shukan Shincho,* July 14, 1994. pp. 128–132.

Dower, John W. *Embracing Defeat: Japan in the Wake of World War II.* New York: W. W. Norton / The New Press, 1999.

————. *War without Mercy: Race and Power in the Pacific War.* New York: Pantheon Books, 1986.

Feiler, Bruce S. *Learning to Bow: Inside the Heart of Japan.* New York: Houghton Mifflin, 1990.

Fogel, Joshua A., and Charles S. Maier, eds. *The Nanjing Massacre in History and Historiography.* Berkeley and Los Angeles: University of California Press, 2000.

Freeman, Laurie Anne. *Closing the Shop: Information Cartels and Japan's Mass Media.* Princeton, NJ: Princeton University Press, 2000.

French, Howard W. "Tired of News That Rocks the Boat? Visit Japan." New York Times News Service, February 16, 2000.

Fujioka, Nobukatsu, and Shudo Higashinakano. *Za Reipu obu Nankin no Kenkyu—Chugoku ni okeru Johosen no Teguchi to Senryaku* [A Study of *The Rape of Nanking*—Methods and Strategy of the "Propaganda War" in China]. Tokyo: Shodensha, 1999.

Gittings, John. "Japanese Rewrite *Guardian* History: Nanjing Massacre Reports Were False, Revisionists Claim." *Guardian,* October 4, 2002. http://www.guardian.co.uk/international/story/0,3604,804169,00.html.

"Goiken ban Saito Juichi Komon Chokugeki Intabyu—Waga Shinchosa Shain ni Tsugu" ["Direct Interview of an Opinion Leader and Advisor Juichi Saito—Advice to You, Our Employees at Shinchosha"]. *Shukan Bunshun,* July 31, 1997. pp. 40–41.

Goodman, David G., and Masanori Miyazawa. *Jews in the Japanese Mind: The History and Uses of a Cultural Stereotype.* Expanded ed. Lanham, MD: Lexington Books, 2000.

Haley, John Owen. *Authority without Power: Law and the Japanese Paradox.* New York: Oxford University Press, 1991.

Hall, Ivan P. *Bamboozled!: How America Loses the Intellectual Game with Japan and Its Implications for Our Future in Asia.* Armonk, NY: M. E. Sharpe, 2002.

————. *Cartels of the Mind: Japan's Intellectual Closed Shop.* New York: W. W. Norton, 1998.

Hardacre, Helen. "Aum Shinrikyo and the Japanese Media." Japan Policy Research Institute. Working Paper No. 19. April 1996. http://www.jpri.org/publications/workingpapers/wp19.html.

Hicks, George. *The Comfort Women: Japan's Brutal Regime of Enforced Prostitution in the Second World War.* New York: W. W. Norton, 1994.

Honda, Katsuichi. *Chugoku no tabi* [A Journey to China]. Tokyo: Asahi Shimbunsha, 1972.

————. *The Impoverished Spirit in Contemporary Japan: Selected Essays of Honda Katsuichi.* Edited by John Lie. Translated by Eri Fujieda, Masayuki Hamazaki, and John Lie. New York: Monthly Review Press, 1993.

————. *The Nanjing Massacre: A Japanese Journalist Confronts Japan's National Shame*. Translated by Karen Sandness. Armonk, NY: M. E. Sharpe, 1999.

"Honsha Gyarappu Seikatsu Ishiki Hatsuno Doji Chosa" ["Together for the First Time, *Yomiuri Shimbun* and the Gallup Organization Conducted a Survey of the Daily Life of the People"]. *Yomiuri Shimbun*, May 3, 1979. pp. 1, 10, 11.

Hora, Tomio. *Nankin Daigyakusatsu Ketteiban* [Nanjing Massacre: Final Edition]. Tokyo: Tokuma Shoten, 1987.

————, ed. *Nankin Daigyakusatsu no Genba e* [At the Site of the Nanjing Massacre]. Tokyo: Asahi Shimbunsha, 1988.

————, ed. *Nankin Daigyakusatsu no Kenkyu* [Research on the Nanjing Massacre]. Tokyo: Banseisha, 1992.

————. *Nankin Jiken o Kangaeru* [Examining the Nanjing Massacre]. Tokyo: Otsuki Shoten, 1987.

Howard, Keith, ed. *True Stories of the Korean Comfort Women*. London: Cassell, 1995.

Hutzler, Charles. "Yuppies in China Protest via the Web—And Get Away with It," *Wall Street Journal*, March 19, 2004, pp. A1–A8.

Ikeda, Daisaku. *Faith into Action: Thoughts on Selected Topics*. Santa Monica, CA: World Tribune Press, 1999.

————. *The New Human Revolution*, Vol. 8. Santa Monica, CA: World Tribune Press, 2002.

Iwase, Tatsuya. *Shimbum ga omoshiroku nai ri yuu* [The Reason Why Newspapers Are Boring]. Tokyo: Kodan-sha, 2001.

Jameson, Sam. "A Veteran American Journalist Looks at the Japanese Media." Japan Policy Research Institute. http://www.jpri.org/WPapers/wp40.html. *Asuteion*, Fall 1997.

Jewell, Richard. Interview by Mike Wallace. "Sixty Minutes II: Falsely Accused." CBSNEWS.com. January 2, 2002. http://www.cbsnews.com/stories/2002/01/02/60II/printable322892.shtml.

Jewell, Richard. Opening Remarks of Richard Jewell before the United States House of Representatives Subcommittee on Crime. Committee of the Judiciary. July 30, 1997. http://www.house.gov/judiciary/375.htm.

Jewell, Richard, and Watson Bryant. Interview by Kenichi Asano. Transcript. October 14, 1997. http://www1.doshisha.ac.jp/~kasano/FEATURES/ATLANTA/atlanta-interview.html.

JIMPOREN. "Mission Statement." Liaison Committee on Human Rights and Mass Media Conduct. http://www.jca.apc.org/~jimporen/mission01.html.

Johnson, Chalmers. *Japan: Who Governs?: The Rise of the Developmental State*. New York: W. W. Norton, 1995.

Kamei, Jun. *Shukanshi no Yomikata* [How to Read *Shukanshi*]. Tokyo: Hanashi no Tokushu, 1985.

Karmon, Ely. "The Anti-Semitism of Japan's Aum Shinrikyo: A Dangerous Revival." In *Anti-Semitism Worldwide: 1998/1999*. Annual report by the Stephen Roth Institute for the Study of Contemporary Anti-Semitism and Racism at Tel Aviv University. Nebraska University Press. http://www.ict.org.il/articles/aum_antisemitism.htm.

Kasza, Gregory J. *The State and the Mass Media in Japan, 1918–1945*. Berkeley and Los Angeles: University of California Press, 1988.

Katayama, Hans. "*Shukan Shincho*: Victim—or Victimizer." *No. 1 Shimbun*, November 15, 1997.

Katz, Richard. *Japan: The System That Soured: The Rise and Fall of the Japanese Economic Miracle.* Armonk, NY: M. E. Sharpe, 1998.

Kerr, Alex. "Alex Kerr's View: Japan: A Land Gone to the Dogs." Interview with Stephen Hesse. *Japan Times,* April 25, 2002.

———. *Dogs and Demons: Tales from the Dark Side of Japan.* New York: Hill and Wang, 2001.

Kim-Gibson, Dai Sil. *Silence Broken: Korean Comfort Women.* Parkersburg, IA: Mid-Prairie Books, 1999.

Kindred, Dave. "A Long Wait in the Shadows after His Moment in the Sun." *Atlanta Journal-Constitution,* August 1, 1996.

"'Kisha Club' Tradition Dies Hard." *Japan Today,* January 30, 2003.

Kobayashi, Yoshinori. "Gomanizumu Sengen Extra—Dai Yon Sho: Dai-Toua Senso—Sofu Tachi no Monogatari" ["'Arrogance-ism' Manifesto—Extra. Chapter 4: Greater East Asia War—Grandfather's Tale"]. *Wascism* 4 (December 3, 2002): 45.

Kono, Yoshiyuko. *Tsuma yo! Waga Ai to Kibo to Tatakai no Hibi* [My Wife! Days of My Love, Hope, and Struggle]. Tokyo: Ushio Shuppansha, 1998.

Krauss, Ellis S. *Broadcasting Politics in Japan: NHK and Television News.* Ithaca: Cornell University Press, 2000.

Kyodo News. "EU Again Calls for End to Press Clubs." *Japan Times,* December 12, 2003.

———. "Nothing to Hide? Press Clubs Stymie Free Trade in Information: EU." *Japan Times,* November 7, 2002.

Landesman, Peter. "The Girls Next Door." *New York Times Magazine,* January 25, 2004.

Lazarus, David. "Poorando ga Otoshita Kage: Aushubittsu ga Abunai" ["'Auschwitz Hangs by a Thread': The Shadow Created by Poland's Democratization"]. *Marco Polo,* December 1992. pp. 142–150.

Lee, Ok Seon. "Personal Testimony." Presentation to the Korean American Students Association. Brown University, Providence, RI, November 16, 2002.

Machacek, David, and Bryan Wilson, eds. *Global Citizens: The Soka Gakkai Buddhist Movement in the World.* Oxford: Oxford University Press, 2000.

Mainichi Shimbun Survey, *Mainichi Shimbun,* January 4, 2001.

Markovits, Andrei S., and Mark Silverstein, eds. *The Politics of Scandal: Power and Process in Liberal Democracies.* New York: Holmes and Meier, 1998.

Matsubara, Hiroshi. "Libel Payouts Soar: Crackdown Has Publishers Running Scared." *Japan Times,* April 3, 2004.

———. "Magazine Muckrakes where Major Media Won't Make Waves." *Japan Times,* November 10, 2002.

McNeil, David. "Media Intimidation in Japan." Discussion Paper 1. *Electronic Journal of Contemporary Japanese Studies,* March 27, 2001. http://www.japanesestudies.org.uk/discussionpapers/McNeill.html.

Miller, George David. *Peace, Value, and Wisdom: The Educational Philosophy of Daisaku Ikeda.* Amsterdam: Rodopi, 2002.

"Nankin Gyakusatsu Attato Iwanaito Nihon wa Toore nainoka" ["Won't Japan Fare Well if It Doesn't Admit It Committed the Nanking Massacre?"]. *Shukan Shincho,* May 19, 1994. pp. 134–136.

Nathan, John. *Japan Unbound: A Volatile Nation's Quest for Pride and Purpose.* Boston: Houghton Mifflin, 2004.

Nishino, Rumiko. *Jugun Ianfu—Moto Heishitachi no Shogen* [Wartime Comfort Women: The Testimony of Former Soldiers]. Tokyo: Akashi Shoten, 1992.

Nishioka, Kensuke. *"Uwasa no shinso" Toppu ya kagyo—Scandal o Oe!* ["The Truth Behind the Rumor": Freelance Reporting—Catch the Scandal!]. Tokyo: Kodan-sha, 2001.

Nishioka, Masanori. "Sengo Sekaishi Saidai no Tabuu; Nachi 'Gasu shitsu' wa Nakatta" ["The Greatest Taboo in Post-War History: There Were No Nazi Gas Chambers"]. *Marco Polo,* February 1995. pp. 170–179.

Nobuhira, Nobuko. "Chinmoku o Yabutta Hokkaido Moto Fujinbu-kanbu 'Watashi wa Ikeda Daisaku ni Reipu sareta'" ["A Former Women's Leader in Hokkaido Breaks Her Silence, 'I Was Raped by Daisaku Ikeda'"]. *Shukan Shincho,* February 22, 1996. pp. 58–63.

Nobuhira v. Ikeda. Tokyo District Court Judgment of May 30, 1996. Tokyo District Court Division 28, Heisei 8 (Wa) Number 10485 Case of Claim for Compensation of Damages; Tokyo High Court Judgment of January 31, 2000. Tokyo High Court Division 11, Heisei 12 (Wa) Number 3364.

Nobuhira v. Ikeda. Tokyo District Court Judgment of May 30, 2000. Tokyo District Court Civil Section 28, Heisei 8 (Wa) No. 10485 Damage Compensation Claims Case. Judgment of First Instance.

NSK. Canon of Journalism. Adopted June 21, 2000. Japan Newspaper Publishers and Editors Association. http://www.pressnet.or.jp/English/about/canon.htm.

Olson, Kyle B. "Matsumoto Sarin Jiken wa Terorisuto no Hanko da: Bei Kagaku Heiki Ken Fukushocho ga Matsumoto de Tettei Kensho" ["The Matsumoto Sarin Incident Is a Terrorist's Crime: Associate Dean of the U.S. Chemical Weapon Research Institute Conducts a Thorough Verification in Matsumoto"]. *Marco Polo,* February 1995.

Ourvan, Jeffrey A. "Damage Control: Why Japanese Courts Should Adopt a Regime of Larger Libel Awards." *New York Law School Journal of International and Comparative Law* 21, no. 2 (2002): 307–321.

Pharr, Susan J., and Ellis S. Krauss, eds. *Media and Politics in Japan.* Honolulu: University of Hawai'i Press, 1996.

"Poll: 82 Percent of Voters Distrust Politicians, Politics." *Daily Yomiuri* (English ed.), July 14, 2002.

Rabe, John. *The Good Man of Nanking: The Diaries of John Rabe.* Translated by John E. Woods. New York: Vintage Books, 1998.

Ramseyer, J. Mark, and Frances McCall Rosenbluth. *Japan's Political Marketplace.* Cambridge, MA: Harvard University Press, 1993.

"Religious Groups Condemn Mori's 'Divine Nation' Remark." *Japan Times,* Friday, May 18, 2000.

Rosen, Jay. *What Are Journalists For?* New Haven, CT: Yale University Press, 1999.

Rubenstein, Richard. *The Cunning of History: The Holocaust and the American Future.* New York: Perennial, 1975.

Sano, Shinichi. "'Shuppan kai Saigo no Kaibutsu' no Shizuka naru Hibi. Saito Juichi" ["Quiet Days of the Last Monster in Publishing Circles: Juichi Saito"]. *Aera,* March 15, 1999. pp. 60–64.

Sayle, Murray. "Letter from Japan: Poison, Why a Puzzling Village Crime Has Unnerved a Nation." *New Yorker,* November 22, 1999.

Schellsted, Sangmie Choi, ed. *Comfort Women Speak: Testimony by Sex Slaves of the Japanese Military.* New York: Holmes and Meier, 2000.

Scruggs, Kathy, and Ron Martz. "FBI Suspects 'Hero' Guard May Have Planted Bomb." *Atlanta Journal-Constitution,* July 30, 1996.

Sigal, Leon V. *Reporters and Officials: The Organization and Politics of Newsmaking.* Lexington, MA: D. C. Heath, 1973.

Smith, Patrick. *Japan: A Reinterpretation.* New York: Pantheon Books, 1997.

Soh, Ok Cha. "Presentation on Korean Comfort Women Issue." Presentation to the Korean American Students Association. Brown University, Providence, RI, November 16, 2002.

Sugihara, Yukiko. *Rokusen-nin no inochi no biza* [Visas for Six Thousand Lives]. Tokyo: Asahi Sonorama, 1990.

Toshikawa, Takao, et al. "Chogin Warera ga ketsuzei 5-cho en o kuu Yudaya shihon jinmyaku tsui ni tsukanda!" ["Finally Unveiled! The Human Network of Jewish Capital That Devours Five Trillion Yen of Our Hard-Earned Taxes through the Long-Term Credit Bank of Japan"]. *Shukan Post,* October 15, 1999, pp 34–35. [Note: Although the author of this article is listed as Takao Toshikawa, the article was changed so drastically that the magazine had to write an apology to him.]

Tanaka, Yuki. *Hidden Horrors: Japanese War Crimes in World War II.* Boulder, CO: Westview Press, 1996.

———. *Japan's Comfort Women: Sexual Slavery and Prostitution during World War II and the U.S. Occupation.* London: Routledge, 2002.

"Tenno Hochu de Ichiji Chudan Nankin Gyakusatsu no Sanjyu mannin kara Nihyaku nin" ["Arguments over the Number of Victims (Ranging from 200 to 300,000) in Nanjing Massacre Temporarily Halted As Emperor's Visit to China Nears"]. *Shukan Shincho,* October 22, 1992.

Timperley, Harold. *The Japanese Terror in China.* New York: Modern Age Books, 1938.

Uno, Masami. *Yudaya ga Wakaru to Nihon ga Miete Kuru: Kudo ka Nihon o Yudaya ga Techu ni Surutoki* [If You Understand the Jews, You Will Understand Japan: When "Hollowing Out Japan" Fall Into the Hands of Jews]. Tokyo: Tokuma Shoten, 1986.

———. *Yudaya ga Wakaru to Sekai ga Miete kuru: Sen Kyuhyaku Kyuju nen Shumatsu Keizai Senso he no Shinario* [If You Understand the Jews, You Will Understand the World: The Scenario Toward "Economic War Catastrophe" in 1990]. Tokyo: Tokuma Shoten, 1986.

U.S. State Department. 18 Jun 52-Working Draft PSB-D-27 (1827) f PSB RE Draft Psychological Strategy Plan for the Pro-US Orientation of Japan-CD385 (Psy. Warfare). National Archives, Washington, D.C.

———. 29 Dec 52-Memo (01770) f PSB t DSD RE National Psychology Program for Japan-CD385(Psy. Warfare). National Archives, Washington, D.C.

Van Wolferen, Karel. "Bourgeoisie—The Missing Element in Japanese Political Culture." Unpublished English-language manuscript for *Ikare Nihon no Churyu Kaikyu.* Translated by Chikara Suzuki. Tokyo: Mainichi Shimbunsha, 1999.

———. "Can Japanese People Control Their Own Fate?" Unpublished English-language manuscript for *Nihon to Iu Kuni o Anata no Mono ni Suru Tameni.* Translated by Kiyomi Fujii. Tokyo: Kadokawa Shoten, 2001.

———. *The Enigma of Japanese Power: People and Politics in a Stateless Nation.* New York: Alfred A. Knopf, 1990.

———. Unpublished, untitled English-language manuscript for "Sukyandaru ni yotte Nihon Kenryoku Kiko wa Ikinobiru" ["Scandals Maintain Japanese Power"]. Translated by Masaru Shinohara. *Chuokoron,* October 1991, pp.186–194.

———. "Why Can't the Japanese Love Japan?" Unpublished English-language manuscript for *Naze Nihonjin wa Nihon o Aise nai no ka: Kono Fuko na Kuni no Yukue*. Translated by Susumu Ohara. Tokyo: Mainichi Shimbunsha, 1988.

Weiner, Tim, Stephen Engelberg, and James Sterngold. "C.I.A. Spent Millions to Support Japanese Right in 50's and 60's." *New York Times*, October 9, 1994. pp. 1, 14.

Williams, Walter. "Journalist's Creed." National Press Club. http://www.press.org/abouttheclub/history-ethics.cfm.

Yamamoto, Eiichi. *Genron no Terorizumu: "Netsuzo Zasshi" Shukan Shincho o Kaibo suru* [Media Terrorism II: Anatomy of a "Fabricating Magazine," *Shukan Shincho*]. Tokyo: Ohtori Shoin, 2002.

———. *Genron no Terorizumu: Shukan Shincho "Netsuzo Hodo Jiken" no Tenmatsu* [Media Terrorism: Full Account of *Shukan Shincho*'s Fabricated Reporting Incident]. Tokyo: Ohtori Shoin, 2001.

"Yomiuri Shimbunsha Yoron Chosa" ["Yomiuri-Shimbunsha Public Opinion Poll"]. *Yomiuri Shimbun*, November 1, 2000. p. 36.

Yomiuri Shimbun Survey. *Yomiuri Shimbun*, November 7, 1999.

Yoshiaki, Yoshimi. *Comfort Women: Sexual Slavery in the Japanese Military During World War II*. New York: Columbia University Press, 1995.

Yoshida, Seiji. *Chosenjin Ianfu to Nihonjin: Moto Shimonoseki Roho-doin-bucho no Shuki* [Korean Comfort Women and the Japanese: The Memories of a Former Shimonoseki Labor Recruit Manager]. Tokyo: Shin-Jinbutsu-Orai-sha, 1977.

———. *Watakushi no Senso Hanzai: Chosenjin Kyosei Renko*. [My War Crimes: The Forced Draft of Koreans]. Tokyo: San-ichi Shobo, 1983.

Selected Interviews Conducted for this Book

Asano, Kenichi. Interview with Adam Gamble. November 9–10, 2002, Boston and Yarmouth Port, MA.

Chomsky, Noam. E-mail to Adam Gamble (in response to a list of questions provided to interviewee). October 16, 2002.

Cooper, Abraham. Interview with Adam Gamble. May 1, 2002, Los Angeles.

Covert, Brian. E-mail to Adam Gamble (in response to list of questions provided to interviewee). December 26, 2002.

Dower, John. Telephone interview with Adam Gamble. May 7, 2002, coauthor in Yarmouth Port, MA, interviewee in Cambridge.

Fujioka, Nobukatsu. Interview with Adam Gamble. April 2, 2003, Tokyo.

Fuyushiba, Tetsuzo. Interview with Adam Gamble. July 5, 2002, Tokyo.

Garfield, Bob. Telephone interview with Adam Gamble. June 12, 2002, coauthor in Yarmouth Port, MA, interviewee in New York.

Haley, John Owen. Telephone interview with Adam Gamble. December 5, 2003, coauthor in Dennis, MA, interviewee in St. Louis, MO.

Hall, Ivan P. Telephone interview with Adam Gamble. June 8, 2003, coauthor in Dennis, MA, interviewee in Honolulu, HI.

Hanada, Kazuyoshi. Interview with Adam Gamble. April 4, 2003, Tokyo.

Honda, Katsuichi. Interview with Adam Gamble. July 5, 2002, Tokyo.

Iwase, Tatsuya. Interview with Adam Gamble. December 19, 2002, Tokyo.

Kamei, Jun. Interview with Adam Gamble. December 18, 2002, Tokyo.

Kamoshita, Ichirio. Interview with Adam Gamble. July 3, 2002, Tokyo.

Kerr, Alex. Interview with Adam Gamble. June 16, 2003, Tokyo.

Kitamura, Hajime. Interview with Adam Gamble. April 2, 2003, Tokyo.

Kono, Yoshiyuki. Interview with Adam Gamble. May 19, 2002, Matsumoto, Nagano.

Lee, Ok Seon. Interview with Adam Gamble. November 17, 2002, Providence, RI.

Maeda, Kunishige. Interview with Adam Gamble. July 8, 2002, Tokyo.

Matsuda, Hiroshi. Interview with Adam Gamble. December 19, 2002, Tokyo.

Mondale, Walter. Telephone interview with Adam Gamble. June 6, 2003, coauthor in Dennis, MA, interviewee in Minneapolis.

Nakamura, Akira. Interview with Adam Gamble. December 20, 2002, Tokyo.

Nishioka, Kensuke. Interview with Adam Gamble. April 2, 2003, Tokyo.

Oda, Makota. Interview with Adam Gamble. April 6, 2003, Kobe, Japan.

Sandberg, Neil. Telephone interview with Adam Gamble. January 16, 2003, coauthor in Yarmouth Port, MA, interviewee in Los Angeles.

Soh, Ok Cha. Interview with Adam Gamble. November 17, 2003, Providence, RI.

Takada, Kiyoshi. Interview with Adam Gamble. April 4, 2002, Tokyo.

Takeuchi, Ken. Interview with Adam Gamble. May 19, 2002, Tokyo.

Tanaka, Kengo. Interview with Adam Gamble. December 19, 2002, Tokyo.

Urushibara, Yoshio. Interview with Adam Gamble. July 5, 2002, Tokyo.

Van Wolferen, Karel. Interview with Adam Gamble. July 20–21, 2002, near Amsterdam.

Wood, L. Lin. Interview with Adam Gamble. August 16, 2002, Atlanta, GA.

INDEX